Fortran 95

Fortran 95

Including Fortran 90, details of High Performance Fortran (HPF), and the Fortran module for variable-length character strings

Martin Counihan

University of Southampton

Published in 1996 by
Taylor & Francis Group
270 Madison Avenue
New York, NY 10016

No claim to original U.S. Government works
Printed in the United States of America on acid-free paper
10 9 8 7 6 5 4

International Standard Book Number-10: 1-85728-367-8
International Standard Book Number-13: 978-1-85728-367-8

Library of Congress Cataloging-in-Publication Data

Catalog record is available from the Library of Congress

Taylor & Francis Group
is the Academic Division of Informa plc.

Visit the Taylor & Francis Web site at
http://www.taylorandfrancis.com

To Elizabeth

Contents

Preface

This is a revised, expanded, and updated version of the original book *Fortran 90* which appeared when Fortran 90 was first launched as an international standard programming language some five years ago. This book conforms to the proposed new Fortran 95 standard, but the new features are clearly marked as such so that the book can be used without difficulty by those who are continuing to use Fortran 90. It is designed to be useful both as a textbook for those new to programming and also as a fully up-to-date reference book for more experienced computer users.

Fortran 95 includes a chapter on High Performance Fortran, the major extension to the language enabling programs to be written to exploit multiple-processor computers to the full. In addition there is an appendix giving details of the module **ISO_VARYING_STRINGS**, the now-standard extension of the Fortran language to handle variable-length character strings.

As well as dealing with the vocabulary and syntax of Fortran, a number of general programming concepts are explained here. The production of annotated, comprehensible, bug-free, and maintainable code is encouraged. Fortran is a large language and it provides the programmer with plenty of latitude for bad as well as good programming practice, so attention is paid to disciplined methods of programming and to consistent coding conventions. The language has evolved over a long period of time, and it has always been considered important that new versions of Fortran should be backward-compatible with earlier versions so that old programs can continue to be used alongside new. So Fortran 95 contains within it virtually all of Fortran 90, which itself contained all of FORTRAN 77. Just a few features of Fortran 90 have been deleted in Fortran 95: they are listed in the first chapter, and where they arise in the course of the book they are indicated as being non-Fortran-95 features.

As a result of its history Fortran 95 has many redundant features which would nowadays be regarded as obsolete. At the same time there are also elegant modern features, such as derived data structures and modules, which are very powerful and encourage up-to-date programming practice. In the main part of this book we concentrate on the modern core of Fortran 95, but all parts of the language, old and new, are included within this book and are indexed for easy reference.

CHAPTER 1

What is Fortran 95?

This introductory chapter describes the evolution of the Fortran programming language and its new extensions. The nature and structure of a Fortran program, its division into separate program units of different types, the existence of intrinsic procedures, the distinction between declarative and executable statements, and the types of data that can be represented in the language, are introduced. Some comments are made about coding conventions.

1.1 The Fortran language family

Fortran is a world-standard computer programming language approved under the auspices of the International Standards Organization (ISO). It is the leading language for scientific computing and it is an evolving language that has existed for over 40 years in various forms. Fortran 90 replaced FORTRAN 77 a few years ago, and in turn is being replaced now by the latest version, Fortran 95. Fortran's evolution has been the key to its longevity: it has developed in response to progress in computer architecture and to new insights in programming language theory, it has been used for solving an increasingly broad range of problems, and it will certainly continue to develop in the future to enable computer users to take full advantage of innovations to come.

Fortran 90 was accepted as an international standard by ISO in 1991 and it was a major expansion of the earlier FORTRAN 77. At the time of writing, Fortran 95 is expected to gain final ISO approval in mid-1996. Fortran 95 will be a relatively minor revision of Fortran 90 and most programs written in Fortran 95 will appear very similar to those in Fortran 90. This book can be used equally well for Fortran 90 as for Fortran 95. The next major revision of Fortran, expected to take place very early in the next century, is already being contemplated and is termed "Fortran 2000" or "f2k".

Although Fortran includes an impressive set of mathematical functions,

1

and is the most advanced high-level programming language for scientific and technical computing, it is not intended only for mathematical work. In fact, Fortran handles text and general datasets with the same flexibility that it handles numbers. So, while containing numerous mathematical examples, this book is intended to be equally valuable to non-mathematicians who will be using Fortran to solve problems of other kinds.

Fortran involves ideas and terminology which have become standard in the world of software engineering, with concepts like "character" and "pointer" and "argument" that are also used in describing other programming languages. These terms have precise technical meanings and are part of the vocabulary that program-writers need to discuss their work. Beginners should try to get used to the terminology even when it sounds rather pompously long-winded, e.g. "structure constructor", and "relational intrinsic operator". This book deliberately uses accurate technical terms as often as possible, since serious Fortran users will need to become familiar with the terminology as well as learning the keywords and syntax of the language itself.

Uniquely among computer programming languages, the evolution of Fortran is self-consciously progressive and open-ended, and arrangements are in place for the steady development of the language beyond Fortran 95. It is intended that the language should be expanded in a modular fashion, extending but not modifying what is already in existence. A module subprogram, which encapsulates new procedures and derived data types in a self-contained package, is a natural way of implementing such extensions to Fortran. The first such module to gain ISO approval, **ISO_VARYING_STRINGS**, is described in detail in Appendix C.

"High Performance Fortran", or HPF, is a much more elaborate extension to Fortran than **ISO_VARYING_STRINGS**. HPF has arisen because new kinds of computer architecture demand to be exploited as efficiently as possible. HPF is for programmers who need to push against the performance envelope of the most advanced parallel-processing systems that exist today.

1.2 Programs and programming

A computer program is simply a sequence of instructions to be carried out by a computer. A computer is a composite mechanical system that works by the transmission of signals and data between components such as keyboards, optical and magnetic disks, semiconductor chips with micron-scale circuits for storing and processing data, visual display screens and printers. A computer system also includes special programs – system software – whose task is to manage the flow of information around the system itself. "Operating systems" are a species of system software. Some computer systems have sophisticated interfaces with telecommunications systems that connect them with other computers, including the global network of computers known as the Internet, and recent years have seen the evolution of "open systems" in that the boundaries between one computer system and others have become blurred.

But what are computers for? Ultimately, computers exist in order to exercise control over equipment external to the computer, or to make calculations and to solve problems that lie outside computer science. A computer might control a production line, or it might predict the likely result of a presidential election, or the likely course of a tornado. To do such jobs, special-purpose programs must be written. Because a computer is a general-purpose tool, it cannot be expected that a special-purpose program will always be installed on the computer for which it was originally written: it may happen that the program will be used on many different computers, perhaps manufactured by different companies and running under the control of different operating systems. One of the main reasons for having a standardized programming language like Fortran is to ensure that a program will be portable from one computer to another. As long as a computer can understand Fortran, it can run any program written in Fortran. Program portability has always been important, but it is all the more vital now that the Internet makes it possible for a program to be distributed with great ease to large numbers of different computers.

Fortran, then, is a standard programming language to allow general-purpose computers to solve specialized problems. The newcomer to Fortran may be surprised to learn that it is supposed to be an easy language, intended to be used not by experts in computer science but by those whose primary specialism is in some other discipline that might be a branch of engineering, physics, chemistry, mathematics, or the environmental and human sciences. For this reason – as well as for reasons of program portability – Fortran does not involve the programmer in the "low-level" technical details of exactly how a particular computer system is designed and how it stores and manipulates information internally. This philosophy is an aspect of what is sometimes called "data abstraction" – allowing the programmer to think of data in terms of idealized concepts (such as that of a real number) while not having to think about how that data is represented physically within a particular computer's hardware. If Fortran is not easy to learn, it is because, in response to demand by its users, it has become a sophisticated and powerful modern programming language and is very extensive. However, most programming tasks can be achieved with recourse to only a fraction of Fortran's features, and most program-writers do not attempt to memorize the whole language. The skill lies not in knowing all of Fortran, but in knowing what it can express and being able to refer to what you want when you want it.

A program written in Fortran will be translated (or "compiled", to use the technical term) into the appropriate low-level machine code by the computer system itself. This leaves the programmer free to concentrate on solving the real problem in hand, whether it be in aeronautics, economic forecasting or

3

whatever. Programmers can cultivate their expertise in their specialist subjects and their involvement with computer science need not extend much beyond the strictly defined boundaries of the programming language. The purpose of a programming language, like that of any language, is that the user should not have to cross its boundaries. The compilation of a program from Fortran into machine code is carried out by a part of the system known as a "compiler". A compiler is itself a piece of software, i.e. a computer program, but one that would not normally be written in Fortran. For all its merits, Fortran is not usually the ideal language for writing system software or compilers. Other languages, such as C, come into their own for such purposes. Compiling a program is not the same as running it: compilation puts instructions into a form understandable to the computer, but only when the compiled program is "run" will the instructions be carried out.

Portability between computers has already been mentioned above, but portability in time is just as important as portability in space. There is now an enormous investment in existing programs written by the scientific community in the past using earlier versions of Fortran. To preserve that investment, Fortran 90 was designed for backwards-compatibility with the previous standard version, FORTRAN 77; and apart from the deletion of a few of the obsolete features Fortran 95 is compatible with Fortran 90. Consequently, Fortran 95 includes a number of archaic features that would not have been included in the language if it were being designed from scratch without the burden of history. The archaic features should be avoided by a newcomer; they are no longer functionally necessary, and in this book they are covered only for the sake of completeness.

What we mean by a "program" generally takes the form of a length of text divided into lines. There might be a couple of dozen lines in a very simple program, or a few hundred in a medium-sized one, or many tens of thousands of lines in sophisticated programs written and maintained by teams of programmers.

Any program will have a starting point and an end point, and instructions between the start and the end will be "executed" in turn when the program runs. Many of the instructions will manipulate data in some way – multiplying numbers together, for example, or concatenating strings of text. However, some instructions can permit a program to branch out into alternative paths, and so in practice most programs are not executed in a fixed linear sequence of instructions. There can be branches, loops, conditionally executed blocks of instructions, and other structures, and a program may have several different possible points of termination.

1.3 Program structure

In general a Fortran program consists of a number of separate "program units", namely

- **A "main program"** When the program as a whole is run, it always starts at the first statement of the main program.
- **An arbitrary number of other program units** These can be called into play when needed by special statements within the main program or within other program units.

A short program could consist only of a main program, but in practice there are usually several program units. Apart from the main program, the other program units fall into two classes:

- "external subprograms", or "external procedures" (introduced in Chapter 7).
- "modules" (dealt with in Chapter 10) that can, for example, be used to contain data that will be made available to different subprograms.

There is a third class of program unit, now outmoded and unnecessary, known as **BLOCK DATA**. Throughout the chapters of this book, small type like this is used when referring to old Fortran features whose use is no longer recommended.

The difference between a module and an external subprogram is that a module contains information made permanently accessible to the program unit that invokes it: invocation is by a once-and-for-all declaration at the start of that program unit. A subprogram, on the other hand, is invoked dynamically (and perhaps repetitively) by action statements during program execution.

Subprograms can be invoked from the main program or from other subprograms. There is even the possibility of "recursive" subprograms that invoke themselves. Subprograms fall into two classes, namely "subroutines" and "functions", differing according to exactly how they are invoked. Normally subroutines are used to switch the flow of execution of the program, while functions are used for repeated calculations.

It should be noted that the terms "procedure" and "subprogram" are synonyms in the Fortran context. They are used interchangeably in this book.

There is another kind of subprogram not so far mentioned, namely a "module subprogram". A module subprogram is a procedure encapsulated within a module. Module subprograms, like external subprograms, are classified as either subroutines or functions, but putting a group of them together in a module can be a useful way of setting out a group of subprograms that have a special relationship with one another and need access to a shared pool of data. Technically, module subprograms are not classified as program units in their own right: it is the module that contains them that is classed as a "program unit".

1.4 Intrinsic procedures

"Intrinsic procedures" are a kind of toolkit provided for the programmer in Fortran. They are a general-purpose set of subprograms that can be invoked from any Fortran program. For example, to calculate the square root of a number a program only needs to use the expression **SQRT(...)**, inserting the number in question between the brackets. **SQRT** is a Fortran "keyword" that simply causes the square root to be calculated. Procedures like **SQRT** are just there, waiting in the background in case they are needed. They are an intrinsic part of the Fortran language. There are well over 100 intrinsic procedures in Fortran 95, and almost all of them (including **SQRT**) take the form of a "function", like a mathematical function, and are called "intrinsic functions". A function is a procedure that can be referred to simply by mentioning its name, even in the middle of a complicated expression; for example **SQRT(21 - SQRT(25))** is an acceptable Fortran expression that calls the **SQRT** function twice and is equal to **4.0**.

Fortran's intrinsic procedures include several standard mathematical functions such as the common trigonometrical and hyperbolic functions. They also include some very useful procedures for frequently needed numeric manipulations, such as finding the absolute magnitude of a number or picking out the largest from a given set of numbers. There are other intrinsic procedures that operate not on numbers but on strings of characters. Yet others are useful for checking up on the characteristics of the computer being used: for example the intrinsic inquiry function **PRECISION** will tell your program what is the limit of your computer's decimal precision. Inquiry functions like this would be unnecessary if all computers were identical, but are very valuable for writing programs to be portable between computers with different characteristics.

There are still other intrinsic procedures that are used for handling vectors and matrices, and for manipulating binary "bits", and for tasks such as the generating of random numbers. They are introduced gradually through this book, but are all listed in Appendix F.

1.5 Statements

A Fortran program or subprogram consists of an ordered sequence of "statements", and the statements can carry out different sorts of tasks. Some statements ("assignment" statements) give a value to a variable quantity: for example

```
n = 256
```

is an assignment statement that sets a variable called **n** equal (for the time being!) to **256**. Assignment statements always have an **=** sign in them. Other kinds of statement are indicated by special keywords, for example a statement that writes out data will begin with the keyword **WRITE**. Fortran statement types are listed in Appendix E; it is a long list, and rather bewildering at first sight, but in practice most programs, like most people's conversation, is built up predominantly out of statements of relatively few kinds.

Statements can be divided into two important classes: "declarative" statements and "executable" statements. The declarative statements can be imagined to take effect once and for all when the program is compiled: they establish what kinds of data are to be manipulated by the program (or subprogram), allow memory space to be allotted to data, and may set up certain relationships between items of data.

The executable statements take full effect only when the program is run: they are action statements that cause items of data to be altered or moved in some way, or that make decisions. Executable statements are sometimes called "procedural" statements and, when the program runs, the computer proceeds through them in turn.

Within a program or subprogram, the declarative statements must be grouped together at the beginning and they are followed by the executable statements in sequence. The difference between a declarative statement and an executable statement is quite fundamental. It is a little like the difference between an adjective and a verb in English. Consider the following program:

```
Cinderella is beautiful
Sisters are ugly, and coarse, and there are two of them
The Prince is rich
Dress Cinderella
Nullify the Sisters
Take Cinderella to the dance
Marry the Prince
```

The first three of these statements do not actually do anything but they set the scene. They could have been stated in any order. They are declarative. The last four statements are executable, in the sense that changes are made to some of the entities referred to in the first three statements. For the executable statements, the order is important.

All Fortran program units have the same basic structure as the Cinderella example above. However, one should be aware that there are different styles and fashions in programming and some programmers prefer to emphasize declarative aspects of programming while others prefer the procedural approach. Fortran is historically a procedural language and earlier versions of it were much more limited in their repertoire of declarative statements than Fortran 95 is.

There are several kinds of declarative statement in Fortran, but by far the most important is known as the "type declaration statement" or TDS. It is so important that most of Chapter 8 is devoted to describing all its possible variations. The TDS can be regarded as Fortran's archetypal declarative statement, the archetypal executable statements being the assignment statement and the **IF** statement that enables the flow of program execution to be controlled according to the values that variables are found to have at the time.

1.6 Data

Items of data may be "constants", unchanging throughout the execution of a program, or they may be "variables" able to be changed. Every variable is identified by a "name". In the example of an executable statement given earlier,

```
n = 256
```

the letter **n** is the name of a variable and the number **256** is a constant. In fact, a set of similar data items may be grouped together in an "array" under a common name: this makes it possible to manipulate large sets of data with very simple statements. Mathematically, these sets of data may be sequences of numbers, or vectors, or matrices, or tensors, or whatever you like, and they may be organized in many different dimensions; they can still be named and handled as single entities. "Array" is the general term used for a set of data going under a single name. Fortran works very flexibly with arrays of almost arbitrary size and can be used to exploit vector-processing facilities on computers of advanced architecture. In fact, the statement above could actually cause a large number of data items each to be set equal to **256** if it had been arranged for the name **n** to represent an array of numbers. The arrangement would be made by stating **n** to be an array in a declarative statement (a TDS) at the start of the program. Thus, the meaning and effect of an executable statement may depend profoundly on the attributes that items of data have been declared to have.

Likewise, most of Fortran's intrinsic mathematical functions will work for arrays: an expression like **SQRT(x)**, if **x** is the name of an array, will calculate the square roots of all the numbers in the array **x**.

Data items may be of a number of different "types". For example, integer numbers and complex numbers are different types. The word "type" is not used loosely: it is a technical term that refers to the nature, and not the particular value, of a single data item. Most programming languages allow for a few different types of data, but Fortran 90 allows, in principle, for an arbitrary variety of types. This is because of a feature known as "user-defined types" or "derived types", by which the programmer may construct a definition of a fresh type of data relevant to the problem in hand. It is easy to draw examples from advanced mathematics: for example, a programmer interested in four-dimensional geometry could define four-component vectors and 4×4 transformation matrices, and could also define what would be meant by the sums and products of such entities. As a more down-to-earth example, the latitude and longitude of a geographical point together comprise a special sort of data item and could be set up as a user-defined type obeying its own rules according to the programmer's wishes. User-defined types can be more flexible than arrays: an array is a set of items all of which must be of the same type, but a user-defined type can be a complicated structure incorporating data of quite different basic types, e.g. mixing numbers and words. So, a single Fortran "name", like **x**, could in this way refer to a mixed package of data such as a person's name, address, telephone number and age.

Another interesting feature in Fortran is that of "pointer" data. The concept of a pointer is not easy to appreciate at first, but one way to illustrate the idea is to take the example at the end of the previous paragraph, of a set of data consisting of a person's name, address, telephone number and age. Imagine that we have a large list of information of this sort. Suppose that we want the set of data for each person to include also a cross-reference to the corresponding information for the person's spouse. There are various ways in which this might be achieved. One way might be to give an index number to each person listed, and to include the spouse's index number in the data set for each person who is married. However, the simplest method in Fortran is to include a "pointer" to a spouse's details. The pointer would have the appearance of an additional data item encapsulating all the spouse's personal details; but in reality it would simply "point" to the other area of memory where the spouse's details are already listed in his/her own right. Using pointers, there is no need to take up unnecessary memory space by repeating chunks of data, nor to set up special codes for cross-referencing between data.

Modules are another very valuable feature of Fortran, and were mentioned above in Section 1.3. Like pointers, modules are difficult to appreciate in the abstract. You have to use them, in real programs, to see how effective they can be. Modules are useful in the architecture of large programs or systems of programs, where they can be used to organize plug-in sets of procedures for particular purposes. In smaller programs, modules are most useful for memory access, i.e. for containing data that is to be used by more than one procedure.

9

1.7 Writing Fortran

In practice, any Fortran program takes the form of text divided into lines. Each line may be up to 132 characters in length. Usually there is one Fortran "statement" per line. Within the line, the statement does not have to start at the first character or end at the end of the line: there may be blank spaces leading or trailing behind the statement. As a rule, blanks may be used to space out parts of a statement to improve legibility.

If desired, it is possible to have several statements on one line, using the semi-colon as a separator. It is also possible to spread one statement over several lines, using an ampersand (&) to mark the break. Also, it is easy to annotate the program with comments – pieces of text which do not actually form part of the program and will be ignored by the compiler. This way of laying out a program is known as "free source form" to distinguish it from an older "fixed form", the latter being a tightly constrained statement layout which originated historically in the format of the now-long-vanished 80-column punched card.

It is important to understand that Fortran will not, usually, solve a conceptual problem for the programmer. The programmer has to solve it. Fortran itself has no creativity, but simply allows the programmer to express the solution (or "algorithm")in a form that can be read and acted upon by a computer. However, although Fortran will not of itself solve the problem facing the programmer, a methodical approach to writing Fortran can assist by helping the programmer to analyze the problem efficiently and perhaps to reduce it to a number of simpler sub-problems. The pattern of program units in a Fortran program often reflects the logical reduction of the original problem into separate parts. In this sense, Fortran is a powerful thinking tool and it can be claimed that you do not really understand the solution to a problem unless you can express it as a successful Fortran program!

Fortran usually offers the programmer more than one correct way of expressing an algorithm. Choices are therefore involved and can be made on the basis of various considerations such as mathematical elegance, speed of computation, economy of memory, and the transparency of the code to a different human reader. Some of these considerations may be irrelevant: for example, such is the speed of today's computers that, for a particular problem, the computation time may be negligible however the program is written. But the history of computing is a beautiful illustration of how increasingly complex tasks are attempted to match the resources available to carry them out and of how leading-edge science always seems to work at the limits of current technology. So, in spite of the prodigious speed and memory capacity of present-day computers, it is just as important as it ever was to design programs that will execute as speedily as possible and will utilize memory as economically as possible. Many of Fortran's apparently arcane features – such as "allocatable arrays" – exist for this reason.

1.8 Coding conventions and typography

Fortran 95 offers its users a good deal of scope for establishing their own conventions about the superficial aspects of writing a program, such as the use of upper- or lower-case letters, margins and choices between equivalent ways of expressing the same things such as **ELSEWHERE** as opposed to **ELSE WHERE**. The Fortran code in this book embodies, for the most part, a set of coding conventions that are summarized in Chapter 14. Programmers often like to disagree with one another about coding conventions and it is possible for individual creativity to express itself harmlessly in the way that a program is presented to the human reader. It is not the purpose of this book to promote one set of coding conventions over another. However, consistency of presentation is extremely important both for an individual and, obviously, for any group of programmers who will need to be able to read and check one another's work efficiently. Consistency itself is more important than the particular set of conventions chosen. It may be legal to refer to a variable as **x** in one line of code and as **x** in the next, but it would not be wise. Fortran is a permissive language, but liberty implies responsibility!

One of the coding conventions used in this book is to express all Fortran keywords and intrinsic procedure names in upper-case letters, and the names of data objects in lower case. Fortran is additionally set in **Courier** typeface. For example, as it will be expressed in this book, **REAL** is a keyword referring to a special class of Fortran data whereas "real" is an English word that may refer to the mathematical concept of a real number.

Sometimes, in the text, double quotes (" ") are used to clarify the meaning if there is any danger of ambiguity between a technical term, or the name of a data object, and the corresponding English word. This should prevent any confusion over words like "automatic" and "name" which have technical as well as English meanings.

Fortran statements and expressions sometimes need to be expressed in generalized forms in a book like this, and then italics are used. For example, the first statement of a program takes the general form

```
PROGRAM program-name
```

but it would never look like that in an actual program: **program-name** merely represents whatever the name of the program might be. If the program is to be called **Extrapolate** then the actual statement would be

```
PROGRAM Extrapolate
```

Italics will also be used for other generalizations such as when discussing procedures with optional arguments such as **RANDOMSEED (SIZE, PUT, GET)**. It could be misleading to print **RANDOMSEED (SIZE, PUT, GET)** because the false impression might be given that it is a valid fragment of Fortran as it stands.

1.9 Fortran 90 features deleted from Fortran 95

Existing users of Fortran 90 should note that Fortran 95 is expected to exclude real **DO**-loop indices, branching to an **END IF** statement from an outer block, the **PAUSE** statement, the **ASSIGN** statement, and "Hollerith" data editing. All the expected differences between Fortran 90 and Fortran 95 are described in context in the appropriate sections of this book. The new features of Fortran 95 that were not present in Fortran 90 are listed in Appendix D.

CHAPTER 2

Getting started

The characters, "lexical tokens" and format used to construct Fortran 95 programs are described, and a simple example program is discussed in detail. The Fortran statements met are the "assignment statement" and the statements **PROGRAM, REAL, READ, WRITE, IF...THEN, ELSE, END IF,** *and* **END PROGRAM.** *Arithmetic operators and the intrinsic function* **SQRT** *are also encountered.*

2.1 The character set

Fortran programs are built up out of the limited set of characters listed below:

Letters: **ABCDEFGHIJKLMNOPQRSTUVWXYZ**
Digits: **0123456789**

The underscore: **_**

Special characters:

=	Equals	**:**	Colon
+	Plus	**!**	Exclamation
-	Minus	**"**	Quote (or double quote)
*	Asterisk	**%**	Percent
/	Slash	**&**	Ampersand
(	Left parenthesis	**;**	Semicolon
)	Right parenthesis	**<**	Less than
,	Comma	**>**	Greater than
.	Decimal point or full stop	**?**	Question mark
$	Currency symbol		Blank
'	Apostrophe (or single quote)		

Most of these characters have specified uses in Fortran. For example, the letters crop up in statement keywords like **WRITE** or **STOP**; the digits and decimal point are used to represent numbers; characters like + and – are used in the usual way for mathematical operations; and so on. Virtually all the Fortran standard characters should exist on any keyboard and it should be possible to display them all on any screen or printer.

It should be noted that Fortran only recognizes one kind of apostrophe or single quote ('). Although a processor may distinguish between an opening apostrophe (') and a closing one ('), they are the same to the Fortran language. A similar thing applies to (double) quote marks – or inverted commas – (").

There are just two exceptional special characters, the currency symbol ($) and the question mark (?), which have no particular roles in standard Fortran itself. However, such characters occur in real life and so they are likely to crop up in programs as elements of character strings, as in the **WRITE** statement

```
WRITE (*,*) "What is your name?"
```

This is an executable statement that, when the program containing it runs, would cause the standard output device – presumably a screen – to display the string of character between the quotation marks, i.e.

```
What is your name?
```

The meaning of (*,*) in the **WRITE** statement will be explained in due course.

With Fortran, output devices will display the characters more or less in the forms tabulated above, although the exact font style may vary. The symbol given as a dollar sign ($) is regarded as a general currency symbol and could appear as £ or whatever according to the country.

The **WRITE** statement above illustrates an important point: in a specified character string (**"What is your name?"**) one may mix lower-case and upper-case letters and the processor may distinguish between them. Almost all modern computer systems do in fact permit the two kinds of letters, but some equipment does not, so Fortran does not insist on the distinction and no such distinction is made in the syntax of the language itself, e.g. in keywords such as **WRITE**. This is why lower-case letters were not listed separately at the beginning of this chapter. As far as the processor is concerned, the statement given above could equally well appear as

```
Write (*,*) "What is your name?"
```

and if the processor is incapable of discriminating between lower-case and upper-case letters, the result of executing the statement might be

```
WHAT IS YOUR NAME?
```

Throughout the rest of this book it will be assumed that the processor can discriminate between upper-case and lower-case letters. However, the programmer must always realize that there is no such distinction in the syntax of the Fortran language itself ("What is your name?" is the English language, not Fortran!). So

```
N = 256
```

is precisely equivalent to the example statement, n=256, encountered in Chapter 1.

It is advantageous for the programmer to develop a style that exploits lower-case and upper-case letters to improve the readability and editability of programs; for example, it is a good idea always to use upper-case letters for statement keywords (like WRITE) and for the names of intrinsic functions, and to use lower-case letters for the names of variables, as in something like

```
x = -b + SQRT(b**2 - 4*a*c)
```

Here, SQRT is Fortran's built-in square root function, mentioned earlier in Section 1.4. It should be remembered that a programmer will normally be working through the medium of some sort of text editor while writing or updating a program. It makes no practical difference to Fortran whether you refer to the square root function as SQRT, Sqrt or sqrt, but it may make a difference to your editor if, for example, a string-search facility is used to find all the usages of that function within a very large program. Consistency is therefore recommended.

Blank spaces are not always relevant to the syntax of Fortran, but they can be used to space things out to improve appearance. The above statement is precisely equivalent to

```
x=-b+SQRT(b**2-4*a*c)
```

but the former is a little easier to read and to check. However, blank spaces may not be embedded within keywords or within the names of procedures. The letters of WRITE and SQRT, for example, may not be broken up with blanks. Furthermore, blanks are not ignored when they appear as elements of fixed character strings such as "What is your name?". In program statements, such strings are always distinguished by being enclosed between quotes or apostrophes.

There is one more important point that must be made about characters in Fortran. It is that any character whatsoever that is representable within the processor may occur in "character context", i.e. as an element of a character string such as "What is your name?". The lower-case letters are a special case of this rule, but it applies equally to any other unusual characters that were not listed in the table earlier but may be available on a particular processor and may appear on keyboards and screens. If a processor is capable of representing the letters of the Greek alphabet, or Japanese kanji characters, or whatever, then they may validly appear in a character context within Fortran. The character set shown at the beginning of this section is a minimum set for conformance with the Fortran standard, but a program may display information in other ways depending on the capabilities of the processor.

15

2.2 A simple program

```
PROGRAM Triangle
REAL :: a, b, c, s, areasq, area

WRITE (*,*) "This program calculates the area of a triangle."
WRITE (*,*) "Type in the lengths of the three sides:"
READ (*,*) a, b, c
WRITE (*,*) "Check: you have input the following lengths"
WRITE (*,*) a, b, c
s = 0.5 * (a+b+c)                    ! Semiperimeter
areasq = s*(s-a)*(s-b)*(s-c)         ! Square of area
IF (areasq<0.0) THEN
   WRITE (*,*) "Error: that is not a real triangle"
ELSE
   area = SQRT(areasq)
   WRITE (*,*) "The area of the triangle is ", area
END IF
END PROGRAM Triangle
```

Here, the first two statements are the declarative part of the program. The **PROGRAM** statement serves to introduce the program and to give it a name (**Triangle**). The statement beginning **REAL** serves the purpose of establishing that **a, b, c, s, areasq** and **area** are to be the names of variables which are real numbers. We shall see later that this **REAL** statement (a special form of what is generally known as a "type declaration statement" or TDS)is in fact not strictly necessary here.

After the first two lines is a blank line. This does absolutely nothing – it will be ignored by the compiler – but is an allowable way of breaking up the program for display purposes.

We now move on to the program's executable statements. The **WRITE** statements are for the output of data. The statement

```
WRITE (*,*) "Type in the lengths of the three sides:"
```

is a Fortran abbreviation for

```
WRITE (UNIT=*,FMT=*) "Type in the lengths of the three &
&sides."
```

If a statement is uncomfortably long, or is too long to fit onto one line, ampersands (the **&** character) can be used to divide it between two lines, as here. It does not really matter where the break between lines occurs. The following statements are equivalent:

```
WRITE (UNIT=*, FMT=*) "Type in values for the lengths &
&of the triangle's three sides"
```

and

```
WRITE (UNIT=*,FMT=*) &
"Type in values for the lengths of the triangle's &
&three sides."
```

It is no mistake that only one **&** appears between the first two lines here, but two between the second and the third. The exact rules for continuing a statement from one line to the next are summarized in Section 2.6.

In principle, **WRITE** statements may be used to output data onto any of a variety of devices that may be connected to the processor: printers, a screen, magnetic tape units, or whatever. Fortran expects each device to have a number, the "unit number", and the **WRITE** statement can specify the unit by including in brackets **UNIT=1**, **UNIT=3**, **UNIT=9**, or whatever. However, to simplify matters any processor is required to have a standard output unit that will automatically be used unless another unit is explicitly specified by number. An asterisk is used to refer to the standard output unit, so we have the specification **UNIT=*** in the **WRITE** statement above. In most modern personal computers the standard output device will be a screen, so this **WRITE** statement will cause the string of characters

```
Type in the lengths of the three sides:
```

to appear on the screen.

What about **FMT=***? This is to do with the format in which a piece of data is to be output (or, for input, the expected format in which it is to be read). Just as the **UNIT** keyword gives the programmer access to the range of available input/output devices, so the **FMT** keyword gives freedom to specify precisely in what style the information is to be displayed: for example, with how many places of decimals a number will be shown. By using the asterisk in **FMT=***, we are taking an easy way out called "list-directed formatting", whereby the format follows certain default conventions according to the nature of the data item (or items) listed in the subsequent part of the **WRITE** or **READ** statement. For the time being, list-directed formatting will be sufficient for us. Format specification is a large topic but not, for everybody, an important one. It is covered in detail in Appendix A.

So, in the example program above, **(*,*)** is a valid abbreviation for **(UNIT=*,FMT=*)** and it means that standard defaults are being used for the i/o devices and for the i/o formats. For most of this book we will imagine that all input is via a keyboard and all output is onto a screen.

The **READ** statement in the example program is

```
READ (*,*) a, b, c
```

and it means that numbers represented by **a**, **b** and **c** are to be input from the keyboard. "Real" numbers are expected, i.e. positive or negative numbers that may include decimal fractions, as opposed to integers or complex numbers or people's names or anything more complicated. **a, b** and **c** are "variables", i.e. entities whose values are not necessarily known when the program is written but are determined later on as the program runs and may be altered from one value to another in the course of the program. Inputting the numbers with a **READ** statement is one such way of giving values to the variables **a, b** and **c**. Selecting the first three letters of the alphabet as the names of these variables is a completely arbitrary choice. We could have used more or less any letters of the alphabet, or indeed sequences of letters. For example, we could have used instead the statement

```
READ (*,*) side_a, side_b, side_c
```

in which case the rest of the program would also have to have **a, b** and **c** replaced **by side_a, side_b** and **side_c**. The detailed rules for the naming of variables are given in the next chapter.

Fortran normally expects a variable to be a real number if its name begins with a letter of the alphabet in the range **a–h** or **o–z**. Names beginning with **i, j, k, l, m** or **n** are expected to represent integer variables, corresponding to numbers without fractional parts. If a variable is neither a real number nor an integer, for example if it is a complex number, Fortran requires this fact to be declared explicitly in advance by a type declaration statement along the same lines as the **REAL** statement above.

The default (list-directed) format is such that **a, b** and **c** in our example can be input from the keyboard in a form such as

```
3, 4, 5
```
or
```
3,4,5
```
or
```
3  4  5
```

or even with the numbers on separate lines as in

```
3(return)
4(return)
5(return)
```

The "delimiter" between the numbers may be a comma, or a blank, or both, or a series of blanks, or it can be the end-of-record code signified by the **return** or **enter** button on most keyboards. Decimal points could be included as in

```
3.0, 4.0, 5.0
```

and obviously the decimal point is mandatory if the variables actually have fractional parts, as in

```
3.5, 4.333, 5.25
```

However,

3½, 4¾, 5¼

would be unacceptable because ½, ¾ and ¼ are not part of the Fortran character set listed at the start of this chapter.

The final number must be followed by a delimiter (e.g. a blank or a **return**) otherwise the processor does not know you have finished. More detailed information on the format of "list-directed" input is given in Appendix A.

If we continue with the example program, **Triangle**, there are two **WRITE** statements that display the given lengths of the sides of the triangle as a check. Then we have

```
s = 0.5 * (a+b+c)        ! Semiperimeter
```

This is the first statement of the program that actually does anything mathematical. It is called an "assignment statement" and it sets the real variable **s** to be equal to half the sum of **a**, **b** and **c**. The asterisk is Fortran's multiplication sign. Assignment statements do not begin with a keyword but are characterized by the = sign. In general, on the right hand side of the = there must be an expression that the processor can calculate. In this example the processor will just have been given numerical values for **a**, **b** and **c** and these will be used to give a numerical value to **s** when the assignment statement is executed. It would not matter if the variable **s** already had a value: if it did, then the previous value would be replaced.

This statement also illustrates the use of the exclamation mark to start a comment. The ! and the text that follows it are treated like blanks by the processor. It is the means by which the programmer can annotate the program.

The next statement is:

```
areasq = s*(s-a)*(s-b)*(s-c)! Square of area
```

If **a**, **b** and **c** represent the lengths of the sides of a triangle then **areasq** is the square of the triangle's area. The expression on the right-hand side is a geometrical formula, the knowledge that the programmer must bring to this program. To finish calculating the area we just have to take the square root of **areasq**, and this is done by calling the intrinsic function **SQRT** that we have already met.

However, there is a potential problem: if the user of the program put in silly values for **a**, **b** and **c** (e.g. **1**, **1** and **99**, which cannot correspond to the sides of a real triangle) then the variable **areasq** could come out to have a negative value. Trying to take its square root would then cause the program to fail, since a negative number does not have a real square root. So the program should first check to make sure that **areasq** is not negative. The check is carried out by control statements that direct the course of the program so that different statements will be executed in different circumstances.

19

The control statements in our example are the **IF...THEN, ELSE,** and **END IF** statements. Their meaning should be obvious, but the details are set out in Chapter 6. In the **IF...THEN** statement, the expression

```
areas<0.0
```

is a "logical expression", that is to say an expression that has not a numerical value but a logical value, i.e. is either true or false. If **areasq** is less than zero then this logical expression has the value "true" and control will then pass to the statement following. If **areasq** is not less than zero, then the logical expression has the value "false" and control will pass down to the statement following **ELSE**. The **END IF** statement indicates the end of the blocks of conditional statements.

Whatever the value of **areasq**, control finally passes beyond the **END IF** statement to the **END PROGRAM** statement that brings execution of the program to a halt. Note that the conditional statements following **IF...THEN** and **ELSE** have been indented to the right purely for cosmetic reasons. Leading blank spaces have no significance in Fortran syntax, but by indenting statements in this way we can make a program considerably easier to read and understand.

The above example has been discussed in fine detail. We have encountered the statement types **PROGRAM, REAL, WRITE, READ,** Assignment (**=**), **IF...THEN, ELSE, END IF** and **END PROGRAM.** We have discussed numeric variables and the names that can be used to represent them, and used **READ** and **WRITE** statements to input and output values of real variables by list-directed formatting on the standard default i/o devices (keyboard and screen). We have encountered real and logical expressions. The real expressions

```
0.5 * (a+b+c)
```

and

```
s*(s-a)*(s-b)*(s-c)
```

illustrate the use of the arithmetic operators * (for multiplication), + (for addition), and – (for subtraction) and of brackets to make sure that things are done in the right order (**s*s-a*s-b*s-c** would be not be same thing at all!). Arithmetic operators in general are described in the next section.

2.3 Arithmetic operators

Fortran's complete list of arithmetic operators is:

**   exponentiation, i.e. raising to a power (e.g. **3**4** is equal to **81**)
* and **/**   multiplication (e.g. **5*6** equals **30**) and division
+ and **–**   addition and subtraction (e.g. **9-27** is equal to **-18**)

These are "binary operators" in the sense that they go between two numbers and produce a result that depends on the two. (However, the minus sign can also be used as a "unary" operator, applied to just one number, e.g. -**b** is the negative of **b**. The plus sign, too, can be a unary operator in the trivial sense that +**10** is equal to **10**.)

The arithmetic operators above can be combined with variables and constant numbers to form expressions such as **b**2-4*a*c**.

The descending order of the operators listed above is their order of precedence, i.e. the order in which they are normally carried out when different kinds occur in the same expression. However, brackets are used to over-ride that order of precedence. In the example just mentioned, **b** is first of all squared, then **4*a*c** is evaluated, then **4*a*c** is subtracted from **b**2**. The result is as if we had instead

    (b**2) - (4*a*c)

When there are two or more operators together on the same level of precedence, the expression is evaluated left to right, i.e. **4*a*c** is equivalent to **(4*a)*c**. With a chain of multiplications, of course, the order does not usually make any difference: **(4*a)*c** is the same as **4*(a*c)**. But in many cases the order is significant, e.g.

    16/8/2 is equivalent to (16/8)/2, equal to 1
    16/8*2 is equivalent to (16/8)*2, equal to 4
    12-6-3 is equivalent to (12-6)-3, equal to 3

The left-to-right rule applies to all the above examples, but there is an exception in the case of the exponentiation operator. When a number of exponentiations are strung together they are evaluated from right to left: so **2.0**0.5**(-1)** is equivalent to **2**(0.5**(-1))**, and is equal to **4.0**.

Note that **2**0.5**-1** would not be a permissible expression because the rules of Fortran do not allow two consecutive numeric operators (in this case, ****-**). Another limitation is that the exponentiation operator should not be used to raise a negative real quantity to a real (as opposed to integer) power: so you should not expect **(-3.375)**(0.333333)** to have the value **-1.5**. Expressions of this sort should either be avoided or should be handled using complex numbers (Chapter 3).

Here are a few more examples of the rules of operator precedence in Fortran expressions:

    3*5+7-9   = (((3*5)+7)-9)   = 13
    21/3*5/7   = (((21/3)*5)/7)   = 5
    2**2**2**2 = (2**(2**(2**2))) = 65536
    4**4/2*2**2 = ((4**4)/2)*(2**2) = 512

However, in practice it is wise to sidestep the question of operator predence by the liberal use of brackets when writing Fortran statements.

2.4 Exercises 2.A

2.A1 Check which of these are in the Fortran character set:

    # A $ @ % [: ; >

2.A2 Evaluate the following:

(i) `3**2**3`   (ii) `4+6/12*2`
(iii) `18/4/2**(-1)`   (iv) `SQRT(4**3**2)`
(v) `9/8*7/6*5/4*3/2`   (vi) `9*8/7*6/5*4/3*2`
(vii) `6-4+1`   (viii) `16.0**3.0/2.0`
(ix) `(-1)**0.5**(-1)`   (x) `2-1**0.5**(-1)`

2.A3 If **a, b, c, d** and **e** are the names of real variables, write Fortran expressions for:
(i) The average of **a, b, c, d** and **e**;
(ii) The root-mean-square of **a, b** and **c**;
(iii) **b**, expressed as a percentage of the total of **a, b, c, d** and **e**;
(iv) The geometric mean of **a** and **b**.

2.A4 Input into a computer the example program (**Triangle**) given earlier. Run the program and test it with different values for **a, b** and **c**. Enhance the program to make it calculate and display not only the area of the triangle but also its perimeter.

2.A5 Write a program to input two numbers and to output the larger of them. The program should communicate clearly with the user, and should use only the elements of Fortran that appear in **Triangle**.

2.5 Names and other lexical tokens

In the discussion so far we have encountered several of what are called "names" in Fortran terminology. These examples were as follows:

the name of a program: **Triangle**
the names of variables: **a, b, c, s, areasq, area, side_a, side_b, side_c**
an intrinsic function: **SQRT**

The names of variables are sometimes referred to a "identifiers". Fortran also permits names for subprograms (user-written functions, subroutines and modules), for user-defined data types, and for certain other objects such as "namelist" groups. The general rule is that names must begin with a letter and may consist of up to 31 "alphanumeric" characters. The alphanumeric characters are the letters, the digits and the underscore.

A blank is not regarded as an alphanumeric character, so blanks may not be included in names, and nor may the other special characters listed in Section 2.1.

Names are just one of the six kinds of "lexical tokens" that Fortran syntax is built up out of. The six are:

Names	(see above)
Keywords	e.g. **PROGRAM, WRITE, READ, IF, FMT, UNIT**
Constants	e.g. numeric constants such as **1.0, 365** and **-66.896**; and character-string constants such as **"Error: that is not a real triangle"** (in quotes or inverted commas)
Operators	e.g. **+, -, **, =** and **>**
Delimiters	e.g. **!** and brackets (parentheses)
Statement labels	(see Chapter 14)

From Fortran's point of view it is possible for names to be identical to keywords, but this is best avoided as it could obviously lead to confusion in the programmer's mind.

We have been using a particular convention for the capitalization (i.e. upper case or lower case) of letters of the alphabet. This convention is just that – a convention – and is not obligatory within Fortran, but it is extremely important to use some sort of capitalization convention to achieve orderly, consistent and attractive programming, particularly when teams of programmers are working together. There is nothing worse than a lengthy program in which the use of upper and lower case is arbitrary or inconsistent.

Our suggested capitalization convention can be summarized as follows:

Upper-case:
Statement keywords (such **READ**)
Names of intrinsic procedures (such as **SQRT**)
Keywords for arguments of intrinsic procedures

Lower-case, but with an initial capital letter:
Name of a program or a program unit
Keywords for arguments of non-intrinsic procedures
Namelist group names
Derived types

Lower-case
Names of variables or of constants

Some of the terms mentioned above may not be meaningful at this stage, but they are listed here for the sake of completeness. You may, of course, choose a different convention from this.

2.6 Fortran source form

The Fortran "source form", i.e. the general format according to which programs should appear, can be of two alternative kinds, namely "free" or "fixed" source form. The latter is now of historical interest only and is summarized further below. Free source form has already been used in the examples of Fortran given so far, and the details are as follows:

(a) A program is divided into records (i.e. "lines") each up to 132 characters in length. Except as mentioned in (g) below, blank characters have no significance, other than to make the code more readable, and they are ignored by the processor.

(b) Normally there is one "statement" per line. A statement may start with a keyword (such as **PRINT**) or it may be an assignment statement (assigning a value to a variable by use of the = sign). A statement may be preceded on the line by blank characters, i.e. it may be indented, and it may be followed by blanks. A statement may also be preceded by an integer number used as a "statement label", a common but generally inelegant feature of Fortran programming discussed in Chapter 14.

(c) Comments may be inserted after statements to guide readers of the code. A comment must always be separated from the statement by the ! character. The ! terminates the statement as far as the processor is concerned, and everything on that line after the ! is treated as commentary. A line is permitted to contain only a comment, and no statement at all, if it begins with a !. A completely blank line will be ignored. However, it must be remembered that a ! that occurs within character context, i.e. as part of a character string specified between single or double quotes, does not start a comment.

(d) A statement may be continued from one line to the next. Continuation is indicated by having an ampersand (&) as the last non-blank character in a line, with the effect that the subsequent line is tacked on to whatever immediately preceded the &.

However, a comment cannot be continued in this way: an & occurring within a comment has no special effect. Also, an & occurring in character context will not normally continue the string on the next line, i.e. it will just be taken as part of the character string, in the same way that a ! in character context has no special effect. However, in a case where it is necessary to continue a character string to the next line, the effect can be achieved by using two &s, putting one at the end of the first line and the other at the beginning of the second.

In fact, it is always acceptable to put an ampersand at the beginning of the continuation line as well as at the end of the preceding line, but unless you are in character context the second ampersand is optional rather than compulsory. When an ampersand starts a continuation line it need not be the first character of the line: there may be leading blanks that the compiler will ignore.

It was mentioned above that the ampersand should be the last non-blank character on a line that is to be continued: but in fact it may be followed by a ! and a comment except when the continuation is within character context.

(e) A statement may be continued over many lines. The only limitation is that a statement may not contain more than 2640 characters.

(f) It is possible to have more than one statement per line. The semi-colon (;)then serves to separate one statement from the next. However, a semi-colon in character context does not have this effect.

(g) Blanks are generally irrelevant to Fortran and they can be used generously to make a program easy to read. However, blanks are significant in one or two respects. They may not be embedded in lexical tokens. A keyword adjacent to a name must be separated from it by a blank. Blanks are not ignored in character context. In most double-keyword combinations a dividing blank is not mandatory but it is good practice to include it.

> In a statement like
>
> **END PROGRAM Triangle**
>
> the blank between **END** and **PROGRAM** is not strictly necessary, i.e.
>
> **ENDPROGRAM Triangle**
>
> would be equally valid. The Fortran keyword-pairs (and in one case, triplet) that are allowed to be run together without a blank space are as follows: **BLOCKDATA, DOUBLEPRECISION, ELSEIF, ELSEWHERE, END-BLOCKDATA, ENDDO, ENDIF, ENDINTERFACE, ENDMODULE, ENDPROGRAM, ENDSELECT, ENDSUBROUTINE, ENDTYPE, ENDWHERE, GOTO, INOUT,** and **SELECTCASE.** Needless to say, for the sake of clarity, it is recommended that the blanks be inserted.

The following contrived examples, all legal Fortran, may help to make the rules clear:

```
PROGRAM                Master                !Version 6

                       READ (*,*) indata

                       WRITE (*,*) "We're off!"

weightedsumofcubes =   a * alpha**3        &
                       + b * beta**3        &
                       + c * gamma**3

remark = "When a statement is continued from one line &
&to the next, but without breaking a character string &
&like this, it doesn't matter whether or not the &
&continuation line starts with an ampersand or not. &
&The two ampersands are only necessary in a character &
&string."
```

```
x=a1; y=a2; z=a3; sum=x+y+z    ! 4 statements, 1 line.

this = &    ! One statement, two lines
that


! This & does not turn the next line into a comment.
```

These are:

- a **PROGRAM** statement with lots of blank spaces and a comment at the end;
- **READ** and **WRITE** statements with leading blank space;
- an assignment statement spaced by ampersands over three lines;
- a character-string assignment statement spaced over six lines with pairs of ampersands;
- a set of four assignment statements on one line, followed by a comment;
- an assignment statement split into two lines and with a comment after the first part; and finally
- a statement consisting only of a comment.

Fixed source form

There is an alternative to the source form described above, namely "fixed" source form that was the usual form in earlier versions of Fortran and is therefore retained in Fortran 95 for the sake of backward compatibility. Fixed source form originated when programs were stored on 80-column punched cards, of which the first 72 columns could be used for Fortran. So, in fixed source form each line must contain 72 characters.

The first six character positions in each line are reserved for the following special purposes:

(i) If the first character is c or *, the whole line is taken as a comment.
(ii) Characters 1 to 5 may contain an integer statement label (see Chapter 14).
(iii) The sixth character is normally blank. A continuation line is indicated by having any non-blank character (other than zero) in sixth position.

Fortran keywords, names, etc. would normally follow after the sixth character. Therefore, in fixed source form, each line may only contain 66 characters of actual code.

2.7 Program structure

When a program is to be written, it is important to approach the task by planning what is to be done before actually starting to do it. I did not write this book by starting at the beginning and working through to the end. I started by clarifying the purpose of the book, then I planned the structure it should have so that it would fit together logically with nothing being left out or duplicated. Only then did I actually start to write it. Planning a laboratory experiment is rather similar: the first step, which is often surprisingly difficult, is to establish precisely what the purpose of the experiment is. The second step is to plan what will be the experimental procedure (analogous to drawing up a structure plan for a computer program). Only then should one actually do the experiment.

This is an aspect of what is sometimes called the "top-down" design philosophy. One starts by taking a broad view, defining the purpose of the task and planning the overall structure of the program that is to be written. Often, at this stage it will become clear that it would be advantageous for the program to be broken down into a number of quasi-independent program units. It must always be borne in mind that a program (or program unit) does not only do calculations: it must also communicate with the outside world (or with other program units) so that data can be passed in and out, otherwise there is no point in doing anything. And of course, it is essential to define at the outset what sort of data is being dealt with, e.g. whether we are doing integer or real-number arithmetic.

It can sometimes be helpful to consider a program as having the general form:

```
PROGRAM statement
Declarative statements (data definition)
Executable statements (data processing):
   data input
   calculations
   data output
END PROGRAM statement
```

The program Triangle, the example given at the start of Section 2.2, can be written as follows in an annotated form to make that structure clear:

```
PROGRAM Triangle

! Declarative statements:
  REAL :: a, b, c        !  The lengths of a triangle's sides
  REAL :: s              !  The semiperimeter of the triangle
  REAL :: areasq         !  The square of the triangle's area
  REAL :: area           !  The area of the triangle

! Data input:
  WRITE (*,*) "This program calculates the area of a &
  &triangle."
  WRITE (*,*) "Type in the lengths of the three sides:"
  READ (*,*) a, b, c
  WRITE (*,*) "Check: you have input the following lengths"
  WRITE (*,*) a, b, c
```

27

```
! Calculations:
  s = 0.5 * (a+b+c)
  areasq = s*(s-a)*(s-b)*(s-c)
  IF (areasq<0.0) THEN
    WRITE (*,*) "Error: that is not a real triangle"
  ELSE
    area = SQRT(areasq)
! Data output:
    WRITE (*,*) "The area of the triangle is ", area
  END IF

END PROGRAM Triangle
```

Comparison with Section 2.2 shows that this version has been made rather more understandable by the liberal use of annotations, particularly where the variables are declared, and by the clear separation between the three phases of execution. Another thing, which may help to make the program easier to read, is that the statements whose execution is conditional on the **IF** and **ELSE** statements are indented to the right. This is an example of a widely used indentation convention for blocks of code controlled by statements such as **IF**. The indentation convention is particularly valuable for its visual impact when dealing with lengthy blocks of conditionally executed code, especially when there is a complex structure of "nested" blocks.

2.8 Exercises 2.B

2.B1 Which of these are valid Fortran names?
   (i) **aramaic**   (ii) **zhq5**   (iii) **balance$**
  (iv) **p998530**   (v) **99in**   (vi) **top_mark**
 (vii) **bakers dozen**   (viii) **baker's dozen**
  (ix) **state_population_estimate_1997**

2.B2 Write a program to read in two numbers and calculate and write the magnitude of their difference as a percentage of their sum.

2.B3 Write a program called **Quad** to solve a quadratic equation expected to have real solutions. The coefficients in the equation are to be input and the solutions output.

2.B4 Write a program (**Mean**) that will input six numbers, calculate and display their average, and calculate and display their root-mean-square deviation from that average.

2.B5 Write a program to convert temperatures in either direction between Celsius and Fahrenheit.

CHAPTER 3

Types of data

Fortran 95 can deal with data items of many different types: in fact with an indefinite range of data types, since there is a facility for "derived" (or "user-defined") data types constructed by the programmer. Derived data types will be explained in Chapter 12. In this chapter we will cover the "intrinsic" data types **INTEGER, REAL, COMPLEX, LOGICAL** *and* **CHARACTER.** *This chapter also deals with the simple but invaluable* **IF** *statement, the intrinsic functions* **ABS, AIMAG, CMPLX, COS, EXP, HUGE, INT, LOG, LOG10, MOD, REAL, SIN, TRIM** *and* **LEN,** *and finally the ASCII character set and the associated functions* **ACHAR** *and* **IACHAR.**

3.1 Integers

As their name implies, integers in Fortran are the whole numbers **0, 1, 2, 3, 4,**... and including the negatives **-1, -2, -3,** ....

Examples of integer constants are

137
+365 (the + sign is unnecessary but may be included)
-9
0
299792458

Constant integers may appear explicitly in programs. Integers may alternatively be represented by names. The usual convention is to represent an integer by a name beginning with a letter in the range **i–n**. Unless otherwise specified (by a type declaration statement, Section 3.6 and Chapter 8) variables with names like

| **istructure** | **j57** | **mlight** |
| **nyear** | **izero** | **ides_april** |

will be therefore be taken by Fortran 95 to be integers.

Arithmetic can be done with integers using the arithmetic operators introduced in Chapter 2. If `i2=2` and `i3=3`,

> `i2**i3` has the value `8`
> `i2*i3`   has the value `6`
> `i2+i3`   has the value `5`
> `i2-i3`   has the value `-1`

and more surprisingly

> `i2/i3`   has the value `0`

The final example arises because of the way the ratio of two integers is interpreted: the exact ratio is calculated, then the fractional part of it is discarded if an integral result is required. Thus, `365/7` has the value `52`. Where negative numbers are concerned, the ratio is cut back towards zero, i.e. `-365/7` has the value `-52`. If we had an assignment statement such as

> `r = i2/i3`

with `i2` and `i3` as above, and `r` being a real variable, the result would still be zero, because the expression `i2/i3` is first interpreted as an integer-valued expression; assigning an integer value to a real variable is something made clearer in the next section.

Fortran has an intrinsic function, `MOD`, which can be very useful in integer arithmetic. `MOD(j,k)` is the value of `j` modulo `k`, i.e. the remainder when `j` is divided by `k`. To be more precise,

> `MOD(j,k)` is equivalent to `j - ((j/k)*k)`

where `j/k` is the integer quotient calculated according to the rounding-down rule mentioned above. Thus

> `MOD(365,7)`   has the value `1`
> `MOD(-365,7)` has the value `-1`
> `MOD(9,5)`   has the value `4`

Below is an example of a program using the `MOD` function.

```
PROGRAM Miles

! Display information and input a number
WRITE (*,*) &
  "This program converts a large number of inches into &
  &miles, yards and inches."
  WRITE (*,*) "Type in the distance in inches: "
READ (*,*) inches
```

```
! Calculation
inch = MOD(inches, 36)
nyards = inches/36
nyard = MOD(nyards, 1760)
mile = nyards/1760

! Output the results
WRITE (*,*) "The result is:"
IF (mile>1) WRITE (*,*) mile," miles"
IF (mile==1) WRITE (*,*) mile," mile"
IF (nyard>1) WRITE (*,*) nyard," yards"
IF (nyard==1) WRITE (*,*) nyard," yard"
IF (inch>1) WRITE (*,*) inch, " inches"
IF (inch==1) WRITE (*,*) inch, " inch"

END PROGRAM Miles
```

This program uses statements of the kind introduced in Section 2.2, except for the **IF** statements. An **IF** statement is simply a conditional form of some other single statement: the keyword **IF** is followed by a bracketed logical expression, followed by something else (in the above examples, **WRITE**) that will be executed only if the logical expression is true. Note that an **IF** statement is not quite the same thing as what is called an **IF** "construct". Using **IF** constructs we would have blocks of code like

```
IF (miles>1) THEN
  WRITE (*,*) miles, " miles"
END IF
```

but in a case like this, where only one action is contingent on the **IF**, it can be put into one **IF** statement as in the program above.

It should be noted that the program **Miles**, above, has no declaration statements at the beginning to state what are the variables to be used (**inches, inch, nyards, nyard, mile**) and what types of variable they are (integers). This is because of the capitalization convention by which these variables, having names starting with letters in the alphabetical range **i–n**, are automatically taken to be variables of integer type, as desired. It would do no harm to add the type declaration statement

```
INTEGER :: inches, inch, nyards, nyard, mile
```

immediately after the **PROGRAM** statement, simply to make it beyond doubt, for anyone reading the program, that these variables are integers. In fact, many authorities on Fortran would insist that type declaration statements should always be included for all the variables in a program for the sake of clarity even when one is not strictly necessary.

One may ask how large an integer may be in Fortran. Obviously a finite processor cannot cope with all of the infinite mathematical set of integers. In fact, the maximum-sized integer is not specified by the Fortran 95 standard but will depend on the processor. It may therefore be important within the running of a program to check what the processor's largest permissible integer is. For this purpose there is an intrinsic inquiry function **HUGE**. If **i** is any variable of type integer, then **HUGE(i)** returns with the largest integer number representable in the processor. (It does not really matter what the value of **i** is.) For example, the statement

```
IF (ABS(nyears)>HUGE(1)/100) CALL Error
```

will transfer control to a subprogram called **Error** if the variable **nyears** gets within two orders of magnitude of the largest permissible integer. The keyword **CALL** is explained in Chapter 7. **ABS** is an intrinsic function that calculates the absolute value of its argument, i.e. a positive number is unchanged but a negative one is changed in sign to become positive.

As well as **HUGE** there is another enquiry function, **RANGE**, which will return the maximum number of digits allowed. In other words, **RANGE(i)** = **INT(LOG10(HUGE(i)))**, **LOG10** being an intrinsic function calculating the logarithm (to base 10) of its argument, and the function **INT** being as described in the next section.

3.2 Real numbers

"Real" numbers are positive or negative numbers not restricted to integral values, in general having fractional parts. They are sometimes called "floating point" numbers and are usually expressed in decimal notation. Real numbers may appear in programs explicitly (i.e. as "real literal constants") in forms such as:

```
-78.915443
1877724.
+3.000
4.65E-9
-0.3E12
-.1E+6
666E6
```

where the last four examples introduce the notation of the "exponent letter" **E** followed by a power of ten, positive or negative, which is to multiply the number. The last example is therefore equal to 666 million. The number **4.65E-9** is equal to 4.65×10^{-9}. Note that a **+** sign is always optional both with the number itself (the "significand") and with the exponent. A decimal point should always appear somewhere unless there is an exponent letter: otherwise the processor cannot distinguish a real number from an integer.

Real variables should normally be represented by names beginning with a letter in the range **a–h** or **o–z**.

It is easy to convert integers into the corresponding real numbers, and vice versa, bearing in mind that when a real number is converted into an integer the fractional part will be discarded. One method of conversion is just to use an assignment statement such as

```
r = i
```

and then if **i=1**, **r** will be set equal to **1.0**. With

```
i = r
```

we would get **i=9** if **r=9.9**. This works because, according to Fortran's rules for assignment statements, type conversion will automatically take place between real and integer numbers if a variable of one type is set equal to an expression of the other type. More elegantly, there is an intrinsic function **INT** that always replaces a real argument by the corresponding integer: so the above example is shorthand for

```
i = INT(r)
```

The function **INT** may of course be combined into expressions, as in

```
ksum = INT(radius_1) + INT(radius_2)
```

and you should perceive that this is not necessarily equal to

```
ksum = INT(radius_1 + radius_2)
```

To convert integers into real numbers, Fortran has an intrinsic function **REAL**, and **r=i** is exactly equivalent to

```
r = REAL(i)
```

In practice the function **REAL** is not often needed in Fortran, since implicit type conversion will happen anyway if an integer appears in a context demanding a real number. However, if we pick up an example from Section 3.1, the **REAL** function may be important in a statement such as

```
r = REAL(i2)/REAL(i3)
```

which is not equivalent to **r=i2/i3**.

It is easy to fall into confusion about how an expression is evaluated if it includes both real and integer numbers. There is a very important rule concerning the effect of a binary arithmetic operator (+, -, *, /, or **) on data of real and/or integer types. Any such operator comes between two "operands", which is why it is called "binary". The rule is that if both operands are integers, the result is an integer, but if one or both of the operands is real then the result is real. So if we have integers **i2=2** and **i3=3** as in our earlier example,

33

```
i2**i3
```

is an integer. Because this rule applies to expressions as well as individual variables,

```
i2*(i2**i3)
```

is also an integer. On the other hand,

```
REAL(i2)/i3
```

is real, because one of the operands is real, and this would be exactly equivalent to

```
i2/REAL(i3)
```

With an expression like

```
r1/i2/i3
```

care is needed because the result may depend on the order in which the divisions occur. In fact, because of the left-to-right rule for operators of the same precedence (Section 2.3), this statement is equivalent to

```
(r1/i2)/i3
```

The expression in brackets is real (because one of its operands is real) and then the whole expression is real because the first operand of the second division is a real expression. However, if we had

```
r1/(i2/i3)
```

then the second division would operate first and would give an integer result because both of its operands are integers. Subsequently the first division, operating between a real variable and an integer expression, would give a real result to the expression as a whole. So, `(r1/i2)/i3` and `r1/(i2/i3)` are both expressions of real type, but of course they have different values.

The lesson to learn from this is that for trouble-free code you should make liberal use of brackets to simplify complicated expressions, and use the REAL and INT functions explicitly, allowing implicit type conversions to occur only in the simplest cases.

The intrinsic function HUGE and RANGE, mentioned earlier in connection with integers, can be used with a real argument, in which case the value of HUGE is the largest real number representable on the processor and RANGE is the number of powers of ten that can be spanned by representable non-zero positive real numbers (normally from 1.0 up to HUGE).

3.3 The `IF` statement and the `IF` construct

It is of fundamental importance that a computer program should be able to direct itself through different executable statements, and often through different sets of procedures, in response to data that is input or is calculated. A program would be very limited indeed if, when it was executed, it always passed through exactly the same set of executable statements in the same order. It is essential that there should be the possibility of conditional changes of direction, unpredictable when the program is written, taking place as the program is executed. These possibilities are provided by execution control statements of various sorts that are covered in detail in Chapter 6, but we have already seen how the flow of a program can be controlled by statements beginning with **IF**.

The **IF** statement is a single statement of the form

```
IF (condition) conditional-statement
```

where **condition** is a relationship that is either true or false, like **mile>1**. Technically, **condition** is known as a "logical expression", something explained more fully in Section 3.9 below. The **conditional-statement** can be any kind of executable statement, except another **IF** statement.

The **IF** construct has the general form

```
Name: IF (condition) THEN
   conditional statements
ELSE IF (condition) THEN Name
   conditional statements


 . . . .


ELSE Name
   conditional statements
END IF Name
```

The construct may, optionally, be given a **Name**. If so, the same name must appear before a colon at the start of the **IF...THEN** statement that opens the construct, and at the end of the **END IF** statement. The same name may also be inserted, optionally, at the end of an **ELSE IF** statement or an **ELSE** statement.

After the opening **IF...THEN** statement, there follows a set of one or more statements that are executed if, and only if, the **condition** in the **IF...THEN** statement is satisfied. If it is not satisfied, the **condition** in the **ELSE IF** statement is scrutinized and, if satisfied, the set of statements following that are executed. There can be any number (including none) of **ELSE IF** statements and associated sets of conditional statements. If the **IF..THEN** condition is not satisfied, nor any conditions attached to **ELSE IF** statements, then finally statements following an **ELSE** statement will be executed. However, it is not necessary for an **ELSE** statement to be present. So the simplest kind of **IF** construct would consist only of three statements such as

```
IF (miles>1) THEN
   WRITE (*,*) miles, " miles"
END IF
```

having no name, no secondary (**ELSE...IF**) conditions, no default (**ELSE**) statements, and only one statement being executed if the **IF...THEN** condition is satisfied. As we have seen, an **IF** construct as simple as this could equally well be replaced by a single **IF** statement.

A slightly more complex **IF** construct is the following:

```
Rootover: IF (snakeskin>0.0) THEN
   droop = 1.0/SQRT(snakeskin)
ELSE IF (snakeskin==0.0) THEN
   droop = 0.0
ELSE
   snakeskin = -snakeskin
   droop = 1.0/SQRT(snakeskin)
END IF Rootover
```

Giving the construct a name (**Rootover**) makes no difference to the execution of the construct, but can help the programmer to keep track of what is going on in code where there may be several **IF** constructs. It is possible for one **IF** construct to be nested inside another, as in

```
First: IF (a>b) THEN
   a = a/2
   Second: IF (a<1.0) THEN
        b = b**2
        a = a*b
   END IF Second
   b = a + b
   IF (b>a) b = b - 1.0
END IF First
```

which also includes an **IF** statement for good measure. This example should make it clear that complex systems of alternative actions can be coded with **IF** constructs.

3.4 Intrinsic procedures

We have now met a number of Fortran's intrinsic functions: **SQRT**, **MOD**, **HUGE**, **ABS**, **RANGE**, **EXP**, **INT**, **LOG10**, and **REAL**. Others introduced later in this chapter are **AIMAG**, **CMPLX**, **COS**, **LOG**, **SIN**, and **TRIM**.

They are invoked simply by having an expression of the general form

FUNCTION (*argument*)

where *FUNCTION* is the Fortran name for the intrinsic procedure in question, and *argument* is the variable of which the function is being calculated. In some cases (**HUGE** and **RANGE**) the value of the function does not, oddly enough, depend on the value of the argument, but only on what type of data item it is. In other cases (**MOD** and **CMPLX**) there may have to be two or even more arguments.

Fortran's intrinsic functions carry out different kinds of task and are classified accordingly. Some of the classifications are:

- "Numeric" functions such as **ABS, AIMAG, CMPLX, INT, MOD** and **REAL**. These do not actually calculate anything but manipulate numeric data in various ways. Many of them are to do with the converting of data from one numeric type to another.
- "Mathematical" functions such as **COS, EXP, LOG, LOG10, SIN** and **SQRT**, which calculate standard mathematical functions.
- "Character" functions, operating on textual data. The character function **TRIM** is explained in Section 3.10 below.
- "Numeric inquiry" functions such as **HUGE** and **RANGE**.

All the intrinsic functions are listed in Appendix F and it is worth looking there to see the full variety of classifications and complete descriptions of each procedure.

3.5 Exercises 3.A

3.A1 What are the values of the following integer expressions, if **n=-8**?
  (i)   **n**2-2**
  (ii) **n/2/2**
  (iii) **MOD(42,n+11)**
  (iv) **MOD(n,-3)**
  (v)   **ABS(n**3-n)**
  (vi) **2**n**

3.A2 Express as ordinary decimal numbers
  (i)   **666E-3**
  (ii) **0.024E6**
  (iii) **1E+1**
  and use the exponent letter (**E**) notation to express the following compactly as Fortran real constants:
  (iv) 2700000000.0
  (v)   0.0000101
  (vi) 10^{-16}

3.A3 What are the values of the following real-number expressions, if **s=-9.0** and **t=14.8**?
  (i)   **s+t/2-1**
  (ii) **s**2+t**
  (iii) **ABS(s+t)**
  (iv) **MOD(s,t)**
  (v)   **MOD(t,s)**
  (vi) **n**2/s**, with **n=-8**
  (vii) **2.0**n**, with **n=-2**

3.A4 Write a program to convert a sum of British currency expressed in pounds and new pence to the old-style pounds, shillings and old pence (a pound contained 20 shillings, each of 12 old pence).

3.A5 The Bohr radius for a very heavy nucleus is given by the formula

$$a_\infty = \frac{4\pi\varepsilon_0 \hbar^2}{m_e e^2}$$

where $\varepsilon_0 = 8.854188\, C^2 N^{-1} m^{-2}$, the permittivity of free space;
$\hbar = 1.054589 \times 10^{-34}\,$Js, the reduced Planck constant;
$m_e = 9.109534 \times 10^{-31}$kg, the mass of the electron;
$e = 1.602189 \times 10^{-19}$C, the charge of the electron;
and the classical electron radius is $r_e = e^2 / (4\pi\varepsilon_0 m_e c^2)$,
where $c = 2.997925\,$ms^{-1}, the velocity of light.

In these units, write a program to calculate and write out the values of a_∞ and r_e.

3.A6 Write a program to read the coordinates of two points in the two-dimensional plane and to calculate and write out the equation of the line joining them.

3.6 The type declaration statement

This section is a preliminary description of a sort of statement that is not dealt with in full detail until Chapter 8.

It has been said that integer numbers are represented by variables whose names start with the letters **i**, **j**, **k**, **l**, **m** and **n**, and real numbers by variables starting with other letters of the alphabet. However, this rule can be overridden by a "type declaration statement" that can take forms like

```
REAL :: negentropy
REAL :: joules, kelvin_temp, energy
INTEGER :: days, weeks, months
```

i.e. the keyword **REAL** or **INTEGER**, followed by a double colon, followed by a list of one or more names. The variables named are thereby declared to be of real or integer type whatever their initial letters might be.

The double colon
In type declaration statements we show a double colon between the type keyword and the list of variables. In fact, the double colon is usually optional and can be omitted except in more complicated cases that will be covered in Chapter 8. Nevertheless, it is best to use the double colon as a general rule, because it is never wrong to do so and it is the distinctive signature of the type declaration statement.

These **REAL** and **INTEGER** statements fall into the special class known as "nonexecutable" or "declarative" statements. They are used to define the nature of data objects once and for all when the program is compiled, but do not change anything during execution. Such statements must occur at the very beginning of the program (or subprogram) immediately after the **PROGRAM** statement. Declarative statements may not be mixed up with executable statements.

Other kinds of type declaration statement are the **COMPLEX, LOGICAL** and **CHARACTER** statements introduced in the remainder of this chapter.

Although it is not always necessary for variables to be declared in type declaration statements, it is recommended that they should be except in the case of the very simple integer variables known as "loop indices" that have not yet been introduced. If variables are always declared, it does not really matter whether the capitalization convention (**i–n** for integers, other letters for reals) is used or not; but nevertheless it is recommended that the capitalization convention be adhered to firmly to make it straightforward for readers of a program to distinguish immediately between integers and real numbers. It is not really too hard to think of suitable names starting with appropriate letters!

3.7 Kinds of real numbers

In fact, real numbers in Fortran are a little more complicated than the discussion in Section 3.2 suggests. The language actually allows for at least two different kinds of real numbers, with different degrees of precision. The first, sometimes called "default precision", is the sort of real number we have been using so far: it provides ample precision for most calculations and is provided automatically by the processor if the programmer does not explicitly demand still higher precision. The second kind of real number, providing more accuracy, is sometimes called "double precision" because on many processors it corresponds to doubling the number of bytes used to store a real number (e.g. from four to eight bytes). Double-precision constants can be set up by using the exponent-letter notation but using a **D** instead of an **E** as in the examples

```
4.65D-9
-0.3D12
-.1D+6
666D6
0.D0
```

The names of double-precision variables should be declared by means of the **REAL** statement, the keyword being followed by the specification of a parameter called **KIND**. For example, this statement could set up five double-precision numbers:

```
REAL(KIND=2) :: splithair, x, y, z, difference
```

It might be possible to use other values of **KIND** for numbers of still greater precision. However, the actual values of **KIND** that might be valid (including **KIND=2**) may vary from one processor to another and, for the sake of program portability, it would be necessary to use special intrinsic inquiry functions (described in Chapter 5) to establish which values of **KIND** are applicable to a particular processor. On a processor representing double precision by **KIND=2**, the above declaration statement would be valid and variables could be assigned by statements such as

```
splithair = 4.65D-9
```

There is also another way of writing a real constant, including its **KIND** parameter, by following the number itself by an underscore followed by the value of the **KIND** parameter. The above statement could therefore be written

```
splithair = 4.65E-9_2
```

as long as **KIND=2** corresponds to double precision, and the other constants listed above could be written

```
-0.3E12_2
-100000.0_2
666000.0_2
0.0_2
```

In fact, in expressions like this the **KIND** parameter may be expressed by a named integer constant as in the example

```
6666000.0_maxprecision
```

(See **PARAMETER**, Chapter 8.)

Optionality of the **KIND** parameter
In type declaration statements such as that given above, **KIND=** may be omitted, i.e. a statement like

```
REAL(2) :: splithair, x, y, z, difference
```

would be valid.

Double precision
Instead of a statement such as

```
REAL(KIND=2) :: splithair, x, y, z, difference
```

one may write

```
DOUBLE PRECISION :: splithair, x, y, z, difference
```

In general, **DOUBLE PRECISION** specifies real numbers having a precision greater than the processor's default real kind. **DOUBLE PRECISION** is equivalent to **REAL(KIND=KIND(0.D0))**, in terms of the intrinsic **KIND** function explained later!

3.8 Complex numbers

Fortran allows for complex numbers as long as the names of complex variables are declared by statements like

```
COMPLEX :: z1, z2, z3, z4
COMPLEX :: omega
COMPLEX :: i
```

Complex constants can be specified by the usual mathematical notation of giving, in brackets, the real part followed by the imaginary part. Examples are

```
z1 = (3.756, 0.051)
z2 = z1**2 - (0.0, 1.0)
z3 = SQRT(z2) - (0.0, -1.0)
omega = (-1.0, 0.0)**(1.0/3.0)
i = (0.0, 1.0)
```

The brackets are needed even in a case like

```
i = SQRT((-1.0,0.0))
```

because, here, one pair of brackets is needed to set apart the argument of the **SQRT** function and another to contain the parts of the complex number.

As the above examples show, complex numbers may be combined in expressions using the usual arithmetic operators. The **SQRT** function works with a complex argument: if the argument is complex, so is the result. In Fortran, the following intrinsic functions are either real functions of real arguments or complex functions of complex arguments, according to the argument types:

SQRT	Square root
SIN	Sine
COS	Cosine
EXP	Exponential function
LOG	Natural logarithm (i.e. the logarithm to base e)

The trigonometrical functions measure angles in radians. The complex **SQRT** function normally yields the principal value with positive real part, and the complex **LOG** function yields the principal value with imaginary part between $+\pi$ and $-\pi$. There is one intrinsic function that always has to have a complex argument and a complex value:

CONJG	Complex conjugate

The following functions may have complex arguments but give real or integer values:

REAL	Real part
INT	Real part, truncated to an integer

AIMAG Imaginary part
ABS Absolute value

Note that if **z** is complex, **INT(z)** is the same as **INT(REAL(z))**, and that **AIMAG((1.0,2.0))** is equal to **2.0**, not **(0.0,2.0)**. The function **LOG10**, which was mentioned briefly in Section 3.4 and gives a base-10 logarithm, is not permitted to have a complex argument.

Finally there is a function, **CMPLX**, which generally has two real arguments and a complex value. It simply forms a complex number, the real and imaginary parts respectively being given as arguments. **CMPLX** is discussed further in Section 5.3.

It is possible to mix complex, real and integer data in Fortran expressions built up out of the arithmetic operators. When each operator takes effect, if either operand is complex, then the result of that operation is complex. This is just an extension of what happens with real and integer data, where an operation gives a real result if either operand is real.

3.9 Logical data

"Logical" data is a non-numeric data type that we have already encountered indirectly: for example, as the logical expression in brackets within the statement

```
IF (miles>0) THEN
```

In general we may have constants, variables and expressions of logical type. They have only two possible values, true and false, and can be thought of as "bits" of information like binary digits. The names of logical variables must be declared initially using the **LOGICAL** type declaration statement, e.g.

```
LOGICAL :: error_flag
LOGICAL :: checksum, kexists, ifmiles
```

A statement like

```
ifmiles = miles>0
```

is a valid assignment statement, setting the logical variable **ifmiles** to be true or false according to whether or not the integer **miles** is greater than zero. The **IF** statement given earlier could then take the form

```
IF (ifmiles) THEN
```

Logical constants are written as either **.TRUE.** or **.FALSE.**, the surrounding dots being an essential part of the syntax. Logical constants could crop up in code like

```
LOGICAL :: condition_1, condition_2
INTEGER :: j, k
READ (*,*) j, k
condition_1 = .TRUE. ; condition_2 = .TRUE.
IF (j>k) condition_1=.FALSE.
IF (k>0) condition_2=.FALSE.
IF (ABS(j+k)>0) condition_1=condition_2
```

There is a set of special operators available for use on logical variables only, namely:

.NOT.   Negation
.AND.   And
.OR.   Or
.EQV.   Logical equivalence
.NEQV.   Logical inequivalence

.NOT. is a unary operator that flips the value of whatever logical quantity follows it. Thus, if **checksum** is a logical variable, .NOT.**checksum** has the value .FALSE. if **checksum** has the value .TRUE., and vice versa. Obviously, .NOT..TRUE. is equal to .FALSE. and .NOT..FALSE. is equal to .TRUE.

The other operators in the list above give results depending on the relationship between two items of logical data. They are binary operators, and stand between the two logical quantities to which they relate. Their meanings are summarized in Table 3.1, with **p** and **q** representing logical variables (or logical constants or expressions). In this table *t* stands for .TRUE. and *f* stands for .FALSE.. Note that a programmer may chose to avoid the rather clumsy constants .TRUE. and .FALSE. by a declaration like

```
LOGICAL, PARAMETER :: t=.TRUE., f=.FALSE.
```

which sets up fixed logical constants called **t** and **f** instead! (For the details of the attribute **PARAMETER**, see Chapter 8.)

The logical operators discussed above may be combined to form more complicated logical expressions like

```
q.AND..NOT.p.NEQV.q.OR.r
```

In evaluating such an expression the operators have an order of precedence. .NOT. comes before .AND., which comes before .OR., which comes before

Table 3.1 Relationships between logical data.

p	q	p.AND.q	p.OR.q	p.EQV.q	p.NEQV.q
t	*t*	*t*	*t*	*t*	*f*
t	*f*	*f*	*t*	*f*	*t*
f	*t*	*f*	*t*	*f*	*t*
f	*f*	*f*	*f*	*t*	*f*

.EQV. or .NEQV.. That is why they were listed in that order above. So, the above example is equivalent to

```
(q.AND.(.NOT.p)).NEQV.(q.OR.r)
```

Since .EQV. and .NEQV. have the same level of priority, an expression like

```
q.EQV.p.NEQV.r.EQV.s
```

could be ambiguous: but then in a case like this Fortran works from left to right, so the expression is equivalent to

```
((q.EQV.p).NEQV.r).EQV.s
```

Brackets may always be used to over-ride the normal order of precedence, as for the arithmetic operators, and even when brackets are not strictly necessary the programmer should use them to make the meaning of an expression as clear as possible. If brackets are always used, it is unnecessary to memorize the order of precedence!

In addition to the operators discussed above, which operate on logical-type data and produce logical values, there are "relational" operators that act on numerical data (and, in some cases, character strings) to produce logical values. In fact one or two of these have already been met: in Section 2.2 we used the expression areas<0.0, and in Section 3.1 we used expressions such as miles>0. The full set of relational operators that can be used between numerical data is:

==	Equal
/=	Not equal
<	Less than
<=	Less than or equals
>	Greater than
>=	Greater than or equals

It is important to realize that these operators, although used to form logical expressions, cannot be used between logical data items. If p and q are logical, we must use p.EQV.q rather than p==q. Also, the double equals sign (==) has a meaning quite different from the single equals sign (=). The = is used in assignment statements and changes the value of whatever is on the left-hand side. The == just compares the existing values of the objects on either side of it and changes neither.

Using both sorts of relational operator we can form quite complicated logical expressions, as in the statement

```
IF (((j/=k).AND.(m>k)).EQV.((j+m)==k)) THEN
```

where j, k and m are integers. Because Fortran has a default order of precedence for all operators it is often possible to get away without all the brackets: the relational operators take precedence over the logical operators and arithmetic operators take precedence over both, so the above statement is equivalent to

```
IF (j/=k.AND.m>k.EQV.j+m==k) THEN
```

but, as said before, the best practice is always to use brackets freely to make the meaning of the code as clear as possible.

Alternative forms of the relational operators:
The operators ==, /=, <, <=, >, and >= have also the synonymous forms .EQ., .NE., .LT., .LE., .GT., and .GE. respectively.

3.10 Characters and strings

So far we have met the numeric data types **INTEGER, REAL** and **COMPLEX**, and the non-numeric type **LOGICAL**. The next data type for us to deal with is **CHARACTER** data.

"Character constants" and "character variables" are not quite the same things as "characters". A character is an explicit individual symbol, such as a letter of the alphabet. Characters can be drawn from the list given at the beginning of Chapter 2, i.e. from the letters, the decimal digits, the underscore, and 21 special characters. In addition, characters could in principle include other more exotic symbols: the total number of permissible different characters is processor-dependent. Usually, upper- and lower-case letters are regarded as distinct characters.

A character constant is an explicit "string" of characters. For example, **"aeiou"** is a character constant. In fact we have already met character constants: early in the previous chapter we used **"What is your name?"**, which is a character constant or fixed-value character string. A character string may be only one character in length; in fact it may have zero length, i.e. have no characters in it at all. In Fortran, character constants are given between a pair of double or single quotes, although in this book we will generally stick to double quotes for this purpose.

We can also have character variables, i.e. names that could represent arbitrary characters or strings of characters. We will often use the common term "character string", or just "string", to denote any character variable or character constant.

Here is a simple example of how character strings can be manipulated within a program:

```
soft = "aei"
hard = "ou"
vowels = soft//hard
WRITE (*,*) vowels
```

which will yield the output

```
aeiou
```

In this example there are three character variables: **soft**, **hard** and **vowels**. These words are being used as the names of character strings, just as they could have been used as the names of numeric variables. The first two statements set the variables **soft** and **hard** to be equal to the constants **"aei"** and **"ou"**. The third statement sets the variable vowels to be the "concatenation" of **soft** and **hard**. The double-slash (//) is the concatenation operator, making a single longer string out of the two strings on either side of it. The concatenation operator can be used with character variables or with character constants: thus

```
vowels = "aei"//"ou"
```

or

```
vowels = "aei"//hard
```

or

```
vowels = soft//"ou"
```

would all have exactly the same effect as **vowels = soft//hard** in the above example.

The "length" of a character string is the number of characters in it (including blanks, which are significant in this context). Strings may obviously have various lengths. **soft**, **hard** and **vowels**, in the above example, have lengths of three, two and five respectively. Before a character variable is used, it must be declared to be of character type: otherwise the name will be assumed to represent a real or integer number. At the same time its length should normally be specified. The example above should therefore be preceded by type declaration statements of the form

```
CHARACTER(3) :: soft
CHARACTER(2) :: hard
CHARACTER(5) :: vowels
```

the lengths of the strings being in brackets after the keyword **CHARACTER**. The lengths of character variables are, of course, unrelated to the lengths of their names.

If there is no bracketed number after **CHARACTER**, the string is taken to have length one, i.e. it consists of just a single character:

```
CHARACTER :: dollarsign, shriekmark, ampersand
```

sets up three character variables each of which will be just a single character; but this statement is exactly equivalent to

```
CHARACTER(1) :: dollarsign, shriekmark, ampersand
```

and many programmers take the view that the length of the character strings should always be declared explicitly even when it is equal to the default value of one.

LEN
In a character type declaration statement, the string length may be preceded by **LEN=** thus:

```
CHARACTER(LEN=5) :: vowels
```

In practice, we may not know in advance the lengths of character variables and the declaration statements will need to allow for the maximum number of significant characters that the variable might contain. For example, consider this:

```
PROGRAM Nomination
CHARACTER(20) :: forename, surname
CHARACTER(41) :: name
CHARACTER(1) :: initial1, initial2
CHARACTER(2) :: initials
WRITE (*,*) "What is your first name?"
READ (*,*) forename
WRITE (*,*) "What is your surname?"
READ (*,*) surname
name = TRIM(forename)//" "//TRIM(surname)
WRITE (*,*) "Thank you. You are ", TRIM(name)
initial1 = forename
initial2 = surname
initials = initial1//initial2
WRITE (*,*) "Your initials are ", initials
END PROGRAM Nomination
```

The **READ** statements here will fill the strings **forename** and **surname** with the names that are input, but there will be blank spaces at the ends to make up 20 characters for each. **TRIM** is an intrinsic Fortran function that takes any string and returns it with trailing blanks removed. The variable **name** will contain the person's forename and surname with one blank space between them, and with trailing blanks to make up its full length of 41 characters. The third **WRITE** statement will output **name** without the trailing blanks. The assignment statements involving **initials1** and **initials2** exploit the fact that a truncation will take place if a longer string is assigned as the value of a shorter string.

Besides the function **TRIM**, mentioned above, another important intrinsic function that has a character string as its argument is called **LEN**, and its value is simply the length of (i.e. the number of characters in) the string. For example, the expression **LEN("Gum")** is an integer equal to **3**.

3.11 The ASCII character set

The ASCII code is a correspondence between a set of characters and the numbers ranging from 0 to 127 (Table 3.2). Since 127 is 1111111 in binary notation, i.e. 128 is 2^7, ASCII is a seven-bit code. Because computer systems use eight-bit "bytes", there is a "spare" bit that means that it is possible to have additional characters corresponding to the numbers 128 to 255: but they are not specified by the ASCII standard. Most of the ASCII "characters" are ordinary printable characters. Those that are not are omitted from Table 3.2, except for some whose usual meaning is indicated in parentheses.

The correspondence between characters and ASCII code numbers would be irrelevant to Fortran if it were not possible to translate the one into the other.

Table 3.2 The ASCII character set.

Character	Code	Character	Code	Character	Code
(null)	0	<	60	^	94
(bell)	7	=	61	_	95
(backspace)	8	>	62	'	96
(return)	13	?	63	a	97
(delete)	16	@	64	b	98
(escape)	27	A	65	c	99
(blank)	32	B	66	d	100
!	33	C	67	e	101
"	34	D	68	f	102
#	35	E	69	g	103
$	36	F	70	h	104
%	37	G	71	i	105
&	38	H	72	j	106
'	39	I	73	k	107
(	40	J	74	l	108
)	41	K	75	m	109
*	42	L	76	n	110
+	43	M	77	o	111
,	44	N	78	p	112
-	45	O	79	q	113
.	46	P	80	r	114
/	47	Q	81	s	115
0	48	R	82	t	116
1	49	S	83	u	117
2	50	T	84	v	118
3	51	U	85	w	119
4	52	V	86	x	120
5	53	W	87	y	121
6	54	X	88	z	122
7	55	Y	89	{	123
8	56	Z	90			124
9	57	[	91	}	125
:	58	\	92	~	126
;	59	]	93	(delete)	127

This can be achieved by two intrinsic functions, **ACHAR** and **IACHAR**. **IACHAR**'s argument is a single character, and its value is the integer corresponding to that character in the ASCII code. **ACHAR** is the inverse function: its argument is an integer and its value is the corresponding character. So **ACHAR(78)** is equal to **"N"**, and **IACHAR("m")** is equal to **109**. If **c** is the name of a character variable, **ACHAR(IACHAR(c))** is equal to **c**. An example of the use of the **ACHAR** and **IACHAR** functions is given in Section 7.3.

3.12 Exercises 3.B

3.B1 Which of these are legal Fortran constants? What are their types?

(i)	**.**	(ii)	**3.**	(iii)	**3.1**
(iv)	**31**	(v)	**0.**	(vi)	**+2**
(vii)	**-E18**	(viii)	**"ACHAR(61)"**	(ix)	**3 500**
(x)	**4,800,000**	(xi)	**"X or Y"**	(xii)	**"X"//"Y"**
(xiii)	**4.8E6**	(xiv)	**5000E-3**	(xv)	**"VAT 69"**
(xvi)	**6.6_big**	(xvii)	**(1,-1)**	(xviii)	**007**
(xix)	**1E**	(xx)	**-630958813365**		

3.B2 Write type declaration statements to declare
   (i)   Three real variables called **power1, power2** and **creeper**;
   (ii) Two integers called **kappa** and **kappa_prime**;
   (iii) A **KIND=3** real variable called **finetune**;
   (iv) Two strings, each of four characters, called **v** and **w**.

3.B3 Using a type declaration statement and three assignment statements, set up complex variables called **c1, c2** and **c3**, and give them the values of the cube roots of –2.

3.B4 Write a program to solve a quadratic equation (with real coefficients) allowing for complex roots.

3.B5 If **gum1** and **gum2** are logical variables both with the value **.TRUE.**, what are the values of
   (i)   **gum1.NEQV.gum2.EQV..NOT.gum1**;
   (ii) **(gum1.NEQV.gum2).EQV..NOT.gum1**;
   (iii) **gum1.OR..NOT.gum2.NEQV.gum1.AND.gum2**.
   (iv) What is the value of (iii) above if **gum1** is **.TRUE.** and **gum2** is **.FALSE.**?

3.B6 Write a Fortran logical expression depending on five integers **n1, n2, m1, m2** and **k**, which will be true if (and only if) the absolute magnitude of the difference between **n1** and **n2** exceeds that between **m1** and **m2** by at least the magnitude of **k**.

3.B7 Write a program to read in two strings of 12 characters each and to write out the first if the second is **"satisfactory"**. (If it is not, write out a message saying so.)

3.B8 Write a program to read four real numbers, taken to be the lengths of the sides of a trapezium in cyclic order, and calculate and write out the area of the trapezium.

3.B9 With a distance to be travelled being input, produce a table of the journey times for average speeds ranging from 40 to 140 kph (in steps of 10 kph).

3.B10 Write a program to read in a sequence of three single characters. If they are all hexadecimal digits the program is to write out the decimal equivalent of the hexadecimal integer that the characters represent. If one or more of the characters cannot be interpreted as hexadecimal digits, an appropriate error message should be written. (Use only the elements of Fortran, including the **IF** construct, that have so far been introduced. Other features of the language, to be introduced later on, will shorten the program considerably!)

CHAPTER 4

Introducing arrays

*This chapter begins with how array variables are declared and used. Then "array constructors" and "array sections" are explained, followed by information about the notation for specifying character substrings and sections of character arrays. The **WHERE** statement and the **WHERE** construct are described. Finally a number of intrinsic functions for arrays are introduced: **ALL**, **ANY**, **COUNT**, **MAXVAL**, **MINVAL**, **PRODUCT** and **SUM**.*

4.1 Declaring arrays

Up to now we have looked at data that may consist of a real or integer number, a complex number or a logical element. We have also looked at items of character data consisting of a string of characters. These have all been "scalar" objects, in the sense that a constant or the name of a variable refers to a single integer, or a single string of characters, and so on. It does not matter that a long string of characters will take up much more memory than a single logical datum: both are regarded as individual scalar data items. An "array", on the other hand, is an ordered set of data items, all of the same type, that can be referred to collectively by a single name. Arrays are an invaluable feature of Fortran and in practice only the very simplest of problems are solved without recourse to them.

A statement like

```
CHARACTER(30) :: surname
```

will establish that **surname** is the name of a variable whose form is a string of 30 characters. It is equally simple to set up instead a list of 50 people's surnames, the declaration statement then taking the form

```
CHARACTER(30) :: surname(50)
```

On either side is it possible to have a space before opening the brackets, so it would be equally valid to write

```
CHARACTER (30) :: surname (50)
```

By following the name (**surname**) with a positive integer in brackets, it is implied that the variable is a one-dimensional array (sometimes called a "vector") with that number of members. There is an equivalent alternative notation, namely

```
CHARACTER(30), DIMENSION(50) :: surnames
```

Here the keyword **DIMENSION** is known as an "attribute specifier", specifying that the variable is an array and indicating how many members it has. This form is convenient if you want to declare several similar arrays: for example

```
CHARACTER (30), DIMENSION (50) :: surnames, forenames, &
   nationalities
```

sets up three arrays each of 50 character strings, each string being 30 characters long, i.e. 4500 characters in all. Each string is an "element" of a 50-strong array.

Arrays of other types can be declared in similar ways, e.g.

```
REAL, DIMENSION(100) :: height, weight
INTEGER, DIMENSION(100) :: kage
```

However, the attribute **DIMENSION** may always be omitted if the dimensions of the arrays are given in brackets after their names, as in

```
REAL :: height (100), weight (100)
INTEGER :: kage (100)
COMPLEX :: roots (25)
LOGICAL :: maskmatrix (32,32)
```

These are all variations of the type declaration statement (Chapter 8). For simplicity it is recommended that the **DIMENSION** attribute be always avoided, and in the rest of this book arrays are indicated simply by specifying their dimensions after the names of the variables as in examples immediately above.

The final example above, the logical array called **maskmatrix**, is an example of a two-dimensional array, specified by having two integers between the brackets following the name. It may be imagined as a matrix with 32 rows and 32 columns, and therefore with 1024 elements in all. An array's number of dimensions is known as its "rank", and may be up to seven, i.e. we could have a seven-dimensional array like

```
INTEGER :: iternary(3,3,3,3,3,3,3)
```

this example having 2187 different elements. The total number of elements in an array is called its "size". In general an array may have a different "extent" in each dimension, and the total size is the product of the extents. So,

```
REAL :: hash (1024,8,26,2)
```

declares an array of rank 4 and size 425984. This array has an extent of 1024 in its first dimension, 8 in its second, and so on. The set of extents (1024,8,26,2) is known as the "shape" of the array.

Incidentally, it is possible for an array to have an extent of only one in one or more of its dimensions. The array

```
REAL :: oddity (1, 1, 1)
```

is, technically speaking, a three-dimensional array, in spite of the fact that it has only one element that might just as well have been expressed as a scalar variable. In fact, it is even possible for an array to have a zero extent in one of its dimensions, and therefore to contain no elements at all. The sense of this will become clearer later when array sections and arrays of variable shape are discussed.

4.2 Using arrays

In the declaration statements given as examples in the above section, the array names are followed by bracketed lists of the extents of the arrays in each dimension. In assignment statements, or in expressions, a similar notation is used to specify a particular single element of an array, e.g.

```
surnames(12) = "Johnson"
```

assigns a value to the 12th element of **surnames**. It does not mean that **surnames** has rank 12. However, **surnames** must have rank of at least 12 in order for **surnames(12)** to exist. To take an example where an array element is on the right-hand side of an assignment statement,

```
x = 1.0 - SQRT(hash(98,1,14,2))
```

takes one element out of the four-dimensional real array **hash**, and uses it to calculate **x**.

To refer to all the elements of an array it would be possible to use a construct like a **DO** loop (see Chapter 6), such as

```
Cuberoots: DO i=1,30
   croots(i) = REAL(i)**(1.0/3.0)
END DO Cuberoots
```

and this would set up a table of cube roots. But this sort of construction is generally not necessary: arrays really come into their own in Fortran because a reference to an array name by itself is equivalent to a reference to all the elements individually. For example, if **x** and **y** are one-dimensional arrays of size 12, then

```
x = y**2
```

is equivalent to

```
x(1) = y(1)**2; x(2) = y(2)**2; x(3) = y(3)**2;
x(4) = y(4)**2; x(5) = y(5)**2; x(6) = y(6)**2;
x(7) = y(7)**2; x(8) = y(8)**2; x(9) = y(9)**2;
x(10) = y(10)**2; x(11) = y(11)**2; x(12) = y(12)**2
```

As a rule, array assignment statements may refer to Fortran's intrinsic functions, as in

```
x = SQRT(y)
```

this being equivalent to 12 scalar assignments and involving 12 calls to the function **SQRT**, if **x** and **y** both have size 12. Functions that can be used like this in array assignment statements are called "elemental" functions because they operate on all the elements of the array that is given as their argument. Other valid statements would be, for example,

```
x = SQRT(x)
```
and
```
x = y/z
```

The variables **x**, **y** and **z** here could be arrays of any shape, but their shapes must be the same. In the latter example, **x(1)** is set to **y(1)/z(1)**, **x(2)** to **y(2)/z(2)**, and so on.

An array assignment statement must have an array on the left-hand side with the same shape as the array (or array expression) on the right-hand side, but an exception to this rule is that we may have a scalar on the right-hand side, in which case all elements of the array are set equal to that same value. For example, going back to the first example of this section,

```
surnames = "Johnson"
```

would set all elements of the array called **surnames** to the same string **"Johnson"**. To show how an array might be used in a program, here is something equivalent to the program shown in Section 2.2:

```
PROGRAM Triangle
REAL :: side(3)
WRITE (*,*) "This program calculates the area of a triangle."
WRITE (*,*) "Type in the lengths of the three sides:"
READ (*,*) side
WRITE (*,*) "Check: you have input the following lengths"
WRITE (*,*) side
```

```
s = 0.5 * SUM(side)              ! Semiperimeter
areasq = s*PRODUCT(s-side)       ! Square of the area
IF (areasq<0.0) THEN
   WRITE (*,*) "Error: that is not a real triangle"
ELSE
   area = SQRT(areasq)
   WRITE (*,*) "The area of the triangle is ", area
END IF
END PROGRAM Triangle
```

This is no shorter than the earlier version of this program and it uses two intrinsic functions (**SUM** and **PRODUCT**) that will be explained at the end of this chapter. However, it illustrates how three variables (originally **a**, **b** and **c**) can be referred to under one name (**side**) so that the program reflects the mathematical symmetry of the problem. Note that **READ** and **WRITE** statements can be used with arrays, with the same effect as if each element of the array had been listed. So, the statement

```
WRITE (*,*) side
```

is equivalent to

```
WRITE (*,*) side(1), side(2), side(3)
```

On the other hand,

```
WRITE (*,*) side(1)
```

would only write the first element.

4.3 Array constructors

So far, we have looked at how variables are declared to be arrays, and at how arrays can be used in assignment statements and **READ** or **WRITE** statements. But how do we initially set values for the elements of an array? It is possible to set each element individually, as in

```
REAL :: x(3)
x(1) = 3.76; x(2) = -7.4; x(3) = 5.19
```

but for rank-1 arrays there is a simpler syntax known as an "array constructor" that looks like

```
x = (/3.76,-7.4,5.19/)
```

The array has its elements specified as a list between a (/ and a /). This notation can be used in an assignment statement, or it can be used when array

55

variables (or named constants) are initially declared, as in

```
REAL :: x(3) = (/3.76,-7.4,5.19/)
```

or

```
INTEGER, PARAMETER :: months(12) = &
(/31,28,31,30,31,30,31,31,30,31,30,31/)
```

(The **PARAMETER** attribute is explained in Chapter 8.) The list in an array constructor may include items that are themselves arrays, so

```
INTEGER :: u(3), v(3), w(3), uvw(9)
u = (/1,2,3/)
v = 4
w = (/3,2,1/)
uvw = (/u,v,w/)
```

has the effect of giving **uvw** the value

```
(/1,2,3,4,4,4,3,2,1/)
```

Also, arrays within array constructors may themselves be array constructors, if you see what is meant. For example, **uvw** above could have been written

```
uvw = (/(/1,2,3/),v,(/3,2,1/)/)
```

Furthermore, a form of implied **DO** can be used in an array constructor. As an example, the table of cube roots given in the previous section is equivalent to

```
croots = (/ (REAL(i)**(1.0/3.0), i=1,30) /)
```

The meaning of this notation should be fairly clear even though the syntax is based on the idea of the **DO** loop described in Chapter 6. Within its own pair of brackets there is a structure comprising an expression, then a comma, then an index ranging between limits separated by another comma. The index name **i** is arbitrary, and the expression may be a function of the index. This structure creates an array element in the structure constructor for each value of the index over the range specified, i.e. 30 elements in the above case.

Another example is

```
ten_units = (/ (1.0, i=1,10) /)
```

which is equivalent to

```
ten_units = 1.0
```

as long as **ten_units** was declared to be a rank-one array of size 10.

One should be aware that an array constructor cannot be used as the parent array in the specification of an array element or array section, i.e. something like

```
neat = (/1,2,3,4,4,4,5,6,7/)(7)
```

is an illegal statement and cannot be used to pick out the seventh element of the constructed array. However, if **miasma** is the declared name of a nine-element rank-one integer array, then

```
miasma = (/1,2,3,4,4,4,5,6,7/)
neat = miasma(7)
```

does the trick.

Since an array constructor is a one-dimensional sequence of values, it can be used to construct only one-dimensional (rank-one) arrays. A one-dimensional array can be reshaped into a multidimensional array of the same size, using a special intrinsic function **RESHAPE**, but details of this are deferred until Chapter 9.

4.4 Array sections

We have so far considered arrays whose elements are labelled by integers ("subscripts")ranging from **1** up to the maximum extent in each dimension. However, subscripts may run from starting points other than **1** with a notation where both the lower and upper subscript limits are given, separated by a colon. For example,

```
REAL :: annual(1900:2025)
```

declares an array with 126 elements, i.e. **annual(1900)**, **annual(1901)**, **annual(1902)**, ... , **annual(2025)**. In a case like this items such as **annual(1)** simply do not exist. This notation can equally well be used for multidimensional arrays, as in

```
LOGICAL :: flipper(-10:10,32,0:20)
```

which is a rank-three array with total size $21 \times 32 \times 21$.

The colon notation is also used to refer to what is called an "array section", which is a subset of a previously declared array. We could have

```
REAL :: annual(1900:2025), decade(10)
     .
     .
     .
     .
decade = annual(1981:1990)
```

where, in the assignment statement, **annual(1981:1990)** is an array section, i.e. a particular set of ten elements from the larger array **annual**. The elements of the array **decade** are being set equal to **annual(1981)**, **annual(1982)**,..., **annual(1990)**. In fact, for array sections, the notation can be extended to allow sets of elements that are not sequential in the original array, by specifying a "stride" after a second colon. So,

```
annual(1904:1996:4)
```

is an array section consisting of every fourth element starting from **annual(1904)** and going up to **annual(1996)**. The three bracketed numbers, separated by colons, are a "subscript triplet" and the general rule is that the processor starts from the first and moves on to the second in steps equal to the third. If **leaps** is a rank-one real array of size 24, then

```
leaps = annual(1904:1996:4)
```

picks out leap years. The stride may be negative and, if it is equal to **-1**, the effect is to give an array section with elements in the reverse order from the original array. Note that sections of the same array may occur on both sides of an assignment statement, as in

```
decade = decade(10:1:-1)
```

which reverses the order of the elements in **decade**, or

```
tenfold = tenfold + tenfold(10:1:-1)
```

where **tenfold** is a rank-one array of size 10. This array assignment statement is a bit like

```
tenfold(1) = tenfold(1) + tenfold(10)
tenfold(2) = tenfold(2) + tenfold(9)
   .
   .
   .
tenfold(10) = tenfold(10) + tenfold(1)
```

except for the very important difference that when we write it out the long way, with ten scalar assignment statements, the last five statements will have quantities on the right-hand side that were changed by the first five statements. The array assignment statement, on the other hand, always uses the original values of all the elements on the right-hand side and the result is therefore not dependent on the order in which a processor might evaluate the elements of the array on the left-hand side.

By applying this notation to each dimension in turn we can form sections of multidimensional arrays. With the rank-three array given by

```
INTEGER :: matrices(4,4,200)
```

it is possible to have sections such as

```
matrices(1:4, 1:4, 1)
matrices(1:4, 4, 98)
matrices(4:1:-1, 4:1:-1, 1:200)
```

The first of these fixes the third subscript as **1** and so gives a two-dimensional array with 16 elements in total, i.e. a "size" of 16. In the second case both the second and third subscripts are fixed, leaving a one-dimensional array of size four. The final example is like the full array but with the element order reversed along two of the three dimensions.

In an array section, any subscript limit may be omitted, in which case it is taken to be the array's lower bound (before the colon) or upper bound (after the colon). So, with the array **matrices** as above, the examples could be written more compactly:

```
matrices(:,:,1)
matrices(:,4,98)
matrices (4:1:-1,  4:1:-1,:)
```

There are some subtleties to the syntax associated with array sections. An array section is an array even if it has only one element or even if it has no elements at all. For example,

```
r(1:0) = 1.0
```

is valid but does nothing because the array section on the left has no elements. Bear in mind that an assignment statement can have an array on the left and a scalar on the right. But,

```
r(1:0) = (/1.0/)
```

is illegal because on the right we have an array of size one (not a scalar!) which is not conformable with the zero-sized array on the left.

In view of the importance of the subscript triplet notation for array sections, it is stated concisely for future reference in Section 4.6 below.

4.5 Exercises 4.A

4.A1 Write statements, which should be as concise as possible, to set up the following one-dimensional arrays:
  (i) The square roots of the first ten positive integers;
  (ii) (/-1,-1, ... (repeated 30 times),1,1, ... (repeated 30 times)/);
  (iii) The first ten powers of π.

4.A2 Write declaration statements to set up two-dimensional arrays to contain examination marks (0–100) and corresponding letter grades (A–F) for each of 300 students in each of 12 subjects. Write code to rescale all the marks so that the average mark is 60 per cent in every subject, and then convert the marks into grades in a sensible way.

4.A3 Write code to set up a two-dimensional array of the binomial coefficients, i.e. the numbers of ways in which m objects may be selected from n, n being a positive integer up to 50.

4.A4 A statistical exercise: if x_n ($n = 1, \ldots, N$) is a set of N values drawn from a distribution with mean X and variance σ, then estimates of X and σ are given by

$$X = \Sigma x_n / N$$

$$\sigma^2 = \Sigma (x_n - X)^2 / (N - 1)$$

and the uncertainty in the estimate X is $\sigma/N^{\frac{1}{2}}$.

On this basis, write a program to read in a series of numbers that are assumed to come from a distribution having a particular mean. The program is to calculate and write out an estimate, X, of the mean of the distribution, together with the uncertainty in it.

4.6 Subscript triplets

Before proceeding further, for future reference it will be useful to define in general terms the notation using colons that was described above to specify array sections. A section of an array specified by **array-name** is defined by

```
array-name (section-subscript, section-subscript,  &
    section-subscript, ...)
```

there being one **section-subscript** for every dimension of the array.

What is a **section-subscript**? A **section-subscript** is either a **subscript-triplet** or a single integer. (A third possibility, a "vector subscript", is introduced in Chapter 9.) If a **section-subscript** is an integer, it could be either a constant or a variable or an integer-valued expression, but it must be a scalar.

However, to form an array section, it would not be permissible for every **section-subscript** to be an integer. If they were all integers, the expression would be a valid one but, instead of representing an array section, it would simply represent a single element of the array and would be a scalar. On the other hand, as long as at least one **section-subscript** is a **subscript-triplet**, then we will be forming an array section and it is important to realize that an array section is itself a kind of array. The array section has a rank equal to the number of **subscript-triplets** among the **section-subscripts**.

What is a **subscript-triplet**? It is

```
subscript1: subscript2: stride
```

a construction in which only the first colon is compulsory and may not be omitted. The effect of the **subscript-triplet** is to pick out the elements of the array whose indices (in this particular dimension) run from **subscript1** to no more than **subscript2** in increments of **stride**. Note that **subscript1, subscript2** and **stride** must be integers (constants, variables or expressions). If *subscript1* is omitted, the effect is as if it were equal to the index at the lower bound of the array in this dimension. If *subscript2* is omitted, it is as if the upper bound were specified. If *stride* is omitted, it is as if it were equal to **1**.

Note that *subscript2* would normally be greater than *subscript1*, but it could be the other way round if *stride* were negative, in which case the selected array elements would be reversed in order from the original array. Note also that an array section will contain no elements (but will still exist!) if there is a *subscript-triplet* that generates no valid index. This would happen, for example, if *stride* were positive but *subscript2* were less than *subscript1*.

If **quintessence** is a rank-five array,

```
quintessence(:,:,:,:,:)
```

is no different from

```
quintessence
```
but
```
quintessence(:,1,:,6,:)
```

is a rank-three array section and

```
quintessence(1,1,9,6,2)
```

is just one element of quintessence, and is a scalar. In

```
quintessence(:,:,:,:,2:1:1)
```

the fifth *subscript-triplet* is **2:1:1**, which generates no indices because you never get to **1** by adding units to **2**; so this array section is a rank-five array with no elements at all!

4.7 Character substrings and arrays of character strings

The subscript triplet notation is very similar to a notation that may be used to pick out a part of a character string. If **lines(10)** is an array of ten character strings, what will the processor understand by lines(1:5)? The answer is, it means the first five elements of the array **lines**, in accordance with all that has been said above. On the other hand, **lines(1)(1:5)** would actually represent the first five characters of the first element of the array!

The situation is that if *character-name* represents any scalar character-string, then

```
character-name (position1 : position2)
```

represents the character string formed by taking the sequence of characters within *character-name* starting from position *position1* and going forward to *position2*. It is a "substring" of *character-name*. If *position1* is omitted, it is taken to be 1, and if *position2* is not given, it is taken to have its maximum value, i.e. the length of the string *character-name*. If L is the length of **character-name**, we must have

$$1 \leq position1 \leq position2 \leq L$$

unless

position1 > *position2*

in which case the substring exists but contains no characters, i.e. it has zero length. The pair

position1 : *position2*

is known as a "substring range".

So, the substring `c(i:j)` would be equal to

`c(i)//c(i+1)//c(i+2)//...//c(j-1)//c(j)`

if `j` is sufficiently greater than `i`.

Now, if we pick up the example given at the start of this section,

`lines(1:4)(1:5)`

is an array section consisting of four substrings, i.e. the first five characters from each of the first four elements of the array **lines**. On the other hand,

`lines(1:5)(1:4)`

is an array section consisting of five substrings each of four characters.

Symbolically, the notation for a subobject of a rank-one character array is

character-array-name (section-subscript) (substring-range)

and if the rank is greater than one there must be that number of *section-subscripts*. If *substring-range* is omitted then we simply have a section of the array as defined in Section 4.6. The *section-subscripts* may not be omitted, i.e.

character-array-name (substring-range)

is not legal, but the desired effect may be got by writing

character-array-name (:,:,:,...,:) (substring-range)

where the number of colons is the rank of *character-array-name*.

The following example may make the notation clear:

```
CHARACTER(30) :: words(2000), test(25)
CHARACTER(10) :: shorter(2000), check
```

```
    .
    .
    .
test = words(176:200)
shorter = words(1:2000)(1:10)
check = words(99)(1:10)
```

The first two of these assignment statements give values to arrays. The third gives a value to the scalar character string **check**. The last two statements could equally well be written

```
shorter = words(:)(:10)
check = words(99)(:10)
```

since an omitted index is taken to have the lowest or highest value possible, according to whether it is before or after the colon. Similar rules apply to multidimensional arrays, as in

```
CHARACTER(30) :: words(30,60,200), halfpage(30,30)
CHARACTER :: capitals(30,60,200)
    .
    .
    .
halfpage = words(:,:30,57)
capitals = words(:,:,:)(:1)
```

Array sections and substrings can also be used in array constructors, as in

```
CHARACTER, PARAMETER :: digits(0:9) = (/ ("01235456789"&
   (k:k), k=1,10) /)
CHARACTER, PARAMETER :: octals(0:7) = digits(:7)
```

This syntax is made clearer in Chapter 8. As a final example, if we have

```
CHARACTER(6) :: concept(3) = (/&
"origin","cattle","potato"/)
```

then **concept(2:)(4:5)** is equal to (/"tl","at"/).

Incidentally, an array constructor is taken to have the same type as the first element in it, and a character-type array constructor consists of strings whose lengths are all the same as those of the first element. So, the character constant

```
(/"or","cattle","potato"/)
```

is exactly equivalent to (/"or","ca","po"/), because the longer elements will be truncated just as they would be if they were given as values to length-two strings by assignment statements.

Remember that the substring notation may not be applied to an expression other than a constant or a variable. So,

```
a//b(i:j)
```

concatenates a string with a substring; it does not take a substring of the concatenation of two strings. And it is not permissible to specify a substring of a substring directly as in

```
p = q(1:m)(n:)
```

which could actually mean something quite different, as we will see in the next chapter when arrays are explained in more detail.

4.8 Masks

The concept of a "mask" arises in the **WHERE** statement, to be explained below, and in several of the intrinsic functions commonly used with arrays.

A mask is a logical array, i.e. an array whose elements are data items of **LOGICAL** type. The word "mask" is appropriate because arrays of this type are most often used to mask arrays of other types, i.e. to identify a subset of their elements on which some other operation is to be carried out.

Suppose, for example, that **a** and **b** are **REAL** arrays of the same shape. Then **a>b** is a logical expression, whose value is **.TRUE.** whenever **a>b**, and it is itself an array of the same shape as **a** and **b**. It is a logical array, i.e. a mask.

Logical arrays can be manipulated by assignment statements like any other type of array, e.g.

```
pickneg = a<0.0
evens = (/.FALSE.,.TRUE.,.FALSE.,.TRUE.,.FALSE.,.TRUE./)
```

4.9 WHERE

Normally, an array assignment statement **a=b** will set each element of **a** equal to the corresponding element of **b**. However, the assignment may be made conditional with a statement such as

```
WHERE (b>a) a = b
```
or
```
WHERE (a<0.0) a = 0.0; a=SQRT(a)
```

The expression **b>a** is a mask of the same shape as the arrays **a** and **b**, and **a<0.0** has the same shape as **a**. The logical array **b>a** could be expressed in array constructor notation as

```
(/ b(1)>a(1), b(2)>a(2), b(3)>a(3), .... /)
```

The general syntax of the **WHERE** statement is

```
WHERE (m) a = b
```

Here, *m* must be of logical type: it could be a variable, or a constant, or an expression. It is necessary for **a** to be an array (otherwise, we could have had **IF** instead of **WHERE**). If *m*, **a** and **b** are all arrays, they must have the same shapes. The assignment **a=b** then takes place conditionally, element by element, according to whether the corresponding element of *m* is true or false. The logical object *m* could be a scalar, in which case the statement is equivalent to

```
IF (m) a = b
```

If **b** is a scalar and *m* and **a** are arrays, then the value of **b** is given to all the elements of **a** that correspond to true elements of *m*.

Here is another simple example:

```
REAL :: angles(500)
WHERE (angles>360.0) angles = MOD(angles,360.0)
```

Going beyond the simple **WHERE** statement, there is a **WHERE** construct by which a number of conditional array assignment statements may be tied together. If **x**, **xl** and **xr** are real arrays of the same shape, we could have:

```
WHERE (x>0.0)
   xl = LOG(x)
   xr = SQRT(x)
ELSEWHERE
   xl = -99.0
   xr = 0.0
END WHERE
```

This **WHERE** construct consists of an opening statement with the keyword **WHERE** followed just by a bracketed logical array; then there is a sequence of array assignment statements; then there can be an **ELSEWHERE** followed by assignment statements conditional on the inverse of the original logical array. Finally, the construct is terminated by an **END WHERE** statement. The **WHERE** construct forms a unit and must not be interspersed with other types of statement. The **WHERE** construct may only contain assignment statements and not (for example) **WRITE** statements.

The **WHERE** statement, and assignment statements within a **WHERE** construct, are often called "masked" array assignments.

Fortran 95 feature not in Fortran 90

WHERE constructs may be nested, and may be named, in the same way as **IF** constructs. An example is

```
Outer: WHERE (out)
  a = b
  c = d
  Inner: WHERE (narrow)
    e = f
      Innermost: WHERE (inside)
          x = y
      END WHERE Innermost
    g = h
  END WHERE Inner
  i = j
  WHERE (outlook) k = 1
END WHERE Outer
```

This consists of three **WHERE** constructs nested inside one another, and a **WHERE** statement that is within the outer **WHERE** construct. For simplicity no **ELSEWHERE** statements are included in this example, but in principle they could also occur.

In Fortran 95, a **WHERE** construct may contain a series of masked **ELSE WHERE** statements, like **ELSE IF** statements in the **IF** construct, as well as a non-masked **ELSEWHERE** that is analogous to **ELSE**. (Notice that, although Fortran does not distinguish between **ELSE WHERE** and **ELSEWHERE**, it is as well to follow the English language and use **ELSE WHERE** when another mask follows it, but **ELSEWHERE** for an unmasked catch-all final part of the construct).

In a Fortran 95 **WHERE** statement or **WHERE** construct, if the data is of a user-defined derived type, then the assignment must be an "elemental" assignment defined by an elemental subroutine (Section 11.3).

4.10 Arrays and intrinsic functions

Arrays can make use of many of Fortran's intrinsic functions, and in this chapter we have already encountered the **SQRT** and **LOG** functions being applied to arrays. Functions that can be applied to arrays are known as "elemental" functions. Fortran's numeric, mathematical and character functions are all elemental, and so are the bit manipulation functions (Appendix B). However, inquiry functions and so-called "transformational" functions that operate on whole arrays are not elemental. Examples of transformational functions are

```
ALL(mask)
ANY(mask)
COUNT(mask)
MAXVAL(array)
```

```
MINVAL(array)
PRODUCT(array)
SUM(array)
```

where the arguments are one-dimensional arrays but the results returned are scalars. The use of multidimensional arrays with these functions is slightly more complicated and additional arguments may be applicable.

The names of these functions make it easy to remember what they do. The argument of **ALL** must be a logical array, and the result is a scalar of logical type and is true if and only if all elements of the argument are true. The function **ANY** likewise returns a true result if any of its elements is true. The function **COUNT** has an integer value equal to the number of true elements in its argument. **MAXVAL** and **MINVAL** operate on arrays that may be of real or integer type, and the results are the highest (**MAXVAL**) or lowest (**MINVAL**) values to be found among the elements. So,

```
MINVAL((/5,99,0,-5,1/))
```

is equal to **-5**. The functions **PRODUCT** and **SUM** operate on arrays that may be real, integer or complex and the result is the product of all the elements or the sum of them. Thus,

```
PRODUCT((/(0.0,1.0),(0.0,1.0)/))
```

is equal to **(-1.0,0.0)**.

Note that **MAXVAL, MINVAL, PRODUCT** and **SUM** have values that are of the same data type as their arguments. For example,

```
SUM((/1,-1,1,-1/))
```

is equal to the integer **0** because the argument is an integer array. Because these functions are not specific to a single data type they are called "generic" functions.

4.11 Exercises 4.B

4.B1 What are the substrings
  (i) `"mulligatawny"(7:8)`   (ii) `"mulligatawny"(1:4)`
  (iii) `"mulligatawny"(6:6)`   (iv) `"mulligatawny"(10:8)`

4.B2 Write type declaration statements to declare
  (i) A zero-length string called **null**;
  (ii) Three strings, each of length 24, called **s1**, **s2** and **s3**;
  (iii) A character-string constant named **me** whose value is your surname;
  (iv) A named character constant of length 1 called **bs** whose value is the backslash character (\).

4.B3 Write statements, which should be as concise as possible, to set up the following one-dimensional arrays:

   (i) `(/.TRUE.,.FALSE.,.TRUE.,.FALSE., ..., (repeated for 50 pairs) /)`;

  (ii) `(/"a","ab","abr","abra", ...,"abracadabra"/)`;

 (iii) The array `razamatazz` but with its elements in reverse order and omitting every third element, where `razamatazz` is the name of a size-30 vector.

4.B4 Write a program to read a list of ten real numbers (real parts) and then another list of the same length (imaginary parts) and then to form the array of complex numbers comprised by the corresponding real and imaginary parts. Then calculate which of the complex numbers has the greatest magnitude, and write it. (Note that `CMPLX` and `ABS` are elemental functions.)

4.B5 If the array `s` is given by

```
CHARACTER(5):: s(6)
s = (/"light","trick","witch","hazel","beach","shore"/)
```

use structure constructors to write down the values of

  (i) `s(1:2)`   (ii) `s(5:)`   (iii) `s(4:3:-1)`

 (iv) `s(1:2)(3:4)`   (v) `s(1)(5:5)`   (vi) `s(5:1:-1)(5:)`

For example, the answer to (vi) is `(/"ch","el","ch","ck","ht"/)`.

4.B6 Write a program to input a string of up to 80 characters that will be interpreted as a line of text. Obtain the words from this string (a "word" being any sequence of letters with non-letter characters at both ends of the sequence) and search the words for palindromes. A palindrome is a word that reads the same in both directions, like "deed". The program should write out any palindromes that it finds.

4B.7 Write code to convert a sequence of x, y, z coordinate triplets into the corresponding sequence of radial coordinates (r, θ, ϕ), and then write out the radial coordinates of the point nearest to the origin. (Hint: look up `MAXLOC` in Appendix F.)

4.B8 Use a `WHERE` statement to halve all the elements of an integer array that are even numbers.

4.B9 Write a program to input a string of up to 20 characters and replace any blank in the string (but not trailing blanks) by an asterisk. Then write out the string, excluding trailing blanks.

4.B10 Write code to take a string that is a series of words (separated by blanks) and reduce it to a string made of their capital letters (e.g. `"North Dakota"` being reduced to `"ND"`).

4.B11 Use a `WHERE` construct to manipulate three two-dimensional square arrays (i.e. matrices) of real type called `a`, `b` and `c`. The object is to double the values of the elements of `a` that correspond in position to negative elements of `b`, unless the corresponding element of `c` is also negative, in which case it is the element of `b` that is doubled in value; and subsequently it is necessary to replace each element of `b` by the greater of the corresponding elements then to be found in `a` and `c`.

4.B12 Use a `WHERE` construct to look at an integer-valued array called `nibble` and form a real-valued array called **chew**. The elements of **chew** are to be the square roots of the elements of **nibble** where the latter are positive and odd, but the cube roots in all other cases.

4.B13 Given an array of 100 real numbers, called **data**, write a **WHERE** construct to halve each element of **data** that exceeds the average value of all of the elements initially in **data**, and to double those which are less than the average.

4.B14 Write another **WHERE** construct, again looking at the array **data** as in the previous example, but halving each element that is closer in value to the largest than to the smallest, and doubling those closer in value to the smallest.

4.B15 Again looking at the array **data** of the previous two examples, write a statement which, if any element of **data** is negative, will add to each element a number (the same for each element) sufficient to bring the value of the lowest element up to zero.

CHAPTER 5

Intrinsic procedures

Intrinsic procedures are facilities provided as a ready-coded adjunct to Fortran and they can be used to carry out a number of commonly-needed tasks and calculations. Here we discuss the procedure **DATE_AND_TIME** *as an example of an intrinsic subroutine, introduce the* **CALL** *statement, and then turn to the mathematical intrinsic functions* **SQRT, SIN, COS, EXP, LOG, LOG10, TAN, SINH, COSH, TANH, ASIN, ACOS, ATAN,** *and* **ATAN2.**

The numeric functions **ABS, AIMAG, CMPLX, INT, MOD, REAL, AINT, ANINT, CEILING, CONJG, DIM, FLOOR, MAX, MIN, MODULO, NINT,** *and* **SIGN** *are explained, and then the numeric enquiry functions* **HUGE, PRECISION, TINY, RANGE,** *and* **EPSILON,** *leading to a more detailed discussion of the* **KIND** *parameter for data types. Then after covering the intrinsic subroutines* **SYSTEM_CLOCK, CPU_TIME, RANDOM** *and* **RANDOMSEED,** *the final part of this chapter is devoted to the array-related functions* **MAXLOC, MINLOC, ALL, ANY, COUNT, MAXVAL, MINVAL, PRODUCT, SUM, SIZE, CSHIFT, EOSHIFT, TRANSPOSE, MERGE, PACK, UNPACK, SPREAD, DOTPRODUCT** *and* **MATMUL** *and to the floating-point manipulation functions* **RADIX, DIGITS, MAXEXPONENT, MINEXPONENT, TINY, EXPONENT, FRACTION, NEAREST, SPACING, RRSPACING, SCALE** *and* **SETEXPONENT.**

5.1 An intrinsic subroutine: DATE_AND_TIME

One of Fortran's intrinsic subroutines is entitled **DATE_AND_TIME** and can be invoked by a statement of the form

```
CALL DATE_AND_TIME &
  (ALL=list, COUNT=nticks, MSECOND=millisecs, &
  SECOND=nsecs, MINUTE=nmins, HOUR=nhours, DAY=nday, &
  MONTH=nmonth, YEAR=nyear, ZONE=minadvance)
```

This subroutine is taken as an example to explain a number of points about intrinsic procedures in general.

Some intrinsic procedures are functions, but some are subroutines, and those in the latter category can only be invoked by a **CALL** statement, an executable statement which has the general form

```
CALL subroutine-name (arguments)
```

although the call may be the "action" part of an **IF** statement such as

```
IF (time==.TRUE.) CALL DATE_AND_TIME (MSECOND=ms)
```

Unlike a function, a subroutine does not have a "value". Information may be passed to and/or from a subroutine through the values of its arguments.

DATE_AND_TIME has ten arguments, indicated by the keywords **ALL**, **COUNT**, **MSECOND**, and so on. These keywords are part of the language and are fixed (except, of course, that it would not matter if lower-case letters were used for them).

The effect of the call is to set the variables represented above by *list*, *nticks*, *millisecs*, etc. to values that will tell the program what the time and date are at the moment the statement is executed. Note that the names *nticks*, *millisecs*, *nsecs*, etc. are arbitrary, and any names for integer variables could be inserted in their place.

The statement

```
CALL DATE_AND_TIME &
  (ALL=list, COUNT=nticks, MSECOND=millisecs, &
SECOND=nsecs, MINUTE=nmins, &
  HOUR=nhours, DAY=nday, MONTH=nmonth, &
  YEAR=nyear, ZONE=minadvance)
```

would have exactly the same effect as

```
CALL DATE_AND_TIME &
  (list, nticks, millisecs, nsecs, nmins, nhours, &
  nday, nmonth, nyear, minadvance)
```

i.e. it is optional to include the attributions of the variables to the keywords. However, it is generally advisable to use the keywords and it is very useful to do so when (as is usually the case with the **DATE_AND_TIME** subroutine) not all the information contained in all the ten arguments is required. If the keywords are not used, then all the arguments must be included, in the correct order, at least as far as the last of them that is needed. So, if the value of the argument **minadvance** is needed, and if keywords are not being used, then all the preceding nine arguments must be included in the argument list before **minadvance**. On the other hand, if only **list** is required, the statement

```
CALL DATE_AND_TIME (list)
```

would be sufficient. The advantage of the argument keywords is that they can appear in any order and they need not all be present. For example, the statement

```
CALL DATE_AND_TIME (MONTH=k1, DAY=k2)
```

could be used if it were only necessary to find the values of the seventh and eighth arguments.

As the keywords suggest, the **DATE_AND_TIME** subroutine yields the local time and date in milliseconds, seconds, minutes, hours, days in the month, months in the year, and years according to the Gregorian calendar. **ZONE** gives the number of minutes that local time is in advance of Coordinated Universal Time. **COUNT** provides a processor-dependent "stopwatch". All the arguments of **DATE_AND_TIME** are integers. The keyword **ALL** can provide a neat way of getting all the information of the other keywords: the corresponding argument, called **list** above, must be an array with nine elements and would be filled with the values **COUNT**, **MSECOND**, etc. in that order. This is our first example of an array being an argument of a subroutine.

Incidentally, a piece of code like

```
CALL DATE_AND_TIME (ZONE=minutes); longitude=minutes/4
```

could give a very rough indication of where the processor is!

There are keywords that may be used with all the arguments of all Fortran's intrinsic procedures, functions as well as subroutines, although it is common to omit the keywords in the cases where there are only one or two arguments anyway and so there is little danger of confusion between them. For example, the intrinsic function **SQRT** could be invoked by an expression such as **SQRT(X=36.0)** using the keyword **X**, but there is no advantage over omitting the keyword and writing **SQRT(36.0)**.

It is possible to omit the keywords for some arguments but not for others, as long as those for which they are omitted (and which are therefore distinguished from one another by their positions in the list) all precede the arguments for which the keyword is included. For example,

```
CALL DATE_AND_TIME (listarray, nods, YEAR=j, DAY=k)
```

would be a valid statement.

DATE_AND_TIME is unusual because of the large number of its arguments and because all of them are optional. Most intrinsic procedures have at least one argument which must always be present. Since **DATE_AND_TIME** has no obligatory argument, the statement

```
CALL DATE_AND_TIME ()
```

could in theory be written although it would be useless. A subroutine with no arguments does not even need the pair of brackets, i.e. we could just have

```
CALL DATE_AND_TIME
```

These remarks are not pointless because it will be seen later that there can be "external" (user-written) subroutines that have no arguments but nevertheless carry out useful tasks.

The situation is slightly different with intrinsic (and external) functions. In the few cases where it makes sense to refer to a function without giving it an argument, the brackets cannot be omitted. For example, **NULL()** is permissible but not simply **NULL**. The reason is that, without the brackets that follow it, a function name would be indistinguishable from the name of an ordinary variable. A subroutine, however, is always distinguished by following the keyword **CALL** and so the brackets may be omitted without ambiguity.

5.2 Mathematical functions

The intrinsic procedures can be divided into several categories, one being the mathematical functions. A complete list of these follows, and more detailed specifications are given in Appendix F. The letter **x** is used to represent the argument, and may be used optionally as an argument keyword, although we will not use a keyword when the function has only one argument.

The following may have either a real or a complex argument and a result of the same type:

SQRT(X)	square root
SIN(X)	sine
COS(X)	cosine
EXP(X)	exponential (power of e)
LOG(X)	natural logarithm

So, **SQRT((-1.0, 0.0))** is equal to **(0.0, 1.0)**. The functions **SQRT** and **LOG** are not allowed to have a negative real argument, and the argument of **LOG** may never be zero. The following functions must have a real argument, and yield a real result:

LOG10(X)	logarithm to base 10
TAN(X)	tangent
SINH(X)	hyperbolic sine
COSH(X)	hyperbolic cosine
TANH(X)	hyperbolic tangent
ASIN(X)	inverse sine (between $\pm\pi/2$)
ACOS(X)	inverse cosine (from 0 to π)
ATAN(X)	inverse tangent (between $\pm\pi/2$)
ATAN2(Y,X)	inverse tangent (in range $\pm\pi$)

In spite of the requirement of non-integer arguments, it is in fact possible to insert integers as arguments of any of these functions, just as an integer may appear on the right-hand side of an assignment statement giving a value to a real or complex variable named on the left. What happens is that implicit type conversion takes place, the effect being as if the function **REAL** had been used for explicit type conversion. For example, the evaluation of **EXP(5)** is equivalent to **EXP(REAL(5))** and is the same as **EXP(5.0)**.

In all the functions above, angles are always taken to be in radians, not degrees.

The last function, **ATAN2**, is unusual in having two arguments. In effect it is very similar to **ATAN**, but its two arguments can be regarded as the coordinates of a point of which **ATAN2** is the bearing and that can lie in the full angular range between ±π. Another way of saying this is that **ATAN2(y, x)** is the "argument", in the mathematical sense, of the complex number **(x, y)**. In a statement like

```
bearing = halfpi + ATAN2(to_north, to_east)
```

the arguments of **ATAN2** must be in the correct order to avoid ambiguity and they are then called "positional" arguments. Alternatively, using the argument keywords **x** and **y**,

```
bearing = halfpi + ATAN2(Y=to_north, X=to_east)
```

and

```
bearing = halfpi + ATAN2(X=to_east, Y=to_north)
```

are equivalent to one another and to the previous example.

5.3 Numeric functions

The "numeric" functions are a group that carry out simple manipulations of numbers. They include the following, introduced in the previous chapter:

ABS(A)	Absolute value of **A** (argument of any numeric type)
AIMAG(Z)	Imaginary part of **z** (complex argument)
CMPLX(X,Y,KIND)	Forms a complex number (real or integer **x** and **y**)
INT(A,KIND)	The fractional part of **A** is removed, giving the integer nearest to **A** whose magnitude does not exceed the magnitude of **A** (argument of any numeric type, but **INT(A) = INT(REAL(A))** if **A** is integer or complex.)
MOD(A,P)	Remainder if **P** is repeatedly subtracted from **A** (real or integer arguments **A** and **P**).
REAL(A,KIND)	Converts **A** to real type (argument of any numeric type)

Most of these will require no further explanation. The function **MOD** may have either real or integer arguments and the result is of the same type as the argument **A**. The function **REAL** can be used to extract the real part of a complex number, or to convert an integer into real type. It is important to realize that this is a different usage of the word **REAL** from that in a type declaration statement: arguably it is a defect of Fortran that **REAL** could represent either a data type, or this function, and for that matter could also be used as the name of a variable. However, the pathological statement

```
REAL :: real = REAL (0)
```

is illegal because a name (of a variable, constant, construct, procedure, derived type or namelist group) may not be used in the same subprogram (technically, within the same "scoping unit") to identify two things. The above statement is illegal because **real** and the second **REAL** are both names, indistinguishable to Fortran, but the former refers to a variable and the latter to an intrinsic procedure. The first **REAL** is not a name at all, but a statement keyword, and so

```
REAL :: real
```

involves no clash of names and would be a legal statement (albeit an unwise one because it would preclude any reference to the **REAL** function elsewhere in the same subprogram).

The **KIND** argument is always optional where it is mentioned in the list above, and if present it can specify a non-default **KIND** parameter for the result's type (see Section 3.7 for non-default real numbers). For example we could have

```
x = REAL (A=number, KIND=k)
```

and in this example **number** is an integer variable being converted to a real number (**x**) with a **KIND** parameter given by the variable **k**. The **REAL** function could be used to convert between real types, as in

```
xhigh = REAL(A=xlow, KIND=2)
```

Similarly, **CMPLX** can be used to form a complex number as in

```
z = CMPLX(X=horiz, Y=vert)
```

or to convert a complex number from one **KIND** to another as in

```
zhigh = CMPLX(X=zlow, KIND=2)
```

So, for **CMPLX**, **x** and **y** may be integer or real, and **x** may be complex if **y** is absent. The other numeric intrinsic functions are:

AINT(A, KIND)	Truncation of **A** to a whole number (similar to **INT**, but with real **A** and a real result)
ANINT(A, KIND)	Nearest whole number to **A** (real **A** and a real result)
CEILING(A)	Nearest integer not less than **A** (real **A** but an integer result)

CONJG(X)   Complex conjugate of **x** (complex argument and result).

DIM(X, Y)   Difference (unsigned) between **x** and **y** (**x**, **y** and the result must all be real or all be integer).

FLOOR(A)   Nearest integer not greater than **A** (real **A** but integer result).

MAX(A1,A2,A3...)   Highest number (indefinite number of arguments).

MIN(A1,A2,A3...)   Lowest number (indefinite number of arguments).

MODULO(A,P)   **A** modulo **P**.

NINT(A,KIND)   Nearest integer to **A** (real **A** but an integer result).

SIGN(A,B)   Gives the first argument the sign of the second.

AINT simply removes the fractional part of a real number, and **ANINT** does a very similar job but goes to the nearest whole real number; so **AINT(-1.7)=-1.0**, **AINT(-0.7)=0.0**, and **AINT(1.7)=1.0**, but **ANINT(1.7)=2.0**.

The **CEILING** function is very similar, but its result is of integer type: **CEILING(A)** gives the integer immediately above **A** in value, i.e. **CEILING(1.3)=2** and **CEILING(-5.8)=-5**. The function **CONJG** must have a complex argument and its result is the complex conjugate of it. The **DIM** function must have two arguments and they can be either both real or both integer. **FLOOR** is another function along the lines of **CEILING**. The argument of **FLOOR** must be real and its result is the integer immediately below. Consequently, if **x** is any number with a fractional part, **FLOOR(x)** is equal to **CEILING(x)-1**. If **x** has no fractional part, i.e. if **REAL(INT(x))** is equal to **x**, then **FLOOR(x)** and **CEILING(x)** are both equal to **INT(X)**.

MAX and **MIN** are very useful functions which may have any number of arguments; the arguments may be real or integer, but not a mixture of the two types. The result is simply the largest (**MAX**) or smallest (**MIN**) of the arguments, i.e. **MIN(-9, -5, 0, 2)** is **-9**.

MODULO is subtly different from **MOD**, the distinction being relevant if either argument is negative. To be precise,

```
MODULO(A,P) = A-P*FLOOR(REAL(A)/REAL(P))
```

whereas

```
MOD(A,P) = A-P*INT((A/P)
```

The final two functions listed above, **NINT** and **SIGN**, have real or integer arguments and the result is of the same type as the arguments.

DBLE and DPROD

There are two intrinsic functions to do with "double precision" real data. **DBLE(A)** is like **REAL(A)** but the result is of double precision type. **DPROD(X,Y)** calculates the double-precision-real product of the default-real arguments **x** and **y**.

Fortran 95 features not in Fortran 90

The **CEILING** and **FLOOR** functions may also have a **KIND** argument (as **INT** and **NINT** may) to give a result of the specified **KIND** of integer.

The **SIGN** function may be used for a special purpose if the processor is configured (as some are) to offer a distinction between real variables of positive and negative zero values.

If the second argument of **SIGN** is a variable or expression of zero value, the value of **SIGN** may be positive or negative. This facility is provided in Fortran 95 because some processors, following an IEEE standard, have one bit pattern for positive zero and another for negative zero.

5.4 Numeric inquiry functions

The precision of real number arithmetic, and the maximum and minimum sizes of real numbers, depend on the processor. To monitor and manage precision Fortran provides a number of utility functions. The functions available include:

HUGE(X)	The largest representable number
PRECISION(X)	An integer equal to the maximum decimal precision, i.e. the maximum number of significant figures
TINY(X)	The smallest representable non-zero positive number
RANGE(X)	An integer equal to the order of magnitude of the largest representable number or, if greater, of the inverse of the smallest. So, **RANGE(X)** is equal to the greater of **INT(LOG10(HUGE(X)))** and **INT(-LOG10(TINY(X)))**
EPSILON(X)	A positive real number almost negligible in comparison with unity, convenient when you simply want to use as small a number as the processor will support (e.g. for numerical differentiation).

Different kinds of real number are distinguished by the **KIND** parameter, which was introduced in Chapter 3. It is a parameter that may be specified in a type declaration statement and it must have a non-negative integer value. When a real constant appears, the **KIND** parameter may follow the value after an underscore, as in

```
-78.915443_normal
1877724._quad
4.65E-9_hiprec
```

where **normal**, **quad** and **hiprec** are named constants given previously in type declaration statements (with the **PARAMETER** attribute, Chapter 8) and having values corresponding to **KIND** parameters valid for this processor.

The **KIND** parameter could alternatively be given explicitly, as in

```
-78.915443_2
```

but this sort of code is unsafe as it may not be portable between processors: the actual values of the **KIND** parameters (**2** in this instance) are not laid down in Fortran. The best thing to do is to use a special intrinsic function, **KIND(X)**, which returns the value of the **KIND** parameter for the number **x**. The default **KIND** parameter is given by, say, **KIND(0.0)**. Real numbers of higher precision can always be specified by a **KIND** parameter as defined by, say,

```
INTEGER, PARAMETER :: hiprec = KIND(0.0D0)
```

where **0.0D0** is a "double precision" number, as mentioned in Section 3.7. Notice that the word **KIND** can be used in three different ways: as a parameter when real data is declared, as an argument keyword in several intrinsic functions, and as the name of a particular intrinsic function. Examples of the three sorts of use are the statements

```
REAL (KIND=hiprec) :: sensitivity
q = REAL(A=k, KIND=2) - AINT(A=1.0, KIND=2)
IF (KIND(r).NE.2) THEN
```

Another example will be given at the end of this section. In addition to **KIND**, there is another intrinsic function provided to help control the use of real numbers of different kinds. It is the function **SELECTED_REAL_KIND(P,R)**, which returns an integer equal to the minimum **KIND** value used by the processor for real numbers of a given precision and range. The argument **P** is the required decimal precision and **R** is the required exponent range, and it is not necessary for both arguments to be present. **SELECTED_REAL_KIND** could be used in a type declaration statement (see Chapter 8) such as

```
INTEGER, PARAMETER :: nreal = SELECTED_REAL_KIND(P=15)
```

which sets **nreal** to be a named integer constant equal to the **KIND** parameter necessary for 15-figure decimal precision. Variables requiring this precision can subsequently be declared by statements like

```
REAL (KIND=nreal) :: x, y, z
```

However, one should first check that **nreal** is positive, because the **SELECTED_REAL_KIND** function will return a negative value if the processor cannot attain the required precision or range. In any program doing serious number crunching it is advisable for the programmer to decide in advance what precision and range are going to be needed. You could have a statement such as

```
IF (SELECTED_REAL_KIND(P=15, R=80) &
/= SELECTED_REAL_KIND(0.0)) STOP
```

to check that non-default kinds are not needed, or

```
IF (SELECTED_REAL_KIND(P=20, R=100)<0) STOP
```

to check that kinds of real numbers are available that will be capable of achieving the needed precision and range. (The **STOP** statement is mentioned in Section 6.7.)

Normally the default precision will be amply good enough for most calculations. Arguably, a program is badly designed if it relies on exceptionally high decimal precision. In the remainder of this book, little more will be said about non-default kinds of data.

Among the intrinsic functions discussed so far there have been the functions **REAL** and **KIND**. It is worth emphasizing yet again that these functions should not be confused with the keywords or parameters **REAL** and **KIND** that can occur in type declaration statements. The statement

```
REAL(KIND=KIND(0.0D0)) :: giga=REAL(2**30)
```

is really quite tricky because it uses the keyword **REAL**, meaning that the data object **giga** is to be of real type, and also the function **REAL**, which converts the integer **2**30** into a real number; and also there is the **KIND** function, which yields the parameter needed by this processor to specify a double-precision number such as **0.0D0**, and the **KIND** keyword that applies that parameter to **giga**!

5.5 Exercises 5.A

5.A1 Write programs to read a number from the keyboard and calculate and display the value(s) of its
 (i) secant
 (ii) inverse hyperbolic sine (arcsinh)
 (iii) logarithm to the base 16

5.A2 Write a program to input a sum of money, an interest rate and a time in years, and to calculate what the sum has grown to after that time if the interest is compounded monthly.

5.A3 A straight line (chord) divides a circle into two unequal parts. Write a program to calculate the area of the smaller part, given the circle's radius and the length of the chord.

5.A4 Write code to find the number of the current month of the year (using **DATE_AND_TIME**) and output its name.

5.A5 If x is a real variable, write a line of code to calculate the natural logarithm of the complex number whose real and imaginary parts are $\cosh(x)$ and $\sinh(x)$.

5.A6 Write a program which will simulate the tossing of a coin (writing out **head** or **tail**) using the millisecond counter of **DATE_AND_TIME** to give an integer of practically random parity.

5.A7 Write a program which will input a sequence of ten integers and calculate their average when the largest one and the smallest one are disregarded.

5.A8 Write a program to find and write the order of magnitude of the number given by **EPSILON** on your processor. Also, find out if the square of this number is representable as distinct from zero.

5.A9 The intrinsic function **SIGN(A,B)** gives the first argument the sign of the second. Write code to do the same job without using this function.

5.6 More intrinsic subroutines: SYSTEM_CLOCK, CPU_TIME, RANDOM and RANDOMSEED

Besides **DATE_AND_TIME**, described at the start of this chapter, there are two other intrinsic subroutines used for timekeeping, namely **SYSTEM_CLOCK** and (in Fortran 95) **CPU_TIME**.

SYSTEM_CLOCK has up to three arguments and is called by a statement of the form

```
CALL SYSTEM_CLOCK (COUNT=i, COUNT_RATE=j, COUNT_MAX=k)
```

The arguments are scalar integers with the keywords **COUNT**, etc. as shown. The **COUNT** argument measures time in the processor's own basic units or "clock counts". It is the same as the **COUNT** argument in the **DATE_AND_TIME** subroutine. **COUNT_RATE** allows the programmer to connect values of **COUNT** with real elapsed time, **COUNT_RATE** being the number of counts per second. **COUNT_MAX** gives the maximum count after which the clock is reset to zero. If the processor does not possess a clock then **COUNT_RATE** and **COUNT_MAX** are returned as zero. **SYSTEM_CLOCK** could be used by statements like

```
CALL SYSTEM_CLOCK(COUNT_RATE=nsec)
   .
   .
   .
IF (nsec>0) THEN
  CALL SYSTEM_CLOCK(COUNT=n)
  milliseconds = 1000*n/nsec
END IF
```

Note that all three arguments of **SYSTEM_CLOCK** are optional, although obviously there is no point in calling it if none are present.

Fortran 95 feature not in Fortran 90

CPU_TIME is an intrinsic subroutine that has one argument, of real type, measuring the "processor time" in seconds. The precise definition of processor time will in general be dependent on the processor. **TIME** is a scalar in standard Fortran 95, but a parallel processor could provide an enhanced version of **CPU_TIME** returning an array of processor times.

There is a very useful pair of intrinsic subroutines used for generating random numbers, **RANDOM** and **RANDOMSEED**. **RANDOM** has a single argument, of real type, which is returned to the program with a random value in the range between **0** and **1**. It does not matter what value (if any) the argument had before **RANDOM** is called. If it is an array variable, then an array of different random numbers will be returned. So, if **x** is a real scalar variable,

```
CALL RANDOM(x)
```

gives **x** a random value between **0.0** and **1.0** (to be precise, $0.0 \le x < 1.0$). A more complex usage is the following:

```
REAL :: radvec(3) = 99.0
   .
   .
   .
DO WHILE (SUM(radvec**2)>1.0)
  CALL RANDOM(radvec)
END DO
```

The **DO WHILE** syntax is explained in the next chapter. This code finds a random point within the three-dimensional unit sphere. It does so by picking a point within a cubic volume and checking to see if it is also within the enclosed sphere. The coordinates are preset to a large value merely to satisfy the **WHILE** condition when the **DO** loop is first entered: subsequently the loop is repeated until a point within the sphere is found.

The subroutine **RANDOMSEED** is to do with the initializing of the random number generator that **RANDOM** will invoke. **RANDOMSEED** has three optional arguments, but no more than one may be present in a particular call, so we could have any of the following

```
CALL RANDOMSEED
CALL RANDOMSEED(SIZE=nints)
CALL RANDOMSEED(PUT=intseedin)
CALL RANDOMSEED(GET=intseedout)
```

Now, **RANDOM** generates random numbers (or, more technically, "pseudo-random" numbers) using internally a set of integers known as the "seed" that changes from one call to the next. The seed determines the subsequent sequence of random numbers. A call to **RANDOMSEED** with no argument will simply reset the seed, and might be used at the beginning of a program to make sure that different runs of the same program would give different sequences of random numbers. A call with the argument keyword **GET** is used to obtain from the processor the current value of the seed. The **PUT** keyword lets the program specify the seed value. Calls with **GET** and **PUT** could be used to record the value of the seed at the start of a simulation, say, and to repeat the run later with the same sequence of random numbers. A complication is that the seed might not be a single integer but a set of integers in a rank-one array. The size of that array (i.e. the number of integers in the seed) is processor-dependent but can be found in a program by calling **RANDOMSEED** with the **SIZE** keyword. Obviously the variables used to hold the seed must be arrays of sufficient size, i.e. in the above example, **intseedin** and **intseedout** must be of size equal to or greater than **nints**.

Although **RANDOM** generates real numbers between **0** and **1**, it is a simple matter to scale the results to simulate, say, the throw of a set of seven dice:

```
REAL :: x(7)
INTEGER :: n(7), ntotal
CALL RANDOM(x)
n = 1 + INT(6.0*x)
ntotal = SUM(n)
```

5.7 Functions for arrays

The intrinsic functions described in this section are

MAXLOC	Location of an array's largest element
MINLOC	Location of the lowest element
ALL	True if all an array's elements are true
ANY	True if any element is true
COUNT	The number of true elements
MAXVAL	Value of the largest element
MINVAL	Value of the lowest element
PRODUCT	Product of all the elements
SUM	Sum of all the elements
CSHIFT	Shift the elements cyclically
EOSHIFT	Shift the elements "end-off"
TRANSPOSE	The transpose of a matrix
MERGE	Merge two arrays selectively
PACK	Pack an array into a rank-one array
UNPACK	Unpack a rank-one array
SPREAD	Replicate an array
DOTPRODUCT	Scalar product of two vectors
MATMUL	Product of two matrices
SIZE	Size of an array

Each of these will be discussed briefly below, with indications of the argument keywords and their meanings. In many cases it is obvious what the keywords mean, e.g. **ARRAY** always refers to an array argument. At first reading, the descriptions below will inevitably seem very complex and you may wonder what on earth these functions are really needed for. In fact, they are very useful for testing, manipulating and reordering the elements of arrays, and doing so with great flexibility and conciseness. They are powerful tools for the programmer who needs to work with arrays of data.

MAXLOC(ARRAY, MASK) looks into an array of real or integer numbers and returns the set of subscripts giving the location of the largest element. The value of **MAXLOC** will be a rank-one array containing the subscripts, so the size of **MAXLOC** is equal to the rank of **ARRAY**. **MASK** is an optional second argument: if present it must be a logical array (or expression) with the same shape as **ARRAY**, and elements of **ARRAY** are disregarded if the corresponding elements of **MASK** are false. For example, if **y** is the array (/1946,1932,1945,1949, 1936/) then

    MAXLOC(ARRAY=y,MASK=y<1946)

is equal to the array (/3/). **MINLOC(ARRAY,MASK)** is exactly like **MAXLOC** except that it indicates the minimum-valued array element.

ALL(MASK,DIM), and others following it in the list above, were introduced in a simple form in Chapter 4. Its first argument is a logical array, **MASK**. In the simple case, where the optional argument **DIM** is absent, **ALL** is a logical function true if all the elements of **MASK** are true. If **DIM** is present, **DIM** (short for "dimension")must be a scalar integer no greater than the rank of **MASK**, and the function then sees if all the values of **MASK** are true along the **DIM**th dimension: the result is then an array of rank one less than that of **MASK**. In other words, **ALL** suppresses the **DIM**th dimension of **MASK** to a value that is true only if all **MASK**'s elements along that dimension are true. For example, if **q** is a six-dimensional logical array and

    f = ALL(MASK=q,DIM=4)

then **f** is a five-dimensional array such that **f(i,j,k,m,n)** is equal to

    ALL(MASK=q(i,j,k,:,m,n))

ANY(MASK,DIM) is like **ALL** except that the result (or an element of the result) is true if any of **MASK**'s elements (or its elements along a particular dimension) is true.

COUNT(MASK,DIM) also operates on logical arrays. In the simple case when the optional argument **DIM** is absent, the function has an integer (not logical) value equal to the number of **MASK**'s true elements. If **DIM** is present, then (as for **ALL** and **ANY**) the result **COUNT** is an array whose shape is reduced from that of **MASK** by the elimination of the **DIM**th dimension. Continuing the previous example,

```
ntrue = COUNT(MASK=q,DIM=4)
```

gives an array such that `ntrue(i,j,k,m,n)` is equal to

```
COUNT(MASK=q(i,j,k,:,m,n))
```

MAXVAL(ARRAY,DIM,MASK) operates on an array of type integer or real and looks for maximum element values. **MASK** is an optional logical array that, if present, must be of the same shape as **ARRAY**; it causes the function to ignore elements of **ARRAY** corresponding to false elements of **MASK**. If **DIM** is present, it has an effect similar to that for the functions **ALL**, **ANY** and **COUNT**, and the result is an array. **MINVAL(ARRAY,DIM,MASK)** is similar to **MAXVAL** but finds the minimum-valued element, or elements, of **ARRAY**. **PRODUCT(ARRAY,DIM, MASK)**, just like **MAXVAL**, has optional arguments **DIM** and **MASK** that make it possible to do more complicated things than were mentioned when we introduced this function in Chapter 4. For example, if

```
kit = (/1,0,6,-5,3,0,0,-2,10/)
```
then
```
PRODUCT(ARRAY=kit,MASK=kit/=0)
```

is equal to **1800**.

SUM(ARRAY,DIM,MASK) is just like **PRODUCT** except that it adds rather than multiplies. The function **SIZE(ARRAY)**, as its name implies, yields the size (i.e. total number of elements) of the array; it may also be used with an optional argument **DIM**, and **SIZE(ARRAY,DIM)** is the extent of the array along its **DIM**th dimension. A simple example of the use of **SIZE** and **SUM** is the calculation of the root mean square (rms) of the elements of an array **x**, by the statement

```
rms = SQRT(SUM(x**2)/SIZE(x))
```

If we wanted the rms value only of alternate members of the array **x**, that could be achieved by

```
rms_odd = SQRT(SUM(x(1::2)**2)/SIZE(x(1::2)))
```
or
```
rms_even = SQRT(SUM(x(2::2)**2)/SIZE(x(2::2)))
```

and if we wanted these two things to be paired as a size-two array, we could have

```
rms_alternates = (/ (SQRT(SUM(x(i::2)**2)/&
SIZE(x(i::2)))), i=1,2) /)
```

CSHIFT(ARRAY,DIM,SHIFT) is a function we have not encountered before. It operates on an array of any type. The result **CSHIFT** is also an array and it is of the same type and shape as **ARRAY**. In the simplest case, where **ARRAY** is one-dimensional, **DIM** must be equal to **1** and the effect of the function is to perform a circular shift of the elements of **ARRAY**. The shift is through **SHIFT** places, **SHIFT** being a scalar integer. So,

```
y = (/"a","b","c","d","e","f"/)
z = CSHIFT(ARRAY=y,DIM=1,SHIFT=-2)&
  //CSHIFT(ARRAY=y,DIM=1,SHIFT=1)
```

gives

```
(/"eb","fc","ad","be","cf","da"/)
```

If **ARRAY** has more than one dimension, then shifting will take place along the dimension specified by **DIM**. **DIM** must be a scalar integer lying in the range from 1 up to the rank of **ARRAY**. In this case, **SHIFT** may be a scalar integer and all elements of **ARRAY** will be shifted by **SHIFT** places around the **DIM**th dimension; but alternatively the different sections

```
ARRAY(i,j,k...,:,...)
```

(where a colon appears in the **DIM**th position) may be shifted **DIM**-wise by different numbers of places, **SHIFT** then being an array whose shape is reduced from that of **ARRAY** by the suppression of the **DIM**th dimension (cf. **ALL**, **ANY** etc. above).

EOSHIFT(ARRAY,DIM,SHIFT,BOUNDARY) is just like **CSHIFT** except that the shifting of elements is not circular, i.e. elements disappear when they fall off one end of a dimension and are not transferred to the other end. **EOSHIFT** is an acronym for "end-off shift". With an array **y** defined as previously,

```
EOSHIFT(ARRAY=y,DIM=1,SHIFT=2)
```

is equal to

```
(/" "," ","a","b","c","d"/)
```

i.e. as we move the array to the right, vacancies are created on the left and these are filled with blank strings of the appropriate length. In the case of numeric or logical data, zero or **.FALSE.** is inserted. If different infill values are required, they can be specified through the optional argument **BOUNDARY**, which like **SHIFT** may be a scalar or an array. For example, if

```
n = (/ (k, k=1,10) /)
```

then

```
EOSHIFT(ARRAY=EOSHIFT(ARRAY=n,DIM=1,SHIFT=4, &
  BOUNDARY=0),DIM=1,SHIFT=-2,BOUNDARY=10)
```

is equal to (`/0,0,1,2,3,4,5,6,10,10/`).

TRANSPOSE(MATRIX), by contrast with the above functions, is extremely simple. It obtains the transpose of a matrix, in the mathematical sense. **MATRIX**, the only argument, must be a rank-two array and may be of any type. If **MATRIX** is an array **m** with shape $(n1,n2)$ and elements $m(i,j)$, and `t=TRANSPOSE(m)`, then `t` has shape `(n2,n1)` and elements $t(i,j) = m(j,i)$.

`MERGE(TSOURCE,FSOURCE,MASK)` is an elemental function returning either `TSOURCE` or `FSOURCE` according to whether `MASK` is true or false. `MASK` must be of logical type; `TSOURCE` and `FSOURCE` may be of any type, but the same, and if they are arrays they must have the same shape. If `MASK` is an array it must have the same shape as `TSOURCE` and `FSOURCE`. If `TSOURCE` and `FSOURCE` are logical, then `MERGE` is equivalent to

`(TSOURCE.AND.MASK).OR.(FSOURCE.AND..NOT.MASK)`

The `MERGE` function acts as a sort of switch, as in the expression

`MERGE(TSOURCE=1,FSOURCE=0,MASK=veracity)`

which could be used to convert a logical variable (`veracity`)into integer type.

`PACK(ARRAY,MASK,VECTOR)` can transform an array whose rank is two or more (`ARRAY`) into a rank-one array. This can be done selectively, keeping only those elements corresponding to `MASK` being true. In other words, `PACK` is constructed by forming the elements of `ARRAY` into a one-dimensional list. The order is determined by running through the subscript values of `ARRAY` from the left as in:

```
ARRAY(1,1,1,...),
ARRAY(2,1,1,...),
ARRAY(3,1,1,...,,
    .
    .
    .
ARRAY(1,2,1,...),
ARRAY(2,2,1,...) ...
```

This is called "array element order". Another example should make the principle clear: if the array `s` is declared by

`REAL :: s(2,3)`

then `PACK(s)` is the one-dimensional array

`(/ s(1,1), s(2,1), s(1,2), s(2,2), s(1,3), s(2,3) /)`

It is permissible for `ARRAY` to have rank one, in which case `PACK` will be very similar to `ARRAY` but excluding elements for which `MASK` is false. Thus, the expression

`PACK(ARRAY=characters,MASK=(characters/=" "))`

eliminates all the blanks from an array of single characters.

The size of `PACK` will be the number of elements in `ARRAY` for which `MASK` is true, but to get a result of predetermined size the optional argument `VECTOR` can be used: it must be a rank-one array whose size will be the size of **PACK** and whose latter elements provide values to pad out **PACK** in default of sufficient **MASK=.TRUE.** elements from **ARRAY**. For example,

```
PACK(ARRAY=(/5,4,3,2,1/),MASK=.TRUE.,VECTOR=(/k,k=1,10/
))
```

has the value

```
(/5,4,3,2,1,6,7,8,9,10/)
```

UNPACK(VECTOR,MASK,FIELD) can be regarded as the inverse of **PACK**. If **VECTOR** is a rank-one array of any type, its elements will be distributed into the array **FIELD** to form the result **UNPACK**. **FIELD** may have any shape, but its type must be the same as **VECTOR**'s. The unpacking of **VECTOR** into **FIELD** is done under the control of **MASK**. Running through the elements of **FIELD** in the usual array element order (see **PACK**), elements from **VECTOR** are inserted sequentially to replace those elements of **FIELD** for which **MASK** is true. Where **MASK** is false, or where the elements of **VECTOR** have already been used up, **FIELD** is unchanged. To take a simple example, if there is such a thing,

```
UNPACK(VECTOR=(/1,2/),&
  MASK=(/.TRUE.,.FALSE.,.FALSE.,.TRUE./),&
  FIELD=(/9,8,7,6/))
```

is `(/1,8,7,2/)`.

SPREAD(SOURCE,DIM,NCOPIES) will replicate the array **SOURCE** by adding an extra dimension of extent **NCOPIES**; each element of **SOURCE** is repeated **NCOPIES** times along the new dimension. The argument **DIM** indicates in which position the new dimension is to be inserted in the list of extents defining the shape of **SOURCE**. So, if the shape of **g** is `(4,4,200)`,

```
SPREAD(SOURCE=g,DIM=3,NCOPIES=10)
```

has the shape `(4,4,10,200)`. A more complicated example: the code

```
v1 = .FALSE.
v2 = EOSHIFT(ARRAY=v1,DIM=1,SHIFT=1,BOUNDARY=.TRUE.)
m1 = SPREAD(SOURCE=v2,DIM=2,NCOPIES=d)
m2 = CSHIFT(ARRAY=m1,DIM=2,SHIFT=(/ (i-1,i=1,d) /))
m3 = 0.0
diagonal_matrix = UNPACK(VECTOR=vector,MASK=m2,FIELD=m3)
```

where the **v**s are size-**d** vectors and the **m**s are $d \times d$ square matrices, is a way of forming a diagonal matrix from the elements of **vector**.

DOTPRODUCT(VECTOR_A,VECTOR_B) forms the dot product (or "scalar product") of the two vectors that are its arguments. If the vectors are integer or real numbers, the dot product is the sum of the products of corresponding pairs of elements. If they are complex (to be more precise, if **VECTOR_A** is complex) then the complex conjugates of the elements of **VECTOR_A** are multiplied with the elements of **VECTOR_B**. If the vectors **u** and **v** are of logical type, then **DOTPRODUCT(u,v)** is equivalent to **ANY(u.AND.v)**.

MATMUL(MATRIX_A,MATRIX_B) forms the matrix product of two numeric matrices. The shapes of the two arguments must fit together, i.e. if **MATRIX_A** has shape **(i,j)** and **MATRIX_B** has shape **(j,k)** then **MATMUL** has shape **(i,k)**. Alternatively, one of the two arguments may be a vector, in which case **MATMUL** takes the product between the vector and the matrix in the conventional way. **MATMUL** may be used with logical instead of numeric data: if **u** and **v** are logical matrices and **w=MATMUL(u,v)**, then **w(i,j)** is **ANY(u(i,:) .AND.v(:,j))**.

5.8 Floating-point manipulation functions

The next set of intrinsic functions to be looked at is to do with the way in which numbers are represented internally within the computer. Although we almost always work with numbers displayed in decimal form, the computer itself may use a base other than ten. There is an intrinsic inquiry function **RADIX(X)** that returns an integer equal to the internal number base being used for real numbers (if **x** is real) or for integers (if **x** is an integer). In fact, most computers use the binary (base two) system. Below, it is assumed that **RADIX** is equal to **2**.

The processor represents a real number **x** in a form that may be modelled as

```
X = ±1 * 2**e * 0.1...
```

where the exponent **e** is a positive or negative integer and **0.1...** is any binary fraction in the range **0.1000...** to **0.1111...** (i.e **0.5** to almost **1.0** in decimal). The integer **e** might typically be formed from eight bits and could then range from **-126** to **+127**. (To represent the case of **x=0**, **e** and all the digits in the binary fraction are set to zero.) The binary fraction might run to, say, 24 places, and since the first place is always **1** this corresponds to 23 bits of information. With the sign bit and the eight bits forming **e**, we therefore have 32 bits representing a real number. This is a common system for representing default-real data in processors with 32-bit "words", but real data of higher-precision **KIND** may use, say, 64 bits and have a higher exponent range and more significant figures. To find out the situation on a particular processor, for numeric data of particular type and kind, there are intrinsic inquiry functions **DIGITS(X)**, **MAXEXPONENT(X)** and **MINEXPONENT(X)**, as well as the function **RADIX(X)** already mentioned. The argument just specifies the type and kind of data (e.g. **DIGITS(0.0)** specifies default real data). **DIGITS** returns the number of significant binary digits, while **MAXEXPONENT** and **MINEXPONENT** return the maximum and minimum values of the exponent **e**.

The function **TINY(X)** returns the value of the smallest positive number that can be represented on the processor.

Other functions give details of the representation of particular numbers. **EXPONENT(X)**, for real **X** of a specific value, gives the (integer) value of the exponent **e** as defined above. **FRACTION(X)** gives the value of the binary fraction **0.1...** defined above, but expressed as a real decimal fraction. **NEAREST(X,S)** returns the real number that the processor will allow nearest to (but not equal to) **X**; the real argument **S** is a flag to indicate whether **NEAREST** is to be above **X** or below it, according to whether **S** is positive or negative. **SPACING(X)** returns the minimum spacing between two real numbers in the neighbourhood of **X**. (If **SPACING** is itself too small to be represented, **TINY(X)** is returned instead.) Another function, **RRSPACING(X)**, returns the very large number that is the reciprocal of the relative minimum spacing between two real numbers near **X**. The definitions are such that

```
RRSPACING(x) * SPACING(x) = ABS(x)
```

for any value of **x**. There is a function **SCALE(X,I)** that scales up a real number **x** by the **I**th power of the processor's internal base, i.e. usually by **2**I**. Finally, there is **SETEXPONENT(X,I)**, a function that changes the exponent part of **x** to the power **I**; in other words, **e** is replaced by **I** in the expression for **x** given near the start of this section.

Specific names of intrinsic functions

Fortran's intrinsic functions have been introduced under names that are "generic". This usually means that the function can accept arguments of more than one type and that the function result has the same type as the argument. For example, **SIN(X)** is real if **x** is real, complex if **x** is complex, and has "double precision" if **x** has double precision. **SIN** is therefore said to be a "generic" function name. Likewise, **HUGE** is "generic" because **HUGE(X)** is a large integer if **x** is an integer and a large real number if **x** is real. However, Fortran also allows for a number of "specific" names, i.e. names under which functions may be referenced when the argument is restricted to being of a specific type. In the case of the **SIN** function, there are specific names **CSIN** and **DSIN** that can be used if the argument and result are to be restricted to complex or double-precision-real types respectively.

In Appendix F there is a complete list of specific names for generic Fortran functions. As a rule there is no point in using specific names and they are a hangover from earlier versions of Fortran in which different function names had to be used for arguments of different types.

What we mean by "specific" and "generic" names can cause confusion. The situation is that all intrinsic functions have a generic name. In many cases (especially the non-mathematical functions like **HUGE** and **ACHAR**) there is only the generic name. Furthermore, the fact that the name is "generic" does not necessarily mean that arguments or results of more than one type are possible: for example **ACHAR** by its nature can only be a character function of an integer variable, but this is still regarded as a "generic" function name. At the same time, some generic names can also be used as specific names when the context demands it: **SIN** is an example.

These complications are best avoided by using only the generic procedure names that we have been using so far and that are listed in Appendix F.1. The "specific" names in Appendix F.2 can be avoided altogether, except in connection with the use of procedure names as the arguments of other procedures, a usage that crops up only very rarely and discussion of which is deferred to Chapter 14.

5.9 Exercises 5.B

5.B1 Under the **MERGE** function, a way was pointed out for converting an item of data from logical to integer type. Write an expression to do the converse, i.e. to convert a binary digit into logical type.

5.B2 Being consistent with the account of **MATMUL** given above, express as clearly as you can in words what **MATMUL(x,y)** would mean if **x** were a logical vector and **y** a logical matrix.

CHAPTER 6

Execution control

Within any program unit, statements are normally executed in the sequence in which they appear, but often it is necessary for program execution to branch along different paths or to loop repeatedly through the same set of statements. Branching and looping may depend on conditions (such as values of data to be read in) that are not known before the program starts to run. Fortran has five "constructs" for controlling the flow of execution through different blocks of executable statements: **CASE, IF, DO, WHERE** *and* **FORALL.**

Besides covering all the details of **CASE, DO** *and* **FORALL,** *this chapter includes reviews of the* **IF** *and* **WHERE** *constructs and describes the* **STOP** *statement.*

6.1 CASE

Different blocks of code may be selected for execution according to different possible values of an expression (the "case expression")which may be of integer, logical or character type. The construct begins with a **SELECT CASE** statement, then there are one or more blocks each starting with a **CASE** statement, and finally an **END SELECT** statement. This very simple example makes a selection according to the value of a logical expression:

```
Switch: SELECT CASE (input(1:1)=="Y")
  CASE (.TRUE.)
  .
  .
  .    (case block)
  .
  .
END SELECT Switch
```

The case expression is specified in brackets at the end of the **SELECT CASE** statement. A **CASE** construct may be given a name, here **Switch**, and if so the name precedes the keywords **SELECT CASE** and is followed by a colon. Here the case expression is the logical expression

```
input(1:1)=="Y"
```

In this example there is only one case block, following the statement

```
CASE (.TRUE.)
```

and it would be a section of code to be executed if and only if the first letter of the character string **input** is a **Y**. The **END SELECT** statement closes the case construct, and unconditional execution of the program continues. Since the construct has a name, its name must be specified at the end after the keywords **END SELECT**.

Here is a more complicated example, with a selection being made according to the value of an integer **nyears**:

```
Wars:   SELECT CASE (nyears)
        CASE (1853:1856)
              war = "Crimean War"
        CASE (1899:1902)
              war = "Boer War"
        CASE (1914:1918)
              war = "WW1"
        CASE (1939:1945)
              war = "WW2"
        CASE DEFAULT
              war = "Peace"
    END SELECT Wars
```

A character variable (**war**) is being given different values according to whether the case expression (**nyears**) lies in certain ranges. The colon notation is used to specify lower and upper (inclusive) limits for the values of the case expression. Both limits need not be present, i.e. **CASE (1914:)** would be satisfied by any value greater than **1913**, and **CASE (:1914)** would be satisfied by any value below **1915**, while **CASE (1914)** would be satisfied only by the value **1914**. In any **CASE** construct, the ranges satisfied by the different blocks may not overlap, so that whatever the value of the case expression there can be no more than one block selected. A **CASE DEFAULT** statement may be used to define a default block that will be selected if the case expression matches none of the other blocks. Obviously there can be no more than one default block.

The next example is a section of code with two **CASE** constructs. The first selects according to the value of an element of a character string and the second according to the value of an integer. The **DO** construct will be explained in proper detail shortly, but here it means that everything between the **DO** and

END DO statements will be executed repeatedly with the integer **i** taking the values from **1** up to the length of a character string called **text**.

```
!    Interpret input text as a number
!    Initialization
     string = ""; npoints = 0
     Rune: DO i = 1, LEN(text)
        Digit: SELECT CASE (text(i:i))
           CASE ("0":"9")
              string=string//text(i:i)
           CASE (",")
              WRITE (*,*) &
              "NB Commas are disregarded"
           CASE (".")
              npoints=npoints+1
              string=string//"."
           CASE ("O")
              WRITE (*,*) &
              "An O has been interpreted as a zero"
              string=string//"0"
           CASE ("I")
              WRITE (*,*) &
              "An I has been interpreted as a 1"
              string=string//"1"
           CASE (" ")
              WRITE (*,*) &
              "A blank has been disregarded"
           CASE DEFAULT
              WRITE (*,*) &
              "There is a fatal error"
              STOP
        END SELECT Digit
     END DO Rune
     Points: SELECT CASE (npoints)
        CASE (0)
           WRITE (*,*) &
           "Check: There was no decimal point"
        CASE (2:)
           WRITE (*,*) &
           "There was more than one decimal point"
           STOP
        CASE DEFAULT
           WRITE (*,*) &
           "Your number was "//string
     END SELECT Points
     text = string
```

The first **SELECT CASE** statement specifies that the **i**th character of the string **text** is the case expression. In the seven blocks following, different actions are taken if this character is a numerical digit, a comma, a decimal point, a letter **O** or **I**, or a blank, or something else. When the construct has been executed the required number of times, i.e. after the **END DO** statement, the character variable **string** will contain a modified version of the original **text**. There is then a second **CASE** construct looking at the number of decimal points that were encountered. The **STOP** statement is explained in Section 8.4.

To summarize: in general the case construct takes the form

```
construct-name:   SELECT CASE (case-expression)
        CASE (case-value-range-list)
          .
          .
          .
        CASE ...
          .
          .
          .
        CASE DEFAULT
          .
          .
          .
  END SELECT construct-name
```

where *construct-name* is an optional name, *case-expression* is an expression and *case-value-range-list* is a value, a range of values around a colon, or a set of such values and/or ranges separated by commas. Each value may simply be a constant or it may be an expression of some sort (technically, an "initialization expression"). Valid **CASE** statements are

```
CASE (p.NEQV.q)
CASE ("A","E","I","O","U")
CASE (SIZE(array))
CASE (1914:1918,1939:1945)
CASE (10**5+1:10**6)
CASE ("A":"Z","a":"z")
```

The last example illustrates a possible difficulty when the case expression is of character type and a **CASE** statement specifies a range of values. The problem is that the range is interpreted according to the processor's own character collation sequence, not necessarily the ASCII sequence, and this may differ from one processor to another. For fully portable code, it would be safer to have something like

```
SELECT CASE (IACHAR(char))
    .
    .
    .
CASE (65:90,97:122)
```

to select characters which are letters of the alphabet.

6.2 IF: review

The **IF** statement and the **IF** construct, described in Section 3.3, are briefly reviewed here. The **IF** statement is, of course, a single statement of the general form

```
IF (condition) conditional-statement
```

where *conditional-statement* can be any executable "action" statement except a further **IF** statement or an **END PROGRAM** or **END SUBROUTINE** statement (Chapter 7).

Technically, a statement such as

```
IF (convergence==.TRUE.) END FUNCTION Iterate
```

could be permitted in Fortran, but this is something of an anomaly and the usage is not recommended.

By the definition of an action statement, the *conditional-statement* is also forbidden to be the start or end of a **CASE**, **DO**, or **WHERE** construct, or a **CASE**, **ELSE**, **ELSE IF**, or **ELSEWHERE** statement, but it may be a **CYCLE** or **EXIT** statement (Section 6.4) or a single **WHERE** statement.

Examples are

```
IF (r>0.0 .AND. s>0.0) qfunc = SQRT(LOG(r)*LOG(s))
IF (SIZE(a)==SIZE(b)) WHERE (b==0.0) b=a
```

The **IF** construct, whose general form is given in Section 3.3, consists of a series of blocks of code separated by **IF...THEN**, **ELSE IF**, **ELSE** and **END IF** statements:

```
IF ... THEN
  .
ELSE IF ... THEN
  .
ELSE IF ... THEN
  .
  .
  .
ELSE
  .
END IF
```

where each block contains executable statements. They are not restricted only to the "action" statements that may be used in a single **IF** statement (see above), but may also include further **IF** statements and additional **CASE**, **IF**, **DO** and **WHERE** constructs. However, when these constructs are nested inside one another, the integrity of each construct must be respected, i.e. if one construct contains another then it must contain all of it. One construct may not overlap another. For this reason

```
Allowance: IF (allow.EQV..TRUE.) THEN
Permission: IF (chance.EQV..FALSE.) THEN
q = r*(f+p/2.0)
END IF Allowance
r = 0.0
END IF Permission
```

is forbidden even if it were not muddle-headed. The desired effect in this instance, if it is the desired effect, could be achieved with a properly nested pair of IF constructs:

```
Permission: IF (chance.EQV..FALSE.) THEN
   Allowance: IF (allow.EQV..TRUE.) THEN
      q = r*(f+p/2.0)
   END IF Allowance
   r=0.0
END IF Permission
```

Of the series of blocks of code within a particular IF construct, divided by the ELSE IF and ELSE statements, at most one block will be executed each time the construct is executed. What happens is that the logical conditions associated with the IF and ELSE IF statements are evaluated in sequence and, as soon as a true condition is found, the associated block is executed. Subsequent ELSE IF are ignored. The ELSE block is executed only if all the conditions attached to the preceding IF and ELSE IF statements are found to be false. When there is an ELSE statement, then exactly one block of code within the construct will be executed. Without an ELSE, it is possible that no blocks will be executed.

More examples of IF constructs are:

```
IF (initialized) THEN; i=0; j=0; k=0; END IF

Clear: IF (x<1.0) THEN
   Sign: IF (x<0.0) THEN
      x = -x
      ind = .TRUE.
   END IF Sign
   x = x + 1.0
ELSE Clear
   x = x - 1.0
END IF Clear
```

6.3 Exercises 6.A

6.A1 Write a program, using a **CASE** construct for execution control, to solve a quadratic equation whose coefficients are real but that may have complex roots.

6.A2 Use a **CASE** construct to look at the initial letter of a character string. If it is a lower-case letter, convert it to upper case. If the string starts with a non-letter character, replace it with an **x**, but if it starts with a blank just remove it.

6.A3 Repeat Exercise 6.A2 but using an **IF** construct instead of **CASE**.

6.A4 Given an integer, write a program that will check if it is the square or the cube (but not both) of a smaller integer and, if so, write a message saying so.

6.4 DO

The **CASE** and **IF** constructs allow a program to execute one block of statements selected from a set of alternative blocks. The **DO** construct (or "**DO** loop") allows a program to execute a single block of statements repeatedly. The block must be enclosed between **DO** and **END DO** statements. In its simplest form, the construct is

```
DO
  .
  . (block)
  .
END DO
```

and this causes execution to loop through the block an indefinite number of times. The following example calculates the value of the number **e** by summing an infinite series:

```
e=1.0; k=1; j=1
DO
  e=e+1.0/REAL(j); k=k+1; j=j*k
END DO
```

The problem here is that the program will apparently never stop unless there is some way of escaping from the **DO** loop. In practice, it will keep looping until an error condition arises when **j** exceeds the processor's range of integers. So how do we get out of a **DO** loop? There is a special statement, **EXIT**, which does this and passes control to whatever statement follows the **END DO**, as in

```
INTEGER :: ifib(100), i
ifib(1)=1; ifib(2)=1; i=3
DO
  ifib(i) = ifib(i-1) + ifib(i-2)
```

```
    i=i+1
    IF (i>100) EXIT
END DO
```

You can also escape from a **DO** loop by a **STOP** (see Section 6.7) or, in a subprogram, by a **RETURN** statement. Another construction is

```
DO WHILE (logical expression)
    .
    .
    .
END DO
```

Here, each time the program is at the top of the loop, the value of the bracketed logical expression is checked, and, if it is not true, then the loop will not be executed and control passes to the statement after **END DO**. The **DO WHILE** construct is exactly equivalent to

```
DO
IF (.NOT.(logical expression)) EXIT
    .
    .
    .
END DO
```

Since the **DO...WHILE** syntax does not enable Fortran to do anything it could not otherwise do, some authorities disapprove of its use.

Note that **DO** loops, like **IF** and **CASE** constructs, may be named. Loop names are not functionally necessary, but it is a good idea to use them as a form of program annotation and self-checking especially when there are nested loops. A loop name, if used, must be given before a colon at the start of the **DO** statement, and must also appear at the end of the **END DO** statement. Here is an example of a named **DO** loop:

```
x = 1.0; y = 1.0; z = 1.0; ncount=0
Lorenz: DO WHILE ((x**2 + y**2 + z**2)<1000000.0)
    xplus = 10.0*(y-x)
    yplus = x*z + 28.0*x - y
    zplus = x*y - 8.0*z/3.0
    test = ABS(xplus) + ABS(yplus) + ABS(zplus)
    IF (test <= 0.000001) EXIT
    ncount = ncount + 1
    IF (MOD(ncount,20) == 0) WRITE (*,*) ncount, &
        " iterations"
    x = x + xplus
    y = y + yplus
    z = z + zplus
    WRITE (*,*) x, y
END DO Lorenz
```

Another type of statement that is used for **DO** loop control is **CYCLE**. The **CYCLE** statement is a way of jumping to the bottom of the block and thence back to the top again, but unlike **EXIT** it does not jump right out of the loop:

```
DO
  WRITE (*,*) "Type the password"
  READ (*,*) inword
  IF (inword/=password) CYCLE
  WRITE (*,*) "That's right. Now type a new password"
  READ (*,*) password
  WRITE (*,*) "The new password is ",password
  EXIT
END DO
```

The user never gets out of this loop unless the correct password is typed in.

Another way of controlling a **DO** loop is with a variable known as a loop index. Historically, this was the usual way of constructing **DO** loops in earlier versions of Fortran. The syntax is

```
DO i = i1, i2, i3
  .
  .
  .
END DO
```

where the loop-control quantities i, $i1$, $i2$ and $i3$ are of scalar integer type. A loop name, of course, may also be included as in the earlier example.

The first loop-control quantity, here called i, is the "loop index" and it is a local variable whose name is arbitrary. The integers $i1$, $i2$ and $i3$ may be variables, constants or expressions, but they must have definite values at the start of the loop. The loop is executed for values of i starting with $i1$ and going up to $i2$ in steps ("strides") equal to $i3$. The stride $i3$ may be omitted from the **DO** statement, in which case its default value is **1**.

Here are two simple examples with constant loop parameters:

```
WRITE (*,*) "Table of cubes:"
DO k = 0, 20
  WRITE (*,*) k, k**3
END DO

WRITE (*,*) "Table of cubes:"
DO k = 0, 1000, 5
  r = REAL(k)/1000.0
  WRITE (*,*) r, r**3
END DO
```

The first of these tabulates the cubes of the integers from 0 to 20, and the second tabulates the cubes of numbers from 0 to 1 in steps of 0.005.

A loop index may have negative stride (*i3*) if its starting point (*i1*) is greater than its end point (*i2*) as in

```
WRITE (*,*) "Table of cubes:"
DO i = 20, 0, -1
  WRITE (*,*) i, i**3
END DO
```

which does the same thing as an earlier example but in the reverse order. Loop control parameters may also be more complicated expressions, as in

```
DO icount = MIN(intalpha, intbeta, intgamma), &
  MAX(intalpha, intbeta, intgamma), jumper+1
```

The loop control parameters are set up when the **DO** statement is first encountered, before looping actually starts, and they cannot be altered by statements within the block. The loop index (i.e. the variable called **i** or **k** or **icount** in the above examples) increases by the "stride" each time the loop repeats, but it should not be altered by statements within the block.

The nesting of loops is a very useful feature of the language, as in

```
Decades: DO nyear = 1910, 2000, 10
  prod=0.0; res=0.0
  Ten: DO n = nyear-9, nyear
        prod = prod + oil(nyear)
        res = res + found(nyear)
  END DO Ten
  WRITE (*,*) nyear, prod, res
END DO Decades
```

It is important not to mix up your loop indices and not to have overlapping loops. It is always a good precaution to name the loops, as in the scheme

```
Outer: DO
  .
  .
  .
  Middle: DO
    .
    .
    .
    Inner: DO
      .
      .
      .
    END DO Inner
    .
    .
    .
  END DO Middle
  .
  .
  .
END DO Outer
```

The **EXIT** and **CYCLE** statements usually have effect with respect to the deepest loop level where they appear, but they can refer to any level if names are appended. If you **EXIT** or **CYCLE** from an inner loop to an outer one, the inner loop will be finished and cannot be re-entered without re-initializing the inner loop index. The following is a fairly complex structure:

```
Outer: DO
   .
   .
   .
   CYCLE Outer
   .
   .
   .
   Middle: DO
      .
      .
      .
      EXIT Middle
      .
      .
      .
      Inner: DO
         .
         .
         .
         EXIT Outer
         .
         .
         .
         CYCLE Middle
         .
         .
         .
      END DO Inner
      .
      .
      .
   END DO Middle
   .
   .
   .
END DO Outer
```

In this example, **CYCLE Outer** has the effect of transferring control down to the **END DO Outer** statement, but it does not actually terminate looping at this level. **EXIT Middle** does stop looping at the middle level because it transfers control to whatever statement follows after **END DO Middle** (not to **END DO Middle** itself) and so it leaves only the outer loop operative. **EXIT Outer** transfers control to the statement after **END DO Outer**, so no loops remain active. **CYCLE Middle** transfers control to **END DO Middle**, terminating the inner loop but leaving the other loops still active.

A complicated example like this is bound to seem confusing at first, but in practice nested loops are extremely useful and the **EXIT** and **CYCLE** statements are soon mastered.

DO loops with statement labels:

There is a form of the **DO** loop that uses a statement label (see Chapter 14) to indicate the bottom of the loop. In this type of **DO** statement, a numerical "statement label" follows the keyword **DO**, and the **END DO** statement must start with the same label. (Alternatively, the labelled **END DO** statement may be replaced by a labelled **CONTINUE** statement.) An example is

```
sumsq = 0.0; DO 6 k=1, kmax
sumsq = sumsq + datum(k)**2; 6 CONTINUE
```

which is equivalent to

```
sumsq = 0.0; DO k=1, kmax
sumsq = sumsq + datum(k)**2; END DO
```

and of course, most simply, to

```
sumsq = SUM(ARRAY=datum(1:kmax)**2)
```

6.5 FORALL (Fortran 95 feature not in Fortran 90)

The **FORALL** statement provides a way of controlling the execution of assignment statements involving sets of "subobjects", i.e. array sections and character substrings, of which the elements are identified by indices. **FORALL** is a bit like a cross between **IF** and **WHERE**. Like **IF** and **WHERE**, **FORALL** may be used either in the form of a single statement or in the form of a construct containing a block of code.

FORALL is primarily intended to allow for the possibility of the parallel processing of assignment statements. The assignments could be applied in parallel for all the elements of specified data objects. An example will help to make the idea clear:

```
FORALL (i=1:n, j=1:n, upside(i,j)/=0.0) &
  down(i,j) = 1.0/upside(i,j)
```

which takes the inverses of all the non-zero elements of **upside**. This is much the same as

```
WHERE (upside/=0.0) down = 1.0/upside
```

but the advantage of a **FORALL** statement is that the logical condition may involve the values of the indices of the elements within **upside** as in

```
FORALL (i=1:n, j=1:n, upside(i,j)/=0.0.AND.i.NE.j) &
  down(i,j) = 1.0/upside(i,j)
```

that inverts only the non-diagonal non-zero members of **upside**.

The general form of the **FORALL** statement is

```
FORALL (triplet-spec, triplet-spec, ..., triplet-spec, &
  mask) assignment-statement
```

There must be at least one **triplet-spec**, and a **triplet-spec** refers to an index of a data object and takes the general form

```
index-name = subscript1: subscript2: stride
```

the **index-name** being the name of a scalar variable. This follows a very similar syntax to an array section, i.e. it picks out values of **index-name** going from **subscript1** to **subscript2** in leaps of **stride**. The stride is taken to be **1** if the second colon and **stride** are omitted in the statement, but neither **subscript** can be omitted. Note that a **subscript** or a **stride** is not allowed to refer to an **index-name** from the same list of **triplet-specs**, i.e.

```
FORALL (i=1:n, j=1:i, upside(i,j)/=0.0) &
   down(i,j) = 1.0/upside(i,j)
```

is not permissible. Incidentally, an **index-name** only has meaning within the scope of the **FORALL** statement (or construct, below) and does not interfere with any variable of the same name outside it.

The **assignment-statement** must have, on the left of the = sign, a variable that is a subobject identified by the set of **index-names**. If it is an element of a rank-n array, there will be n **triplet-specs** and therefore n **index-names**. The assignment statement is executed for the elements picked out by the **triplet-specs**, which may be subject also to the truth of a condition **mask**.

The optional condition **mask**, if present, is a scalar logical expression that may involve the **index-name** variables as well as other variables. If **mask** involves the invocation of procedures, they must be **PURE** procedures (see Section 11.2) such as Fortran's intrinsic functions.

The **assignment-statement** must be an assignment statement (or a pointer assignment statement, see Chapter 13) giving a value to a subobject. The subobject must involve all the **index-names** as indices. No **index-name** may be redefined by the statement. The expression on the right of the assignment statement, like a **mask**, must not involve procedures that are not **PURE**.

The general form of the **FORALL** construct is

```
Name: FORALL (triplet-spec, triplet-spec, ..., &
   triplet-spec, mask)
   .
   .
   .
statements
   .
   .
   .
END FORALL Name
```

And this follows much the same rules as a single **FORALL** statement. The **statements** may be assignment statements, following the same rules as mentioned above. Additionally, the **statements** block may include other **FORALL** statements, **WHERE** statements, and nested **FORALL** and **WHERE** constructs. Here is an example of a **WHERE** statement within a **FORALL** construct:

```
REAL :: x(10,30), y(10,30), z(10)
    .
    .
    .
FORALL (i=2:10:2, z(i)>0.0)
  WHERE (x(i,:)==0.0) x(i,:) = REAL(i)
  y(i,:) = REAL(i)/x(i,:)
END FORALL
```

In the following example, the notionally parallel nature of **FORALL** execution is important:

```
REAL :: a(10, 300)
    .
    .
    .
FORALL (m = 1:10)
  WHERE ((m /= 1).AND(m /= 10))
    a(m,:) = a(m-1,:) + a(m+1,:)
  ELSE WHERE (m == 1)
    a(m,:) = a(10,:) + a(2,:)
  ELSEWHERE
    a(m,:) = a(9,:) + a(1,:)
  END WHERE
END FORALL
```

Here, the right-hand sides of some assignments involve elements of **a** that are changed by being on the left-hand sides of other assignments. But what is intended, and what will happen, is that the right-hand sides should all refer to the elements of **a** as they were before the **FORALL** was entered. What will happen is that all the mask expressions are first calculated, then all the right-hand expressions are calculated where (and only where) the mask is true, and only then will the left-hand variables (the elements of **a** in this case) have their values changed.

It should be remembered that the keyword **FORALL** may not be split into **FOR ALL**.

6.6 WHERE: review

The **WHERE** statement and **WHERE** construct, described in detail in Section 4.9, are to carry out masked array assignments. Broadly speaking, **IF** is more appropriate for scalar assignment statements and **FORALL** for assigning values to array elements or array sections dependent on the values of indices.

In the example above,

```
WHERE (x(i,:)==0.0) x(i,:) = REAL(i)
```

is a valid **WHERE** statement. Whenever it is executed, the integer i will have a particular value, so that the array section $x(i,:)$ will be a one-dimensional array with thirty elements, and **REAL(i)** is a scalar.

- In Fortran 90, **WHERE** constructs may only contain array assignment statements.
- In Fortran 95, a **WHERE** construct may also contain further **WHERE** statements and nested **WHERE** constructs. Although a **WHERE** construct may be nested in a **FORALL**, the reverse is not true.
- In Fortran 95, an assignment may be an elemental (Section 11.3) defined assignment.

Ideally, **WHERE** statements and constructs should allow a parallel-processing system to carry out array assignments on all elements of the array independently, i.e. "elementally". The benefit may be lost if the calculations for the different elements are interdependent or if non-elemental functions are involved. For example,

```
WHERE (x>0.0) y = LOG(x)
```

works elementally and (if the processor permits) in parallel, and the **LOG** function is only called for the elements of x that have positive values; but

```
WHERE (x>0.0) y = LOG(x)/SUM(LOG(x))
```

involves a non-elemental function (**SUM**) of the logarithms of all the elements of x, not just the individual elements selected by the mask $x>0.0$. Apart from being unsafe code (because it could fail by trying to calculate the logarithm of a non-positive number) this statement is wasteful because calls to **LOG** will be duplicated.

6.7 STOP

On the subject of execution control there is one type of statement that still needs to be mentioned. Very simple but very important, it is the **STOP** statement. **STOP** halts the execution of the program. The only other statement that should normally halt a program is **END PROGRAM**, but **STOP** can appear anywhere within the program and it can be made conditional as in

```
IF (time>overrun) STOP
```

The **STOP** statement may, optionally, be followed by a "stop code" or "access code" consisting of either a character constant or a string of up to five digits. The idea is that the stop code should be accessible to the user after the program has stopped and can be used to indicate exactly where it stopped. This is important for debugging lengthy programs that may have numerous **STOP** statements dotted about them. So, we can have statements like

```
IF (time>overrun) STOP "Too Late"
```
or
```
CASE (1999); STOP 1999
```

Exactly how the stop code is output is a matter for the processor's operating system, not for Fortran, since by definition it happens when the Fortran program is no longer running.

PAUSE

The statement **PAUSE** can be used to halt execution of the program temporarily, with the possibility of resumption under the user's control. **PAUSE** can be followed, like **STOP**, by a stop code.

6.8 Exercises 6.B

6.B1 Use a **DO** loop to calculate the factorial of an integer.

6.B2 Given a character string which consists of letters of the alphabet, write code to put the letters into alphabetical order and produce a new string consisting of the reordered letters.

6.B3 Write a program that will calculate an integer value from a character-string sequence of digits, i.e. to calculate the value **10** from the string **"10"**.

6.B4 Write a program that will find the largest prime factor of an integer.

6.B5 Write a program to test whether a character string would be valid as the name of a Fortran variable.

6.B6 Write a program to input a word and write out its vowels.

6.B7 Write a program that repeatedly reads words typed in until a predetermined password is encountered.

6.B8 Picking up the example at the end of Section 6.6, given a rank-one array **x** of 100 real numbers, write code to produce an array that contains the logarithms of the positive-valued elements of **x**, but normalized (i.e. scaled) by the average of the logarithms so that the average value of the array produced is **1**. Note that the size of the array produced will depend on the number of positive elements of **x**, and therefore it cannot be declared at the outset. Since allocatable arrays etc. (Chapter 12) have not yet been introduced, the array produced will have to take the form of an expression or an array section, not a whole named array.

6.B9 Calculate and display the average of an arbitrary number of input numbers.

CHAPTER 7

Introducing external procedures

We have already come across several of Fortran's intrinsic procedures, both functions and subroutines. This chapter explains how the programmer can write and use additional "external" functions and subroutines. External procedures are not only useful for carrying out calculations not covered by the intrinsic procedures; they are necessary also for the clear organization and subdivision of any large Fortran program.

The statements covered here are FUNCTION, SUBROUTINE, END FUNCTION, END SUBROUTINE, and CALL. The important keyword INTENT is also introduced. This chapter includes extended sets of exercises.

7.1 Functions

A function is used to calculate a result whose value will generally depend on the values of "arguments" given each time that the function is invoked. A function is like a mini-program and has an overall structure deliberately similar to a main program: it starts with a title statement, followed by non-executable declaration statements, and then the series of executable statements finishing finally with a version of the END statement. An example is

```
FUNCTION Cot(x)
REAL :: Cot
REAL, INTENT(IN) :: x
REAL :: s, c
IF (x==0.0) THEN
  WRITE (*,*) "Error: cotangent function called with &
  &zero argument"
  Cot = HUGE(x)
ELSE
  s = SIN(x); c = COS(x); Cot = c/s
```

109

```
END IF
END FUNCTION Cot
```

This piece of code would be provided alongside a main program. Whenever there is any reference to **Cot** in the main program (or for that matter anywhere else in the program as a whole, including other functions) this function will be entered and the cotangent will be calculated. When the **END FUNCTION** statement is reached, control returns back to wherever the reference to **Cot** was made.

With the function **Cot** defined as above, references to **Cot** must have one argument, and the argument must have a real value. This argument is called **x** within the function, but elsewhere a reference to **Cot** can have as its argument the name of any variable, or a constant, or an expression. The name **x** as it appears above is an arbitrary choice, and **x** is called a "dummy" argument, because it stands in for whatever "actual" argument will be supplied when the function is invoked. Valid invocations of **Cot** (occurring in the main program, for example) are the expressions

```
Cot(y)
Cot(0.1)
Cot(pi - SQRT(q**2 + p**2))
```

or even

```
Cot(alpha + ATAN((Cot(beta)+Cot(gamma)))
```

the **Cot** function being called three times by the last example.

It is fundamental to understand clearly the distinction between "dummy" arguments and "actual" arguments. A dummy argument is a variable with a name local to the function itself, and should be declared at the start of the function along with other variables used in the calculation of the function's value. An "actual" argument is supplied at execution time when the function is referred to elsewhere in the program, and the actual argument need not be the name of a variable. The actual arguments in the above examples are

```
y
0.1
pi - SQRT(q**2 + p**2)
alpha + ATAN((Cot(beta)+Cot(gamma)))
beta
gamma
```

Leaving aside techniques involving modules (Chapter 10), it should be considered that a function's arguments are the only way in which data can enter it. Except as arguments, a function does not have access to data items used elsewhere in the program. Conversely, data items used within a function (except the arguments) are internal to the function and are unknown to the rest of the program, even if the names of variables in the function and variables elsewhere have similar names. Variables internal to the function should be declared by type declaration statements within it.

In the example of the **Cot** function above, the first statement

```
FUNCTION Cot(x)
```

declares that this is the start of a subprogram that is an external function and it gives it the name **Cot**. (The use of an initial capital is a suggested convention, not a necessity. **COT** or **cot** would have the same effect.) After the name, **(x)** means that the function has a single argument that is being given the local ("dummy")name **x**.

After the **FUNCTION** statement is a set of declarative statements that set up the necessary variables. First we have

```
REAL :: Cot
```

and this is needed because a function (unlike a subroutine) has a value in its own right, and **Cot** is intended to have a value of **REAL** type.

As a matter of fact, there is another way of specifying that the function **Cot** has a real value: the **FUNCTION** statement itself may be prefixed by the keyword **REAL** as in

```
REAL FUNCTION Cot(x)
```

The function name does not then need to appear in a type declaration statement. Corresponding prefixes can be used also for function values of other types, e.g.

```
INTEGER FUNCTION Nfactorial(n)
COMPLEX FUNCTION Gamma(z)
CHARACTER(20) FUNCTION All_Upper_Case(string)
LOGICAL FUNCTION Cone(z)
DOUBLE PRECISION FUNCTION Finetune(p, q)
```

The function type is never mentioned, however, in **END FUNCTION** statements.

Since it is not necessary to use type-prefixed **FUNCTION** statements, and sometimes it can be cumbersome to do so (in Chapter 11 we shall meet other prefixes!), the practice is not recommended.

The next statement in **Cot**,

```
REAL, INTENT(IN) :: x
```

declares that the variable **x**, which is the argument of the function, is of real type. It also specifies what is known as an **INTENT** attribute for **x**. The **INTENT** of an argument is whether it represents information flowing into the procedure or out of it. In this example, it is obvious that the former is intended, i.e. the function receives the value of **x** when the function is invoked. Later, however, we shall come across cases of external procedures that use arguments as a way of passing information out. The **IN** above means that information goes in, and if it were going out we would have **INTENT(OUT)**. It is also possible to have **INTENT(IN OUT)** for an argument that can be used to pass information either way.

At this stage it will seem rather pointless to declare the **INTENT** of any argument, because any argument can be used to pass data either in or out, or both, if the **INTENT** attribute is omitted entirely. Instead of the above statement we could have simply

```
REAL :: x
```

The specification of the **INTENT** attribute is optional in almost all cases. It is for the sake of more advanced applications, when the **INTENT** specification can be useful to the compiler, and for the sake of program clarity, that it is recommended that all procedure arguments should have specified **INTENT**.

The remainder of the function **Cot** is straightforward to understand. The final declarative statement,

```
REAL :: s, c
```

affirms that **s** and **c** are variables of **REAL** type. The executable statements

```
IF (x==0.0) THEN
  WRITE (*,*) "Error: cotangent function called with &
  &zero argument"
  Cot = HUGE(x)
ELSE
  s = SIN(x); c = COS(x); Cot = c/s
END IF
```

calculate the required cotangent, and assign a value to **Cot** accordingly. It is obligatory that a value be given to **Cot**. Finally we have

```
END FUNCTION Cot
```

which ends the subprogram and, on execution, returns control to the point in the main program or elsewhere from which **Cot** was invoked.

Instead of

```
END FUNCTION Cot
```

the statement can have the abbreviated form **END FUNCTION** or even just **END**.

It has to be understood that the data type of a function's name is the type of its value, and this is not necessarily the same type as its argument or arguments. For example, a logical function **Cone** could have a complex argument, the function value being true or false according to whether the complex argument **z** has a real part of greater or lesser magnitude than its imaginary part:

```
FUNCTION Cone(z)
LOGICAL :: Cone
COMPLEX, INTENT(IN) :: z
```

```
Cone = .FALSE.
IF (ABS(REAL(z))>ABS(AIMAG(z))) Cone = .TRUE.
END FUNCTION Cone
```

Functions may have more than one argument, as in

```
FUNCTION Average (r1, r2, r3, r4)
REAL :: Average
REAL, INTENT(IN) :: r1, r2, r3, r4
Average = 0.25 * (r1 + r2 + r3 + r4)
END FUNCTION Average
```

In this example the four arguments are all of the same type, and their order is immaterial, but in general it has to be ensured that the proper order of the dummy arguments is adhered to whenever the function is called. This is obvious from the cases of some of the intrinsic functions already met: for example CMPLX(a,b) is not the same as CMPLX(b,a).

It is usually best for a function to receive information through its argument and return information through its value, i.e. to have arguments of INTENT (IN) only. But, if argument values are changed within a function, then the new values will be passed back to the program unit from which the function was called. When arguments are to be changed, it is often more appropriate to use not a function, but the other type of procedure, namely a subroutine.

Statement functions

Within a program unit it is possible to have a sort of simplified one-line function that can be used only within that program unit. It is specified by a non-executable statement that might typically look like this:

```
Fun_name(x, y, z) = x/y + y/z + z/x
```

i.e. an arbitrary function-name, followed by a bracketed list of arguments, followed after an = by an expression giving the value of the function in terms of the arguments. All arguments and other quantities must be scalars or single elements of arrays. Here is another example:

```
Croot (a) = a**(1.0/3.0) !    Cube Root Function
```

Such a statement is known as a "statement function" and must appear before any of the executable statements. Its use is not recommended.

There is one final point that needs to be made about functions. A function may involve ancillary variables (such as s and c in Cot above) that are not arguments. If the function is called repeatedly as the program executes, such variables are not "remembered" from one call to the next. Until we meet the attribute SAVE in Chapter 11, and ways of "pooling" data in modules (Chapter 10), all local variables within functions (and also within subroutines) must be regarded as strictly temporary. Anything that a function calculates must be recalculated afresh each time the function is called.

7.2 Exercises 7.A

7.A1 Write a function to calculate the volume of a sphere given its radius.

7.A2 Write a complex function to calculate the inverse sine of its (complex) argument.

7.A3 Write as simple a function as you can to calculate the sine of an angle by adding up the terms of the series

$$\sin(x) = x - x^3/3! + x^5/5! - x^7/7! \ldots$$

until additional terms do not seem to make much difference. Do not use any Fortran intrinsic functions, and do not use the power operator (**).

7.A4 The escape velocity from a star or planet is $(2GM)^{1/2}/R$ where G is equal to $6.673 \times 10^{-11} \, \mathrm{N \, m^{-2} \, kg^{-2}}$. Write a function that calculates the escape velocity as a fraction of the velocity of light $c = 299792 \, \mathrm{km \, s^{-1}}$. The function must include a logical argument of INTENT (OUT) which is returned false if the object is a Black Hole.

7.A5 Write a function called Ind_int_arcsin to calculate the indefinite integral of the inverse sine function using the equation

$$\int \arcsin(x) \, dx = x \arcsin(x) + (1 - x^2)^{1/2}$$

7.A6 The "radiation length" L_R for a material of atomic weight A and atomic number Z is given by

$$L_R = Z^2 B / (716.4A)$$

where $B = \ln(184.15/Z^{1/3}) + Z^{-1} \ln(1194/Z^{2/3}) - 1.202.(\alpha)^2 .Z^2$
$+ 1.0369(\alpha)^4 .Z^4 - 1.008(\alpha)^6.Z^6/(1 + (\alpha)^2.Z^2)$
and the value of α is 1/137.036. Express the radiation length as a Fortran function.

7.A7 A logarithm to base 10 can be computed approximately by the formula

$$\log_{10} x = a_1 t + a_3 t^3$$

where $t = (x-1)/(x+1)$, and $a_1 = 0.86304$, $a_3 = 0.36415$, as long as x is within the range $(10)^{-1/2} \leq x \leq (10)^{1/2}$.

Use this to calculate the logarithm to base 10 of any positive number. The square root of 10 is 3.162277660 and its inverse, of course, is 0.3162277660. Your function should be as fast as possible and should not defeat the object of the exercise by calling any of the Fortran intrinsic functions or using the power operator (**).

7.A8 Try to write an integer square root function, i.e. calculating the square root of an argument that can be assumed to be a perfect square. It should not rely on real-number arithmetic and should be faster (and more reliable) than using INT(SQRT(I))!

7.A9 Write a function to calculate the natural logarithm of any positive real number. Use the approximation

$$\ln(1 + x) = a_1 x + a_2 x^2 + \ldots + a_8 x^8$$

where the "a"s are as follows:

$a_1 = 0.99999\ 64239$

$a_2 = -0.49987\ 41238$

$a_3 = 0.33179\ 90258$

$a_4 = -0.24073\ 38084$

$a_5 = 0.16765\ 40711$

$a_6 = -0.09532\ 93897$

$a_7 = 0.03608\ 84937$

$a_8 = -0.00645\ 35442$

This approximation is valid in the range $0 \le x \le 1$ so it can be used to get the logarithm of a number between 1 and 2. To calculate the logarithm of a number below 1, use $\ln(y) = -\ln(1/y)$. To calculate the logarithm of a number greater than 2, use the relation $\ln(y) = \ln(2) + \ln(y/2)$, dividing the number by 2 repeatedly until we have a number in the right range for the series approximation above and using $\ln(2) = 0.69314\,71805\,59945$.

7.A10 Using **RANDOM**, write an integer function that will simulate the throw of two dice, adding their results. If a double is thrown, an extra throw is allowed in addition.

7.3 Subroutines

Subroutines are simpler than functions. While a function has a value, and is called by any mention of its name, a subroutine is called only by a special kind of statement, the **CALL** statement, as in the main program

```
PROGRAM Process
CALL Read_Data
CALL Analyze
CALL Display_Results
END PROGRAM Process
```

Read_Data, Analyze, and **Display_Results** are the names of subroutines to which execution is directed in turn by the **CALL** statements. They do not themselves have values and, in this example, they do not have arguments either. A subroutine can be more or less any block of code, not necessarily calculating anything in particular. At the end of it, control returns back to the calling program at the point immediately following the **CALL** statement. In the above example three subroutines are called from the main program, but in general any subroutine may be called from anywhere in the program as a whole, including functions and other subroutines.

Information may be passed into and/or out of a subroutine through arguments, as in:

```
PROGRAM Process
REAL :: x(100), y(100), xprime(100), yprime(100)
LOGICAL :: readcheck
CALL Read_Data(x, y, readcheck)
IF (readcheck) CALL Analyze (x, y, xprime, yprime)
CALL Display_Results (xprime, yprime, readcheck)
END PROGRAM Process
```

This illustrates, incidentally, that procedure arguments may be arrays. A subroutine is written very much like a main program except that it usually has arguments after its name and it begins with a **SUBROUTINE** statement. The above program could call the subroutine

```
SUBROUTINE Display_Results (a, b, go)
REAL, INTENT(IN) :: a(100), b(100)
LOGICAL, INTENT(IN) :: go
IF (.NOT.go) THEN
  WRITE (*,*) "The data was not input correctly"
ELSE
  .
  .
  .
  (Display a scatter diagram of a against b)
  .
  .
  .
END IF
END SUBROUTINE Display_Results
```

Here, as in a function, we have dummy arguments (**a**, **b** and **go**) whose names are local to the subroutine and need not be the same as the names of the actual arguments in the calling program. The dummy arguments here are associated with the actual arguments **xprime**, **yprime**, and **readcheck** by their corresponding positions in the argument lists in the **CALL** and **SUBROUTINE** statements. The arrays **xprime** and **yprime** have the same shapes as the dummy arguments **a** and **b**, i.e. they are rank-one arrays of 100 elements. Although other possibilities exist, and these will be explained in Chapter 11, for the time being it can be taken that actual arguments and dummy arguments, when they are arrays, must be declared to have matching shapes. It is also possible for procedures to have arguments that are character strings, in which case the actual and dummy argument strings need not be of exactly the same lengths, but the actual argument may not be shorter than the dummy argument.

```
SUBROUTINE Compare_Strings_20 (string1, string2, equivalent)
CHARACTER (20), INTENT (IN) :: string1, string2
LOGICAL, INTENT (OUT) :: equivalent
CHARACTER (20) :: s1, s2
equivalent = .FALSE.! Initialization

! Sees if two character strings are equivalent to one
!another, disregarding the distinction between upper-case
!and lower-case letters.

! Work on s1 and s2, leaving string1 and string2 unchanged.
s1 = string1; s2 = string2
```

```
! The matter is immediately settled if there are different
!numbers of trailing banks.
IF (LEN(TRIM(s1)) /= LEN(TRIM(s2))) RETURN

! Replace all upper-case letter case by the corresponding
lower-case ones
DO n = 1, 20
j1 = IACHAR(s1(n:n)); j2 = IACHAR(s2(n:n))
IF (j1>64.AND.j1<91) THEN
   j1 = j1 + 32
   s1(n:n) = ACHAR(j1)
END IF
IF (j2>64.AND.j2<91) THEN
   j2 = j2 + 32
   s2(n:n) = ACHAR(j2)
END IF
END DO
IF (s1==s2) equivalent = .TRUE.
END SUBROUTINE Compare_Strings_20
```

In this example, two of the arguments are 20-character strings. When the subroutine is called, the corresponding arguments must also be character strings each containing at least 20 characters, and their leftmost 20 characters are transmitted to the subroutine as the values of **string1** and **string2**. The subroutine would be called by a statement such as

```
CALL Compare_Strings_20(teststring,&
"North Dakota         ", check)
```

as long as **teststring** is the name of a sufficiently long character string and is defined when the call is made, the second argument has enough trailing blanks to make at least 20 characters, and **check** is the name of a logical variable.

The above subroutine includes a new type of statement, **RETURN**. The **RETURN** statement, which may occur in any subroutine or function, has the same effect as jumping down to the **END FUNCTION** or **END SUBROUTINE** statement and returning immediately to where the procedure was called from in the calling program. In the case of a function, though, it has to be remembered that the function must have been given a value before you return from it.

Although the use of a **RETURN** statement can sometimes be handy, it is never necessary, as execution control constructs can be used so that the actual return always takes place at the **END FUNCTION** or **END SUBROUTINE** statement that finishes the procedure. It is therefore suggested that the **RETURN** statement be avoided.

There are a number of commonsense restrictions on the way that actual arguments may be associated with dummy arguments in subroutines and in functions. A variable that is an actual argument may be accessible within the subroutine, not only via the corresponding dummy argument, but also in some other way: this could happen through host or use association in relation to modules (Chapter 10) or simply via an additional argument. In such circumstances, the value of the variable may only be altered within the procedure via the dummy argument.

If there is any overlap among the actual arguments given to a procedure, then the overlapping bits may not be defined or redefined within the procedure. An example is a subroutine with two arguments, both of which are ten-element arrays, called by the statement

```
CALL MIX (x(1:10), x(6:15))
```

Because the arguments overlap with the elements `x(6:10)`, these particular elements may not be redefined within `MIX`. Similar comments would also apply if we were talking about overlapping substrings of characters. As another example of the same sort of thing, consider

```
SUBROUTINE Product (a, b, ab)
REAL :: a, b, ab
ab = a * b
END SUBROUTINE Product
```

This is all very well, but

```
CALL Product (alpha, beta, alpha)
```

is illegal because the dummy arguments **a** and **ab** are here being made to overlap (in **alpha**) and so it is illegal for the subroutine to redefine either of them (specifically, **ab**). However,

```
CALL Product (alpha, alpha, beta)
```

is legal because, although the first two arguments are being made to overlap, the subroutine does not attempt to redefine either **a** or **b**. Declarations of **INTENT** help to make things clearer:

```
SUBROUTINE Product (a, b, ab)
REAL, INTENT (IN) :: a, b
REAL, INTENT (OUT) :: ab
ab = a * b
END SUBROUTINE Product
```

and the illegality of

```
CALL Product (alpha, beta, alpha)
```

can then be interpreted in terms of the rule that an **INTENT(IN)** argument must remain unchanged by the procedure.

ENTRY

Usually a procedure is invoked by the name supplied in its first statement, the **FUNCTION** or **SUBROUTINE** statement, and it starts executing from that statement; but it is possible to allow a procedure to be entered at different points under different names and with different arguments. This is done by inserting an **ENTRY** statement at each alternative entry point. A silly example is:

```
SUBROUTINE Powers(x)
REAL:: x           ;      STOP
ENTRY Fifth (x)    ;      x=x**5    ;     RETURN
ENTRY Fourth (x)   ;      x=x**4    ;     RETURN
ENTRY Cube (x)     ;      x=x**3    ;     RETURN
ENTRY Square (x)   ;      x=x**2    ;     RETURN
END SUBROUTINE Powers
```

This is not intended to be called at all under the name **Powers**, but by statements like **CALL Fifth(y)** or **CALL Fourth(z)** that will return with **y** or **z** raised to the power **5** or **4**. In general an **ENTRY** statement consists simply of the keyword **ENTRY** followed by the name by which it will be called, followed by a bracketed list of arguments. Multiple **ENTRY** statements may also be used in a function subprogram, in which case the appropriate entry names (rather than the overall function name) must be given a value.

Internal procedures

Functions and subroutines are normally either "intrinsic" or "external" or are "module procedures" (Chapter 10). A fourth possibility is that of "internal procedures". An internal procedure looks very much like an external procedure, but is placed inside another "host" program or subprogram. It must be inserted towards the end of its host, immediately before the host's **END** statement and following a special separator statement, **CONTAINS**. An internal procedure may only be accessed from its host, not from other parts of the program. Unlike an external procedure, an internal procedure has automatic access to all the variables defined in its host program as well as the data transmitted as its arguments.

7.4 Exercises 7.B

7.B1 Write a subroutine to arrange three numbers in increasing order of magnitude.

7.B2 There is a simple way of finding the day of the week for any date in the twentieth century. You take the two-digit year number (i.e. without the "19"), add to it what you get when you divide it by 4 (rounding down to a whole number), add on to that the number of the day within the month, and then add on a "month code" equal to:

0 for January	1 for May	5 for September
3 for February	4 for June	0 for October
3 for March	6 for July	3 for November
6 for April	2 for August	5 for December

Finally, take the result of this modulo 7 (i.e. take the remainder when you divide by 7) and the number you are left with points to the day of the week, i.e. 1 for Monday, 2 for Tuesday, and so on. Write a subroutine to do this. Three arguments should be the integers forming the date (input to the subroutine) and a fourth argument (output) should be the character-string name of the day.

7.B3 Write a subroutine to return the probability value for a non-negative integer n from the Poisson distribution of mean A. The probability value is

$$A^n.\exp(-A)/n!$$

where $n!$ is the factorial function of n. Having done that, extend the function so that it will give an appropriately interpolated result if it is called with a (positive) non-integer value for n.

7.B4 Write a subroutine to solve a quadratic equation

$$ax^2 + bx + c = 0$$

where the coefficients a, b and c may be complex numbers and the solutions of the equation may be complex values of x.

7.B5 The "error function" that is defined mathematically by

$$\text{erf}(x) = 2\pi^{-1/2} \int_0^x \exp\left(-t^2\right) dt$$

can be well approximated for non-negative values of x by

$$\text{erf}(x) = 1 - \exp(-x^2).(a_1 t + a_2 t^2 + a_3 t^3)$$

where $t = (1 + px)^{-1}$; $p=0.47047$; and the as are: $a_1 = 0.3480242$, $a_2 = -0.0958798$, $a_3 = 1 - a_1 - a_2$
Using the fact that $\text{erf}(-x) = -\text{erf}(x)$, write a Fortran function to yield $\text{erf}(x)$ for any real x.

7.B6 Write a subroutine to solve the general cubic equation, allowing for complex coefficients and complex solutions. A cubic equation may be written in the standard form

$$x^3 + a_2 x^2 + a_1 x + a_0 = 0$$

Notice that if we started with an equation in which x^3 had a different coefficient, i.e.

$$a_3 x^3 + a_2 x^2 + a_1 x + a_0 = 0$$

then we could get to the standard form by dividing through by a_3. To solve the cubic equation in the standard form, two auxiliary quantities must first be computed:

$$q = a_1/3 - a_2^2/9$$

$$r = (a_1 a_2 - 3a_0)/6 - a_2^3/27$$

Then, let $T = q^3 + r^2$ and $t = T^{1/2}$.

If $T > 0$, the equation has one real solution and a conjugate pair of complex solutions. If $T < 0$, all the solutions are real. If $T = 0$, all the solutions are real but at least two are equal to one another. To calculate the solutions, more auxiliary quantities must be computed:

$$s_1 = (r + t)^{1/3} \qquad\qquad s_2 = (r - t)^{1/3}$$

and then the solutions are

$$x_1 = (s_1 + s_2) - a_2/3$$

$$x_2 = -(s_1 + s_2)/2 - a_2/3 + i\sqrt{3}\,(s_1 - s_2)/2$$

$$x_2 = -(s_1 + s_2)/2 - a_2/3 - i\sqrt{3}\,(s_1 - s_2)/2$$

where i is the imaginary unit. Incidentally, the solutions satisfy the symmetry relations

$$x_1 + x_2 + x_3 = -a_2$$

$$x_1 x_2 + x_2 x_3 + x_3 x_1 = a_1$$

$$x_1 x_2 x_3 = -a_0$$

When the calculations are made, t may be imaginary and s_1 and s_2 may be complex. In taking the cube roots to get s_1 and s_2 when they are complex, it may be necessary to know that the Fortran operation

y ** z

computes the "principal value" of **EXP (z * LOG(y))**. The **LOG** function may not have zero argument, and if it has a complex argument then the **LOG** is taken to have an imaginary part between $\pm\pi$. If s_1 and s_2 are complex, they should be complex conjugates.

7.B7 When a particle moves with velocity β through a medium of refractive index n, the "Cerenkov angle" θ_c is given by

$$\theta_c = \arccos(1/\beta n)$$

The velocity β must be high enough for βn to exceed 1. The particle will emit Cerenkov light, the number of visible-spectrum photons per metre of pathlength being approximately

$$N_\gamma = 50000\sin^2(\theta_c)$$

Write a subroutine yielding θ_c and N_γ when β and n are given.

7.B8 From two successive complex numbers **z1** and **z2**, a third is generated by taking

z3 = 0.5*(z1 + z2) + c*(z1 - z2)

where **c** is an imaginary constant. Hence, an indefinite sequence of complex numbers can be generated, given two to start things off. Write a program to model what is going on and investigate the convergence of the sequence for different values of **c**.

CHAPTER 8

More about data; the type declaration statement

This chapter begins with a closer look at characters, including the definition of character constants and the operators used with character data. The intrinsic functions **LEN, LEN_TRIM, TRIM, IACHAR, ICHAR, ACHAR, CHAR, LGE, LGT, LLE, LLT, ADJUSTL, ADJUSTR, INDEX, SCAN, VERIFY,** *and* **REPEAT** *are explained.*

Then the type declaration statement is described in detail: all the possible type specifications, attribute specifications, and ways of declaring character-string lengths and array shapes.

Finally, defined operators are covered and there is an introduction to procedure interfaces.

8.1 More about characters

Fortran's handling of character data has already been introduced in preceding chapters. Unlike other data types, character data involves the complication that a single item may be a string consisting of an arbitrary number of individual characters. Character constants are specified simply by putting them between quotation marks or apostrophes. So **9** is an integer, **9.0** is real, **"9"** is a character, and **"Nine"** is a character string. A string may be of any length, including zero or one, so a single character is just a special case of a character string. As in the cases of numeric and logical data, names are used to represent variable character data. Names may also be used as a convenience to stand in place of character constants. Apart from cases where an **IMPLICIT** statement has been used (see end of Section 8.4) the names of character strings must always be declared, using a **CHARACTER** type declaration statement, at the start of the program or subprogram. Normally the lengths of the strings must also be specified at that time.

The character constants mentioned above, **"9"** and **"Nine"**, were specified as usual between double quotes. But what happens if quote marks are going to crop up in the character string itself? The assignment statement

```
remark = "Use "==" instead of ".EQ.", please."
```

does not make a string containing

```
Use "==" instead of "EQ", please.
```

To get over this problem, there are two additional rules.

First, a character constant may be enclosed in single quotes (apostrophes) rather than in double quotes, in which case double quotes may occur freely between the single quotes. (Conversely, single quotes may occur freely in a string delimited by double quotes.) So, we could have statements like

```
remark = 'Use "==" instead of ".EQ.", please.'
class = 'CONFIDENTIAL'
quote = '"'
apostrophe = "'"
destination = "It's a cul-de-sac"
```

Second, if the delimiting character itself is to occur within the string, this can be achieved by showing it twice successively. So,

```
remark = "Use ""=="" instead of "".EQ."", please."
quote = """"
apostrophe = ''''
destination = 'It''s a cul-de-sac'
```

are equivalent to the corresponding statements above. More complicated examples can be contrived, like the character constant

```
'Distinguish "it''s" from "its''"'
```

which actually looks like

```
Distinguish "it's" from "its'"
```

and

```
"Between quotes, """" means """
```

which looks like

```
Between quotes, "" means "
```

In practice the choice of two kinds of delimiter, and the doubling convention if a delimiter is to appear in the string, together give the programmer plenty of flexibility. In fact, it is possible to stick always to one sort of delimiter for all character constants, using the doubling convention when necessary. In this book, double quotes (") will be used as the delimiter.

It should be remembered that the Fortran character set does not distinguish between opening and closing double quote marks (" and "), nor between opening and closing single quote marks (' and '). In the ASCII character set these characters are `ACHAR(147)`, `ACHAR(148)`, `ACHAR(145)` and `ACHAR(146)` respectively, but do not appear on a standard keyboard. The keyboard has an angled single quote `ACHAR(96)`, as well as a straight single quote, `ACHAR(39)` (often used as an apostrophe) but there is only one kind of double quote mark ("), `ACHAR(34)`. If single quotes (apostrophes) are used to delimit a character string constant, they must be the straight quote from the keyboard as in 'James', not `James' (or 'James').

Non-default character types

Just as a processor may support more than one kind of integer, and more than two kinds of real number, it may also support character data of more than one kind. For example, if a processor uses `KIND=2` to specify a set of two-byte characters, then we might have for example

```
CHARACTER(KIND=2) :: runder = 2_"r"
```

(The `KIND` parameter in a character constant must come in front, the reverse of the case with real numbers!)

8.2 Operators and intrinsic functions for character data

There are a number of operators and intrinsic functions that may be applied to character data. We have already encountered the concatenation operator, `//`. Other operators that can be used are the relational operators `==`, `/=`, `>`, `>=`, `<`, and `<=`, giving logical results. For example,

```
(string1=="Sir").AND.(string2>string3)
```

is a logical expression with the value `.TRUE.` if `string1` is `"Sir"` and if also `string2` is "greater than" `string3`. When strings are compared in this way, if their lengths are different, then the shorter of the two is first padded out to the right with blanks. Then, strings are compared one character at a time, working from the left, until differing characters are encountered. The "greater" is then defined by the character which occurs later in the processor's character collating sequence (see the functions `CHAR` and `ICHAR` below).

Rather than use `>`, `>=`, `<`, and `<=` to compare character strings, it is usually better to use the special character functions `LGT`, `LGE`, `LLT` and `LLE`, explained below, which give an ordering according to the ASCII sequence and are therefore processor-independent.

The intrinsic functions for characters or character strings are listed in Table 8.1, showing the keywords that may be used with the arguments and with an indication of the types of the arguments and results (`C`=character, `I`=integer, `L`=logical).

The first of these, `LEN`, simply returns the length of the character string given as the argument. So, `LEN("New Zealand")` is an integer with value 11. A line of code that calculates the number of times a given character (`char`)

Table 8.1   Intrinsic functions for characters or character strings.

Name	Argument type	Result type
`LEN(STRING)`	c	I
`LEN_TRIM(STRING)`	c	I
`TRIM(STRING)`	c	c
`IACHAR(C)`	c	I
`ICHAR(C)`	c	I
`ACHAR(I)`	I	c
`CHAR(I)`	I	c
`LGE(STRING_A,STRING_B)`	cs	L
`LGT(STRING_A,STRING_B)`	cs	L
`LLE(STRING_A,STRING_B)`	cs	L
`LLT(STRING_A,STRING_B)`	cs	L
`ADJUSTL(STRING)`	c	c
`ADJUSTR(STRING)`	c	c
`INDEX(STRING,SUBSTRING,BACK)`	cs (BACK=L)	I
`SCAN(STRING,SET,BACK)`	cs (BACK=L)	I
`VERIFY(STRING,SET,BACK)`	cs (BACK=L)	I
`REPEAT(STRING,NCOPIES)`	STRING=C, NCOPIES=I	c

appears in a given string (**string**), using **LEN** and the logical array function
COUNT, is

```
COUNT((/ (char==string(i,i), i=1,LEN(string)) /))
```

LEN_TRIM is similar but does not count trailing blanks, i.e. **LEN_TRIM**
(**"Four "**) is **4**. The function **TRIM** returns a character string with the trailing
blanks removed. Obviously, **LEN(TRIM(c))** is equal to **LEN_TRIM(c)** for any
character string **c**. **TRIM** could be used in a statement such as

```
WRITE(*,*) TRIM(output)," is the answer."
```

to display some text without having to worry about the number of significant
characters in it.

The functions **IACHAR** and **ICHAR** convert a character into an integer code,
and their arguments must therefore be individual characters, i.e. strings of
length one. In the case of **IACHAR** the resulting integer is the standard ASCII
seven-bit code (0–127) corresponding to the character: thus, **IACHAR("0")**
has value **48**. The ASCII codes are given in Table 3.1. For a character outside
the ASCII set the result may be processor-dependent. With the function **ICHAR**
the code may be a different non-ASCII one, according to the particular processor. Note that the character set could in principle be much larger than the
ASCII set; **IACHAR** and **ICHAR** could yield values above **127**, and even above
255 if the processor allowed characters to be defined by more than one byte.

ACHAR and CHAR are the inverse functions to IACHAR and ICHAR: they yield a character corresponding to the integer code given as the argument. With ACHAR, the codes are the ASCII codes in the range 0–127, and for larger arguments the result will be processor-dependent. For example, ACHAR(97) is "a", ACHAR(36) is the currency symbol, and ACHAR(13) is a carriage return. With CHAR, the codes may depend on the processor in a sequence consistent with the ICHAR function. For most purposes the IACHAR and ACHAR functions should be sufficient, and ICHAR and CHAR can be avoided.

To illustrate the use of IACHAR and ACHAR, a lower-case letter can be converted to upper case by:

```
n=IACHAR(letter)
IF (n>=97.AND.n<=122) letter=ACHAR(n-32)
```

Note that ACHAR can be used to specify characters beyond the Fortran standard character set and perhaps not appearing on your keyboard:

```
CHARACTER, PARAMETER :: bell=ACHAR(7), cent=ACHAR(91)
```

The functions LGE, LGT, LLE and LLT are for comparing character strings according to the ASCII codes of the individual characters taken left-to-right. Since the alphabet is a subset of the ASCII set, these functions may be used to test the alphabetical ordering of strings, but it must be borne in mind that upper-case and lower-case letters have different ASCII codes. LGE means "lexically greater than or equal to", LGT is "lexically greater than", and so on. For example, LGE(STRING_A="A",STRING_B="Z") is .FALSE. because STRING_A does not follow STRING_B in the ASCII collating sequence, because A does not follow Z in the alphabet. However, lower-case letters follow upper-case ones, so LGE(STRING_A="a",STRING_B="Z") is .TRUE..

Also, LGE(STRING_A="Six",STRING_B="Sixty") is .FALSE., because, in comparing strings of different lengths, the shorter string is extended with blanks to the right to match the length of the longer string, and the blank character (ASCII code 32) comes before any of the alphabet.

ADJUSTL and ADJUSTR are string-to-string functions that replace leading blanks by trailing blanks (ADJUSTL) or trailing blanks by leading blanks (ADJUSTR). Thus the value of ADJUSTL(" Preface ") is "Preface ", but on the other hand ADJUSTR(" Chapter One ") is " Chapter One". It is useful that the function-of-a-function TRIM(ADJUSTL(...)) will remove both leading and trailing blanks from a string.

INDEX is a function that carries out the useful job of looking for substrings within strings. If c2 is a substring of c1, then INDEX(STRING=c1, SUBSTRING=c2) yields the first starting point (counting characters from the left) of an occurrence of c2 within c1. So the expression

```
INDEX(STRING="Birmingham", SUBSTRING="ming")
```

is equal to 4, and

```
INDEX(STRING="Birmingham", SUBSTRING="i")
```

is equal to **2**. **INDEX** is zero if **SUBSTRING** is not a substring of **STRING**. If **SUBSTRING** has zero length, **INDEX** is normally returned with the value **1**. The optional argument **BACK** is a logical variable taken to be **.FALSE.** if it is not otherwise specified, but if **BACK=.TRUE.**, the function looks for the last (instead of first) occurrence of **SUBSTRING** within **STRING**; in other words

```
INDEX(STRING="Birmingham", SUBSTRING="i", BACK=.TRUE.)
```

is equal to **5**. If **BACK=.TRUE.** and **SUBSTRING** has zero length, **INDEX** is given a value of one more than the length of **STRING**.

SCAN(STRING, SET, BACK) does a job similar to **INDEX**, but it looks for any of a number of individual characters within **STRING**. The argument **SET** is a string defining a set of individual characters, and **INDEX** points to the first occurrence of any one of them within **STRING**. For example,

```
SCAN(STRING="Strength", SET="aeiou")
```

has the value **4**. As in the case of the **INDEX** function, the optional **BACK** argument will make **SCAN** look for the position of the last occurrence, i.e. **SCAN(STRING="Counihan", SET="aeiou",BACK=.TRUE.)** has the value **7**.

VERIFY(STRING, SET, BACK) is, in a sense, the opposite of **SCAN**. It checks to see if all the characters in **STRING** occur within **SET**, and if not it yields the position (within **STRING**) of the first character not found in **SET**. If **BACK** is present with value **.TRUE.**, **VERIFY** gives the position of the last character in **STRING** that is not in **SET**. If every character in **STRING** occurs in **SET**, **VERIFY** has the value zero whether **BACK** is **.TRUE.** or **.FALSE.** For example, the logical expression

```
VERIFY(STRING=intprint, SET="0123456789")==0
```

has the value **.TRUE.** if **intprint** is the name of a string containing only decimal digits.

Finally, **REPEAT** is a function that concatenates a number of copies of the same string, i.e. **REPEAT(STRING=" ",NCOPIES=80)** is a character string consisting of 80 blanks.

8.3 Exercises 8.A

8.A1 What are the values of:

(i)	**LEN("Test_string")**	(ii)	**TRIM(" ")**
(iii)	**ACHAR(111)**	(iv)	**CHAR(" ")**
(v)	**LGE("Q","S")**	(vi)	**LLE("T","α")**
(vii)	**LLE("6","1")**	(viii)	**LLE("5","e")**

8.A2   Write code to remove the first character of a string called **x** if (and only if) that character is a numeric digit.

8.A3   Write code to trim off all leading blanks of a string called **x**, replace them by trailing blanks and write the result.

8.4 The general form of the type declaration statement

A simple form of the type declaration statement (TDS) was introduced as early as Section 2.2, and since then several elaborations of it have been mentioned when necessary. At this point it is appropriate to give complete details of the syntax of the TDS, although there are still one or two features that will not be fully explained until later chapters. In its various forms the TDS is probably the second most common statement type in Fortran (after the assignment statement) and it is essential to understand it well.

The purpose of a TDS is to declare the characteristics of named data items. The statement may at the same time serve the additional purpose of giving initial values to them.

In general a TDS consists of three parts in this order: first a single "type specification", second an optional list of "attribute specifications", and third an "entity declaration list". The type specification and the attribute specifications which may follow it are separated by commas. The attribute specifications are separated by a double colon from the entity declaration list.

Omitting the colon in a TDS
In the simplest cases where there are no attribute specifications and initial values are not given to any data, it is permissible for the entity declaration list to follow the type specification without the intervening double colon. However, it is recommended that the double colon should always be used.

A simple example of a TDS is

```
LOGICAL, SAVE :: a, cq, cr
```

where **LOGICAL** is the type specification, **SAVE** is an attribute specification, and the entity declaration list contains the three names **a, cq, cr**. A more complicated example is

```
CHARACTER(2), PARAMETER :: unit(3) = (/"mm","cm","dm"/)
```

and here the type specification is **CHARACTER(2)**, there is one attribute specification, **PARAMETER**, and the entity being declared is the array called **unit(3)**. Initial values are being given to the elements of **unit(3)**.

The primary purpose of a TDS is to declare the existence of data objects of a certain type. A single TDS must refer to a single type. The type is given by the

129

type specification and it must be one of the following:

```
INTEGER (KIND=...)
REAL (KIND=...)
COMPLEX (KIND=...)
LOGICAL (KIND=...)
TYPE (type-name)
CHARACTER (length-selector, KIND=...)

DOUBLE PRECISION
```

The bracketed **KIND** parameters that may occur here are optional and can usually be forgotten about. After the type specification there can be the following range of possible attribute specifications, which will be discussed in turn further below.

```
PARAMETER
SAVE
PUBLIC
PRIVATE
EXTERNAL
INTRINSIC
OPTIONAL
INTENT (specification)
POINTER
TARGET
ALLOCATABLE
DIMENSION (specification)
```

Finally, there are the entities actually being declared. The entity declaration list at its simplest is a series of the names of entities that are of the type given in the type specification and which have special qualities indicated by the attribute specifications. These entities are usually variables, but could be named constants or even the names of functions. Their names must follow the usual Fortran naming rules. A name in the entity declaration list of a TDS may have additional information appended to it if it is an array or if it is of character type, and it may be given an initial value.

The possible type specifications are explained in more detail below.

INTEGER (KIND=...)

This indicates that the data declared here is of integer type. There may be a **KIND** parameter if the processor may support integers of unusual precision, but Fortran does not require this to be possible, so this specification will almost always consist simply of the keyword **INTEGER**. An example is:

```
INTEGER :: i, j, k, input_unit, gamma
```

It is recommended that the names of integer data should have initial letters in the range **i–n**.

Although it is usually recommended that every variable should be declared in a type declaration statement, exceptions can be made for the trivial integers used as indices in **DO** loops or in the "implied **DO**" syntax of (say) an array constructor.

REAL (*KIND=...*)

This indicates data of real type. The bracketed **KIND** parameter will rarely be needed, but it allows for real numbers of unusual precision. Examples:

```
REAL :: estimate_1, estimate_2, result, error
REAL (KIND=KIND(0.0D0)) :: hairsbreadth_x, hairsbreadth_y
```

It is recommended that the names of real data should start with letters outside the range **i–n**.

For simple scalar data objects of real and integer type, whose names fit the initial-letter convention and which have no special attributes, there is no need to use a TDS at all although it is recommended that one does so.

COMPLEX (*KIND=...*)

The data following this would be complex numbers. The **KIND** parameter, if present, means that each complex number is equivalent to a pair of real numbers of the specified kind of precision. Example:

```
COMPLEX :: omega1, omega2, z
COMPLEX, PARAMETER :: i = (0.0, 1.0)
```

LOGICAL (*KIND=...*)

This specification indicates data of logical type. The **KIND** parameter, as in the case of integers, allows for processors to have more than one way of representing such data, but this would be meaningless on most processors and we can disregard it. Example:

```
LOGICAL :: decision
```

TYPE (*type-name*)

This type specification makes it possible to declare data objects of special user-defined types, or "derived" types. Derived types are described in Chapter 14.

CHARACTER (*length-selector, KIND=...*)

This indicates data of character type. Whenever character data is declared, the length of each item must be indicated and this can be done by means of a length selector following the keyword **CHARACTER**. The selector specifies a length that will apply to all the items listed later in the statement.

The length-selector here is not mandatory, because the same job can be done by means of a selector appended to each item's name in the entity declaration list. There is a superficial advantage in specifying character string lengths in the entity declaration list, because then strings of different lengths may be declared in the one statement. However, on balance, it is recommended that the lengths should be specified after **CHARACTER** even if this demands more statements, since the syntax can otherwise become more confusing.

A **KIND** parameter may be specified with the **CHARACTER** keyword if the processor supports non-default character sets.

As a result of Fortran's history, the **CHARACTER** keyword, with the length selector following it, may take any one of the forms below:

```
CHARACTER

CHARACTER (expression)
CHARACTER (LEN=expression)
CHARACTER *(expression)

CHARACTER *constant

CHARACTER (*)
CHARACTER (LEN=*)
CHARACTER *(*)
```

The first of these, with no length selector, could be used to declare character strings of length one, i.e. individual characters, and is therefore equivalent to **CHARACTER(1)**.

The three forms in the following group are equivalent and one may as well stick to the first form, i.e.

```
CHARACTER (expression)
```

Here, *expression*, the length of the character string, must be an expression of non-negative scalar integer type. It may simply be a constant, or a constant expression, or it may be a more complicated expression involving variables. However, if it involves variables then they must be accessible and have values when this TDS appears. Accessibility could be through a data module, or (within a procedure) through a dummy argument, or by reference to an intrinsic function. We could have, for example,

```
CHARACTER (128)
CHARACTER (64*128)
CHARACTER (n)
```

```
CHARACTER (1 + LEN(TRIM(z)))
```

as long as the integer **n**, and the character string **z**, have been previously made accessible. In this way, lengths of strings can be set dynamically rather than fixed when the program is compiled. When a non-constant expression is used to declare the length of a string that is not a dummy argument, the string is known as an "automatic" data object.

Another form listed above was

```
CHARACTER *constant
```

and here **constant** would simply be a non-negative integer value. In other words, lengths can be specified by things like

```
CHARACTER *128
```

but this notation offers no advantage over

```
CHARACTER (128)
```

and is best avoided. The list of forms given above ended with three more which are equivalent to one another, i.e.

```
CHARACTER (*)
CHARACTER (LEN=*)
CHARACTER *(*)
```

all of which use an asterisk to mean that the length of the character string is to be assumed from elsewhere. Sticking to the first and simplest of these forms,

```
CHARACTER (*)
```

should be used:
- (a) when the length can be taken from an explicit initial value given to the string later in the statement;
- (b) in a procedure, to declare a dummy character-string argument whose length will be taken from the program unit where the call is made; or
- (c) in a function whose value is a character string, when declaring the name of the function; the asterisk can be used if its length is to be assumed from a declaration made in the program unit from which the function is called.

In cases (b) and (c), the length will therefore be determined, not on compilation, but on execution and could be different each time the procedure is actually called.

Here are a few more examples of character TDSs:

```
CHARACTER(1) :: initial1, initial2, initial3
CHARACTER(20) :: name_of_state, name_of_city
CHARACTER(12*nwords + 24) :: page
CHARACTER(*) :: input_data
CHARACTER(1) :: letter
```

```
CHARACTER(20) :: forename, midname, surname
CHARACTER(12) :: q = "CONFIDENTIAL"
CHARACTER, PARAMETER :: star = "*"
CHARACTER(*), PARAMETER :: origin = "Made in Thailand"
CHARACTER(nchars+6) :: line1, line2, line3, line4
CHARACTER(*) :: surname = "Spock"
CHARACTER(*) :: title = "Mr. "//surname
CHARACTER(1) :: bell = ACHAR(7)
```

In summary: the **CHARACTER** TDS should begin with

CHARACTER(*expression*)

where the ***expression*** is equal to the lengths of the strings declared in the statement. If the expression is not merely a constant but is a "specification expression" evaluated at execution, we have an "automatic" length. Alternatively, the statement may begin with

CHARACTER(*)

when the length is going to be ascertained from an explicit initial value given later in the statement, or by argument-passing (or function-name-passing) to a procedure. To minimize the likelihood of confusion, it is recommended that other forms of syntax be avoided.

IMPLICIT

Unless declared by a TDS to be of a different type, variables are assumed to be of integer type if their names begin with letters of the alphabet in the range **i–n**. Otherwise, they are assumed to be real. This initial-letter convention may be changed within a program unit by a special non-executable statement, **IMPLICIT**. Some examples will make its use clear:

IMPLICIT REAL (a-z)

means that all variables are interpreted by default as real numbers.

IMPLICIT INTEGER (a, e, i, o, u), REAL (b-d, f-h, j-n, p-t, v-z)

means that names starting with a vowel are to be taken as integers, and others as real numbers.

IMPLICIT CHARACTER (a-z)

means that all names (unless individually specified otherwise) are taken to be the names of character strings.

IMPLICIT TYPE(Encrypt) (a-z)

means that all names will refer by default to the data type **Encrypt**. Since **Encrypt** is not an intrinsic type this must be a derived type (see Chapter 12). Finally,

IMPLICIT NONE

means that there is no initial-letter data type convention imposed in this part of the program, and therefore that the programmer will specify explicitly the types of all variables.

The usage of the **IMPLICIT** statement is controversial among Fortran programmers. The view taken in this book is that (i) it is helpful to adhere to the standard initial-letter convention to distinguish between real and integer data, but at the same time (ii) it is recommended that the types of all variables should be declared explicitly anyway, except for integer **DO** loop indices, and (iii) the **IMPLICIT** statement, being unnecessary, should not be used.

8.5 Attributes

The set of possible attribute specifications in a TDS was listed in the previous section. Each attribute may be specified no more than once in one TDS. Many of the attributes are mutually exclusive and many can apply only to certain sorts of data (e.g. to procedure arguments), so in practice it is unusual for a TDS to include more than one or two attribute specifications. When there is more than one attribute specification, they may be given in any order. The meaning of each attribute is explained below.

PARAMETER

A data object with the **PARAMETER** attribute has a fixed value, i.e. it is a "named constant" that will not be changed during the running of the program. The value must be appended to the name in the statement's entity declaration list (see Section 8.7). Examples:

```
REAL(KIND=2), PARAMETER :: e = 2.718281828459045235
CHARACTER(*), PARAMETER :: country = "Lithuania"
```

SAVE

This is an attribute that may apply to data items (other than arguments) occurring in subprograms. It means that the items will retain their values after the subprogram has executed. In other words, **SAVE** is a way of retaining the value of data between subsequent calls to a function or subroutine. The **SAVE** attribute has no effect if it is specified in a main program. Example:

```
INTEGER, SAVE :: number_of_times_called
```

PUBLIC and PRIVATE

These two "accessibility attributes" are only applicable to data items declared in a module (Chapter 10). **PRIVATE** means that the items are not accessible (via a **USE** statement) to any other program unit outside the module. It could be advisable for data to be declared **PRIVATE** if it is used only within module procedures and if there could be an unintended clash of names with other data in program units using the module. **PUBLIC** means the opposite, i.e. that the data is accessible by another program unit using the module. Example:

```
REAL, PRIVATE :: input_buffer(1025)
```

EXTERNAL

This is applicable not to ordinary data items but only to the names of functions. It indicates an external function. It is important to declare the **EXTERNAL** attribute with a function name if that name is to be passed as an argument to another procedure (Chapter 14). Within such a procedure, **EXTERNAL** can indicate the dummy argument that corresponds to that function name.

INTRINSIC

The **INTRINSIC** attribute means that a function name is that of a Fortran intrinsic function. This attribute needs to be specified only in rather unusual circumstances.

OPTIONAL

This attribute can be used when the dummy arguments of procedures are declared. It indicates arguments that need not necessarily be included in the actual argument list when the procedure is called. A procedure with optional arguments must have an interface (see Section 8.9). Examples:

```
COMPLEX, OPTIONAL :: croot1, croot2
REAL, OPTIONAL, EXTERNAL :: Smoothing_function
```

INTENT (specification)

Like **OPTIONAL**, this is an attribute that may apply to procedures' dummy arguments. **INTENT** permits the programmer to ensure that an argument is used

(a) only for data coming in to the procedure;
(b) only for data going out; or
(c) for data flowing both ways.

This is done by a specification, in brackets, which may be **IN, OUT** or **IN OUT** respectively. An argument with **INTENT(IN)** cannot be changed by the procedure, and one with **INTENT(OUT)** is initially undefined and must be defined by the procedure. The attribute **INTENT(IN OUT)** embraces both possibilities and need not be used except as a form of program annotation. Example:

```
REAL, INTENT(IN) :: vector(3), rotation_matrix(3,3)
REAL, INTENT(OUT) :: new_vector(3)
```

It is not normally necessary to specify an argument's **INTENT** at all. However, **INTENT (IN OUT)** is not always equivalent to not specifying **INTENT**. If an actual argument is going to be a constant, then it can only have **INTENT (IN)** and **INTENT(IN OUT)** will not do. **INTENT (IN OUT)** means that it must be possible for information to pass in or out of the procedure through the argument in question.

Fortran 95 feature not present in Fortran 90

The **INTENT** specification is mandatory for the arguments of **PURE** and **ELEMENTAL** procedures (see Chapter 11).

POINTER and TARGET

These two attributes can apply when pointers are being used; they will be discussed in Chapter 13. If a procedure argument has either of these attributes, or if a function's value has the **POINTER** attribute, the procedure must have an interface (see Section 8.9).

ALLOCATABLE

The **ALLOCATABLE** attribute is applicable only to arrays. It will be dealt with in Chapter 12.

DIMENSION (specification)

The **DIMENSION** attribute is used only with arrays. **DIMENSION** indicates that array variables are being declared and it is followed by a bracketed specification of the shape of the arrays.

Alternatively, shapes may be given for individual arrays as part of the entity declaration list, in which case they override a shape specified with **DIMENSION**. The situation is rather like that for character strings, where string lengths may be given globally, for the whole set of entities declared in a statement, or individually.

Because arrays may be declared simply by specifying a shape for each array in the entity declaration list, the **DIMENSION** attribute is not actually necessary at all. So, the TDS

```
COMPLEX, DIMENSION(4,4) :: gamma1, gamma2, gamma3, &
   gamma4, gamma5
```

is equivalent to

```
COMPLEX :: gamma1(4,4), gamma2(4,4), gamma3(4,4), &
   gamma4(4,4), gamma5(4,4)
```

Array specifications following **DIMENSION**, and array specifications following an item in the list, can be constructed in exactly the same ways. These ways are covered in more detail in the next section.

Statements equivalent to data attribute specifications

All the data attributes (**PARAMETER, SAVE**, etc.) that may occur in a TDS may, equivalently, be given by separate statements, "attribute specification statements" (ASSs). An ASS does not specify the data objects' types, which must still be given in a TDS or assumed from the initial letter of the names. An ASS may not duplicate or contradict an attribute already given in a TDS. Some examples of ASSs are:

```
SUBROUTINE Integrate (Rfunction, g, h, i, j, name)

REAL :: Rfunction
EXTERNAL Rfunction              !Double colon forbidden!
INTEGER :: g, h
INTENT (IN) :: g, h, i, j       !Double colon optional!
CHARACTER(*) :: name
OPTIONAL :: name                !Double colon optional!
SAVE :: ncalls                  !Double colon optional!
DIMENSION iflags(6)             !Double colon forbidden!
PARAMETER (del=0.0002)          !Double colon forbidden!
```

In addition, in a module (Chapter 10) there may be a **PRIVATE** statement such as

```
PRIVATE :: workspace            !Double colon optional!
```

This may happen without any list of variables, i.e. we can have just the **PRIVATE** keyword by itself:

```
PRIVATE
```

which means that all data declared in the module are **PRIVATE**. Subsequent to this, a **PUBLIC** statement

```
PUBLIC :: x, y, z !Double colon optional!
```

will make the named objects accessible outside the module again.

ASSs had their origin at a time when many programmers avoided TDSs and relied on the initial-letter convention alone to specify real and integer data. However, it is now recommended that TDSs should be written for virtually all data objects, and all data attributes should be specified in a TDS, avoiding the need for ASSs.

8.6 Array specifications

The simplest kind of array specification is the sort shown in the above example, where the shape of the array is given by a list of its extents in each dimension. A shape **(4,4)** means that there are two dimensions, i.e. a rank of two, and a total of 16 elements making up the whole array. This is a simple example of an "explicit shape" specification list. In fact, Fortran distinguishes between four different sorts of array specification, namely "explicit shape", "assumed shape", "deferred shape" and "assumed size" arrays.

Explicit shape

Explicit shape specification lists such as **(4,4)** or **(3,3,3)** or **(100)** or **(4,20,2)** declare arrays whose elements would be referenced by indices running from **1** to **4** (twice), **1** to **3** (three times), **1** to **100**, and in the final case **1** to **4**, **1** to **20**, and **1** to **2**. Alternatively, starting points different from **1** can be set using the colon notation, the shape **(4,4)** being equivalent to **(1:4,1:4)**. If we have

```
REAL :: alpha(-3:3,0:9)
```

then the array's rank is two and there are 70 elements, and individual elements can be referenced by expressions such as **array(n,m)** with n taking any integer value from **-3** to **3** and m from **0** to **9** inclusive. It is possible to have mixed declarations in that some, but not all, dimensions are given with the colon notation:

```
REAL :: alpha(-3:3,0:9), beta(20,0:1), gamma(20,20)
```

Moreover, the bounds need not be given as specific integers. A declaration like

```
REAL :: xyz(3,npoints), r(npoints,npoints), checksum(0:k)
```

is possible if **npoints** and **k** are the names of integer constants. In fact, when the declaration is made in a procedure and the object is not a dummy argument, the bounds need not even be constants: they can be integer variables or expressions as long as they will have ascertainable values when the TDS is encountered. The array is then known as an "automatic array", since its shape is not fixed until the procedure is called (and may differ from one call to another). Here is an example:

```
SUBROUTINE Falsetto (n, w)
USE Printer_data
INTEGER, INTENT(IN) :: n
CHARACTER(*), INTENT(IN):: w
REAL :: r(0:n-1,0:n-1)
```

```
CHARACTER(1) :: ch(2*LEN(w))
CHARACTER(1) :: page(linelength, pagelength)
   .
   .
   .
```

This subroutine uses the argument **n** to fix the bounds of both dimensions of a rank-two array **r**, and it uses the length of the character string argument **w** in order to determine the size of an array **ch** containing single characters. The dimensions **linelength** and **pagelength** are presumably specified within the module **Printer_data**.

The bounds of explicit-shape arrays may be given by fairly complicated "specification expressions", but there are certain restrictions. In particular, a specification expression may not normally involve a reference to any non-intrinsic function. In the example above, **LEN** is of course an intrinsic Fortran function. Obviously, in order to have a definite value a specification expression must include only variables that are accessible as dummy arguments or (using modules, Chapter 10) as module data or by host association. The situation is the same as for the specification expressions that can be used to set the lengths of automatic character strings (see Section 8.4, under **CHARACTER**).

Fortran 95 feature not in Fortran 90

Specification expressions may involve **PURE** external procedures.

Assumed shape

A dummy argument in a procedure may have an assumed shape, which means that its rank is known but its shape is taken from that of the corresponding actual argument whenever the procedure is called. An assumed shape is specified by giving a series of colons, one colon for each dimension. In the following example there are two dimensions, i.e. the array being declared has rank two, but the extents in each dimension will be determined only as and when the function is called. The extents need not be the same, i.e. this need not be a square matrix:

```
FUNCTION N_positive_elements (matrix)
INTEGER :: N_positive_elements
REAL, INTENT(IN) :: matrix(:,:)
   .
   .
   .
```

With an assumed-shape array it is possible to specify that a lower bound other than **1** will be used in the procedure, by giving the lower bound before the colon. So,

```
REAL :: matrix(0:,0:)
```

means that the lower bounds are both **0**, but this does not affect the total numbers of elements.

An assumed-shape array can only be a dummy argument within a procedure. Also, it can only be used if the procedure has an **INTERFACE** in the program unit from which it is called: the meaning of this will become clear in Section 8.9.

Deferred shape

The third kind of array specification is a "deferred shape" specification, but this involves allocatable arrays or array pointers (Chapters 12 and 13) and it would be premature to give details here. Deferred-shape arrays are specified with the same colon notation as assumed-shape arrays, but without the possibility of specifying lower index bounds.

Assumed size

The fourth and final class of array specification is the "assumed size" specification. Like an assumed shape, an assumed size is a possible feature of a dummy-argument array in a procedure. Assumed-size arrays are usually regarded as an over-complex and unnecessary feature of Fortran and their use is not recommended. The notation for declaring an assumed size includes an asterisk. To take the simplest example,

```
REAL FUNCTION Chi (a, b, z)
REAL :: a, b, z(*)
    .
    .
    .
```

means that the arguments **a** and **b** are scalars but **z** is an array. Within the function, **z** has rank one, but the corresponding actual argument could be an array of any rank. The rank of the actual argument is not passed on and does not become the rank of the dummy argument **z**. The array **z** always has rank one. However, **z** is given the same total number of elements as the actual argument had, i.e. **z** assumes the size of the actual argument.

In the above example the lower bound of **z**'s dimension would be **1**, but as we have previously seen it is possible to give a different lower bound before a colon: with

```
REAL :: a, b, z(1025:*)
```

the array **z** has elements **z(1025)**, **z(1026)**, **z(1027)**, and so on up to an index which will exceed by 1025 the size of the actual argument corresponding to **z**.

There are one or two further possibilities with assumed-size arrays. For one thing, the actual argument need not be the name of an array, but could just be an array element, in which case what is passed is the series of elements starting at the one given and going on to the end of the array (in normal array element order, see Chapter 15). In other words, with

```
klap = (/2,5,7,1,1,0,7,9,5,4,0,0/)
n = 6
CALL Turn (klap(n))
   .
   .
   .
SUROUTINE Turn (k)
INTEGER :: k(*)
   .
   .
   .
```

the dummy argument array **k** in the subroutine will have size seven and the value (/0,7,9,5,4,0,0/).

Things can get a little more complicated with assumed-size character arrays, since the elements of the actual and dummy arguments may be character strings of different lengths! Then, the size assumed for the dummy argument will be whatever is needed to accommodate all the characters in the actual argument array. Suppose we have the following code:

```
toffee = (/"and","pat","cob","try","owl"/)
CALL Twist (toffee)
   .
   .
   .
SUBROUTINE Twist (tripe)
CHARACTER (5) :: tripe(*)
```

then **tripe** will be (/"andpa","tcobt","ryowl"/), i.e. with size three. As with non-character data, the first part of an array can be left out by giving, as actual argument, one element (or a substring of an element) to be taken as the starting point of what is passed to the procedure:

```
toffee = (/"and","pat","cob","try","owl"/)
CALL Twist (toffee(3)(2:3))
   .
   .
   .
SUBROUTINE Twist (tripe)
CHARACTER (2):: tripe(*)
```

Here, the actual argument is a substring (**"ob"**) consisting of the second and third characters from the third element of toffee. The subroutine will receive the contents of toffee starting from that substring, giving tripe the value (/"ob","tr","yo","wl"/). The call

```
CALL Twist (toffee(3)(2:2))
```

would have had exactly the same effect.

So far, in our examples of assumed-size specifications, we have had dummy argument arrays of rank one. Arrays of greater rank are possible, but then all dimensions except the last must be specified as in an explicit shape specification. Only the last dimension is left indeterminate with an asterisk. In the example immediately above, if we had

```
CHARACTER (2) :: tripe(2,*)
```
then tripe would have been a rank-two array taking the shape (2,2).

8.7 The entity declaration list

Having dealt with type specifications and attribute specifications, it only remains to describe the entity declaration list that comes at the end of a TDS. The task is made easy because the most complicated aspects of entity declaration are those to do with character string lengths and array shapes and these have already been covered exhaustively above.

For scalar data of non-character type, the entity declaration list will simply consist of a series of names separated by commas, each possibly being given an initial value by an "initialization expression" following an = after the name. The following are examples of valid lists:

```
a, b, c, d=0.0, e=5.5, f
karavan = 4520988765, k2 = 2**64, kstore1, kstore2, &
  kstore3
check1=.TRUE., check2=.TRUE., check3=.TRUE., checksum
q = (0.39967, -1.03847)
```

There are a number of restrictions on the use of an initialization expression in a TDS. Initialization expressions are compulsory whenever the **PARAMETER** attribute is present. An initialization expression is forbidden when declaring a dummy argument, function result or automatic object, and it is also incompatible with the **ALLOCATABLE and POINTER** attributes. Any data object that is declared with an initialization expression will be saved, in the sense that it is given the **SAVE** attribute even if **SAVE** was not explicitly included in the attribute list. Note that data initialization takes place once and for all before program execution: data in a procedure may be initialized but are not re-initialized each time the procedure is called.

Initialization expressions are subject to a number of technical restrictions. They may not involve variables and the only functions allowed are intrinsic integer or character functions, inquiry functions (except **ALLOCATED**), and the transformational functions **REPEAT, TRIM, TRANSFER,** and **RESHAPE**. Defined operators (Section 8.9) are not allowed and the exponentiation operator (**) is only allowed with an integer power.

When declaring arrays, array constructors may be used as initialization expressions (if necessary with implied-**DO** variables) as in

```
kpow(32) = (/ (2**m, m=1, 32) /)
```

When declaring character data, initialization expressions may involve substrings and character functions, e.g.

143

```
alphabet = (/ ("abcdefghijklmnopqrstuvwxyz"(j:j), j=1, 26) /)
blank_page = REPEAT(" ",1750)
```

It has already been mentioned that the length of character data may be specified alongside the name in the entity declaration list. The notation is similar to that which can be used to do the same job after the **CHARACTER** keyword but is a little more limited. The permissible forms are

```
charname*(expression)
charname*constant
charname*(*)
```

where *charname* is the object's name, *expression* is an integer expression as in Section 11.9, *constant* is a specific integer, and the *(*) notation is similar in effect to **CHARACTER(*)**. With any of these forms, an array specification could also be inserted between *charname* and the character length specification. In an extreme case, we could therefore have a specification such as

```
CHARACTER :: chimera(*)*(*)
```

which is an assumed-size assumed-length character array equivalent to

```
CHARACTER, DIMENSION(*) :: chimera*(*)
```

but the simplest notation is of course

```
CHARACTER(*) :: chimera(*)
```

This variety of different notations arises from the history of Fortran and is not an attractive feature of the language. To keep things simple and clear, it is strongly recommended that you always give character length specifications with the **CHARACTER** keyword and always give array shapes with the arrays' names, avoiding the use of the **DIMENSION** keyword. In other words, specify string lengths always on the left of the double colon and array sizes always on the right. So,

```
CHARACTER(20) :: chimera(30)
```

is an array of 30 strings each of 20 characters.

Fortran 95 features not in Fortran 90

Pointers (Chapter 13) may be initially disassociated by pointer assignment to **NULL()**.

Initialization of derived-type data is allowed, as in

```
TYPE (Link), PARAMETER :: empty = Node(0, NULL())
```

This example involves a derived type (Chapter 12) with a pointer component (Chapter 13).

The DATA statement

As an alternative to initializing data in a TDS, or in an initial assignment statement, there is a special statement type, **DATA**, which exists in order to give initial values to variables. It works only for ordinary variables, i.e. not for dummy arguments, automatic objects, and the like. As an example, to illustrate the details of the syntax, suppose that variables have been declared by the TDS

```
INTEGER :: i1, i2, kappa(4), mult(20), ncells(-10;10,-10:10)
```

Then initial values could be declared by

```
DATA i1, i2, i3 /0,0,20/, kappa /14,71,0,33/, &
  mult /20*1/, ((ncells(i,j),i=-10:10),j=-10,10) /441*0/
```

which is hardly less complicated than it looks. The **DATA** statement consists of a list of sets, the sets in the above example being

```
i1, i2, i3 /0,0,20/
kappa /14,71,0,33/
mult /20*1/
((ncells(i,j),i=-10,10),j=-10,10) /441*0/
```

Each set consists of a list of names followed by a list (between slashes) of initial values. The first set puts **i1**, **i2** and **i3** equal to **0**, **0** and **20** respectively. The second set gives values to the four elements of the array **kappa**. The third set illustrates a "repeat" notation in the list of values, where an integer before an asterisk is equivalent to that number of occurrences of the value; the 20 elements of the array **mult** are all set to **1**. The final set in our example shows how an implied **DO** notation can be used to run through elements of an array.

The **DATA** statement does almost nothing that cannot be done in other ways (especially with array constructors) and it should be avoided. The only thing that a **DATA** statement can do that is not otherwise possible in Fortran is to allow integer variables to be assigned the values of integer constants specified in binary, octal or hexadecimal form. Such integers are written with their digits within a pair of quotes, and preceded by the letter **B, O** or **Z** (for binary, octal or hexadecimal). Thus, **B"10001"** and **O"21"** and **Z"11"** could represent the decimal number 17 in **DATA** statements.

8.8 Summary

Leaving aside some relatively unimportant options, the type declaration statement should begin with one of

```
INTEGER
REAL or REAL(KIND=KIND(0.0D0)
COMPLEX or COMPLEX(KIND=KIND(0.0D0)
LOGICAL
CHARACTER(...)
TYPE(...)
```

In the case of **CHARACTER**, the brackets contain the length of the strings, determined either by a constant or by a non-constant expression ("automatic" data) or by an asterisk ("assumed length"). **TYPE** is dealt with in Chapter 12. The type specification may be followed by optional attribute specifications:

PARAMETER or **SAVE** for ordinary variables
EXTERNAL or **INTRINSIC** for function names
INTENT and/or **OPTIONAL** for dummy arguments
ALLOCATABLE, **POINTER**, and **TARGET**: see Chapters 12 and 13

Then there is an entity declaration list consisting of variables' names separated by commas. There may be an array specification after each name. An array specification should be of one of these kinds:

- explicit shape (including "automatic" arrays)
- assumed shape (for dummy arguments, using colons)
- deferred shape (see Chapters 12 and 13)

Finally, the name of a variable may be followed by an = sign and an initialization expression, giving a starting value to the object named. If the **PARAMETER** attribute is specified, an initialization expression is compulsory and the object is technically a "named constant" rather than a variable.

8.9 Defined operators; introducing interfaces

Just as external functions can be written as a supplement to Fortran's own set of intrinsic functions, likewise it is possible to have user-defined operators to supplement the intrinsic operators (+, -, *, **, //, >, etc.). This section explains how new operators can be created.

Most of Fortran's intrinsic operators are "binary" operators, i.e. they operate between two quantities to produce one result. Sometimes the operation is symmetrical, as for multiplication (*) or addition (+), and sometimes it is not, e.g $p**q$ is not the same as $q**p$. There are two or three "unary" intrinsic operators, operating on a single quantity (+ and - may be used as unary operators, and the logical operator **.NOT.** is always unary).

A new "defined" operator is linked to an external function of one or two arguments, so that any reference to the operator is a reference to the function. This is achieved with the help of an "interface block".

For present purposes, an interface block is a block of declarative statements that refer to an external procedure and that must be inserted in a subprogram if the procedure in question is to be called from that subprogram. The purpose of an interface block is to tell the calling subprogram something about the called procedure. An interface block contains, within it, the declarative statements that also appear within the external procedure itself. For a defined operator associated with an external function, the interface block has the form

```
INTERFACE OPERATOR (.op.)
  FUNCTION Name (argument1, argument2)
  declaration-statements
  END FUNCTION Name
END INTERFACE
```

Here, *op* is the operator being defined, and it must consist of a series of up to 31 letters, surrounded by a pair of dots. The function details must correspond to an external function, and a reference to the operator in an expression of the form

```
argument1.op.argument2
```

obtains the value of *Name(argument1, argument2)*.

If the operator is to be unary, only one argument would be specified in the function and the reference would take the form

```
.op.argument
```

An example is the interface block

```
INTERFACE OPERATOR (.Inv.)
  FUNCTION Inverse_Vector (v)
  REAL :: Inverse_Vector(3)
  REAL, INTENT(IN) :: v(3)
  END FUNCTION Inverse_Vector
END INTERFACE
```

which defines **.Inv.** as a unary operator that can be applied to any real array of rank one and size three. Note that this is a unary operator, with one argument, although the argument happens to be an array with more than one element.

With one argument there may be little to choose between a function-name reference and a defined-operator reference, but with two arguments the usefulness of a defined operator is more apparent. Consider this example:

```
FUNCTION Vector_Multiplication (v1, v2)
REAL :: Vector_Multiplication
REAL, INTENT (IN) :: v1(*), v2(*)
Vector_Multiplication = DOTPRODUCT(v1, v2)
END FUNCTION Vector_Multiplication
```

with interface

```
INTERFACE OPERATOR (.X.)
  FUNCTION Vector_Multiplication (v1, v2)
  REAL :: Vector_Multiplication
  REAL, INTENT (IN) :: v1(*), v2(*)
  END FUNCTION Vector_Multiplication
END INTERFACE
```

147

This means that expressions like `r.X.t` or `x.X.(/1.89,-5.71,20.04/)` can be used freely to calculate the dot product of any pair of real vectors.

Besides defining operators of a new form (`.Inv.` and `.X.` in the examples above) it is possible to redefine Fortran's existing intrinsic operators. If in the example immediately above we had the **INTERFACE** statement

```
INTERFACE OPERATOR (*)
```

this would have the effect of turning the ordinary multiplication operator into a dot product operator in the case of real vectors. This technique is known as "overloading".

It must be emphasized that defined operators arise as a feature not of the procedure itself but of the interface. Since different program units may in principle have different interfaces to the same procedure, different operators could be used for the same task in different parts of a program, or conversely we could have the same operator being used for different tasks. And, with overloading, it is possible to completely confuse Fortran's intrinsic operators: for example the functions of * and / could be interchanged! Unless it is your objective to produce cryptic code, it is best to avoid overloading intrinsic operators and to put all the interfaces to defined operators into one module (Chapter 10) accessed by the whole of your program!

In the evaluation of Fortran expressions, defined unary operators take higher precedence than any other operators, just as if they were single-argument function-name references. By contrast, defined binary operators have a lower precedence than other operators. Naturally, parentheses can and should be used to avoid any ambiguity in the order of evaluation.

As a final example, the following procedure and interface make it possible to concatenate strings using a plus sign (+) as an alternative to the usual // operator:

```
FUNCTION Concat (c1, c2)
CHARACTER (*), INTENT(IN) :: c1
CHARACTER (*), INTENT(IN) :: c2
CHARACTER (LEN(c1) + LEN(c2)) :: Concat
Concat = c1//c2
END FUNCTION Concat

INTERFACE OPERATOR (+)
  FUNCTION Concat (c1, c2)
  CHARACTER (*), INTENT(IN):: c1
  CHARACTER (*), INTENT(IN):: c2
  CHARACTER (LEN(c1) + LEN(c2)):: Concat
  END FUNCTION Concat
END INTERFACE
```

but notice that this will not work with arrays of character strings.

Procedure interfaces are often required for purposes other than the defining of a new operator. An interface is always required if, as in the above example, we have a character function whose result is not of constant length and cannot be assumed from the program unit that calls the procedure. Although the lengths of the arguments **c1** and **c2** are assumed from the call, the length of **Concat** itself is got from the specification expression **LEN(c1)+LEN(c2)** and this fact can only be revealed to the calling program by means of an interface. Such an interface starts with the simple interface statement

INTERFACE

if no operator is being defined.

Another circumstance that requires a procedure to have an interface in the calling subprogram is when the procedure has optional arguments.

8.10 Exercises 8.B

8.B1 (i) Write a TDS to declare an array (called **zbanks**) of 30 complex numbers.

(ii) Write a TDS to declare three optional logical dummy arguments.

(iii) Write a TDS, intended for use in a procedure, for a 20×20 matrix of real numbers and also a vector of 45 real numbers. All are to have their values saved between calls to the procedure.

(iv) Write a TDS for an array of 100 named integer constants, called **squares**, with the index running from **0** to **99**, fixing their values to be equal to the squares of the integers from 0 to 99.

(v) Write a TDS for a dummy argument which is of length-12 character type. Its name is to be **julius** and it is an assumed-shape array of rank two.

(vi) Write a TDS for an array of 100 real variables called **inverse_squares**. They are to be given the initial values of the inverse squares of the integers ranging from **1** to **100**.

(vii) Write a TDS for a scalar character constant whose value is your name. Call it **moniker**.

8.B2 Set up a defined binary operator **//** to concatenate two integers, e.g. to make **1995** out of **19** and **95**, the result being an integer.

8.B3 Set up defined binary operators analogous to **<**, **==** and **>** that will operate between character strings to compare the strings according to alphabetical order, ignoring the difference between upper- and lower-case letters and ignoring all non-alphabetic characters.

CHAPTER 9

Arrays and data manipulation

This short chapter deals with a number of topics to do with the manipulation of data. Some aspects of arrays are covered: array element order, the **RESHAPE** *function, and vector subscripts. "Bits" are introduced. Finally, internal files and the* **TRANSFER** *function are explained.*

9.1 Array element order; array constructors revisited; RESHAPE

A Fortran array is a set of scalar elements ordered in up to seven dimensions, forming what can be visualized as a hyper-rectangular array. Nevertheless, in a sense any array may be regarded as a continuous linear sequence of elements. Within the processor's memory, an array of any rank will usually be stored in an uninterrupted sequence of memory locations. Moreover, a statement such as

```
WRITE (*,*) table
```

where **table** is an array of any shape, will output a series of values depending on the size, but not the detailed shape, of the array **table**. In Fortran, all the elements of an array form a sequence in what is known as "array element order", which was mentioned briefly when the **PACK** function was discussed in Section 5.7. In the trivial case of a rank-one array, this is simply the order of increasing subscript, i.e. the array **q(-3:3)** gives the sequence

```
q(-3), q(-2), q(-1), q(0), q(1), q(2), q(3)
```

For a rank-two array, the array element order is given by letting the first subscript run repeatedly, i.e. the array **q(2,3)** gives the sequence

```
q(1,1), q(2,1), q(1,2), q(2,2), q(1,3), q(2,3)
```

In general, whatever the rank, "array element order" is given by letting earlier subscripts vary more often than later ones.

Array element order is relevant not only to **READ** and **WRITE** statements but also to assumed-size arrays whereby a procedure's argument is passed as a sequence of elements rather than as an array of determinate shape.

It is sometimes convenient to rearrange the elements of an array into another array of different shape. This can be done by assignment statements, looping through all the elements, as in

```
DO j = 1, 32
  DO i = 1, 32
     v(32*(j-1)+i) = w(i, j)
  END DO
END DO
```

which forms a rank-one array from the elements of a rank-two array. Another example is

```
DO k = 0, 1023
  i = 1 + MOD(k,32)
  j = 1 + k/32
  w(i, j) = v(k+1)
END DO
```

which does the opposite. Another way of re-ordering the elements of an array would be to **WRITE** and **READ** "internal files", and this will be explained further below. Yet another approach would be to use array constructors with "implied **DO**" loops, as in

```
v = (/ ((w(i,j), i= 1, 32), j= 1, 32) /)
```

or a mixture of techniques:

```
DO j = 1, 32
  w(1:32, j) = (/ v (32*j-31: 32*j) /)
END DO
```

These last two examples do the same jobs as the earlier two above. Array constructors with implied-**DO** loops can be extremely powerful, although an array constructor can only be used to define a rank-one array. An example of an array constructor with nested implied-**DO** loops is

```
harlequin = (/ ((casque(j,17-i).OR.(i==j), i= 1, 16), &
  j= 1, 16) /)
```

which is a rank-one logical array of size 256, whose elements depend on a rank-two logical array called **casque**.

Any array may be empty, i.e. may have no elements. This is not the same as having elements that are zero-valued (if of numeric type) or blank (if of character type). However, the array constructor

```
(//)
```

should not be used to represent an empty rank-one array, because an array constructor must represent not only the elements of the array but their types, and the type is taken as that of the first element in an array constructor. An empty array of, say, **REAL** type could be written as

```
(/(0.0, i=1,0)/)
```

which has no elements because **0** is below **1**, but it is nevertheless real because **0.0** is a real constant. On the other hand,

```
(/(0.0, i=1,1)/)
```

which is just the same as

```
(/0.0/)
```

is a size-one array whose element happens to have the value zero. Bear in mind that a size-one array is not the same as a scalar. Moreover, an empty array or a size-one array could have any shape – it does not have to have rank one, although array constructors can only be written for rank-one arrays.

This discussion began with a consideration of how the elements of an array can be used to form another array of different shape. In fact, the most straightforward method in Fortran is to use **RESHAPE**, an array-valued intrinsic function provided specifically for reshaping arrays. **RESHAPE** can be referenced with the argument keywords

```
RESHAPE (SOURCE, SHAPE, PAD, ORDER)
```

and the last two arguments, **PAD** and **ORDER**, are optional. Let us suppose firstly that **PAD** and **ORDER** are absent. The argument **SOURCE** can be an array of any sort, and its elements are rearranged to form the result **RESHAPE**. The elements of **RESHAPE** are therefore of the same type as those of **SOURCE**. However, the shape of **RESHAPE** is given by the argument **SHAPE**, which is a rank-one integer array specifying, as one would expect, the desired extents of the dimensions of **RESHAPE**. The rank of **RESHAPE** is therefore equal to the size of **SHAPE**, which must be positive and no greater than seven. The effect of the function is to take the elements of **SOURCE** and place them into **RESHAPE** in normal array element order, **RESHAPE** having the shape specified by **SHAPE**. Using again our earlier examples,

```
v = RESHAPE(SOURCE=w, SHAPE=(/1024/))
```

and

```
w = RESHAPE(SOURCE=v, SHAPE=(/32,32/))
```

If **SOURCE** has more elements than **RESHAPE**, the unwanted elements will not be used. If **RESHAPE** has more elements than **SOURCE**, then the argument **PAD** must be present, and it must be an array of the same type as **SOURCE**. The elements of **PAD** are used, in array element order, to fill the remainder of **RESULT**, if necessary running through **PAD** more than once. So,

```
xout = RESHAPE(SOURCE=xin, SHAPE=(/100/), PAD=(/0.0/))
```

forms the rank-one real array **xout** using the elements of **xin**, padding **xout** with zeros if **xin** has fewer than 100 elements.

Arrays can of course, have zero size. The **SPREAD** function allows us to construct zero-size arrays of high rank: starting from the rank-one empty real array

```
empty_1 = (/(0.0, i=1,0)/)
```
then
```
empty_2 = SPREAD (empty_1, DIM=1, NCOPIES=0)
```

is a rank-two zero-sized array, and

```
empty_3 = SPREAD (empty_2, DIM=1, NCOPIES=0)
```

is a rank-three zero-sized array, etc,. etc.

In **RESHAPE**, the optional argument **ORDER** provides an opportunity of placing the elements of the array yielded by **RESHAPE** not in normal array element order, but as if some of its dimensions were switched around. **ORDER** must be an integer array of the same size and rank (one) as **SHAPE**, but containing the integers **1, 2, 3, ...** in a permuted order. The array **ORDER** then tells the processor in what order it should run through the dimensions of **RESHAPE** when fixing its elements. If **ORDER** is omitted, it is like having **ORDER=(/1,2,3,.../)** and so on up to the rank of **RESHAPE**. This means that if **twist** and **metric** are 4 × 4 arrays, and

```
twist = RESHAPE(SOURCE=metric, SHAPE=(/4,4/), &
    ORDER=(/2,1/))
```

then **twist(i,j)=metric(j,i)**. In this example, **RESHAPE** is being used to do what the **TRANSPOSE** function does.

Using the array transformation functions and array constructors, it is often possible to specify a complex multidimensional array in one statement, as in

```
iternary =  RESHAPE(SOURCE = (/(i, i=0, 2186)/), &
    SHAPE = (/3,3,3,3,3,3,3/), &
    ORDER = (/7, 6, 5, 4, 3, 2, 1/))
```

9.2 Vector subscripts

Section 4.4 dealt with "array sections", i.e. the notation for picking out a subset of the elements of an array. This was done with a colon notation, as in the simple rank-one example

```
decade(10:1:-1)
```

The three integers, separated by colons, form what is known as a "subscript triplet", specifying a starting index, a final index, and a "stride" (Section 4.6). "Vector subscripts" are a further tool for forming array sections, permitting a set of indices to be specified in any order. The idea is that, instead of a subscript triplet, a rank-one integer array is given that contains the desired indices in the desired order. Thus, if we have an array

```
npick = (/10, 9, 8, 7, 6, 5, 4, 3, 2, 1/)
```

then the array section mentioned above could be specified equally well by

```
decade(npick)
```

In other words, an array may have an index that is itself a rank-one array. In **decade(npick)**, if **npick** were a scalar integer then we would just have a single element of the array; but because **npick** is an array so is **decade(npick)**. Another example: with the vector subscript

```
u = (/4,9,1,6/)
```

the array section **x(u)** consists of the elements **x(4)**, **x(9)**, **x(1)** and **x(6)** in that order.

A vector subscript may be any integer expression of rank one, as long as its elements are within the bounds of the array of which it is a subscript. With the arrays

```
INTEGER :: matrices(4,4,200), triad(3), mum(3,3)
```

and if, say,

```
triad = (/196,2,34/)
```
then
```
mum = matrices(3:1:-1,2,triad)
```

is the rank-two array with elements

```
mum(1,1) = matrices(3,2,196)
mum(2,1) = matrices(2,2,196)
mum(3,1) = matrices(1,2,196)
mum(1,2) = matrices(3,2,2)
mum(2,2) = matrices(2,2,2)
mum(3,2) = matrices(1,2,2)
mum(1,3) = matrices(3,2,34)
mum(2,3) = matrices(2,2,34)
mum(3,3) = matrices(1,2,34)
```

As this example illustrates, it is possible to have an array section in which different dimensions have different forms of subscript, i.e. we can have a mixture of single subscripts, subscript triplets, and vector subscripts.

A multidimensional array may have more than one vector subscript. For example, if

```
isquare = RESHAPE(SOURCE=(/ (k**2, k=1, 64) /), &
   SHAPE=(/8,8/))
```

and we have the vector subscript `k3=(/1,2,3/)`, then

```
knine = RESHAPE(SOURCE=isquare(k3,k3), SHAPE=(/9/))
```

is the rank-one array `(/1,4,9,81,100,121,289,324,361/)`. Here, isquare is an 8×8 array of integers, and `isquare(k3,k3)` is an array section with two vector subscripts that happen to be equal.

A vector subscript may have more than one element of the same value, in which case it forms what is called a "many-one" array section. For example, given the array of single characters

```
chars = (/("abcdefghijklmnopqrstuvwxyz_"(i:i), i=1, 27)/)
```

and the vector subscript given by

```
name = (/13,1,18,20,9,14,27,10,1,13,5,19,27,3,15, &
   21,14,9,8,1,14/)
```

then `chars(name)` is a many-one array section consisting of 21 single-character elements such that

```
WRITE (*,*) chars(name)
```

spells out

```
martin_james_counihan
```

If a vector subscript has many repeated elements, the resulting array section could be much greater in size than the array of which it is a section.

There are just a few restrictions on the use of vector subscripts: in particular, a many-one array section may not appear as the variable on the left side of an assignment statement and an array with a vector subscript may not be used as the argument of a procedure that will redefine it (`INTENT(IN)` should be used). Also, a pointer assignment statement (explained later in this book) may not have as its target an array section with a vector subscript.

There are other games we can play. An array may have itself as a vector subscript, so if, say,

```
z = (/1,3,4,2/)
```

then `z(z)` is `(/1,4,2,3/)` and `z(z(z))` is `(/1,2,3,4/)`.

Also, a vector subscript does not have to take the form of an array constructor: it could be a named array variable or even a rank-one array-valued function result as in the expressions

```
r(locations_of_cells)
r(Indices_of_Positive_Values(r))
```

9.3 Bits

The Fortran language allows for a number of different data types, described in Section 8.4, including derived data types constructed out of the basic types real, integer, character, etc.

In addition, it is possible to manipulate data in the form of sequences of binary bits, each bit having the value 0 or 1. In a way, **LOGICAL** data is binary and a logical array is rather like a sequence of bits, but in fact a data element declared **LOGICAL** is not normally stored in a single memory bit. So, "bits" in Fortran have nothing directly to do with **LOGICAL** data. Instead, an item of data declared as **INTEGER** may be interpreted as a sequence of binary bits. One integer will contain a large number of bits: commonly 32 or 64. The exact number for a particular processor can be ascertained by calling the intrinsic inquiry function **BIT_SIZE**.

When an integer is being regarded as a sequence of bits, ordinary integer arithmetic will generally be irrelevant. The integer's value when it is taken as an ordinary integer will, in general, differ from its value when the bits are interpreted as a binary number. A Fortran **INTEGER**, of course, may be negative, but a sequence of binary digits can only be positive. So, instead of the operations of ordinary integer arithmetic, a special set of intrinsic procedures exists so that bits (sometimes called "bitstream" data) can be manipulated. The details are set out in Appendix B.

9.4 Exercises 9.A

9.A1 Given that **r** is an array declared by the TDS

```
REAL :: r(4)
```

which of the following expressions are arrays equal to **r**?

(i) `r(1:4:1)`   (ii) `r(1:4)`   (iii) `r(1:)`
(iv) `r(1)`   (v) `r(:4)`   (vi) `r(:4:1)`
(vii) `r(4:1)`   (viii) `r(1::1)`   (ix) `r(::1)`
(x) `r(:)`   (xi) `r(4)`   (xii) `(/ r(1), r(2), r(3), r(4) /)`
(xiii) `(/ (r(i), i=1,4) /)`   (xiv) `r((/1,2,3,4/))`
(xv) `r((/ (i, i=1,4) /))`

9.A2 Using the information in Appendix B, write a function that will convert a length-32 logical array into the corresponding stream of 32 bits, assuming that **BIT_SIZE(1)=32**.

9.A3 Write a function to convert a string of 32 bits (represented as an integer variable, and assuming **BIT_SIZE(1)=32**) into a positive hexadecimal number (in the form of a length-eight character string representing eight hexadecimal digits).

9.A4 Use **RESHAPE** in an assignment statement setting the first 48 elements of an

157

8×8 matrix, in normal array element order, equal to the elements of a size-48 vector. The matrix is called **chessboard** and the vector is called **six_rows**. They are to be of logical type. The 16 elements of **chessboard** which are not filled by **six_rows** are to be filled with alternating .**TRUE**. and .**FALSE**. values.

9.A5 If **vowels = (/"a","e","i","o","u"/)**, **khard = (/1,4,5/)** and **ksoft = (/2,3/)** what are the values of

(i) **vowels(khard)**   (ii) **vowels(ksoft)**   (iii) **khard(ksoft)**

(iv) **vowels((/4,2/))**   (v) **vowels(khard)//vowels(2)**

9.5 Internal files; TRANSFER

Some parts of this section will not be completely understandable without reference to Appendix A, which deals with the input and output of data, and in particular to format specifiers (see Appendix A.2).

However, "internal" files are not really files at all: they are simply areas of the processor's memory being treated as if they were sequential-access formatted files. Data can be written to or read from internal files using **WRITE** and **READ** statements, but there is no transfer of information outside the processor. Internal files can be very useful for changing the type interpretation of data: you can write to an internal file in one format, then read from it in another format.

Internal files can only be used with the **READ** and **WRITE** statements. All the other i/o statements are inapplicable to them, and "non-advancing" i/o is not possible (see Appendix A). An internal file is not only internal to the processor; it is internal to the program and cannot be used to transfer information between different programs or to save data from one program run to another. In fact, an internal file is a local entity that cannot even be used to transfer data between program units except by the usual methods of data association.

An internal file is no more than a character variable. To read or write an internal file, the unit number is replaced by the name of the character variable. An example should make the principle clear:

```
WRITE (UNIT=digit_string, FMT="(I6)") nref
```

This statement requires **digit_string** to have been previously declared in the usual way as a character variable of length six or more. The integer **nref**, assuming it has a defined value, is written into the string **digit_string**, taking up six character positions. If the length of **digit_string** is greater than six, it will be padded out with trailing blanks. The precise meaning of **FMT="(I6)"** is explained in Appendix A. Subsequently,

```
READ (digit_string, "(5X,I1)") junits
```

will yield the last digit of the number. The statement

```
READ (digit_string, "(F6.0)") ref
```

will yield the original number but now as a variable of real type. If the integer `nref` had been, say, `524288`, then `digit_string` would be given the value `"524288"`, `junits` would be the integer `8`, and `ref` would be the real number `524288.0`. Within the processor's memory, the internal representations of `nref`, `digit_string` and `ref` would be quite different, since they are variables of different types.

The next example shows how an internal file `WRITE` statement can be used for concatenation:

```
CHARACTER(10) :: title
CHARACTER(30) :: forename, midname, surname
CHARACTER(100) :: name
   .
   .
   .
WRITE (name, "(A,1X,A,1X,A,1X,A)") title, forename, &
   midname, surname
```

This is equivalent to

```
name = title//" "//forename//" "//midname//" "//surname
```

In the above examples, the internal files called `digit_string` and `name` were scalar variables regarded as having one record. If the internal file is an array, then each element of the array is regarded as a "record" of the internal file, taken in normal array element order. An internal file may be an array section, but not with a vector subscript.

If `names` is a character array, the statement

```
READ (names(1:2),"(A12)") forename, surname
```

reads a file of two records, each being a length-12 string. This statement involves "format reversion" and is equivalent to

```
forename = names(1); surname = names(2)
```

except that the `READ` statement, unlike the assignment statements, will ignore leading blanks in the elements of `names`. Moreover,

```
WRITE (names(1:2),"(2A12)") forename, surname
```

is equivalent to

```
names(1:2) = (/forename, surname/)
```

but the `WRITE` statement will give an error if the elements of `names` have lengths less than 12. Notice that, in our previous examples, it would be possible for `digit_string`, `nref`, `junits`, `ref`, `title`, `forename` etc. to be arrays as long as they are declared as such and as long as the internal files conform in shape with the data.

When data is input to a Fortran program (say, by reading a magnetic tape) it cannot normally be interpreted properly unless each data item is of a type known within the program. The data types that are read must correspond to the variables named in the input list. This can lead to difficulties when, as sometimes happens, the contents of a file are not known in advance. Suppose `intin` is a size-100 integer array and we have

```
READ(UNIT=7, FMT="(100I10)") intin
```

then what happens if in fact the file contains 100 real numbers? Or an unpredictable mixture of integer and real numbers? Fortunately Fortran provides an intrinsic function, **TRANSFER(SOURCE, MOLD, *SIZE*)**, which can be used to change the type interpretation of a piece of data within the processor, i.e. when it has already been read in. For example, the above statement could be followed by

```
realin = TRANSFER(SOURCE = intin, MOLD = 0.0, SIZE = 100)
```

and this would put values into the real-valued array `realin` by reinterpreting the source data. It is very important to understand that **TRANSFER** does not convert data between types: the functions **REAL**, **INTEGER**, etc. do that. **TRANSFER** leaves unchanged the bit-patterns within the processor's memory, but simply interprets them in a different way.

TRANSFER(SOURCE, MOLD, *SIZE*) gives a result whose internal representation is exactly the same as **SOURCE**, but whose type is that of **MOLD**. **SOURCE** may be an array. *SIZE* is an optional argument discussed below. **TRANSFER** works for any data type, including a derived type.

Normally if **MOLD** is scalar the result is a scalar, whereas if **MOLD** is an array the result will be a rank-one array of sufficient size to hold the contents of **SOURCE**. The result of **TRANSFER** is never an array of rank greater than one. For example,

```
TRANSFER(SOURCE=(1.0,2.0), MOLD=(/0.0/))
```

produces a size-two, rank-one real array whose elements are the real and imaginary parts of the complex number `(1.0,2.0)`.

The *SIZE* argument, if it is present, must be a scalar integer. Its effect is to ensure that the result is an array and to fix its size. If *SIZE* is specified and does not match the size of **SOURCE**, then in forming the function result it is possible that the trailing part of **SOURCE** may be lost or that the trailing part of the result may be left undefined. So,

```
TRANSFER(SOURCE=(/1.0,2.0,3.0,4.0/), MOLD=(0.0,0.0), &
SIZE=2)
```

produces a size-two complex array whose members are `(1.0,2.0)` and `(3.0,4.0)`. The expression

```
TRANSFER((/-7.0,5.1,6.4/),(0.0,0.0),1)
```

has the value (/(-7.0,5.1)/), while

```
TRANSFER((/-7.0,5.1,6.4/),(0.0,0.0))
```

is a scalar with the value (-7.0,5.1).

If the argument **ch** is of character type, **TRANSFER(SOURCE=ch, MOLD=1)** will give an integer-type result of processor-dependent value preserving the bit-pattern of **ch**; this could be used in conjunction with bit manipulation functions.

Incidentally, **TRANSFER(SOURCE=array, MOLD=array)** provides a neat way of replacing an array of any shape by the corresponding rank-one array containing the same elements. This could otherwise be done using the **RESHAPE** function.

The **TRANSFER** function means that a formatted **READ** statement can be made very flexible and the data unravelled later, e.g.

```
READ (UNIT=in, FMT="(A)") chararray
   .
   .
   .
header = TRANSFER(SOURCE=chararray(1:5), MOLD="",&
SIZE=5)
length = TRANSFER(SOURCE=chararray(6:10), MOLD=1)
IF (length>0.AND.length<(recmax-7)) THEN
  rdata = TRANSFER(SOURCE=chararray(11:), &
       MOLD=(/0.0/), SIZE=length)
   .
   .
   .
```

where **header**, **length** and **rdata** are of character, integer and real types respectively. A long program that reads records of different sorts from different devices could in this way use a single generalized **READ** statement.

Notice that

```
REAL :: h (1000)
INTEGER :: i (1000)
   .
   .
   .
(read r from an external device)
   .
   .
   .
i = TRANSFER(SOURCE=h, MOLD=1, SIZE=1000)
```

allows elements of the data read as real numbers into **r** to be interpreted instead as integers by referring to **i** instead of **r**. This code does a similar job to that sometimes done with the now obsolete **EQUIVALENCE** statement.

Initialization expressions may make reference to the **TRANSFER** function, so a declaration of the sort

```
INTEGER :: i = TRANSFER("counihan", 1)
```

is possible.

Finally, the point must be clearly understood that **TRANSFER** is not an alternative to the writing and reading of an internal file. **TRANSFER** works at a lower level and the effect of **TRANSFER**ring an integer into a real number (say) is not easily predictable and will in general depend on the particular processor's methods of representing integer and real data as sequences of bits. Manipulating internal files, on the other hand, will always translate an integer like **64** into the real number **64.0** because internal files are based on characters, not on bits. The result of **TRANSFER** will be processor-independent only when the type transfer is between real and complex types, since a complex number is defined in Fortran as an ordered pair of real numbers.

9.6 Exercises 9.B

9.A1 Write a function that reverses the digits of an integer.

9.A2 Write a function that uses an internal file to convert between a character string and a real number, it being assumed that the string contains digits etc. representing a real number.

CHAPTER 10

Modules

Modules can be of great importance in organizing the structure of any large Fortran program. They enable data to be communicated between subprograms, they are useful for encapsulating sets of related subprograms, and they have a role in the writing of "generic" procedures, which can operate on arguments of different types. This chapter explains the use of modules for sharing data and for containing procedures. There is a discussion of the different forms of data association (argument, host, and USE), a detailed description of the USE statement, and finally an account of how modules can be used in relation to procedure interfaces.

10.1 Data modules

So far we have considered only three different kinds of program units, namely the main program, subroutines, and functions. Program execution always starts with a main program, from which subroutines and functions (collectively called "procedures") may be called. Procedures may call on other procedures in turn. Whenever a procedure is called, a list of arguments is used to pass data in either direction between the two program units, the calling and the called. In the case of functions, of course, the function name itself transfers data back from the function. If a procedure is written to carry out a simple self-contained operation, like calculating a simple mathematical function, then data transmission by argument passing may be good enough, but in general it can be very useful, if not essential, to have a way in which program units can share larger sets of data in a more flexible and open way. Modules provide a method of doing this.

Normally a name given to a variable (or to a named constant) is meaningful only within a particular program unit. A declaration like

```
CHARACTER(80) :: line(60)
```

is only known to the main program or procedure in which it appears. If this statement were to be repeated in different program units, the processor would assume that it referred to different things, and distinct areas of memory would be allocated. In other words, the names of variables in Fortran are usually "local" entities. Using modules, however, it becomes possible for the same sets of data to be accessible to a number of different program units.

Suppose, as an example, that a program needs to use an array of character strings representing a page of text together with some integer and logical data items related to it. The form of the data might be specified by the declaration statements

```
CHARACTER(80) :: line(60)
INTEGER :: linelength, linesperpage, numpage
LOGICAL :: checkin, checkspell, checkout
```

To have access to this data in different procedures, these declaration statements could be encapsulated in another kind of program unit called a "module", consisting simply of the statements above topped and tailed by **MODULE** and **END MODULE** statements:

```
MODULE Textpage
CHARACTER(80) :: line(60)
INTEGER :: linelength, linesperpage, numpage
LOGICAL :: checkin, checkascii, checkspell, checkout
END MODULE Textpage
```

The module can then be invoked in any other program unit simply by supplying the statement

```
USE Textpage
```

The name **Textpage** is of course arbitrary. The general form of the **MODULE** statement is simply the keyword **MODULE** followed by a name that may be chosen according to the usual Fortran rules, like the name of a variable or a procedure. The **END MODULE** statement is similar, just like an **END FUNCTION** or **END SUBROUTINE** statement, and it is not compulsory to repeat the module's name; in fact **END** by itself would suffice. As will be seen later, the **USE** statement can be a little more complicated than is indicated here, but basically it consists of the keyword **USE** followed by the name of a module.

A program may include many different modules as long as they have different names. A particular program unit may invoke a number of modules by having a series of **USE** statements. **USE** statements are non-executable and they must appear at the very beginning of a program unit immediately following the **PROGRAM** (or **SUBROUTINE**, etc.) statement and before any other non-executable statements. A module may itself invoke a further module, e.g. we could have

```
MODULE Textpage
USE Language
CHARACTER(80) :: line(60)
INTEGER :: linelength, linesperpage, numpage
LOGICAL :: checkin, checkascii, checkspell, checkout
END MODULE Textpage
```

but it is not permissible for a module to invoke itself, directly or indirectly. So, the module **Language** may not have a **USE Textpage** statement, or a circularity would be created.

The next example is a data module containing information about metals, and it shows that a module can be used to hold a database of fairly complex design. It must be stressed that this module does not actually "do" anything. It has no executable statements. Its purpose is to declare the structure of a set of data that can subsequently be utilized in other program units.

```
MODULE Metals
INTEGER :: number_of_metals, namelengths(100)
CHARACTER(20) :: metal_name(100)
REAL :: weight(100), density_0(100), density_100(100),&
    tempmelt(100), conductivity_0(100),&
    conductivity_100(100), pricerange(2,100)
LOGICAL :: data_has_been_read_in
END MODULE Metals
```

This could be invoked (by the statement **USE Metals**)in different subroutines to carry out tasks like reading the data from a disk file, modifying the data, rewriting the disk file, and making calculations that need access to this dataset. For example, to estimate the conductivity of a particular metal at a particular temperature we could write a function such as

```
FUNCTION Conductivity (metal, temperature)
USE Metals
REAL :: Conductivity
REAL, INTENT(IN) :: temperature
REAL :: c0, c100
CHARACTER(20), INTENT(IN) :: metal
Conductivity = -99.0! default function value for an
!unrecognized metal
DO i = 1, number_of_metals
  IF (metal/=metal_name(i)) CYCLE
  c0 = conductivity_0(i)
  c100 = conductivity_100(i)
  Conductivity = c0 + temperature*(c100-c0)/100.0
  EXIT
END DO
END FUNCTION Conductivity
```

This is obviously much simpler than transmitting all the data through a long list of arguments.

With a module, a large or complex set of data need only be designed and declared once. This saves memory, keeps programs shorter, avoids error, and avoids passing clumsy long lists of arguments to procedures. In fact subroutines need have no arguments at all. A main program could simply look like

```
PROGRAM Economic_Prediction
CALL Startup
CALL Calculate
CALL Display
END PROGRAM Economic_Prediction
```

with the associated subprograms being, say,

```
SUBROUTINE Startup
USE Basedata
USE Workspace ...

SUBROUTINE Calculate
USE Workspace
USE Results ...

SUBROUTINE Display
USE Results
USE Output_Formats ...

MODULE Basedata ...

MODULE Workspace ...

MODULE Results ...

MODULE Output_Formats ...
```

In this example the four modules could contain all the data declarations and the subroutines could contain only executable statements after the **USE** statements. The program as a whole consists of eight program units. This sort of design can give the programmer great flexibility: for example, the module called **Output_Formats** could be written in two or three completely different versions to interface with different display devices that could be connected to the processor.

In a module, variables should be declared with the **SAVE** attribute if their values are intended to be preserved between calls to program units that **USE** the module (and if the module is not perpetually in **USE** through the main program). If a module is not perpetually in **USE** from somewhere or other, un**SAVE**d variables could become undefined.

Modules encourage a systematic approach to the design, management, and use of a program or system of programs. When important data is kept in modules, the programmer's work can become focused more on the careful design of the data structures rather than on procedures. Modules take on a life of their own, central to how we perceive the program, while procedures can be regarded as mere ancillaries that carry out operations on the data modules. In many application areas that depend on large data sets, this sort of programming style ("declarative" or "data-oriented" programming) is far more appropriate than the "stream-of-consciousness" style that concentrates on the flow of control between subroutines and functions.

This section was headed *Data modules* and we have seen that a module may contain a number of data declarations. The declarations may be type declaration statements of any kind. We shall see later that modules may also contain declarations of derived types (Chapter 12), procedure interfaces (Chapter 11) and namelist groups (Appendix A). They may also include procedures, as explained in the next section.

COMMON

There is an alternative to using a data module for "sharing" data between different program units. The alternative, an old construction that goes back to Fortran's early days, is the "COMMON block". An example of the syntax is

```
COMMON /Pool/ rnums(10), arr(3,3,3), intflag
```

Between slashes, **Pool** is the (arbitrary) name of the common block and can be used in different program units to refer to a single shared area of memory. Data are to be found there according to the ordered list of names and array shapes that follows: in this example, some arrays of real numbers and integers with the local names **rnums**, **arr** and **intflag**. The data does not also need to appear in type declaration statements unless further attributes have to be specified. The data in a common block can have different local names in different program units, i.e. the names and array shapes that follow the slashes can vary, but they will everywhere refer to the same items of data.

The name of the common block can be omitted, in which case the statement refers to a special area of memory known as "blank common". The syntax is like this:

```
COMMON // rnums(10), arr(3,3,3), intflag
```

10.2 Exercises 10.A

10.A1 Write a data module to contain in a convenient form the names of the days of the week, the names of the months, and the usual numbers of days in the months.

10.A2 Write a data module to contain the mathematical constants π and e and the first 20 powers of 2.

10.A3 Write a data module containing a two-dimensional "spreadsheet" of 30 rows and 10 columns, each cell containing data in the form of a string of 12 characters. An ancillary array is to contain single-character indicators to say which cells contain values and whether the values are to be interpreted simply as words or as integers or real numbers.

10.3 Module procedures

The procedures we have so far met have been "external" procedures, i.e. subroutines and functions that are external to the main program. External procedures are extremely useful and in practice they form the bulk of almost all large Fortran programs. They have the incidental advantage that they need not necessarily be supplied in the Fortran language: in principle it is possible for a Fortran program to call external procedures that are in another language or in precompiled machine code. Almost everything that can be achieved with Fortran can be done using a set of external procedures, a main program, and data modules.

Nevertheless, Fortran allows for another kind of procedure, "module procedures", which are specified within modules. Like external procedures, module procedures are either of the "subroutine" or the "function" variety; they look very similar to external procedures and are invoked in exactly the same way by **CALL** statements or function references. However, a module procedure may only be invoked from parts of the program to which the module is plugged in by **USE** statements (or from another module procedure in the same module). Module procedures must always be supplied in Fortran.

There are a number of reasons why module procedures can be useful. If a module defines the structure of a special set of data, and if there are also some specialized procedures needed for operating on that data, then it can be appropriate to include the procedures as well as the data in the one module. Even if no special data set is involved, it can be handy to use a module to hold a "library" of related procedures. A programmer may create a set of procedures with a frequently encountered problem in mind, e.g. reading disk files in various formats, and putting them into a module that could be copied and used in a number of different programs. Another point is that procedures with the same name can sit in different modules, and then the programmer can switch between different versions of the same procedure just by changing a **USE** statement.

A special statement, **CONTAINS**, is required when a module contains module procedures. The general form of a module is

```
MODULE Name
  USE statements
  declarative statements
CONTAINS
  module procedures
END MODULE Name
```

When this module is invoked by a **USE** statement in any other subprogram, that subprogram has access to the data sets declared in the module and may call any of the procedures that follow the **CONTAINS** statement. It also has access to the additional modules, if any, identified by **USE** statements at the beginning of this module. The declarative statements may be a mixture of type declaration statements and the other kinds of declaration mentioned at the end of the last section, but may not include executable statements.

After **CONTAINS**, there is a set of one or more module procedures. Module procedures are exactly the same in form as external subroutines or functions, each starting with a **SUBROUTINE** (or **FUNCTION**) statement and finishing with a suitable **END** statement. All the sorts of subroutines and functions explained in Chapters 7 and 11 may occur as module procedures rather than as external procedures.

There is one very important difference between module procedures and external procedures, namely that a module procedure has direct access to the data declared in the module before the **CONTAINS** statement. This is called the "host association" of data, and the module is said to be the "host" of its module procedures. Entities declared before the **CONTAINS** statement are shared by host association among all the module procedures following.

Here is an example of a module with data and procedures:

```
MODULE Polynomial
REAL :: c(0:3)

CONTAINS

SUBROUTINE Show_Coefficients
WRITE (*,*) c
END SUBROUTINE Show_Coefficients

FUNCTION Poly(x)
REAL :: Poly
REAL, INTENT(IN) :: x
Poly = c(0) + x*(c(1) + x*(c(2) + x*c(3)))
END FUNCTION Poly

FUNCTION Inverse_Poly(y)
REAL :: Inverse_Poly
REAL, INTENT(IN) :: y
REAL :: scratchpad(4)
      .
      .
      .
```

*(finds an approximate real solution to the cubic equation **y=Poly(x)**, with **Poly** as defined as above)*

      .
      .
      .

```
Inverse_Poly = ...
END FUNCTION Inverse_Poly

SUBROUTINE Switchback
c(0:3) = c(3:0:-1)
END SUBROUTINE Switchback

END MODULE Polynomial
```

The subroutines **Show_Coefficients** and **Switchback**, and the functions **Poly** and **Inverse_Poly**, can be accessed by any other program unit that has the statement

```
USE Polynomial
```

These module procedures may also access one another: for example the function **Inverse_Poly** will include calls to **Poly**. Moreover, the data declared at the beginning of the module above (the array **c**) is also directly accessible to all the module procedures and to other parts of the program using the module. To avoid a clash of names, however, the programmer should obviously avoid the use of the name **c** for any other, different, piece of data in any module procedure.

At the same time, a module procedure may have data items internal to itself and not accessible outside it. This is the situation if a module procedure has some type declaration statements of its own: the items declared will be "local" variables and will not be accessible by host association outside the module procedure. For example, the function **Inverse_Poly** above includes a data array called **scratchpad**, and this is a local variable not accessible anywhere else. The argument **y** in **Inverse_Poly**, and also the argument **x** in **Poly**, are names local to those procedures and not accessible to the rest of the module, but they are also dummy arguments and are therefore accessible (by "argument association", not "host association"!) from wherever the functions are called.

Note that if one of a module's own data declarations is repeated within a module procedure, the effect is to set up a separate local variable and therefore to prevent the module procedure from accessing the module's data. Consequently,

```
MODULE Pointless
REAL :: x
CONTAINS
SUBROUTINE Double
REAL :: x
x = 2.0 * x
END SUBROUTINE Double
END MODULE Pointless
```

will achieve nothing because, within the subroutine, **x** is a local variable and is not the same piece of data as the **x** declared before the **CONTAINS** statement! But, if the subroutine's **REAL** statement were removed, then its **x** would be host-associated to the original **x**, and a statement **CALL Double** would double the value of **x**.

10.4 Data association by argument, host and USE

"Local" variables have no significance whatsoever outside the program unit in which they are declared: they have the "scope" of a single program unit. However, data may be shared between program units by "association". There are three distinct forms of association:

- Arguments of procedures allow data to be passed between program units as the program is executing. Just as a door has two sides, an argument exists both as a "dummy" argument in the procedure itself and as an "actual" argument in a calling program. When a procedure is invoked, there is "argument association" between the actual arguments and the dummy arguments. In the case of a function, a similar thing happens with its value. Although "argument association" passes a value between one program unit and another, the names of arguments should be declared separately in the two program units.
- When variables are declared at the beginning of a module that also contains module procedures, then the variables are also accessible within the module procedures by "host association".
- When a **USE** statement connects a module to a subprogram, the variables declared at the start of the module (i.e. before any **CONTAINS** statement) are said to be "**USE** associated" to the subprogram.

The three kinds of association (argument, host and **USE** association) should be kept quite distinct from one another. A crucial point is that argument association happens dynamically as the program executes, with values being passed from one memory location to another. By contrast, host association and use association are static relationships that are established once and for all when the program is compiled. Host association and use association do not involve any copying or duplication of data: they are merely forms of shared access to particular memory locations.

    USE association normally means that all the variables declared in a module (except those local to module subprograms) are accessible within any subprogram which **USE**s the module. However, it can sometimes be helpful to limit this association to a subset of the module's variables. This can be achieved with the help of two attributes that can be applied to type declaration statements in a module, namely **PRIVATE** and **PUBLIC**. Data having the **PRIVATE** attribute cannot be **USE**-associated, while data having the **PUBLIC**

attribute can. The default situation is **PUBLIC**, but this can be reversed with the single statement

```
PRIVATE
```

which, occurring at the beginning of a module, will make all the data non-**USE**-accessible unless it is countermanded by specifying **PUBLIC** in the TDS referring to a particular piece of data. It is also possible to have **PRIVATE** and **PUBLIC** statements listing data items that have already been declared in **TDS**s.

The **PUBLIC** and **PRIVATE** attributes can be applied not only to variables but also to other objects such as named constants and the names of module procedures. For example, suppose we have a complicated module called **Charsets** that, among many other things, defines an operator called **.intersect.** that identifies the characters that are common to two character strings, i.e.

```
string1.intersect.string2
```

is a string consisting of the characters that are to be found both in **string1** and in **string2**. The module **Charset** must contain a function linked to the **.intersect.** operator. However, if **Charset** starts with

```
MODULE Charset
PRIVATE
PUBLIC :: OPERATOR (.intersect.)
   .
   .
   .
```

then it makes the operator usable in any program unit that **USE**s **Charset**, while keeping hidden all the other entities in **Charset**. This will be made a little clearer by Section 10.6. More generally, to have

```
MODULE Name
PRIVATE
PUBLIC :: list of entities to be accessible from outside
   .
   .
   .
```

is a more positive and safer way of allowing **USE** association than doing it the other way around with

```
MODULE Name
PRIVATE :: list of entities not to be accessible from &
           outside
   .
   .
   .
```

10.5 USE in detail

USE statements are non-executable statements that must be positioned before anything else after a PROGRAM, SUBROUTINE, FUNCTION or MODULE statement. Each USE statement points to a module and gives the subprogram access to a set of data and/or module procedures. This could, potentially, give rise to problems if the same names have been used to represent different variables in different parts of the program. If there is a data module such as

```
MODULE Coordinates
REAL :: x(60), y(60), z(60), units
REAL :: xlimits(2), ylimits(2), zlimits(2)
REAL :: scalex, scaley, scalez
INTEGER :: npoints
LOGICAL :: provisional(60)
END MODULE Coordinates
```

then there would be a conflict if it were used by another subprogram which already had other variables called (say) x and y. To avoid this sort of problem, the USE statement may specify a different local name for data within a module. There is also a form of the USE statement that limits access to a chosen subset of the things in the module. The following examples show the syntax:

```
USE Coordinates, nplaces => npoints
USE Coordinates, xhere => x, yhere => y, zhere => z
USE Coordinates, x => y, y => x
USE Coordinates, ONLY: xlimits, ylimits, zlimits
USE Coordinates, ONLY: z
USE Coordinates, ONLY: zhere => z
```

The first of these gives full access to the module coordinates, but a different local name (nplaces) is to be used here in place of the module's name (npoints) for that particular data item. After this USE statement, the name npoints would not refer to the data in the module at all and could be used for something completely different. The combination => is used to link the new local name with the module name. This is similar to the notation we will come across later for pointer assignment (Chapter 13). In the second example above, the local names xhere, yhere and zhere are linked to the data objects known in the module as x, y and z. Incidentally, when a local name is set up in this way, there is no need to mention it in a TDS in the same subprogram: it is assumed to have the same properties as were declared in the module. So, xhere, yhere and zhere are 60-element arrays.

It is permissible for a program unit to have more than one USE statement referring to the same module and it is possible for one data object to have more than one local name. If the first three statements above were put together at the top of the same subprogram, the effect would be to give access to all the module's data items but with **npoints** having the local name **nplaces**, **x** having the local names **xhere** and **y**, **y** having the local names **yhere** and **x**, and **z** having the local name **zhere**. All the other data items in the module would keep their original names.

The fourth, fifth and sixth examples above show how the keyword **ONLY** is used to give partial access to a module. The fourth would be used in a subprogram where access is wanted only to the variables **xlimits**, **ylimits** and **zlimits**. The fifth gives access only to **z**. The sixth also gives access only to **z**, but imposes the local name **zhere**. A **USE** statement with **ONLY** does not cancel out another less restrictive **USE** statement; if a program unit has a **USE** statement without the **ONLY** qualifier for a particular module, then all parts of the module are accessible even if the same module is also invoked by a **USE...ONLY** statement. A set of **USE...ONLY** statements gives access to all the items named. If the three final examples above occurred together, the combined effect would be to give access to **xlimits**, **ylimits**, **zlimits**, and **z**, the last having the local name **zhere** as well as the name **z**.

All that has been said above about local names and partial access to modules applies not only to data, but also to module procedures (and other entities, such as interface blocks, that will be met in later chapters). This means that the statement

```
USE Polynomial, Tell => Show_Coefficients
```

(referring to the example in Section 10.3) gives full access to the module **Polynomial** but the subroutine **Show_Coefficients** is to be referred to locally as **Tell**. The statement

```
USE Polynomial, ONLY: Tell => Show_Coefficients
```

means that no other parts of the module, apart from this subroutine, are accessible here.

As a rule it is a good idea to avoid renaming data and other entities in **USE** statements. When the same item is referred to by different names it generally leads to confusion rather than clarity. On the other hand, **USE** statements with the **ONLY** keyword are a useful form of "positive vetting", to ensure that data sets in different parts of the program are not inadvertently confused, and they make it easier for the programmer to remember exactly what is to be accessed in each module. For example,

```
USE Iocontrol, ONLY: Printer => P6, &
    printer_output_format => printer_output_format_6
```

could be used to select a particular printing function (**P6**) and associated format data (**printer_output_data_6**) from a library (**Iocontrol**) of module procedures and data for input and output.

10.6 Modules and interfaces

Procedure interfaces were introduced in Section 8.9, and will be returned to in Section 11.1. A procedure is given an "explicit" interface in another subprogram by supplying an interface block among the declarative statements at the start of that subprogram. The interface block must contain copies of declarative statements for the procedure in question, declaring the characteristics of the dummy arguments and, where applicable, the function's result. There are many circumstances in which procedures need to be given explicit interfaces and it is potentially a tedious chore to write all the necessary interfaces in many subprograms in a large program involving several different procedures. The chore is simplified considerably, however, by the use of modules to contain interface blocks. For example, if we pick up an example from Chapter 8, the module

```
MODULE Vector_X
INTERFACE OPERATOR (.X.)
  FUNCTION Vector_Multiplication (v1, v2)
  REAL :: Vector_Multiplication
  REAL, INTENT (IN) :: v1(*), v2(*)
  END FUNCTION Vector_Multiplication
END INTERFACE
END MODULE Vector_X
```

provides an explicit interface to the procedure **Vector_Multiplication**. Once this module has been set up, it is only necessary to include the statement

```
USE Vector_X
```

in any subprogram that is going to make use of the operator **.X.**. It is envisaged here that **Vector_Multiplication** is supplied as an external function; but in fact it could equally well be supplied as a module procedure within **Vector_X**, in which case the full interface block is unnecessary because the information required is already available in the module; in other words

```
MODULE Vector_X
INTERFACE OPERATOR (.X.)
MODULE PROCEDURE Vector_Multiplication
END INTERFACE
CONTAINS
FUNCTION Vector_Multiplication (v1, v2)
  REAL :: Vector_Multiplication
  REAL, INTENT (IN) :: v1(*), v2(*)
  Vector_Multiplication = DOTPRODUCT(v1, v2)
END FUNCTION Vector_Multiplication
END INTERFACE
END MODULE Vector_X
```

175

could be used. The meaning of this will be made a little clearer in the next chapter. For present purposes it is sufficient to notice that the module contains the function `Vector_Multiplication` as a module procedure, and the linkage to the `.x.` operator is achieved by means of an abbreviated interface block. The `USE` of this module allows any other subprogram to have access to the operator `.x.` and to the procedure `Vector_Multiplication`. If it is desired that the latter should be referenced only indirectly through `.x.`, and never explicitly, then a statement

```
PRIVATE :: Vector_Multiplication
```

could be inserted at the start of the module.

10.7 Exercises 10.B

10.B1 A database is to consist of a set of up to 3000 names, postal addresses, and telephone numbers, in addition to each of which there is a 12-character code for administrative purposes. Design a data module to contain this information in a suitable form. Then, write specifications (in English, not Fortran!) for a number of module procedures that could operate on the database to carry out as many useful tasks as you can think of in ten minutes.

10.B2 The inverse hyperbolic functions can be expressed as

$$\text{arcsinh}(x) = \ln(x + (x^2 + 1)^{1/2})$$

$$\text{arccosh}(x) = \ln(x + (x^2 - 1)^{1/2}) \qquad\qquad (x \geq 1)$$

$$\text{arctanh}(x) = \tfrac{1}{2}\ln((1 + x)/(1 - x)) \qquad\qquad (0 \leq x^2 < 1)$$

$$\text{arccosech}(x) = \text{arcsinh}(1/x)$$

$$\text{arcsech}(x) = \text{arccosh}(1/x)$$

$$\text{arccoth}(x) = \text{arctanh}(1/x)$$

Write these functions as a set of module procedures.

CHAPTER 11

More about procedures

Pure, elemental and recursive procedures are explained here, as are procedure interfaces and most of the advanced features that require procedures to have explicit interfaces. The final section deals with the ways in which arrays and character strings can be used as the arguments of procedures or as the values of functions. This chapter includes numerous exercises, some of which could easily form the basis of extended projects.

11.1 Interfaces and procedures

The concept of a procedure interface has been introduced gradually in this book. Section 8.9 explained that a special kind of "interface block" headed by a statement of the form

```
INTERFACE OPERATOR (.op.)
```

is needed at the start of a subprogram so that a certain external function will be invoked whenever the defined operator `.op.` is used in that subprogram. It was also mentioned that other kinds of interface blocks are required for certain other purposes. In Section 10.6 it was pointed out that interface blocks to procedures can be placed within modules for convenience, so that only a USE statement needs to appear in the subprograms that call the procedures in question. However, if the procedure is not external but is a module procedure, then what may be needed (in addition to a USE statement for the module procedure itself) is a simplified version of an interface block in which the procedure's name is mentioned in a MODULE PROCEDURE statement.

The concept of a procedure interface is a subtle and important one. Technically, every procedure has an "interface". Its interface is the information that specifies exactly how the procedure can be invoked. The information consists of the procedure's name, the characteristics and attributes of its arguments, the characteristics of its value (in the case of a function) and so on. This information must somehow be available within any subprogram that invokes the procedure, the reason being that a Fortran program will normally be compiled subprogram by subprogram and it cannot be assumed that while the processor is compiling one subprogram it will be able to scrutinize others to get the interface information needed to make sense of a procedure reference.

An important distinction has to be made between an "implicit" interface and an "explicit" interface. An external procedure, when used in the most straightforward way (as in Chapter 7), is said to have an "implicit" interface because all the information that is needed to invoke the procedure is implicit in how the procedure is referred to. For example, if a subprogram contains the statements

```
CALL Countout (gong, x, y)
n = Lonsdale (eubank)
```

then the types and other characteristics of the arguments **gong, x, y**, and **eubank** should be known within the subprogram, probably by having been declared in TDSs at the start of it, and no more information need be supplied about the interfaces of **Countout** and **Lonsdale** to this subprogram.

An intrinsic procedure, on the other hand, is said to have an "explicit" interface, because the form of reference to an intrinsic procedure is explicitly defined as part of the Fortran language, and does not have to be deduced from the context of a particular invocation. A module procedure, likewise, always has an explicit interface because the **USE** statement that gives access to the module will at the same time give direct access to the declarative statements within the module procedure that define the characteristics and attributes of the arguments.

An interface block starts with an **INTERFACE** statement. Interface blocks are required (a) if an external procedure's interface needs to be made explicit, or (b) if a module procedure's interface – which is explicit anyway – needs to be enhanced. An interface block is always inserted near the start of the subprogram that is to invoke the procedure in question. In case (a), the "interface block" contains a set of declarative statements, i.e. copies of the **FUNCTION** or **SUBROUTINE** statement, the TDSs declaring the dummy arguments and (if applicable) the function result variable, and finally the **END FUNCTION** or **END SUBROUTINE** statement. In case (b), the interface block will need a slightly more complex form of the **INTERFACE** statement, and the module procedure's name is specified with a **MODULE PROCEDURE** statement. A very simple interface block for an external procedure is:

```
INTERFACE
FUNCTION Triangle_Area (x1, x2, x3, y1, y2, y3)
REAL :: Triangle_Area
REAL, INTENT(IN) :: x1, x2, x3, y1, y2, y3
END FUNCTION Triangle_Area
END INTERFACE
```

i.e. it starts with the statement **INTERFACE**, finishes with the statement **END INTERFACE**, and between them there is a repetition of the **FUNCTION** (or **SUB-ROUTINE**) statement, argument type declaration statements, and **END FUNC-TION** (or **END SUBROUTINE**) statements that would also be given in the procedure definition itself. An interface block may contain interfaces to more than one procedure, as in

```
INTERFACE

FUNCTION Triangle_Area (x1, x2, x3, y1, y2, y3)
REAL :: Triangle_area
REAL, INTENT(IN) :: x1, x2, x3, y1, y2, y3
END FUNCTION Triangle_Area

FUNCTION Quad_Area (x1,x2,x3,x4,y1,y2,y3,y4)
REAL :: Quad_Area
REAL, INTENT(IN) :: x1, x2, x3, x4, y1, y2, y3, y4
END FUNCTION Quad_Area

END INTERFACE
```

The general form of an interface block is either

```
INTERFACE
     .
   interface body to external procedure
     .
   interface body to external procedure
     .
   interface body to external procedure
     .
     .
     .

END INTERFACE
```

or alternatively

```
INTERFACE generic-specification
     .
   interface body to external procedure
     .
   interface body to external procedure
     .
     .
     .
   MODULE PROCEDURE proc, proc, ...
     .
   MODULE PROCEDURE proc, proc, ...
     .
     .
     .

END INTERFACE
```

In the former case, the interface simply contains "interface bodies" for an arbitrary number of external procedures that are supplied in any order. Each interface body is a set of declarative statements associated with a particular function or subroutine:

```
FUNCTION/SUBROUTINE statement

USE statements, if relevant to characteristics of
arguments (and function result)

Type Declaration Statements for arguments (and function
result)

END FUNCTION/SUBROUTINE statement
```

In the second form of interface block, a *generic-specification* follows the keyword **INTERFACE**. The *generic-specification* may refer to the definition of an operator (Section 8.9) or to the setting-up of a generic name for several related procedures (Section 11.8) or to a defined assignment (Section 12.10). When there is a *generic-specification*, the external procedures represented by the interface bodies and the module procedures listed in the **MODULE PROCEDURE** statements must all be connected in that they will be different "specific" procedures corresponding to one "generic" form of invocation.

An external procedure always needs an explicit interface within any subprogram that calls it if any of the following is true:

1. the procedure is **ELEMENTAL** (Section 11.3);
2. there are **OPTIONAL** dummy arguments (Section 11.7);
3. a dummy argument is an assumed-shape array (Section 8.6), a pointer or a target (Chapter 13);
4. the procedure is a function with an array or pointer as its result;
5. the procedure is a function whose value is a character string of "automatic" length, i.e. a non-constant (and non-assumed) length given by a specification expression (Section 11.9).

Even if Conditions 1–5 do not apply, an external procedure needs an explicit interface to a particular subprogram if it is called from that subprogram under any of the following circumstances:

1. when it is called with an argument keyword (Section 11.6);
2. when it is a subroutine invoked through a defined assignment (Section 12.10);
3. when it is a function invoked through a defined operator (Section 8.9).
4. when it is invoked by a generic name rather than specific one (Section 11.8); or
5. when it is a **PURE** procedure (Section 11.2), and it is being called in circumstances that require it to be **PURE** (for example, if it is being called *from* another **PURE** procedure).

Even if it is not strictly necessary to provide an interface to a procedure, it is not an error to do so and it is wise to provide interfaces liberally rather than depend on remembering the rules listed above. Some authorities on Fortran believe that explicit interfaces should always be provided to all procedures to improve program reliability, since a high proportion of programming errors arise from incorrect data association when procedures are called.

11.2 PURE procedures *(Fortran 95 feature not in Fortran 90)*

A "pure" procedure is one that has no side-effects.

A pure function calculates and returns its value, but its argument or arguments must have INTENT (IN) and may not be changed within the function. A pure subroutine, however, may have arguments of INTENT (OUT) or (IN OUT), as well as INTENT (IN). In both pure functions and pure subroutines, local variables – those whose scope is limited to the procedure itself – may be manipulated, but not variables of wider scope linked with the procedure by the USE association of a module or by host association.

A pure procedure may not read or write external files or carry out other i/o operations. Internal files may be written or read, but any that are written must have names local to the procedure so that no information may leak out. If a pure procedure makes reference to another procedure, that also must be pure. Otherwise, we could have an illogical situation where the procedure referred to could generate side-effects on the "pure" procedure's behalf.

Intrinsic functions are always pure, and can therefore be referred to from within any other pure procedure. Intrinsic subroutines are pure if they are elemental (e.g. MVBITS) but not otherwise.

A pure procedure is declared as such in its header statement by prefixing the keyword FUNCTION or SUBROUTINE with PURE, e.g.

```
PURE FUNCTION Quintessence (x)
REAL :: Quintessence
REAL, INTENT(IN) :: x
   .
   .
   .

END FUNCTION Quintessence
```

The INTENT specification is compulsory: all the arguments of a pure procedure must have declared INTENT, except in the unusual cases of arguments that are dummy procedures (Chapter 14) or pointers (Chapter 13). For the first line, the syntax

```
REAL PURE FUNCTION Quintessence (x)
```
or

181

```
PURE REAL FUNCTION Quintessence (x)
```

would also be allowed but neither is recommended. Finally, the **END FUNC-TION** statement does not include the word **PURE** but the word **FUNCTION** is not optional and must be there.

If a pure procedure has a dummy procedure name as an argument (Chapter 14), the corresponding actual argument must be pure and it must either be an intrinsic procedure or it must have an explicit interface in the pure procedure where (through its dummy name) it is being referenced.

Pure procedures may not be recursive (Section 11.4 below). Moreover, local variables within a pure procedure may not be saved from one call to the next, so the **SAVE** attribute is not allowed, and neither may their values be initialized. Also, pure procedures may not **STOP**!

A pure procedure requires an explicit interface if a reference to it appears in a context that requires the procedure to be pure. An example would be if the procedure is called from within another pure procedure.

It would be fair to ask why the programmer should declare any procedure to be **PURE**, since to do so involves a number of restrictions and appears to give no additional functionality. Any program with pure procedures would, apparently, be unaffected if the keyword **PURE** were deleted wherever it occurs. So why bother?

Actually, there are two contexts in which procedures have to be pure, namely in Fortran 95 specification expressions (Section 11.9) and in the **FORALL** construct (Section 6.5). Specification expressions are a minor issue and, by themselves, would not justify the introduction of the **PURE** keyword and the rules associated with it. The real reason for specifying **PURE** procedures is shown by **FORALL** and is to do with the spread of parallel-processing systems that can take advantage of the fact that multiple calls to pure procedures may be made in any order or simultaneously. Purity, therefore, may not make the programmer's job easier, but in principle it can facilitate greater program efficiency and speed of execution, particularly when the program is to be run on an advanced parallel-processing system.

11.3 ELEMENTAL procedures *(Fortran 95 feature not in Fortran 90)*

Many of Fortran's intrinsic procedures, both in Fortran 95 and in Fortran 90, are "elemental". In Fortran 95 it is also possible for users to write elemental procedures of their own. An elemental procedure is specified as such by having the keyword **ELEMENTAL** in place of **PURE**, e.g.

```
ELEMENTAL FUNCTION Quintessence (x)
```

It is never necessary to specify a procedure to be both **ELEMENTAL** and **PURE** because all elemental procedures are also pure. In fact, of the prefixes **ELEMENTAL**, **PURE**, and **RECURSIVE**, no more than one can ever be used at once. All the constraints on pure procedures, mentioned in the previous section, apply also to elemental procedures. However, to be elemental involves additional restrictions.

Speaking loosely, the point of an elemental procedure is that it is defined in terms of scalar dummy arguments but can be referenced either with a scalar or with an array as the actual argument; if with an array, the effect is as if the procedure were called repeatedly for each element of the array. This allows whole-array operations to be written compactly and it can simplify the implementation of parallel processing on machines capable of it.

Within an elemental procedure, all the dummy arguments must be scalars and may not be pointers or procedure names. If we have an elemental function, its result must be treated as a scalar within the function. However an elemental function's actual argument, by which it is called from elsewhere, may be an array, in which case the result is also an array of the same shape.

An elemental procedure may be a subroutine rather than a function. When an elemental subroutine is called, either

1. all the actual arguments must be scalars, or
2. all the actual arguments whose **INTENT** is **OUT** or **IN OUT** may be arrays, but they must have the same shape; and those whose **INTENT** is **IN** must either have the same shape again or must be scalars.

An example may help to clarify this:

```
ELEMENTAL SUBROUTINE Matrix_Diff_Square (a, b, q, z)
REAL, INTENT (IN) :: a, b, q
REAL, INTENT (OUT) :: z

 ! Each element of z is to be set equal to the square
 ! of the difference between the corresponding elements
 ! of a and b, divided by q.

z = ((a-b)**2)/q
END SUBROUTINE Matrix_Diff_Square
```

This could be invoked elsewhere by code such as:

```
REAL :: d(10, 10), e(10,10), f(10, 10), g = 10000.0
 .
 .
 .

CALL Matrix_Diff_Square (d, e, g, f)
```

In this example, three actual arguments are arrays and, following the rules, they have the same shape. One actual argument (**g**) is a scalar but in theory it could equally well have been an array as long as its shape was the same

(10, 10) as the other arguments. There is just one circumstance – when a dummy argument is used in a specification expression (Section 11.9) – in which the actual argument is restricted to being a scalar.

When one is working with user-defined derived data types (Chapter 12), defined assignments may be elemental. In fact, if the defined assignment is to be used in a **WHERE** construct, it must be elemental.

Every elemental procedure requires an explicit interface in a program unit that invokes it.

11.4 **RECURSIVE** procedures

Normally a procedure may not invoke itself, either directly or indirectly. In some circumstances, though, it can be convenient to let this happen, and it is made possible by putting the keyword **RECURSIVE** before the procedure's name in the first line of the procedure. This can be applied both to functions and to subroutines, but in the case of a function an extension has to be made to the syntax of the **FUNCTION** statement: if, for example, a function called **Iris** is to be made recursive, its first line could be

```
RECURSIVE FUNCTION Iris (juniper) RESULT (berry)
```

The meaning of **RESULT (berry)** is explained below. Subroutines are simpler, just requiring the keyword **RECURSIVE** as in

```
RECURSIVE SUBROUTINE Metamorphosis (jekyll, hyde)
```

How can recursive procedures be used? An example is this subroutine to put a sequence of characters into alphabetical order:

```
RECURSIVE SUBROUTINE Order (caps)
CHARACTER(1) :: caps(:), store
LOGICAL :: disorder
disorder = .FALSE.
DO kount = 1, SIZE(caps)-1
  IF (LGT(caps(kount),caps(kount+1))) THEN
    store = caps(kount)
    caps(kount) = caps(kount+1)
    caps(kount+1) = store
    disorder = .TRUE.
  END IF
END DO
IF (disorder) CALL Order (caps)
END SUBROUTINE Order
```

This works by putting a disordered sequence into something closer to alphabetical order and then calling itself again. (The colon notation **caps(:)** is explained in Section 11.9, and **SIZE** in Section 12.2.) The next example is a recursive subroutine that will show the running total of an indefinite series of input numbers:

```
RECURSIVE SUBROUTINE Add_In (k)
INTEGER :: k, knew, number
READ (*,*) number
IF (number/=0) THEN      ! A zero terminates
   knew = k + number
   WRITE (*,*) knew
   CALL Add_In (knew)
END IF
END SUBROUTINE Add_In
```

This is started by **CALL Add_In(0)**, and finished when a zero is input.

In the case of a recursive function, to avoid a possible ambiguity, the function's result value must be given a name different from that of the function itself. The result name that will be used within the function must therefore be specified in brackets after the keyword **RESULT** at the end of the function statement. Then, within the function, any reference to the actual function name will be taken as a recursive call to the function.

A popular textbook example of a recursive function is the factorial, which can be written:

```
RECURSIVE FUNCTION Factorial (n) RESULT (nfac)
INTEGER :: nfac, n
SELECT CASE (n)
CASE (1)
   nfac = 1
CASE DEFAULT
   nfac = n * Factorial (n-1)
END SELECT
END FUNCTION Factorial
```

Here the result is called **nfac**, a local variable declared in the first line. The result variable **nfac** and the function value **Factorial** must necessarily be identical in type, so there is no need to declare both. If their type is not specified by a prefix to the function statement itself, it must be specified by a type declaration statement referring to the result variable. In the above example, the presence of **RESULT (nfac)** means that the second line may not be

```
INTEGER :: Factorial, n
```

Within this recursive function, the name **Factorial** can only occur as a call to the function and is not used to assign a value to the function.

Recursive procedures can sometimes make life simpler for the programmer, but they can lead to inefficient code and it is usually possible to carry out the task in another way. The factorial function above can be calculated much more simply by the one-liner

```
nfac = PRODUCT ((/ (i, i=1,n) /)) !n!
```

11.5 Exercises 11.A

11.A1 Write a pure function to convert radians to degrees.

11.A2 Write an elemental function to calculate $n!$, the factorial of its argument.

11.A3 Write a fast elemental subroutine to calculate the square, cube, fourth and fifth roots of one of its arguments. *Hint*: only call $\log(x)$ once.

11.A4 Write a recursive function to calculate a definite integral of the function $\sin^n(x)$, the arguments being the power n and the limits of integration.

11.A5 Write a recursive subroutine that will find a solution of the equation

$$x - 3\cos(x) = c.$$

It should work by starting from a rough estimate of the solution, finding a better estimate, and then calling itself again, until the estimate is very close to the exact solution. The subroutine's arguments should be the number c and the current estimate of the solution of the equation.

11.A6 The Ackerman function, $\text{ACK}(m, n)$ is a function of two non-negative integers. It is defined by:

$$\text{ACK}(0, n) = n + 1$$

$$\text{ACK}(m, 0) = \text{ACK}(m - 1, 1)$$

$$\text{ACK}(m, n) = \text{ACK}(m - 1, \text{ACK}(m, n - 1)) \text{ if neither } m \text{ nor } n \text{ is zero}$$

Write a recursive function to give $\text{ACK}(m, n)$, and use it to investigate the function's properties.

11.A7 Write a recursive function to calculate Fibonacci numbers $\text{Fib}(i)$, where i is a positive integer, based on

$$\text{Fib}(n) = \text{Fib}(n - 1) + \text{Fib}(n - 2)$$

starting from $\text{Fib}(1) = \text{Fib}(2) = 1$. What can you do to make the function work as fast as possible?

11.A8 A program makes frequent use of the functions

$$t_{m,n}(\theta) = \sin^m(\theta).\cos^n(\theta)$$

and of the indefinite integrals

$$T_{m,n}(\theta) = \int t_{m,n}(\theta) \, d\theta$$

where m and n are positive integers. As long as $m + n$ is not zero, the integrals can be reduced using the formulae

$$T_{m,n}(\theta) = (m + n)^{-1}.t_{m+1,n-1}(\theta) + (n - 1)/(m + n) . T_{m,n-2}(\theta)$$

$$= -(m + n)^{-1}.t_{m-1,n+1}(\theta) + (m - 1)/(m + n) . T_{m-2,n}(\theta)$$

Write a function procedure for $t_{m,n}(\theta)$ and another for $T_{m,n}(\theta)$, the latter using the reduction formulae above and referring to the former. The functions are to work for any non-negative values of m and n. The procedure for $T_{m,n}(\theta)$ should be written as a recursive function.

Use your procedures to tabulate values of $T_{2k,2k}(2\pi)$ for values of k ranging from 0 to 20.

11.A9 An interesting function of a positive integer (investigated by Dijkstra) is defined by

```
FUSC(1) = 1
FUSC(2*n) = FUSC(n)
FUSC(2*n + 1) = FUSC(n) + FUSC(n+1)
```

Write a recursive function to yield **FUSC(n)** and use it to look into the function's properties. What is its average value for the values of n lying between 9900 and 10100?

11.6 Argument keywords

The idea of argument keywords has already been explained in the context of intrinsic procedures. When a procedure has several arguments, keywords are a foolproof way of avoiding confusion between them, instead of relying simply on the order in which they are specified. With user-written procedures, keywords are not set up in the procedure definition itself, but are set up in an interface block, by listing the desired keyword names in the order of the arguments in the **FUNCTION** or **SUBROUTINE** statement. So, with a function like

```
FUNCTION Distance (x1, x2, y1, y2)
REAL :: Distance
REAL, INTENT(IN) :: x1, x2, y1, y2
Distance = SQRT((x1-x2)**2 + (y1-y2)**2)
END FUNCTION Distance
```

we could use an interface such as

```
INTERFACE
FUNCTION Distance (Xa, Xb, Ya, Yb)
REAL :: Distance
REAL, INTENT(IN) :: Xa, Xb, Ya, Yb
END FUNCTION Distance
END INTERFACE
```

and, in any program unit containing that interface, the function could be called by a statement such as

```
s = Distance (Xa=1.576, Ya=34.88, Xb=pt3x, Yb=pt3y)
```

As this example shows, the arguments need not have the same names in the interface block as in the procedure itself (they are all "dummy" arguments), although they must correspond in order. The argument names used in the interface block become the keywords. Where the function is actually called using the keywords, the arguments can be in any order.

Note that a procedure may be given two (or more) different interface blocks in different parts of a program; this means that different keywords may be used in different places for the same procedure! This sort of confusion should, of course, be avoided.

Where an interface block makes it possible for argument keywords to be used, they may nevertheless be omitted, but not beyond a point in the argument list where the order of the arguments differs from that specified in the procedure itself. Thus, the statement above is equivalent to

```
s = Distance (1.576, Ya=34.88, Xb=pt3x, Yb=pt3y)
```
and to
```
s = Distance (1.576, pt3x, Yb=pt3y, Ya=34.88)
```

Notice that it is only by the occurrence of an = sign that the processor knows that a keyword is being used and it is only through the interface that the name of the keyword is specified.

Whenever one is writing and using external procedures that have multiple arguments, it is good practice to supply interfaces with argument keywords. In fact, one interface block could be put together containing interfaces for all the program's external procedures. This block could be put into a module, and accessed by a **USE** statement at the start of every program unit.

11.7 Optional arguments

One use of argument keywords is to control a situation where not all of the procedure's arguments need necessarily be present each time it is invoked. (A good intrinsic example of this is the subroutine **DATE_AND_TIME**, described in Chapter 5.) An argument that need not be given is known as an "optional" argument, and in an external procedure it would be declared by having a special attribute, **OPTIONAL**, in the TDS. We could have a function starting with

```
FUNCTION Addemup (s1, s2, s3, s4, s5, s6)
REAL :: Addemup
REAL, INTENT(IN) :: s1, s2
```

```
REAL, OPTIONAL, INTENT(IN) :: s3, s4, s5, s6
   .
   .
   .
```

which means that the arguments **s3**, **s4**, **s5**, and **s6** need not actually be present. In other words, **Addemup** may be called with any number from two to six arguments. Within such a function it is usually necessary to have some way of knowing whether or not an optional argument has actually been specified, and this is done with an intrinsic inquiry function, **PRESENT**, which may be called from within the procedure. If **A** is the name of an argument, **PRESENT(A)** is a logical function that is true if and only if **A** has been specified in this particular call to the procedure. The above function could therefore be completed with the statements

```
   .
   .
   .
Addemup = s1 + s2
IF (PRESENT(s3)) Addemup = Addemup + s3
IF (PRESENT(s4)) Addemup = Addemup + s4
IF (PRESENT(s5)) Addemup = Addemup + s5
IF (PRESENT(s6)) Addemup = Addemup + s6
END FUNCTION Addemup
```

If a procedure has any optional arguments, an interface must be supplied. An interface block for the above function could be

```
INTERFACE
FUNCTION Addemup (S1, S2, S3, S4, S5)
REAL :: Addemup
REAL, INTENT(IN) :: S1, S2
REAL, OPTIONAL, INTENT(IN) :: S3, S4, S5
END FUNCTION Addemup
END INTERFACE
```

and valid forms of reference to the function would be, for example, the statements

```
a = Addemup(10.8, 22.1)
b = Addemup(1.0, 2.3, 3.6)
c = Addemup(S1=0.0342, S2=0.0788, S5=0.0066)
d = Addemup(S3=heathrow, S2=gatwick, S1=stansted)
```

Note that keywords do not necessarily have to be used when there are optional arguments; but without keywords it would only be possible to omit a series of arguments from the back end of the procedure's argument list.

As an example of the use of optional arguments and keywords, suppose that a function, to be called **Convert_Angle**, is to have two arguments, namely an angle in degrees and an angle in radians. Whenever the function is used only one argument must be present and the angle is to be converted from degrees to radians, or from radians to degrees, either way according to which argument is present. The converted value is to be returned as the function's value. The function is to write an error message if neither or both are present. Whenever the function is used, a keyword must be used to indicate whether the argument is in radians or in degrees. The function could be as follows:

```
FUNCTION Convert_Angle (radians, degrees)
REAL :: Convert_Angle
REAL, OPTIONAL, INTENT(IN):: radians, degrees
CHARACTER(*), PARAMETER :: err=&
  "Convert_Angle should be called with exactly one&
  & argument"
LOGICAL :: r, d
r=PRESENT(radians)
d=PRESENT(degrees)
IF (r.EQV.d) THEN
  WRITE (*,*) err
  Convert_Angle = 0.0
ELSE
  IF (r) Convert_Angle=radians*57.2958
  IF (d) Convert_Angle=degrees/57.2958
END IF
END FUNCTION Convert_Angle
```

and a suitable interface would be

```
INTERFACE
  FUNCTION Convert_Angle (Radians, Degrees)
  REAL :: Convert_Angle
  REAL, OPTIONAL, INTENT(IN) :: radians, degrees
  END FUNCTION Convert_Angle
END INTERFACE
```

11.8 Generic procedures

Procedure interfaces can be extremely useful if we want to use a single name (or a single operator) to invoke any of several different procedures, the choice depending on the nature of the arguments. This is what happens with intrinsic functions when a "generic" name is used and when the result's type depends on the argument's type. To take a very simple example, suppose we want a procedure to "multiply" a character by an integer, and to work whichever way round the arguments are given. This would require two functions such as

```
FUNCTION Multcn(c,n)
CHARACTER(1), INTENT(IN) :: c
INTEGER, INTENT(IN) :: n
CHARACTER(n):: Multcn
Multcn = REPEAT(c,n)
END FUNCTION Multcn

FUNCTION Multnc(n,c)
CHARACTER(1), INTENT(IN) :: c
INTEGER, INTENT(IN) :: n
CHARACTER(n) :: Multnc
Multnc = REPEAT(c,n)
END FUNCTION Multnc
```

and either could be invoked through the name **Mult** as long as there is the generic interface:

```
INTERFACE Mult

FUNCTION Multcn(c,n)
CHARACTER(1), INTENT(IN) :: c
INTEGER, INTENT(IN) :: n
CHARACTER(n) :: Multcn
END FUNCTION Multcn

FUNCTION Multnc(n,c)
CHARACTER(1), INTENT(IN) :: c
INTEGER, INTENT(IN) :: n
CHARACTER(n) :: Multnc
END FUNCTION Multnc

END INTERFACE
```

(In this example, **Multcn** and **Multnc** are "automatic-length" strings as described in Section 11.9.) Whenever the generic function name **Mult** is referred to, control will pass either to **Multcn** or to **Multnc** according to the order of the arguments. In general, any set of procedures may be referenced by one generic name as long as (a) they are all functions or all subroutines, and (b) the characteristics of the arguments will narrow the choice down to one specific procedure from among the set, so that there is ultimately no ambiguity. The "characteristics" of the arguments means their types, keywords, shapes (if arrays) and whether they are present or not!

Not only can a set of procedures be referenced by a single generic name, but alternatively they may (if functions) be referenced by a single generic operator. The following enables "multiplication" to be defined between integer and logical variables:

```
FUNCTION Pnm (n, m)
INTEGER :: Pnm
```

```
INTEGER, INTENT(IN) :: n, m
Pnm = n*m
END FUNCTION Pnm

FUNCTION Pnq (n, q)
INTEGER :: Pnq
INTEGER, INTENT(IN) :: n
LOGICAL, INTENT(IN) :: q
Pnq = n;     IF (.NOT.q) Pnq = -n
END FUNCTION Pnq

FUNCTION Pqn (q, n)
INTEGER :: Pqn
INTEGER, INTENT(IN) :: n
LOGICAL, INTENT(IN) :: q
Pqn = n;     IF (.NOT.q) Pnq = -n
END FUNCTION Pqn

FUNCTION Pqr (q, r)
LOGICAL :: Pqr
LOGICAL, INTENT(IN) :: q, r
Pqr = q.AND.r
END FUNCTION Pqr
```

The interface will be headed by

```
INTERFACE OPERATOR (*)
```

and contain all the declarative parts of the external function definitions above. This would permit the asterisk to be used freely between integer and logical data, either way round, with the meaning as defined.

To summarize: the **INTERFACE** statement may simply take the form

```
INTERFACE
```

in which case the interface may be specifying the names of external procedures, the types and shapes of function results, and the types, shapes, keywords and optionalities of the arguments. The number of procedures specified is arbitrary and there need be no connection between them. Alternatively, the statement may take the form

```
INTERFACE Name
```

where **Name** is a "generic name" for a set of two or more related procedures specified in the block. The third possibility is

```
INTERFACE OPERATOR (.op.)
```

where **.op.** is the name of an operator, either of the form **.xyz....** or of the same form as an intrinsic operator being "overloaded". The interface block must then contain one or more functions (and no subroutines) and the functions must have either one or two arguments (unary or binary operator). If there is more than one function, the operator is a "generic" one.

A further kind of **INTERFACE** statement is described in Section 12.10.

In the above examples, the sets of functions being given generic names were external functions. The same sort of thing holds good also for external subroutines. However, things can be done differently in the case of module procedures, because it is not necessary to have explicit interfaces for module procedures within the same module. Instead, an interface block which provides a generic name or operator for a set of module procedures may be of the form:

```
INTERFACE ...
    MODULE PROCEDURE list
END INTERFACE
```

where *list* is just a list of the names of the module procedures being bundled together. Going back to the earlier example, if the functions **Pnm**, **Pnq** etc. had been module procedures in the same module, the interface to define the operator could have been simply

```
INTERFACE OPERATOR (*)
    MODULE PROCEDURE Pnm, Pnq, Pqn, Pqr
END INTERFACE
```

The **MODULE PROCEDURE** statement can also be used in the context of defined assignment (see Section 12.10).

11.9 Arrays and strings in procedures

It has already been indicated frequently that arrays and character strings may be used in procedures just as they can in a Fortran main program. The purpose of this section is to summarize the rules governing the use of arrays and strings as variables in procedures, especially when the variable is an argument of the procedure or, in the case of a function, is the function's value. Some of what follows has already been mentioned in Section 8.6. Moreover, there remain some usages of arrays that can be important with reference to procedures but still remain to be fully explained in Chapter 12 ("allocatable" arrays) and in Chapter 13 ("array pointers")and that will therefore be referred to only very briefly in this section.

All the techniques described in this section are different ways of making procedures more flexible by allowing them to use arrays (or strings) under circumstances where it would be unduly restrictive to specify their shapes and sizes once and for all when the program is written. In other words, they are ways of permitting procedures to work with variable-shape arrays and variable-length strings.

In a slightly different sense, we have already dealt with a powerful method of invoking procedures with array arguments of arbitrary shape through "array assignment" and **WHERE** (Sections 4.9 and 6.6), using elemental procedures (Section 11.3). However, although elemental procedures may be called with array-valued actual arguments, they always have scalar dummy arguments, i.e. an elemental procedure has the internal appearance of a procedure whose arguments are all scalars. This section is concerned with non-elemental procedures.

Character strings

A character string must always be declared in a type declaration statement (TDS – Section 8.4) with a length that is specified in some way. In the simplest cases, the length is specified by a scalar integer constant as in

```
CHARACTER (120) :: line_of_text
```

When a character string is a dummy argument of a procedure its length may be specified explicitly, as in the above example, as long as the length matches that of whatever the actual argument is when the procedure is invoked.

Alternatively, a dummy argument of character type may have its length specified not by an integer constant but by a scalar integer "specification expression". The concept of a specification expression is an important one since it arises in connection not only with character strings but also with "automatic" arrays.

Specification expressions

A specification expression is a restricted kind of expression that may depend only on:

1. variables whose values are known within the procedure by **USE** association or (for a module procedure) by host association;
2. variables that are other dummy arguments of the same procedure;
3. references to a number of intrinsic functions, i.e.
   (a) elemental functions of integer or character type, having integer or character arguments;
   b) **SELECTED_INT_KIND, SELECTED_REAL_KIND, TRIM, REPEAT** and **TRANSFER,** with integer or character arguments;
   (c) Array enquiry functions (except **ALLOCATED**), numeric enquiry functions, **BIT_SIZE, KIND, LEN** and **NULL**;
   except that, when an inquiry function is applied to another dummy argu-

ment, the characteristics of that dummy argument should have been specified before this specification expression is encountered. In other words, TDSs (and different entities within them) should appear in the correct order if the specification expression for one dummy argument depends on another;

4. **Fortran 95 feature not in Fortran 90:** specification expressions, besides intrinsic functions, may involve non-intrinsic **PURE** functions (Section 11.2).

The following is a very simple example of how a specification expression may be used to specify the length of a character-type dummy argument:

```
SUBROUTINE Infiltrate (string, nchars)
INTEGER, INTENT(IN) :: nchars
CHARACTER(nchars), INTENT(IN OUT) :: string
   .
   .
   .
```

The specification expression here is simply the variable **nchars**. More complicated specification expressions appear in

```
SUBROUTINE Analyze (z, zm, m, a)
USE Database
REAL, INTENT(IN) :: a(:,:)
INTEGER, INTENT(IN) :: m
CHARACTER (SIZE(a) + 1), INTENT(OUT) :: z
CHARACTER (m*SIZE(z) + 1), INTENT(OUT) :: zm
   .
   .
   .
```

where the array **a** is an assumed-shape array (see Section 8.6, and further below in this section; **SIZE** is discussed in Section 12.2).

Incidentally, a character string variable does not have to be a dummy argument in a procedure for its length to be given by a specification expression rather than a constant. A character string that is an ordinary local variable may also have its length specified in that way, as long as the specification expression obeys the rules listed above. Such a variable is sometimes called an "automatic" data object. For example, in

```
SUBROUTINE Double (word, length)
INTEGER, INTENT(IN) :: length
CHARACTER (length), INTENT(IN) :: word
CHARACTER (2*length) :: word2
   .
   .
   .
```

the variable **word2** is an automatic object whose length is given by the specification expression **2*length**, although **word2** is not a dummy argument of the procedure.

Assumed-length strings

Besides using a specification expression, there is another way of allowing a character string which is a dummy argument to have non-fixed length. It is to have an "assumed-length" string, declared using an asterisk as described in Section 8.4. For example,

```
SUBROUTINE Infiltrate (string)
CHARACTER(*), INTENT(IN OUT) :: string
INTEGER :: nchars
nchars = LEN(string)
    .
    .
    .
```

is an alternative method to that given in the similar example above. Another example is

```
SUBROUTINE Compare (name1, name2, result)
CHARACTER(*), INTENT(IN) :: name1, name2
LOGICAL, INTENT(OUT) :: result
    .
    .
    .
```

and of course the strings **name1** and **name2** must correspond to actual arguments, whose lengths were defined in the calling program. The asterisk in the **CHARACTER** statement means that the lengths of the dummy arguments **name1** and **name2** will be determined when the subroutine is called.

Assumed-length character strings may be used a little more widely than just as dummy arguments: they may be used for other character variables or parameters, whose lengths are assumed from initialization expressions (Section 8.7), or for character-valued functions (see below).

Generally speaking, it is preferable for non-fixed-length character-type dummy arguments to be of assumed length, i.e. using the asterisk notation, rather than being declared with specification expressions. In fact, there is a case for avoiding specification expressions altogether for dummy arguments since they tend to make the language over-complex without any great benefit.

Below is an example of a subroutine, **Eicheck**, with a character string argument of assumed length. Within the subroutine, the length of the argument can be found simply by using the intrinsic **LEN** function. The subroutine looks into the string for occurrences of the diphthong **ei**, and changes them to **ie** except after **c**:

```
SUBROUTINE Eicheck(string)
CHARACTER(*) :: string
CHARACTER(*), PARAMETER :: ei="ei", ie="ie", c="c"
INTEGER :: length
length = LEN(string)
IF (length<3) RETURN
DO ipoint=2, length-1
  IF (string(ipoint:ipoint+1) /= ei) CYCLE

  IF (string(ipoint-1:ipoint-1) == c) CYCLE
  string (ipoint:ipoint+1) = ie
END DO
END SUBROUTINE Eicheck
```

The first **CHARACTER** statement here declares the dummy argument **string** to be of assumed length, its length being assumed from the actual argument wherever the subroutine is called. The second **CHARACTER** statement declares three local character strings also to be of assumed length, except that their lengths (two, two and one) are assumed from the initialization expressions that follow in the same statement.

Character-valued functions

Function values, like arguments, may be character strings of non-fixed length. Again, there are two ways of allocating these. The function's length may be "automatic", given by a specification expression, or it may be indicated by an asterisk and assumed. If it is automatic, the procedure must have an explicit interface.

If the length is assumed (a practice officially declared to be obsolescent in Fortran 95!), it must be assumed from a length specified in the program unit that invokes the function. Thus

```
FUNCTION All_Upper_Case(string)
CHARACTER(*) :: All_Upper_Case
   .
   .
   .
```

has a value whose length is assumed from wherever it is called from, where it could be specified by a declaration statement such as

```
CHARACTER(10), EXTERNAL :: All_Upper_Case
```

As another example, the procedure

```
SUBROUTINE Caller (n1, n2, n3)
USE Database
```

```
INTEGER, INTENT(IN) :: n1, n2, n3
CHARACTER(n1+n2+n3), EXTERNAL :: Called
  .
  .
  .
```

could include a function reference such as

```
WRITE (*,*) Called (flag)
```

With the function `Called` beginning

```
FUNCTION Called (flag)
USE Database
CHARACTER(*) :: Called
LOGICAL, INTENT(IN) :: flag
  .
  .
  .
```

Notice that the subroutine `Caller` declares `Called` to be an external function of character type, its length being given by a specification expression. This is then assumed as the length of the function's value within `Called`.

Arrays as arguments

If a procedure has a dummy argument that is an array, there are four different possibilities for how the array's shape might be determined:

1. It may have a fixed shape, declared explicitly with bounds that are constants. This shape must correspond exactly to the shape of the actual argument.
2. It may have "assumed shape", declared using a colon for each dimension. The shape is assumed from that of the actual argument. Note that an assumed-shape array cannot be anything other than a dummy argument of a procedure. Other arrays cannot have assumed shape.
3. It may have "assumed size" (Section 8.6).
4. It may be an "array pointer", a kind of deferred-shape array described in Section 13.5.

Of these four possibilities, 3 is strongly discouraged, 4 is an advanced feature of Fortran that is not commonly needed, but 2 is recommended for general use whenever a dummy argument is an array. Fixed-shape arrays (1) may be simplest, but they are somewhat restrictive and there is a case for saying that a programmer should always use the "assumed-shape" method when it is necessary for a dummy argument to be an array. As a simple example of an assumed-shape array, if a program unit with an array variable declared by

198

```
REAL :: x(0:9)
```

calls a function called **Fun** with **x** as its real argument, and if the function starts with

```
FUNCTION Fun(z)
REAL, INTENT(IN) :: z(:)
    .
    .
    .
```

then **z** takes on a size of **10**, and its indices range from **1** to **10** (not **0** to **9**!). If we wanted the indices of **z** to run up from **0**, the final statement could be

```
REAL, INTENT(IN) :: z(0:)
```

which is still an assumed-shape declaration since the upper bound will assume whatever value is necessary to fit in all the elements that the actual argument might have. It is only the extents of the actual argument in each dimension, not the pairs of index bounds, that are transmitted from the actual to the dummy argument. However, it is only the lower index bound, not the upper, that may be stated in an assumed-shape array declaration. A statement such as

```
REAL, INTENT(IN) :: x(:99)        ! illegal!
```

would be illegal. However, the lower bound is not limited to being a constant integer: it can be determined by any valid specification expression. So, for example, we could have

```
FUNCTION Fun(z, minimum_index)
INTEGER, INTENT(IN) :: minimum_index
REAL :: z(minimum_index:)
    .
    .
    .
```

although it is hard to imagine how this sort of programming would be useful!

A nice example (which was the subject of a discussion initiated by David Serafini on the comp-fortran-90 mailbase discussion list in 1994) is the following:

```
SUBROUTINE Foo(arg)
INTEGER, INTENT(OUT) :: arg (:,:)
INTEGER :: local (SIZE(arg, 1), SIZE(arg, 2))
    .
    .
    .
```

The point of this is that the dummy argument **arg** must have determined characteristics, including a shape, assumed from the actual argument whether the **INTENT** is **IN**, **OUT**, or **IN OUT**. Specifying **INTENT(OUT)** just means that the argument's value goes out, it does not mean that its characteristics as a data

199

object do not come into **Foo**. When **Foo** is called, there will have to be a defined actual argument that will determine the shape of the variable **local**. Note that **local** is an automatic array whose shape is given here by specification expressions using the **SIZE** function (Section 12.2).

When a dummy argument is an array of non-fixed shape, e.g. when it has assumed shape, the procedure must have an explicit interface.

Finally, it must be emphasized that an elemental procedure (with scalar dummy arguments) is always preferable to a non-elemental procedure (with array dummy arguments) when there is a straight choice between the two.

Arrays as values

A function may have an array as its value, in which case its shape may either be fixed or it may be an "automatic" array with its shape given by a specification expression. The rules governing specification expressions were listed earlier in this section. An array-valued function must have an explicit interface.

This function has an array as its argument and as its value:

```
FUNCTION Inverse_Vector (v)
REAL :: Inverse_Vector(3)
REAL, INTENT(IN) :: v(3)
Inverse_Vector = v/DOTPRODUCT(v,v)
END FUNCTION Inverse_Vector
```

and a suitable interface would be

```
INTERFACE
FUNCTION Inverse_Vector (v)
REAL :: Inverse_Vector(3)
REAL, INTENT(IN) :: v(3)
END FUNCTION Inverse_Vector
END INTERFACE
```

Inverse_Vector((/1.0,0.0,3.0/)) is equal to **(/0.1,0.0,0.3/)**.

Another example is the procedure starting with

```
FUNCTION Function_title (argument)
REAL :: Function_title (8)
      .
      .
      .
```

whose value is a rank-one array with eight elements. More generally, **Function_title** could be an automatic array. If the argument were also an array, and if the function's value were to have the same number of elements as the argument, we could have

```
FUNCTION Function_title (argument)
REAL :: argument (:)
REAL :: Function_title (SIZE(argument))
    .
    .
    .
```

Here, the value of **Function_title** is an automatic array but the argument is an assumed-shape array.

Longer examples

A fuller example of a procedure based on an assumed-size array is the following, which fills an array with prime numbers:

```
SUBROUTINE Primes (p)
INTEGER, INTENT(OUT) :: p(:)
!   The subroutine must be called with p having at least
!   3 elements.
LOGICAL :: prime
INTEGER :: n, index
n = SIZE(p)   !  We're looking for the first n primes
p(1) = 2
p(2) = 3
index = 3
i=3
Odd_Integers: DO
    i=i+2           ! = 5, 7, 9, ...
    prime = .TRUE.
    Factors: DO j = 3, NINT(SQRT(REAL(i))), 2
        IF (MOD (i, j) == 0) THEN
            prime = .FALSE.
            EXIT Factors
        END IF
    END DO Factors
    IF (prime) THEN ! We've found a prime
        p(index) = i
        index = index + 1
        IF (index>n) EXIT Odd_Integers
    END IF
END DO Odd_Integers
END Subroutine Primes
```

The next example features fixed-shape function values, an assumed-shape dummy argument, and various automatic arrays:

```
FUNCTION Polycentroid (vertices)
!
! To calculate the coordinates of the centroid of a convex
! polygon from the coordinates of its vertices.
!
! The argument contains the coordinates of the vertices in
! cyclic order.
!
! This algorithm is valid only for a convex polygon.

INTERFACE
  FUNCTION Triarea (t)
  REAL :: Triarea
  REAL :: t (3,2)
  END FUNCTION Triarea
  FUNCTION Tricentre (t)
  REAL :: Tricentre (2)
  REAL :: t (3, 2)
  END FUNCTION Tricentre
END INTERFACE

REAL :: Polycentroid (2)
REAL :: vertices (:,:)

INTEGER :: nvertices
REAL :: triangles (SIZE (vertices, 1)-2, 3, 2)
REAL :: triareas (SIZE (vertices, 1)-2), tricentres(SIZE
(vertices, 1)-2)-2,2)
REAL :: area, areabycentroid(2)
nvertices = SIZE (vertices, 1)

! initialize summations
area = 0.0
areabycentroid = 0.0

! Set up array of triangles' corners' vertices.
! The i'th triangle's corners are the first, (i+1)'th and
! (i+2)'th vertices of the polygon.

Triangle:   DO i = 1, nvertices-2
Corner:   DO icorner = 1, 3

IF (icorner==1) ivert = 1
IF (icorner>1) ivert = i + icorner
```

```
triangles(i, icorner,:) = vertices(i,:)

END DO Corner

! Now obtain the area and centroid of each triangle
! and add up their areas
! and make a weighted sum of their centroids.

triareas (i) = Triarea (triangles(i,:,:))
tricentres(i,:) = Tricentre (triangles(i,:,:))
area = area + triareas(i)
areabycentroid = areabycentroid + &
tricentres(i,:)*triareas(i)

END DO Triangle

! Now calculate the overall centroid

Polycentroid = areabycentroid/area
END FUNCTION Polycentroid

FUNCTION Triarea (t)
REAL :: Triarea
REAL :: t (3,2)
!
! This function is to return the area of the triangle of
! which the coordinates of the corners (a 3x2 array)
! are supplied as the argument t.
!
END FUNCTION Triarea

FUNCTION Tricentre (t)
REAL :: Tricentre (2)
REAL :: t (3,2)
!
! This function is to return the coordinates of the
! centroid of a triangle. The coordinates of the triangle's
! corners (a 3x2 array) are supplied as the argument t.
!
END FUNCTION Tricentre
```

As a final example, consider a function that calculates the "harmonic mean" H of a set of n numbers a_1, ..., a_n. The harmonic mean of a set of numbers is defined by

$$H^{-1} = (a_{+1} + a_{2-1} + a_{3-1} + ... + a_{n-1})/n$$

and the function below uses an assumed-shape array as its argument:

```
FUNCTION Harmonica (array)
! Declarative statements
REAL :: Harmonica
REAL :: array(:), sum
INTEGER :: number
LOGICAL :: nil

! Initialization
Harmonica = 0.0
sum = 0.0
number = SIZE(array)
nil = .FALSE.

! Calculation
DO index = 1, number
  nil = (array(index)==0.0)
  IF (nil) EXIT
  sum = sum + 1.0/array(index)
END DO
! Termination
IF (.NOT.nil) Harmonica = number/sum
END FUNCTION Harmonica
```

It is worth noticing that data initialization has not been carried out here in the type declaration statements, i.e. we have not used code like

```
REAL :: Harmonica = 0.0              ! illegal!
REAL :: array(:), sum = 0.0
INTEGER :: number = SIZE(array)      ! illegal!
LOGICAL :: nil = .FALSE.
```

mainly because this kind of initialization only takes place the first time that the function is called. On any subsequent calls the variables will start with the values left behind from the previous call (as if the **SAVE** parameter had been used). Initialization within a TDS in a procedure means initialization once only and therefore will not have the desired effect in this function. Moreover, the first and third statements above are illegal anyway, because initialization in a TDS is not permitted for a function result (**Harmonica**) and because an "initialization expression" may not involve the bounds of an array whose shape is assumed.

Although data initialization within a type declaration statement is not appropriate in this example, it may be appropriate for a variable such as a counter that is to keep a running total of how often a function is called throughout the running of the program as a whole; and it is necessary for a fixed-value "named constant" declared with the **PARAMETER** attribute.

11.10 Exercises 11.B

11.B1   Write a unary operator yielding a randomly-chosen logical value.

11.B2   Write a function which can be called with up to a dozen integer arguments. Its value is to be the integer closest to their average.

11.B3   Write a real array-valued function, called **Cross**, with two arguments both of which are also real arrays. The arrays are of rank one and size three, representing three-dimensional vectors, and the result is to be the vector product ("cross product") of the two arguments.

11.B4   Write a function called **Hebrew**, whose argument and value are both character strings of (different) variable lengths. The argument is to be any word, and the result is to be the same word but with the vowels removed.

11.B5   An operator is needed which, acting between two real numbers, gives their geometric mean. Write a function and interface to do the job. What can you do about the case where the two numbers are of opposite signs?

11.B6   Write a function and interface with a defined operator so that any real number (including a negative one) can be raised to an arbitrary real power. If the result is mathematically a complex number, the function's value is to be equal to its real part. Use the symbol ****** as the defined operator, overloading the intrinsic exponentiation operator.

11.B7   Look again at the subroutine **Eicheck** in Section 11.9. Will it always work as intended? What will it do to **"Pompeii"**? "Correct" it!

11.B8   Write a subroutine with two arguments: first, an arbitrary-length array of real numbers and, second, a single real number. The subroutine is to rescale the elements of the array so that their average becomes equal to the second argument (or, if the second argument is not present, to unity).

11.B9   Write a function whose argument is a string of any length, returning a randomly-chosen single character from that string (use the **RANDOM** function).

11.B10   Write a function to say whether or not a number is in the Fibonacci sequence

1, 1, 2, 3, 5, 8, ...

and another to see if it is in the meta-Fibonacci sequence:

1, 3, 4, 7, 11, 18, 29, ...

Then, write a function to say if a number is a super-Fibonacci number, i.e. if it occurs in both the Fibonacci and meta-Fibonacci sequences. These functions should be written for time-efficient multiple reference, by setting up tables of the different sorts of numbers, not by doing all the calculations from scratch every time.

11.B11 Write an operator **.s.** that will concatenate two strings putting one blank space between them. In other words, **"Mel".s."Gibson"** is to be equal to **"Mel Gibson"**.

11.B12 A set of data consists of n pairs of coordinates x and y, and it is presumed that the data can be fitted to a linear relationship

$$y(x) = a + bx$$

Estimates of a and b are given by the formulae

$$a = (S_y.S_{xx} - S_x.S_{xy})/D$$

$$b = (S_1.S_{xy} - S_x.S_y)/D$$

where S_1 is equal to n and S_x, S_y, S_{xx}, and S_{xy} are respectively the sums over the n coordinate pairs of the quantities x, y, x^2, and xy. The quantity D is given by

$$D = S_1.S_{xx} - S_x^2$$

This formula assumes equal uncertainties on all the measurements, i.e. gives equal weight in the sums to all the n points. Write a subroutine that will calculate the estimates of a and b given, as input, arrays of values of z and y.

11.B13 Write functions to convert each way between (a) an array of logical data, and (b) an integer which, if expressed in binary form, would represent the logical data as a sequence of **1**s (true) and **0**s (false).

11.B14 Write a recursive function that, by repeated concatenations, converts an array of single characters into a scalar character string.

11.B15 Write an elemental function **Len(integer)**, i.e. something like the intrinsic character string function **LEN** function but with an integer as argument. It is to give the number of decimal digits in the integer supplied as the argument.

11.B16 Write the functions **Triarea** and **Tricentre** called by the function **Polycentroid** in the example in Section 11.9.

11.B17 An elemental function is needed for the purpose of calculating square roots as quickly as possible but not with high precision. The intrinsic function **SQRT** would be too slow and unnecessarily accurate. It is sufficient to calculate square roots to within one per cent of the precise values. Speed is all-important, but it does not matter how much memory space is taken up.

11.B18 Set up a subroutine **Fast_trig** to take any angle in radians and return the sine, cosine, and tangent each to within one per cent as quickly as possible.

11.B19 Look at the function **PARITY** in Section 15.3. Write a version of it that will work for a rank-one arbitrary-size array. (The **dim** argument will not be necessary.)

11.B20 Look at the **POPCNT** function in Section 15.3, and refer to Appendix B for information about "bits". Write **POPCNT** as an elemental external function.

11.B21 The Mandelbrot set is based on the transformation of a complex number that is obtained by squaring it and adding to it another (constant) complex number c:

$$z \rightarrow z^2 + c$$

Write a complex-valued elemental function **Mandelbrot(z,c,iterations)** whose value will be the result of carrying out the above transformation a number of times given by the integer argument **iterations**.

CHAPTER 12

Advanced array features and derived types

*This chapter begins with a description of allocatable arrays, involving the statements **ALLOCATE** and **DEALLOCATE** and the function **ALLOCATED**. Then a few further intrinsic functions (**LBOUND**, **UBOUND**, **SHAPE** and **SIZE**) are dealt with, and details of the different classes of arrays are tabulated. The latter part of the chapter is devoted to derived types ("structures") and to defined assignment.*

12.1 Allocatable arrays

"Allocatable arrays" are Fortran's most direct tool for dynamic memory management, in other words for letting arrays have variable bounds. Already, in connection with procedures, we have come across other forms of arrays with non-constant shape (Section 11.9), namely automatic arrays, assumed-shape arrays and assumed-size arrays; but these all involve fixing an array's shape when a procedure is entered. Allocatable arrays have nothing directly to do with procedures.

An allocatable array is a variety of "deferred-shape" array. (There is another variety, the "array pointer", dealt with in Section 13.5.) An allocatable array is initially declared with a certain rank, i.e. a certain number of dimensions, but the extent of each dimension (the "bounds") can be set and may be changed during the running of the program. This can be very valuable when a processor is limited in memory and it means that a program may expand and contract its memory requirements during running to minimize the demands made on the processor. For example, a program may need a large amount of memory to read a database, but may then carry out an analysis using just a small fraction of the input information: using allocatable arrays, most of the memory needed at input could be released by the program when it proceeds to the analysis stage.

An allocatable array is declared in a type declaration statement (TDS) by specifying the attribute **ALLOCATABLE**, and at that point its rank is specified by giving an array specifier with a series of colons, one colon for each dimension. This is a "deferred-shape" specification. The following are examples of the declarations of allocatable arrays of ranks one, two, three and four:

```
INTEGER, ALLOCATABLE, SAVE :: bitstream(:)
REAL, ALLOCATABLE :: matrix1(:,:), matrix2(:,:)
CHARACTER(1), ALLOCATABLE :: pages(:,:,:)
LOGICAL, ALLOCATABLE :: truthtable(:,:,:,:)
```

An allocatable array may not be a function value or a procedure's dummy argument. So, although an allocatable array is declared using the same colon notation as an assumed-shape array, there should never be any confusion between the two: dummy arguments may have assumed shape and other variables may be allocatable, but not the other way round.

The bounds of allocatable arrays are set by a special executable statement, **ALLOCATE**, that simply lists the names and shapes of the arrays. The **ALLOCATE** statement causes the required amount of memory space to be allocated to the arrays named. Examples are

```
ALLOCATE (bitstream(4097))
ALLOCATE (matrix1(45,90), matrix2(45,180), &
pages(65,30,1))
```

Following the usual notation for array shapes, lower and upper bounds may be specified:

```
ALLOCATE (truthtable(0:1,0:1,0:7,14))
```

In an **ALLOCATE** statement the bounds may be expressions. Moreover, they are not restricted to the "specification expressions" allowed for automatic arrays (Section 11.9), but may be scalar integer expressions of more or less any kind, as long as they have definite values when the **ALLOCATE** statement is executed. So, we could have an arrangement such as

```
REAL, ALLOCATABLE :: rmem(:)
   .
   .
   .
READ (*,*) n
ALLOCATE (rmem(2*n))
   .
   .
   .
```

Statements such as the following would also be possible:

```
ALLOCATE (workspace(120*nrecords, 15))
ALLOCATE (bytes(npersons, LEN(names)))
```

```
ALLOCATE (scratchpads(dataset(1:1),3,SIZE(dataset)))
```

but not

```
ALLOCATE (results(npoints), display(SIZE(results)))
```

because a bound of one array may not depend on an array inquiry function whose argument is another array that is being allocated within the same **ALLOCATE** statement. (For the meaning of **SIZE**, see Section 12.2.) However, it would be quite possible to have the sequence of two statements:

```
ALLOCATE (results(npoints))
ALLOCATE (display(SIZE(results)))
```

The **ALLOCATE** statement may have, after the list of arrays, a status variable for the purposes of error-checking. It is given with the keyword **STAT** as in

```
ALLOCATE (display(SIZE(results)), STAT=k)
```

or

```
ALLOCATE (a(2), b(3), c(55,4), STAT=icheck)
```

The name after **STAT=** is arbitrary, but it must be a scalar integer variable. After execution of the **ALLOCATE** statement, the status variable (in this instance, **icheck**) will be zero if the allocation was successful, but will be positive if there was an error. If **STAT=...** is not included, then an error in executing the statement will cause the program to terminate.

The **ALLOCATE** statement gives space to an array, but the space can be later released with a **DEALLOCATE** statement. The syntax is just like that for **ALLOCATE** except that the names of the arrays are not followed by their shapes:

```
DEALLOCATE (bitstream, matrix1, matrix2, pages, &
STAT=iflag)
DEALLOCATE (truthtable, workspace, bytes)
```

DEALLOCATE may only be used on allocatable arrays that have actually been allocated, and **ALLOCATE** may only be used on a previously allocated array if it is deallocated first.

It can be useful to have a way of checking, during program execution, whether or not space has been allocated to an array. To do this there is an intrinsic function **ALLOCATED**. The **ALLOCATED** function has one argument, which must be the name of an allocatable array, and it has the logical value **.TRUE.** or **.FALSE.** according to whether the array is currently allocated. So, it is possible to have statements like

```
IF (ALLOCATED(scratchpads)) DEALLOCATE(scratchpads)
```

and

```
IF (.NOT.ALLOCATED(results)) ALLOCATE(results(4,100))
```

When allocatable arrays are used, a problem may arise if an array is allocated within a procedure and then the program returns back to the program unit that invoked the procedure. Under these circumstances the array will in effect be lost, even if the procedure is entered again later. In fact, it will not even be possible to deallocate the array later because its allocation status will have become undefined. There are two ways around this problem: one is to give allocatable arrays the **SAVE** attribute, in which case they are not lost on returning from the procedure, and the other way is to put allocatable arrays into modules. With modules, the arrays are preserved as long as the modules are being used by whatever program units are executing.

Fortran 95 feature not in Fortran 90

Contrary to what is said in the previous paragraph, in Fortran 95 local allocatable arrays that would otherwise get "lost" are automatically deallocated (i.e. without the need for a **DEALLOCATE** statement) on return from any procedure.

12.2 Intrinsic procedures for arrays

There are intrinsic functions **LBOUND** and **UBOUND** that yield the lower and upper bounds on the subscripts of whatever array is given as the argument. If arrays were declared by

```
REAL :: a(21:30), b(10)
```

then **LBOUND(a)** is **21**, **UBOUND(a)** is **30**, **LBOUND(b)** is **1**, and **UBOUND(b)** is **10**. The values of **LBOUND** and **UBOUND** are, obviously, integers, whatever the types of the arguments. With multidimensional arrays, **LBOUND** and **UBOUND** are rank-one integer arrays containing the sets of lower and upper bounds. So with

```
LOGICAL :: c(0:2,0:2,0:2,0:3)
```

LBOUND(c) is equal to **(/0,0,0,0/)** and **UBOUND(c)** is **(/2,2,2,3/)**.

In fact **LBOUND** and **UBOUND** may have an optional second argument, the keywords being **LBOUND(ARRAY, DIM)** and **UBOUND(ARRAY, DIM)**. If **DIM** is present it must be a scalar integer no greater than the rank of the argument **ARRAY**, and then the function yields the subscript bound relevant to the dimension indicated by **DIM**. Using the previous example, **UBOUND(ARRAY=c, DIM=4)** is equal to **3**. If the argument **ARRAY** is an array expression or section, rather than just the name of an array variable, then **LBOUND** will be given equal to **1** and **UBOUND** will be the extent of the appropriate dimension.

SHAPE is a very straightforward intrinsic function, having a single argument which may be any array. Its value is a rank-one integer array specifying the argument's shape, i.e. with the series of dimensional extents. So, the expression

```
SHAPE(RESHAPE(SHAPE=a,SOURCE=b))
```

is just the array **a**.

The intrinsic function **SIZE**, which has already cropped up in various examples in the course of this book, is very simple. With a single argument, which must be an array, **SIZE** is the total number of elements in it. There is an optional second argument, the keywords being **SIZE(ARRAY, DIM)**, in which case **SIZE** is the extent of **ARRAY** along the dimension labelled by the integer **DIM**. So, if **SHAPE(a)** is **(/4,5,100/)**, then **SIZE(a)** is equal to **2000** and **SIZE(ARRAY=a,DIM=2)** is **5**.

12.3 Summary: classes of arrays

Fortran's different types of array were mentioned in Section 8.6, when the type declaration statement was being described, and again in Section 11.9 in connection with procedure reference. However, it is such an important topic that it is worth summarizing the situation in Table 12.1.

Constant-shape arrays and automatic arrays are both forms of "explicit-shape" array. Allocatable arrays and array pointers are forms of "deferred-shape" array.

Table 12.1 Classes of arrays.

Array type	Context	Comments
Constant shape	Permissible for any purpose	The simplest form of array, but the shape must be fixed when the program is written
Automatic	Not usable for a dummy argument	Declared with a "specification expression"; cannot have **SAVE**; may be a function value
Assumed shape	Only used for dummy arguments	Declared with colons (and possibly a lower bound)
Allocatable	Not usable as a dummy argument, function value or structure component	Declared with colons alone; permits flexible memory management as the **ALLOCATE** statement is executable, not declarative
Array pointer	May be used when an allocatable array may not	Declared with colons alone; may use **ALLOCATE** like an allocatable array; requires pointer syntax
Assumed size	Only dummy arguments	Declared with an asterisk; usage not recommended

213

12.4 Exercises 12.A

12.A1 (i) Write type declaration statements for an allocatable rank-two array of complex numbers, to be called **cmatrix**, and an allocatable rank-one array of length-12 character strings, to be called **rivernames**.

(ii) Write statements to allocate the shape **(4,4)** to **cmatrix** and allocate 200 elements to **rivernames**.

(iii) Write code that will deallocate **rivernames** if it has already been allocated, and will then allocate 150 elements to it.

12.A2 Write code that will take a character string, of whatever length, and produce a vector of that size containing the individual characters that formed the string.

12.A3 With the array declared by

```
INTEGER:: spreadsheets (1:12,1901:2050,1:20,0:199)
```

what are the values of

(i) `LBOUND (spreadsheets)`

(ii) `SHAPE (spreadsheets)`

(iii) `SHAPE (spreadsheets(1:1,:,:,:))`

(iv) `UBOUND (spreadsheets(1:1,:,:,:))`

(v) `SHAPE (spreadsheets(1,:,:,:))`

(vi) `UBOUND (spreadsheets(1,:,:,:))`

(vii) `LBOUND (ARRAY=spreadsheets(:,1967,:,:),DIM=2)`

(viii) `SIZE (spreadsheets(1:10,1967,:,:))`

(ix) `UBOUND(LBOUND(spreadsheets(1:10,1967,:,:))`

(x) `SIZE(SHAPE(spreadsheets(2,:,1967,:)))`

12.5 Derived types

"Derived types" are special non-standard types of data that may be set up by the Fortran programmer. A derived type is defined in a block headed by a **TYPE** statement and subsequently data of that type can be declared by a variant of the TDS. Functions and operators, and the meaning of assignment (=), may be defined for use with a derived type.

A derived type (often called a "structure") is built up ultimately from components of intrinsic types. A "derived type constructor", analogous to an array constructor, is used to specify the values of all the components making up a particular structure. To extract an individual component from a structure, there is a special notation involving the **%** character.

There are two main ways in which derived types are useful. One is to let the programmer use unusual mathematical structures, e.g. geometrical figures, arcane algebras, quaternions, sets, and groups. The other is to set up a shorthand to work with large or complex data sets, whether it be entries in a bibliography, pages of text, printer drivers, or radionuclide decay data.

A block of non-executable code, headed by a derived-type definition statement, must be provided among the declaration statements at the start of any program unit where the new type is to be used. This block of code must declare the name of the type and specify how an item of this type is built up from items of intrinsic type. For example, if complex numbers were not already an intrinsic type in Fortran, they could be derived with the definition block

```
TYPE Complex
REAL :: x, y
END TYPE Complex
```

which simply declares that a new data type, `Complex`, is to consist of a pair of real numbers. The details of complex arithmetic would be a matter for function definitions and operator definitions subsequently.

Usually, the derived-type definition statement simply consists of the keyword **TYPE** followed by a name. This statement is followed by one or more statements declaring, in order, the components of the structure. These component declarations are very similar in syntax to ordinary type declaration statements, except that:

1. the only attribute specifiers available are **DIMENSION** and **POINTER**;
2. character lengths must be constants;
3. array bounds must be constants, except only that a pointer component may be an array pointer (Section 13.5); and
4. initial values of components cannot be specified in the derived-type definition.

Finally, the block is finished with an **END TYPE** statement optionally suffixed by the type-name.

It should be noticed that allocatable arrays are not allowed to be structure components. This is the basic reason why the **VARYING_STRING** data type (Appendix C) has been implemented in terms of a structure containing an array pointer.

Fortran 95 feature not in Fortran 90

Contrary to (4) above, Fortran 95 allows for the default initialization of derived type objects, as in the type definition

```
TYPE Coord3
REAL :: x(3) = (/0.0, 0.0, 0.0/)
END TYPE Coord3
```

A more complex example of a derived type definition is:

```
TYPE Mail
CHARACTER(10) :: title
```

215

```
CHARACTER :: initials (3)
CHARACTER(30) :: surname
CHARACTER(30) :: address (5)
CHARACTER(10) :: postcode
INTEGER :: telephone
LOGICAL :: gender
INTEGER :: refnumber, spouseref, entrydate
END TYPE Mail
```

This sets up a data structure that could form the basis of a mailing list. Note that components of different intrinsic types may be included among the components of a structure, and so may arrays.

Once a structure has been defined, variables of that type can be declared by type declaration statements of the form

```
TYPE (Quaternion) :: rho, sigma, phi
TYPE (Mail) :: newentry, spouse
TYPE (Currency_rates) :: yesterday, today, forward1, &
forward2
```

It is essential to understand the distinction between a statement like

```
TYPE Mail
```

which introduces the definition block for the type itself, and

```
TYPE (Mail) :: dud
```

which declares that a particular variable will be of that type. Although both start with the keyword **TYPE**, these two statements do quite different jobs. The type definition block must come first and could be provided most conveniently by being written once and for all in a module accessible to the whole program. The TDS is really just like any of the TDSs described in Chapter 8; it may have all the possible attribute specifications, just like an intrinsic TDS, and it may declare arrays. For example,

```
TYPE (Mail) :: retirees (5000)
```

declares an array with 5000 elements, each being a structure of the type called **Mail**. If **Mail** is defined as above, then **retirees** will actually contain a total of 55 000 character strings, 20 000 integers, and 5000 logical data items!

If a set of coordinates in three-dimensional space is represented by

```
TYPE Coord3
REAL :: x(3)
END TYPE Coord3
```

then TDSs using that definition are

```
TYPE (Coord3) :: neworigin
TYPE (Coord3) :: redgiants(50)
```

Although **Coord3** comprises an array, **x(3)**, it is important to understand that the type **Coord3** is not of itself an array or a scalar, any more than the type **REAL** is of itself either an array or a scalar. The variable **neworigin** is of type **Coord3**, but is a scalar, even though the array **x** subsists in it. The variable **redgiants** is also of type **Coord3**, but is an array of size 50.

It will be seen below that a variable of a derived type may be initialized when it is declared by a TDS. Such initialization overrides a Fortran 95 default initialization in the type definition itself.

SEQUENCE

A derived-type definition block may include the single-word statement **SEQUENCE** after the initial **TYPE** statement but before the statements defining the components. The effect is to make the derived type a "sequenced" structure, which means that any object of this type will be ultimately resolved into individual numbers or characters in the same way wherever the object is declared. This is necessary if such an object is to appear in a **COMMON** or **EQUIVALENCE** statement.

12.6 Structure constructors

It has been explained above how a derived type is defined and how a variable of that type would be declared. But how are actual values given to the components of a derived-type structure? It can be done with a "structure constructor" which takes the general form

```
Typename (component1, component2, component3,....)
```

i.e. the values of the components are simply listed in brackets after a reference to the type name. So, using some of the examples from the previous section, we could have assignment statements such as

```
retirees(1) = Mail ("Prof.", (/"H", "J", ""/), "Wallace",&
  (/("", i=1, 5)/), 0, .TRUE., 386740, 386741, 211090)
locus = Coord3 ((/56.923, 20.768, 91.004/))
```

We can have more complicated expressions such as

```
locus = Coord3 ((/r*COS(theta)*COS(phi), &
r*SIN(theta)*COS(phi), r*SIN(phi)/))
```

Note that array constructors are used when the structure components are arrays. If a structure component were an array of rank greater than one, then the structure constructor could contain a reference to the **RESHAPE** function, within which the elements could be represented in the form of a rank-one array constructor.

The ordinary rules of assignment apply if there is any difference of detail between the list in the structure constructor and the list that originally defined the structure. So, for example,

```
locus = Coord3 (1)
```

would set all the elements of the array **a(3)**, within **locus**, equal to **1.0**.

Another example (which could define, for example, a plane in three-dimensional space) is the type

```
TYPE Vtriplet
REAL :: v1(3), v2(3), v3(3)
END TYPE Vtriplet
```

with variables defined by, say,

```
TYPE (Vtriplet) :: pa, pb, floor
```

and with actual values being set by assignment statements such as

```
pa = Vtriplet (0.0,0.0,0.0)
pb = Vtriplet ((/0.34,0.81,0.08/),(/0.88,0.00,0.55/), &
   (/0.60,0.28,0.31/))
floor = Vtriplet (a,b,(/c,d,e/))
```

where the variables **a** and **b** are 3-vectors and **c**, **d** and **e** are scalars.

A structure may be given an initial value, or it may be a named constant, e.g.

```
TYPE (Vtriplet), PARAMETER :: &
pb = Vtriplet ((/0.34,0.81,0.08/),(/0.88,0.00,0.55/), &
   (/0.60,0.28,0.31/))
```

12.7 Structure components

Given a variable that is a structure, whose components have defined values, how can the values of those components be obtained? This is the inverse of the task performed by a structure constructor. It is done by giving the component name after the variable's name, separated by the **%** symbol. With the structure

```
TYPE Date
  INTEGER :: day, month, year
  CHARACTER(10) :: dayname
  LOGICAL :: holiday, public_holiday
END TYPE Date
```

and data

```
TYPE (Date) :: q = Date (25, 5, 1992, "Monday", &
    .FALSE., .TRUE.)
```

then **q%day** is the integer **25**, **q%holiday** is the logical item **.FALSE.**, and so on. This also holds equally good for variable names, e.g. with

```
q = Date (n1, n2, n3, daystring, flaga, flagb)
```

then the expression

q%dayname

is equivalent to the name **daystring**. This kind of thing can be applied to arrays, e.g. going back to the earlier examples

retirees%telephone

is an array of 5000 integers, consisting of the component **telephone** from each of the 5000 structures in the array **retirees**. A similar thing can be done if the component itself is the array, e.g. **neworigin%x** is simply the array **x** which is within the structure **neworigin** of type **Coord3**. And, with the type **Vtriplet** above, **pb%v2** is the array **(/0.88,0.00,0.55/)**. However, this notation is forbidden when the structure itself and the component are both arrays, because an ambiguity would arise: it would not be clear what sort of array

retirees%initials

is supposed to be, since there are three elements of **initials** in each of 5000 elements of **retirees**. So, in general,

a%b

means the component called **b** within the derived-type variable called **a**, and it is an array if either **a** or **b** (but not both!) is an array. Notice that **a** may be an array element, so we could have

redgiants(1)%x

which would be the 3-vector of the coordinates of the first red giant. However, in **a%b** it is not permissible for **b** to be an array element, it must simply be the bare component-name from the structure definition block. This means that the expression

a%b(i)

is the **i**th element of **a%b**. It does not necessarily refer to the **i**th element of **b**. In fact **a%b(i)** refers to the **i**th element of **b** only if the structure **a** is scalar and the component **b** is an array.

12.8 Structures of structures

If derived-type structures were composed only of data items of intrinsic types, life would be interesting but not fascinating. In fact, components of a structure may themselves be derived-type structures. This example sets up a special type, **Coord**, to represent coordinate pairs in two-dimensional space; and then a further type, **Circle**, is set up to represent circles; but the definition of **Circle** involves a data item of type **Coord**:

```
TYPE Coord
  REAL :: x, y
END TYPE Coord
TYPE Circle
  TYPE (Coord) :: centre
  REAL :: radius
END TYPE Circle
```

This means that structure constructors may be nested, e.g.

```
ring = Circle (Coord(1.0,-1.0), SQRT(2))
```

and that we can have components of components:

```
ring%centre%y
```

would be equal to **-1.0**. This can be extended over several levels, e.g. the type

```
TYPE Sixcircles
  TYPE (Circle) :: round(6)
END TYPE Sixcircles
```

which consists of a set of six circles, each based on a coordinate pair and a radius. Then, if **hex** is a scalar of type **Sixcircles**, there can be components

```
hex%round(5)
hex%round
hex%round(1:3)
hex%round%radius
hex%round%centre(1)
hex%round%centre%x(2)
hex%round%centre%y
```

These expressions represent respectively the fifth circle in **hex**, an array (of type **Circle**) of all six circles, an array formed with the first three circles, a real array of the circles' radii, the centre (type **Coord**) of the first circle, the **x** component of the centre of the second circle, and an array of the **y** components of the centres of the six circles!

It is important to remember that a type definition may include other derived-type structures only if the latter have previously been defined. However, a structure may have a component that is of the same type as itself if that component has the **POINTER** attribute (Section 13.2).

12.9 Procedures and operators with derived types

Like those of intrinsic type, data items of derived type may be used as the arguments of procedures. Functions of derived-type data may be used to define special operators. The following example shows data items representing points and circles in two dimensions, together with a function that will calculate the area of overlap between two circles:

```
MODULE Ringtypes
  TYPE Coord
  REAL :: x, y
  END TYPE Coord
  TYPE Circle
  TYPE (Coord) :: centre
  REAL :: radius
  END TYPE Circle
END MODULE Ringtypes

MODULE Ringover
  INTERFACE OPERATOR (.over.)
    FUNCTION Overlap(c1,c2)
    USE Ringtypes
    REAL :: Overlap
    TYPE (Circle), INTENT(IN) :: c1, c2
    END FUNCTION Overlap
  END INTERFACE
END MODULE Ringover

FUNCTION Overlap(c1,c2)
  USE Ringtypes
    REAL :: Overlap
    TYPE (Circle), INTENT(IN) :: c1, c2
  REAL :: x1, x2, y1, y2, d, r1, r2, ca1, ca2, s, a1, &
    a2, trisq
  x1 = c1%centre%x; x2 = c2%centre%x
  y1 = c1%centre%y; y2 = c2%centre%y
  d = SQRT((x1 - x2)**2 + (y1 - y2)**2)
  r1 = c1%radius; r2 = c2%radius
  IF (d>(r1+r2)) THEN
    Overlap = 0.0; RETURN
```

```
    ELSE IF (D<ABS(r1-r2)) THEN
      Overlap = MAX(r1,r2)**2*3.14159; RETURN
    ELSE
      ca1 = (r1**2 + d**2 - r2**2)/(2.0*r1*d)
      ca2 = (r2**2 + d**2 - r1**2)/(2.0*r2*d)
      s = (r1+r2+d)/2
      a1 = ACOS(ca1) ; a2 = ACOS(ca2)
      trisq = s*(s-r1)*(s-r2)*(s-d)
      Overlap = (a1*r1 + a2*r2 - SQRT(trisq))*2.0
    END IF
  END FUNCTION Overlap

  MODULE Rings
    USE Ringtypes ; USE Ringover
  END MODULE Rings
```

Here, the type definition blocks have been put into a module called **Ringtypes**. The function itself, **Overlap**, is an external function and is not therefore in any module. It is necessary to provide an interface for the function **Overlap**, because an operator is being defined, and this interface is put into a module called **Ringover**. The function itself, **Overlap**, uses the derived types and therefore includes a **USE Ringtypes** statement. Finally, a combination module, **Rings**, brings together **Ringtypes** and **Ringover** so that any program unit using these need contain only the statement

```
  USE Rings
```

Here is another example where a new type, **Location**, is defined and may be operated on with a function **Distance**:

```
  MODULE Locdef
    TYPE Location
    REAL :: dlatitude, dlongitude
    END TYPE Location
  END MODULE Locdef

  MODULE Interdistance
    INTERFACE OPERATOR (.to.)
      FUNCTION Distance (a,b)
      USE Locdef
      REAL :: Distance
      TYPE (Location), INTENT(IN) :: a, b
      END FUNCTION Distance
    END INTERFACE
  END MODULE Interdistance

  FUNCTION Distance(a,b)
    USE Locdef
```

```
  REAL :: Distance
  TYPE (Location), INTENT(IN) :: a, b
  REAL, PARAMETER :: rdn = 57.296, rds = 6330000.0
  REAL :: ta, tb, pa, pb, ra, rb, direct, aa(3), bb(3), &
     absq(3)
  ta = a%dlongitude/rdn    ;    tb = b%dlongitude/rdn
  pa = a%dlatitude/rdn     ;    pb = b%dlatitude/rdn
  aa(1) = sin(ta)          ;    bb(1) = sin(tb)
  ra = cos(ta)             ;    rb = cos(tb)
  aa(2) = ra*sin(pa)       ;    bb(2) = rb*sin(pb)
  aa(3) = ra*cos(pa)       ;    bb(3) = rb*cos(pb)
  absq = (aa - bb)**2
  direct = sqrt(sum(absq))
  Distance = 2.0*rds*asin(direct/2)
END FUNCTION Distance
```

This function would be invoked by any expression of the form

paris.to.moscow

from any program unit with access to the appropriate modules, if **paris** and **moscow** are defined data items of type **Location**.

In the above examples, derived type data occurs as arguments but the function values themselves are of an intrinsic (real) type. But in general a function result itself may be of derived type, as in

```
FUNCTION Loop (c)
  USE Ringtypes
  TYPE (Circle) :: Loop
  TYPE (Coord), INTENT(IN) :: c(3)
  REAL :: csq1, csq2, csq3, top, bot, xcent, ycent, &
     radsq, rad
  csq1 = c(1)%x**2 + c(1)%y**2
  csq2 = c(2)%x**2 + c(2)%y**2
  csq3 = c(3)%x**2 + c(3)%y**2
  top = (c(2)%y - c(3)%y)*(csq1 - csq2) -(c(1)%y - &
     c(2)%y)*(csq2 - csq3)
  bot = (c(1)%x-c(2)%x)*(c(2)%y-c(3)%y) -(c(2)%x- &
     c(3)%x)*(c(1)%y-c(2)%y)
  xcent = 0.5 * top / bot
  ycent = 0.5 * (csq1 - csq2- 2.0 * xcent * (c(1)%x- &
     c(2)%x)) / (c(1)%y - c(2)%y)
  radsq = (xcent - c(1)%x)**2 + (ycent - c(1)%y)**2
  rad = SQRT(radsq)
  Loop = Circle (Coord (xcent, ycent), rad)
END FUNCTION Loop
```

This function uses the types **Coord** and **Circle** that we met in previous examples, and forms the circle that passes through a set of three points **c**. It is not mandatory to have an interface for the function **Loop** because no operator is being defined.

12.10 Defined assignment

Defined operators were covered in Section 8.9, and in some ways it would have been logical to deal with "defined assignments" at the same time. Both are special types of procedure interface; a defined operator permits a function reference to be made through an operator and a defined assignment permits a subroutine to be called through a form of assignment statement (=). However, defined assignment is especially useful in the context of derived types and so has been deferred until this chapter.

First of all, recall that the general form of the assignment statement is

```
variable = expression
```

and this simply gives the variable on the left the value of the expression on the right, as long as they are of the same types and have conformable shapes. This applies also to objects of the same derived type: the components of the variable are set equal to the corresponding components of the expression. But we do not always have to have the same types and shapes on each side of an assignment statement. It is permissible for the expression to be a scalar and the variable an array, in which case all the array's elements will be set to the value of the expression. If the variable and the expression are of different numeric types, then the expression will be converted to the variable's type as if by the intrinsic function **INT**, **REAL** or **CMPLX**. If the variable and the expression are character strings of different lengths, the expression will be either truncated or padded to conform to the length of the variable. Those are the rules of "intrinsic" assignment.

"Defined assignment" permits the assignment statement to be given a meaning when it would normally be undefined, i.e. in cases where the variable and the expression are of different types that would normally be incompatible. It also permits the rules of intrinsic assignment to be redefined, or "overloaded", with something different from usual. Defined assignment is specified with a subroutine having exactly two dummy arguments and having an interface of the form

```
INTERFACE ASSIGNMENT(=)
   SUBROUTINE ...
      .
      .
      .
```

```
END SUBROUTINE ...
END INTERFACE
```

the first line meaning that the subroutine can be invoked by using the = sign in an assignment statement. When this happens, the variable on the left-hand side will be the first argument of the subroutine and the expression on the right will be the second.

As an example, suppose we want to define the assignment **a=b** when **a** is a real scalar variable and **b** is of the type **Circle** used in previous examples above. In this case, suppose we want the number **a** to be set equal to the area of the circle **b**. This could be achieved with

```
SUBROUTINE Discus (a, b)
USE Ringtypes
REAL, INTENT (OUT) :: a
TYPE (Circle), INTENT (IN) :: b
REAL, PARAMETER :: pi=3.14159265
a = pi * b%radius**2
END SUBROUTINE Discus
```

where, to define the type **Circle**, the module **Ringtypes** has been included. It is necessary to have an interface whenever a subroutine is to be used to define assignment, and in this case there would be

```
INTERFACE ASSIGNMENT (=)
   SUBROUTINE Discus (a, b)
   USE Ringtypes
   REAL, INTENT (OUT) :: a
   TYPE (Circle), INTENT (IN) :: b
   END SUBROUTINE Discus
END INTERFACE
```

There are a few things to notice about this example. The dummy arguments **a** and **b** are arbitrarily named and need not even be the same between the subroutine and the interface. The first argument has **INTENT (OUT)** and the second has **INTENT (IN)**, since the purpose of the subroutine is to give a value to the former based on the latter. In fact, Fortran will assume **INTENT (OUT)** and **INTENT (IN)** in these circumstances, so it is not actually necessary to give the **INTENT** attributes at all in this example. However, it is conceivable that the value of the variable **a** might depend not only on the expression **b** but also on the initial value of **a**; so **INTENT (INOUT)** is possible for the first argument of a defined assignment.

A defined assignment will be invoked whenever the objects on either side of the = match the combination of types and/or shapes given for the arguments in the interface block. The interface block could contain interfaces to different subroutines, corresponding to different type/shape combinations of the arguments, and it would then be a "generic" interface. Suppose that we wished to define assignments in either direction between integers and single characters: a suitable generic interface would be

```
INTERFACE ASSIGNMENT (=)

  SUBROUTINE C_to_I (i, char)
  INTEGER :: i
  CHARACTER(1) :: char
  END SUBROUTINE C_to_I

  SUBROUTINE I_to_C (char, i)
  CHARACTER(1) :: char
  INTEGER :: i
  END SUBROUTINE I_to_C

END INTERFACE
```

and the corresponding subroutines could be similar but including the executable statements

```
i = IACHAR(char) - 48
```
and
```
char = ACHAR(i + 48)
```

respectively.

Defined assignments can be great fun, and one more example will not go amiss:

```
MODULE Gettype
  TYPE Grab
  CHARACTER(1) :: c
  END TYPE Grab
END MODULE Gettype

MODULE Getint
  INTERFACE ASSIGNMENT (=)
    SUBROUTINE Smash (c, g)
    USE Gettype
    CHARACTER(1), INTENT(OUT) :: c
    TYPE (Grab), INTENT(IN) :: g
    END SUBROUTINE Smash
  END INTERFACE
END MODULE Getint

MODULE Getget
  USE Gettype
  USE Getint
  TYPE (Grab) :: get
```

```
END MODULE Getget

SUBROUTINE Smash (c, g)
USE Gettype
CHARACTER(1), INTENT(OUT) :: c
TYPE (Grab), INTENT(IN) :: g
READ (*,*) c
END SUBROUTINE Smash
```

With this, in any program unit headed by

```
USE Getget
```

a statement such as

```
qwerty = get
```

will lead to the character variable on the left (whatever its name) being evaluated by reading in one character from the keyboard.

12.11 Exercises 12.B

12.B1 (i) Write a derived-type definition block for a data type to be called **Species**, which is to describe a species of animal. The type is to be composed of a name (a 12-character string), the average weight, length and height of the animal (three real numbers), how many legs it has (an integer), and whether or not it can swim (logical). Choose sensible names for the components.

(ii) Write a type declaration statement for four scalar objects of type **Species**, calling them **panda**, **shark**, **whale** and **butterfly**.

(iii) Write a type declaration statement for a rank-one array of objects of type **Species**, having 15 elements and being named **big_cats**.

(iv) Write an assignment statement using a structure constructor to say that the **whale**, as in (ii) above, is called **cetus_____**, on average has a weight of 4578.0 kg, a height of 2.86 m and a length of 12.71 m, has no legs, and can swim.

(v) Write an assignment statement using a structure constructor to say that the fifth element of the **big_cats** array, as in (iii) above, has the name **snow_leopard**, average weight 46 kg, height 0.69 m and length 1.35 m, and has four legs, and can swim.

(vi) Write an assignment statement using a structure component to change the average weight of the **whale**, first set in (iv) above, to 4287 kg.

(vii) Write an assignment statement using a structure component to say that the **snow_leopard**, in (v) above, cannot swim.

12.B2 Write derived-type definition blocks for
(i) a person, the components being a 40-character name and a three-integer date of birth;

     (ii) a married couple, the components being two persons (husband and wife) and a date of marriage; and

    (iii) a family, the components being a married couple and an array with up to eight children.

    (iv) If **robinson** is the name of a variable of the **family** type, as in (iii) above, write expressions for the year of marriage of the couple who head this family, and for the value of the wife's name.

12.B3 (i) Write a function to calculate the two points of intersection of two circles, following the example in Section 12.8.

    (ii) Write code to allow the + operator to be used between two circles, defining the sum of two circles in a sensible way so that it will be possible also to define the difference between two circles in a consistent way.

12.B4   Write code to set up a special type (**Fuzzy**) composed of two real numbers to represent an estimate of the value of something together with the statistical error on that estimate. Write functions with defined operators to add, subtract, multiply and divide **fuzzy**s together, combining the errors according to the correct statistical procedure for uncorrelated errors. Using generic interfaces, include other functions so that the proper results are given also when **fuzzy**s are combined with ordinary real numbers. Write a square root function for a **fuzzy** argument.

12.B5 (i) Devise a derived type to represent efficiently sparse vectors, i.e. large rank-one arrays of real numbers, almost all of which are zero, only a few being non-zero. Write functions to carry out basic arithmetic operations between sparse vectors.

    (ii) Devise a derived type to represent sparse square matrices, i.e. data equivalent to a real rank-two square array with extents that may be very large but with only a few elements having non-zero values. Allow for a dimensionality up to 1024×1024, but with no more than 512 non-zero elements. The idea is to avoid storing all the zeros and thereby save space. Write a function to form the product of two sparse matrices.

12.B6   Write a subroutine and an interface block defining assignment when a variable of integer type is set equal to one of length-one character type. The integer is to be set equal to the ASCII code of the character or to zero for an unrecognizable character.

12.B7   The game of "Life" is based on a large two-dimensional rectangular array of cells, each of which is either "alive" or "dead". Each cell has eight nearest neighbours, i.e. the cells immediately above, below, to either side, and in the four diagonal directions from it. The state of the array changes generation by generation, with cells dying or being born. Each time, the fate of each cell depends on the number of live neighbours it had in the passing generation. A live cell will die if it had fewer than two or more than four live neighbours and will survive otherwise. A previously dead cell will come to life if it had two or three live neighbours. As parts of a program to model the game of life, devise a derived data type to represent the array of cells and write a subroutine that takes the array from one generation to the next.

There is an alternative set of rules for "Life", i.e. a cell with three live neighbours will become (or remain) alive, a cell with two live neighbours remains however it was, and all other cells become (or remain) dead. Investigate the game and compare the two sets of rules.

12.B8   Write a function subprogram that will take (as argument) a rank-one arbitrary-size array of real numbers and will return (as the function's value) the geometric mean of the array's elements. Design the subprogram so that it can deal efficiently with very large arrays containing large numbers, taking precautions against overflow and taking appropriate action if there is a zero element. The geometric mean of a set of n numbers is defined as the nth root of their product, i.e. the logarithm of their geometric mean is the mean of their logarithms.

12.B9   Set up a user-defined type that is a physically dimensioned real variable, i.e. a real number associated with powers of the fundamental MKSA dimensions, mass, length and time; ignore electric current in ampères (A). Write appropriate ancillary procedures, including a special output subroutine to write out a value in an appropriate format.

12.B10   Construct data types to represent lines and planes in three-dimensional space, with a function to calculate the line of intersection of two planes.

12.B11   Set up a new derived data type, a "rational" number, being the ratio of two integers not sharing a common factor.

This will involve a procedure to reduce two integers by dividing both by their highest common factor. This could use Euclid's algorithm working from the fact that the highest common factor of a and b is the highest common factor of b and c, where c is the remainder left when a is divided by b.

Write functions to carry out all the normal arithmetical operations on rational numbers.

12.B12   Design derived data types and operators to manipulate gravitating point masses in three-dimensional space. The basic data type should be a point associated with a mass. There should be an "addition" (centroid) operator, a totalized gravitational potential function, etc. This could be developed into a system for computing the path of a light test particle through a set of heavy point masses that could have time-varying positions.

12.B13   Look at the function **COPY_SCATTER** in Section 15.3. Write a version of it to be used when all the arguments have rank two.

CHAPTER 13

Pointers

"Pointers" are a powerful and elegant feature of Fortran, but unfortunately they are notoriously difficult to understand when you first meet them, mainly because it is not immediately clear what sort of problem they are there to solve. This chapter first explains the use of pointers in the simplest of circumstances, in relation to ordinary scalar data of intrinsic type. This is straightforward but will not seem terribly useful. Later sections will extend the idea to derived-type structures (Section 13.2), function results and dummy arguments (Section 13.3), and arrays (Section 13.5), and it is in these contexts that most powerful practical applications of pointers arise.

13.1 Simple pointers

Normally, there are two aspects to any data object in Fortran. First, there are the various attributes that describe what sort of object it is: its type, its name, its shape if it is an array, its length if it is a character string, and the other attributes that can be set by a type declaration statement (TDS). This set of details is sometimes known as the "descriptor" of the data. Second, there is the actual value of the object. When a data object is first declared, the data descriptor is fixed and memory space is set aside to hold the value of the data. If the TDS includes data initialization, that memory space will be filled with the initial data values immediately.

It is very important to distinguish clearly between the data descriptor, which is unaffected by the value of the data, and the value itself. The value may occupy a large amount of memory, especially if the object is a long character string, an array, or a derived-type structure. The descriptor will occupy relatively little space, but is essential for making sense of the data's value, because the content of an area of memory is meaningless unless the processor knows whether it is to be interpreted as a real number, a character, or whatever.

A TDS, then, normally sets up a data descriptor (name, type, etc.) and reserves memory to hold its value, and it may fill that memory with an initial value. A "pointer", however, is a data object that does not have its own reserved area of memory. In other words, a pointer is a data descriptor without its own space for a value. A pointer, as its name suggests, "points" to memory space occupied by the value of some other variable, the "target". At its simplest, a pointer can be regarded as a name that can be associated and disassociated dynamically with memory space occupied by other data. A pointer-name can therefore be used as an "alias".

A particular pointer can only point to data of a particular type. A pointer must be declared with a TDS giving its name, type, etc., and the attribute specification list must include the keyword **POINTER**. The effect is to establish a data descriptor, including the pointer's name, but without memory of its own to hold a value. It follows that there can be no initial value given when a pointer is declared (except with the **NULL** function described later below). When the program is executing, the pointer may be associated with a variable of the appropriate type by means of a special statement, a "pointer assignment" statement. Variables to which a pointer may be associated need to be declared initially with a special attribute, **TARGET**. The TDSs

```
REAL, TARGET :: a, b, c, d, e, f
REAL, POINTER :: p
```

set up the pointer **p** and the six real variables **a**, ..., **f** which can be targeted. A pointer assignment statement has a form such as

```
p => a
```

which would mean that the name **p** will henceforth refer to the memory space occupied by the value of the target variable **a**. After such a statement, **p** could be used as an alternative name for **a**, either in statements like

```
b = p**2/2.0
WRITE (*,*) p, b
```

or in

```
p = c + SQRT(d)
```

which, since **p** "points" to **a**, actually changes the value of **a**.

The pointer assignment statement (**=>**) by itself does not change the value of anything: it simply connects the named pointer to the named target. The general syntax of the pointer assignment statement is

```
pname => tname
```

where **pname** is the name of a pointer (i.e. a variable previously declared with the **POINTER** attribute) and **tname** is the name of a target. As far as we are concerned for the time being, **tname** must be the name of a variable previously declared with the **TARGET** attribute, but some exceptions to this will be mentioned later. The pointer and the target must be of the same type. Once a pointer assignment statement has been executed, the pointer is said to be "associated" with the target, but if the same pointer subsequently appears on the left side of another pointer assignment statement, the first association is broken and the second takes effect.

There is an intrinsic inquiry function, **ASSOCIATED**, which can be used to determine whether or not a pointer is associated with a target. **ASSOCIATED** (**pname**) is logical and has the value **.TRUE.** if **pname** points to any target and **.FALSE.** if it does not. This function has an optional second argument which may specify a particular target: the argument keywords are **POINTER** and **TARGET**, and the logical expression

```
ASSOCIATED(POINTER=pname, TARGET=tname)
```

is true if and only if **pname** is associated with **tname**.

As a simple example, this code fragment finds the value of the largest of six numbers:

```
REAL, TARGET :: a, b, c, d, e, f
REAL, POINTER :: p
   .
   .
   .
p => a
IF (b>p) p => b
IF (c>p) p => c
IF (d>p) p => d
IF (e>p) p => e
IF (f>p) p => f
WRITE (*,*) p
   .
   .
   .
```

This is a rather artificial example, since it does no more than

```
WRITE (*,*) MAX(a,b,c,d,e,f)
```

but the principle should be clear. The name **p** is being used to point to one of the six numbers **a**, ..., **f**. The value of **p** does not, itself, occupy any additional memory space, because **p** does not have a "value" in its own right. The above code could be written with **p** being an ordinary non-pointer variable, and with ordinary assignments (**=**) instead of the pointer assignment statements, but a little more memory would be taken up. In the above example, using a pointer has saved a trivial amount of memory space, but later we will come across array pointers that can in principle save a good deal of memory.

Any variable with the **POINTER** attribute may also be used as a target, and it is not necessary to declare the **TARGET** attribute as well as **POINTER**. If we have

```
REAL, POINTER :: p, q, r
REAL, TARGET :: a, b, c
```

then the statements

```
r => b
p => r
```

associate **r** with **b** and then **p** with **r**. Because **r** is a pointer, the effect of the second statement is actually to associate **p** with the target currently pointed to by **r**, i.e. to **b**. In other words, targeting is "transitive". The statements

```
r => a
q => r
p => q
```

associate **p** directly with the value of **a**, and the processor does not "remember" that this happened via **q** and **r**. If **q** or **r** is subsequently disassociated from **a**, **p** still points to **a**. Note that a target may be pointed to by more than one pointer: the code above leaves the target **a** pointed to by the three pointers **p**, **q** and **r**.

If **r** is a pointer and if a statement like

```
p => r
```

is executed at a time when **r** is not associated with a target, the effect is not to link **p** and **r** in any way but to leave **p** "hanging", and if **p** was previously associated with something else it will become disassociated.

There is a special statement, **NULLIFY**, which can be used to disassociate a pointer. The keyword **NULLIFY** is followed by a bracketed list of pointer names. Examples are

```
NULLIFY (p)
NULLIFY (q, r)
IF (ASSOCIATED(POINTER=p, TARGET=r)) NULLIFY (p)
```

A pointer declared within a procedure could be left with undefined status on return from that procedure to another program unit, so it is usually wise to declare pointers with the **SAVE** attribute.

Pointers can be of character type and may point either to a complete character string or to a substring, as long as the pointer was declared with a length matching that of the target. If the target is a substring, it must be part of a string declared with the **TARGET** attribute. The following code indicates how pointers could be used to work on a long character string while keeping memory utilization to a minimum.

```
! Wipe out the start of chapter 5
CHARACTER(*), TARGET   :: document
CHARACTER(9), POINTER  :: phrase
```

```
CHARACTER(2000), POINTER       :: startchapter
CHARACTER(9), PARAMETER        :: heading = "Chapter 5"
CHARACTER(1), PARAMETER        :: blank = " "
    .
    .
    .
Erase: DO icatch = 1, LEN(document)-1999
  phrase => document(icatch:icatch+9)
  IF (phrase/=heading) CYCLE
  startchapter => document(icatch:icatch+1999)
  startchapter = REPEAT(blank,2000); EXIT
END DO Erase
```

It was explained earlier that a pointer has a name and specifies the attributes of a particular type of data, but does not have its own memory space to hold a value. The pointer assignment statement, however, associates a pointer with memory space containing the value of an ordinary data object, the "target", and the pointer name can then be used as an alias for that target. Besides that, there is another way of associating a pointer with memory space without using a pointer assignment statement. It can be done by using the **ALLOCATE** statement, which we met in Chapter 12 in connection with allocatable arrays. The **ALLOCATE** statement can be used with the names of pointers, in which case the effect is simply to associate the pointer with an area of memory for data storage. So, if we have the statements

```
REAL,POINTER :: x
ALLOCATE (x)
```

the first establishes **x** as the name of a real scalar data object and the second allocates space to hold the value of **x**. Unlike the situation when a pointer is associated with an object previously declared as a target, there is no other name for the piece of data. In fact, the above two statements have much the same effect as

```
REAL :: x
```

ALLOCATE is an executable statement and it allocates memory space during the running of the program. Moreover, memory so allocated may be deallocated by the **DEALLOCATE** statement, just as for arrays (Section 12.1). This might seem rather pointless in the case of a single real variable, but it could be useful for efficient memory management if, say, a long character string were involved. For example,

```
CHARACTER (2**20), POINTER :: megabyte
    .
    .
    .
ALLOCATE (megabyte)
```

.
.
.

```
DEALLOCATE (megabyte)
```

sets up a one-megabyte character string and later allocates and deallocates the memory space dynamically. (Note, however, that the inquiry function **ALLO-CATED** must have an allocatable array as its argument and cannot be used to check the allocation status of a pointer.)

Fortran 95 feature not in Fortran 90

There exists an intrinsic function **NULL** of pointer type. The "value" of **NULL()** is a disassociated pointer. It can be used in a type declaration statement to initialize a pointer to have disassociated status, as in

```
REAL, POINTER :: x => NULL()
```

For more details, see Appendix F.

POINTER and TARGET

As an alternative to including **POINTER** or **TARGET** as an attribute in TDSs, it is possible to use separate "attribute specification statements" such as

```
TARGET :: x, y, z(12,12), jswitch
POINTER :: sheet(:,:)
```

These are declarative statements and must appear near the beginning of a program unit following the type declaration statements.

13.2 Pointers and derived types

Pointers are not restricted to being of intrinsic data types such as **REAL** or **CHARACTER**. A pointer may also be of derived type, as in

```
TYPE (Partnumbers), POINTER :: assembly1, assembly2
```

and this could point to any variable of that type as long as it has the **TARGET** attribute, such as those declared by

```
TYPE (Partnumbers), TARGET :: UKspec, USAspec, Pilotspec
```

The type **Partnumbers** could have been defined by the block

```
TYPE Partnumbers
  CHARACTER(24)  :: shortname
  INTEGER   :: nbits, idbit(30), nbit(30)
  LOGICAL   :: stockflags(30)
END TYPE Partnumbers
```

and there is no need for **POINTER** or **TARGET** specifications to be included within the type definition block. Just as for intrinsic-type data, derived types may be used in pointer assignment statements and as arguments of the functions **ASSOCIATED** and **NULLIFY**:

```
NULLIFY(assembly2)
IF (ASSOCIATED(assembly1)) assembly2 => USAspec
```

The name of an associated pointer may be used in structure components, e.g.

```
assembly1 => Pilotspec
item = assembly1%shortname
assembly1%stockflags = stockstatus
```

The third of these statements is an array assignment statement, because the component **stockflags** is an array, although the complete objects declared to be of type **Partnumbers** are scalars. The idea that a pointer may itself be an array will be discussed in Section 13.5.

A derived-type pointer, like one of intrinsic type, can have memory space allocated to it dynamically by **ALLOCATE** and **DEALLOCATE** statements, as in the scheme

```
TYPE (Errormatrix), POINTER :: pmeasured, temp, pfitted
.
.
.
ALLOCATE (pmeasured)    ! Space for data input
.
. (read in data "pmeasured")
.
ALLOCATE (temp, pfitted)    ! Space for calculation
.
. (using "temp" for temporary workspace,
. calculate "pfitted" from "pmeasured")
.
DEALLOCATE (pmeasured, temp)! Space no longer needed
.
. (write out result "pfitted")
.
DEALLOCATE (pfitted)    ! Space no longer needed
.
.
.
```

Here, the objects called **pmeasured**, **temp** and **pfitted** are derived-type structures and they could occupy a great deal of memory space; their components could include large arrays. The **ALLOCATE** and **DEALLOCATE** statements are being used to keep the program's memory requirements to a minimum during program execution.

So far in this section we have been considering pointers to structures of derived type. In addition, it is possible for a structure to have a component that is a pointer. For example,

```
TYPE Employee
  CHARACTER(30) :: name, jobtitle
  CHARACTER(10) :: idcode
  INTEGER :: ntelephone, idepartment, igrade
  CHARACTER(50), POINTER :: salarydatum
END TYPE Employee
```

The pointer **salarydatum** could be associated with data stored separately, e.g. in the array **salaries** as below:

```
TYPE (Employee) :: staff(3500)
CHARACTER(50), TARGET :: salaries(3500)
CHARACTER(10) :: code
INTEGER :: iselect
 .
 .
 .
code = staff(iselect)%idcode
DO i = 1, 3500
  IF (code==salaries(i)(1:10)) THEN
      staff(iselect)%salarydatum => salaries(i)
      EXIT
  END IF
END DO
 .
 .
 .
```

This selects the identity code (**idcode**) of a particular employee from the array **staff**, then runs through the array **salaries** until an element of **salaries** is found whose first ten characters correspond to that code. Then the **salarydatum** pointer for that particular staff member is associated with that element of **salaries**.

If pointers are used like this, cross-references can be created between different arrays of data. As another example, we could have a bibliography with data objects of the structure given by

```
TYPE Book
  CHARACTER(50) :: title, author, publisher
  INTEGER :: iyear, isbn1, isbn2
  LOGICAL :: statusflags(6)
  CHARACTER(200) :: notes
END TYPE Book
```

and a title index with elements of the type

```
TYPE Booktitle
   CHARACTER(50) :: title
   TYPE (Book), POINTER :: ref
END TYPE Booktitle
```

and an author index with elements

```
TYPE Bookauthor
   CHARACTER(50) :: author
   TYPE (Book), POINTER :: ref
END TYPE Bookauthor
```

The necessary TDSs might be

```
TYPE (Book), TARGET :: bibliography(400)
TYPE (Bookauthor) :: authorindex(400)
TYPE (Booktitle) :: titleindex(400)
```

and there could be procedures to read the bibliography from a disk file, create author and title indices, use the indices to interrogate the bibliography, make changes to the bibliography, and write the modified bibliography back onto disk. The important thing is that the bulk of the information is actually kept in a single array, **"bibliography"**, while the author index and title index are relatively short and can be scanned through relatively quickly. A similar job could be done without pointers, using a system of reference numbers, but the system would then be more complex, probably less memory-efficient, and possibly more error-prone.

It is possible for a structure to have, as a component, a pointer to a data object of the same type as the structure itself. The best-known example of this sort of thing is a "linked list", i.e. a set of data items each of which "points" to another member of the set, thereby linking them all together into an ordered sequence. Consider first the type

```
TYPE Link
   REAL :: x
   TYPE (Link), POINTER :: nextlink
END TYPE Link
```

and suppose that there are several objects of this type:

```
TYPE (Link), TARGET :: alpha, beta1, beta2, beta3, &
   gamma, ....
```

then we could have a situation where, say,

```
alpha%x = 0.34
alpha%nextlink => beta2
beta2%x = 0.79
beta2%nextlink => gamma
```

```
gamma%x = 0.04
gamma%nextlink => beta1
```

and so on. Each **Link** in the chain contains a real number and a pointer to the next link. We have created a sort of pseudoarray, i.e. a set of data items ordered into a particular sequence. In that example, each link in the chain had its own name (**alpha**, **beta2**, etc.). By using **ALLOCATE** statements, however, it is possible to be much more clever and to create a chain of arbitrary length while giving a name only to the first item. Using the same type **Link** as above, we could have

```
TYPE (Link), TARGET :: alpha
TYPE (Link), POINTER :: beta, gamma
READ (*,*) alpha%x
beta => alpha
DO i = 1,100
  ALLOCATE (gamma)
  beta%nextlink => gamma
  gamma%x = SQRT(ABS(1.0 - beta%x**2))
  NULLIFY (gamma%nextlink)
  beta => gamma
END DO
```

It is worth working through the meaning of this in some detail. First, there is a statement declaring **alpha** to be a targettable object of type **Link**. We will see shortly why it is given the **TARGET** attribute. The second TDS sets up names (**beta** and **gamma**) for two pointers of type **Link**. Being pointers, they have no memory space associated with them at this stage and both of them are going to be used dynamically to represent different data objects at different times as the program runs.

We then start the executable part with the **READ** statement, which simply allows a value to be given to the first component of **alpha**.

The **DO** loop is going to create a linked list of data items of the type **Link**, starting from **alpha**, and on each occasion the name **beta** will be used for the previously created member of the list and **gamma** will be used for a newly created member. So, before entering the **DO** loop, we have to start things off by pointing **beta** to the initial item, **alpha**. (That is why **alpha** was given the **TARGET** attribute.)

The first statement within the **DO** loop is **ALLOCATE(gamma)**. This has the effect of allocating memory space to hold data under the name of the pointer **gamma**. This is, as declared earlier, of the type **Link**.

Next is a pointer assignment statement, and this points the second component of **beta** to the newly allocated memory space of the object **gamma**. In other words, the previous member of the list points to the new one that is being created.

Next, a value is given to **gamma%x**, the first component of **gamma**: in this example, it is a simple algebraic function of the preceding value **beta%x**.

The next statement, the **NULLIFY** statement, defines the association status of the second component of **gamma**, i.e. the pointer **gamma%nextlink**. When the statement **ALLOCATE(gamma)** was executed earlier, the pointer **gamma%-nextlink** was created but its association status was undefined. In fact, the association status of any pointer is initially undefined. The **NULLIFY** statement ensures that **gamma%nextlink** is, for the time being, disassociated, in the sense that it would be given the result **.FALSE.** by the intrinsic function **ASSOCIATED**. (A reference **ASSOCIATED(gamma%-nextlink)** would give an error without the **NULLIFY** statement.) To summarize: at this point in the **DO** loop, memory space has been allocated for a new object called **gamma**, the second component of the previous object (**beta**) points to **gamma**, the first component of **gamma** has been given a value, and the second component of **gamma** has "disassociated" status.

The final statement within the loop points **beta** to **gamma**; this means that **beta** no longer represents the previous object in the chain, but now represents the new object that has just been set up. The first time we go through the loop, this statement switches **beta** from pointing to the first object in the chain, **alpha**, and points it instead to the second object. The second time we go through the loop, this statement stops **beta** from pointing to the second link and points it to the third: this is interesting because the second link is then left with no name at all, although it consists of actual data occupying actual memory space. Subsequently, it will be possible to get access to this data only through the pointer **alpha%nextlink**.

When the program goes through the **DO** loop on the second and subsequent times, the statement **ALLOCATE(gamma)** causes additional new memory space to be associated with the pointer **gamma**, and the previous association of **gamma** is broken off. Incidentally, this situation is different from the case with allocatable arrays: to **ALLOCATE** a currently allocated array is an error, but to **ALLOCATE** a currently-allocated pointer is not.

In our example, when the **DO** loop has been executed 100 times there will be 101 objects in memory, each containing a real value and a pointer to the next one. The first in the chain has the name **alpha**, and the last is still pointed to by **beta** and **gamma**, but the other 99 are not directly accessible. To look through the chain of data we would need code such as

```
beta => alpha
DO
  WRITE (*,*) beta%x
  IF (.NOT.ASSOCIATED(beta%nextlink)) EXIT
  beta => beta%nextlink
END DO
```

which uses the pointer **beta** to run from one link to the next. You know you are at the end of the list when a link is reached whose forward pointer has "disassociated" status.

This example has been explained in detail because it teaches some very important facts about the effect of the **ALLOCATE** and **NULLIFY** statements on pointers, because of the interesting concept of nameless data and because it shows how pointers within derived types could be used to invent pseudo-arrays if ordinary arrays did not already exist in Fortran!

The type called **Link**, above, included a pointer component so that one object could point to another. However, if a type were constructed with two pointer components, then each object could point to two others. For example, a family tree could in principle be constructed on the basis of the type:

```
TYPE Person
  CHARACTER(30) :: name
  INTEGER :: nyearofbirth
  TYPE (Person), POINTER :: mother, father
END TYPE Person
```

While on the subject of derived-type structures, there is a question that arises about the meaning of assignment statements between structures that have pointer components. Taking the example of the type **Person** immediately above, and having

```
TYPE (Person) :: candidate, brother
  .
  .
  .
candidate = brother
```

the assignment statement is equivalent to

```
candidate%name = brother%name
candidate%nyearofbirth = brother%nyearofbirth
candidate%father => brother%father
candidate%mother => brother%mother
```

the last two being pointer assignments and not ordinary assignments. In other words, an ordinary assignment statement between structures is equivalent to ordinary assignments between their non-pointer components and to pointer assignments between their pointer components. Of course, the programmer is at liberty to change this by providing a defined-assignment subroutine as in Section 12.10.

13.3 Pointers and procedures

When a procedure has an argument that is normally an ordinary variable or expression, the actual argument may be a pointer as long as it has a definite target at the time. This is true of intrinsic procedures as well as external procedures or module procedures. Using a pointer in this context is just like using it on the right-hand side of an ordinary assignment statement, and the pointer is no more than an alias for its target.

A slightly more complicated situation arises if a dummy argument is declared with the **POINTER** attribute within a procedure. In that case, the corresponding actual argument must also be a pointer, and an explicit interface to the procedure must be provided so that the processor always "knows" that a pointer argument is expected. When the procedure is referenced, what happens is that the dummy argument pointer is associated with the target of the actual argument. On return from the procedure, the actual argument is associated with the target of the dummy argument, but if the latter target is local to the procedure and is not saved (with the **SAVE** keyword) then the actual argument will be left with undefined association status. Incidentally, a dummy argument that is a pointer is not allowed to be declared with the **INTENT** attribute. Here is an example of a procedure with pointer dummy arguments:

```
SUBROUTINE Switchpoint (a, b)
CHARACTER(*), POINTER :: a
CHARACTER(*), POINTER :: b
CHARACTER(LEN(a)), POINTER, SAVE :: c
IF (LEN(a)/=LEN(b)) THEN
   NULLIFY (a, b)
ELSE
   c => a    ! Point c to the target of a
   a => b    ! Point a to the target of b
   b => c    ! Point b to the target of c
   NULLIFY (c)
END IF
END SUBROUTINE Switchpoint
```

It is also possible for a dummy argument to have the **TARGET** attribute, but here again it is necessary to provide an explicit interface to the procedure. The following procedure has both **TARGET** and **POINTER** arguments:

```
SUBROUTINE Randomfork (from, toleft, toright)
USE Typedefs
TYPE (Structure), POINTER :: from
TYPE (Structure), TARGET :: toleft, toright
REAL :: x
```

```
CALL RANDOM (x)
IF (x>0.5) THEN
  from => toleft
ELSE
  from => toright
END IF
END SUBROUTINE Randomfork
```

To round off this section, it remains to consider the case where a function result is a pointer. This is allowed in Fortran, but (as for pointer and target arguments) an explicit interface is then needed. The next example has as its argument a character string object that itself is a pointer, and the function result is a pointer to one individual character within that string:

```
FUNCTION Pickstar (string) RESULT (star)
CHARACTER(1), POINTER :: star
CHARACTER(*), POINTER :: string
IF (ASSOCIATED(string)) THEN
  k = SCAN (string,"*")
  IF (k==0) THEN
    NULLIFY (star)
  ELSE
    star => string(k:k)
  END IF
ELSE
  NULLIFY (star)
END FUNCTION Pickstar
```

When a function's value is a pointer, the **RESULT** notation must be used as in a recursive function.

13.4 Exercises 13.A

13.A1 Based on the type **Link** in Section 13.2, write a program that will read in and store indefinitely long sequence of integers from the keyboard. The input of the number 9999999 is to be used to indicate that the sequence has ended. After that, the program should calculate and write the average of the numbers.

13.A2 Write a function whose argument is a rank-one assumed-shape real array and that converts the array into a linked list of the type **Link** in Section 13.2. The function's result is therefore to be a scalar pointer of derived type.

13.A3 The derived type

```
TYPE Character_Chain
  CHARACTER(1) :: q
  TYPE (Character_Chain), POINTER :: qnext
END TYPE Character_Chain
```

244

could perhaps be used for variable-length chains of characters. This could offer some advantage over ordinary character strings because the latter cannot vary in length during program execution. Try to write a subroutine and interface to define the concatenation operator (//)for these character chains (but not for arrays of them!), a function like the intrinsic **LEN** function, and a subroutine that will write out a **Character_Chain**. This project could be developed much further, e.g. with functions to convert data between **Character_Chain** and ordinary character string types.

13.5 Array pointers

Towards the end of Section 13.1 it was shown that pointers can be used to economize on memory space if they are associated with long character strings. Likewise, pointers can be associated with derived-type structures (Section 13.2). In both these cases the pointers themselves were scalar, although pointing to large or complex structures. But pointers do not necessarily have to be scalar: Fortran allows for pointers to be arrays, in which case they have properties similar in many respects to the "allocatable arrays" described in Section 12.1.

Array pointers are declared with the **POINTER** attribute and with an array specification using the same colon notation as an allocatable array, as in the TDSs

```
COMPLEX, POINTER, DIMENSION(:) :: coefficients, roots
REAL, POINTER :: rates(:,:)
CHARACTER(2048), POINTER :: k2(:)
CHARACTER, POINTER :: tiestring(:,:,:)
TYPE (Person), POINTER :: family(:)
```

These statements fix the ranks of the arrays by the numbers of colons after each name, but the shapes are not fully determined at this stage.

Array pointers may point to array targets, or to sections of them, which would therefore need to be declared with the **TARGET** attribute as in

```
INTEGER, TARGET :: jobcodes(180)
```

Array pointers cannot be given the **ALLOCATABLE** attribute, because in a sense they are allocatable anyway. However, array targets may be allocatable arrays:

```
INTEGER, TARGET, ALLOCATABLE :: jobcodes(:)
```

Array pointers, like scalar pointers, may be used in pointer assignment statements. The targets need not be whole arrays: array sections are allowed, but not with vector subscripts. If the target is an allocatable array, it needs to have been allocated before the pointer assignment statement is executed.

One effect of an array pointer assignment statement is to determine the shape of the pointer: the pointer's extent in each dimension, and the bounds of its subscripts, are taken from the target array. Once an array pointer is associated with a target, it may be used in an ordinary assignment statement, representing its target's value. The inquiry function **ASSOCIATED** may be used with an array pointer just as with a scalar pointer.

It is possible to make use of array pointers without having named targets at all, with the statements **ALLOCATE**, **NULLIFY** and **DEALLOCATE**. Although these statements have been met previously in this chapter, it is worth reviewing here what they will do with array pointers as arguments.

ALLOCATE can be used to fix the shape of an array pointer and at the same time to create memory space to which it will point. The syntax is just like that for allocatable arrays and in fact the same statement could allocate a mixture of pointers and allocatable arrays, e.g.

```
ALLOCATE (rates(0:3,0:3), family(nlinked), &
jobcodes(143), STAT=mtest)
```

NULLIFY disassociates target space previously associated with its arguments, but does not deallocate it, i.e. the memory space still exists and may hold data, but is no longer pointed to by this pointer. It is important to remember that the **ALLOCATE** statement, with a pointer argument, allocates new space but like **NULLIFY** does not deallocate the old space. **ALLOCATE** can therefore be used repeatedly with the same pointer argument to create an unlimited amount of "hidden" memory.

The following example illustrates the use of an array pointer, the **ALLO-CATE** statement, and an assumed-shape array:

```
     .
     .
     .
REAL, POINTER :: x(:,:)
     .
     .
     .
ALLOCATE (x(1000, 1000))
     .
     .
     .
CALL Analysis(x)
     .
     .
     .

SUBROUTINE Analysis(z)
REAL, INTENT(IN) :: z(:,:)
     .
     .
     .
```

When **Analysis** is called, **z** takes its shape from **x**'s allocation. Because **Analysis** has an assumed-shape dummy argument, it needs an explicit interface.

To disassociate a pointer and also to deallocate the memory space it is necessary to use the **DEALLOCATE** statement, but this is only applicable if the pointer was originally allocated by an **ALLOCATE** statement: if the pointer was associated with a named target by means of a pointer assignment statement, **DEALLOCATE** cannot be used. Also, if an array pointer is associated with an allocatable array, then the allocatable array cannot be deallocated through the pointer: in fact, it is not permitted to **DEALLOCATE** an array pointer that is currently associated with an allocatable array.

To avoid confusion, it is best to distinguish sharply between two styles of array pointer usage:

1. not using data with the **TARGET** attribute, and without using pointer assignment statements, but using **ALLOCATE** and **DEALLOCATE** statements, and possibly associating the array pointers to assumed-shape dummy argument arrays by procedure reference;
2. using named **TARGET** data (which could be allocatable arrays), associated with the array pointers by use of pointer assignment statements.

Case 1 is very similar to the straightforward use of allocatable arrays described in Section 12.1, but with the crucial difference that an array pointer may be used in circumstances where an allocatable array may not, i.e. as a dummy argument, a function value, or a derived-type structure component. So we have array pointers being used *in place of* allocatable (or other kinds of) arrays.

Case 2 above is more likely to arise if the data is primarily stored in large allocatable arrays and the array pointers are used to latch onto parts of that data, i.e. with array pointers being used as ancillaries *alongside* target arrays of other sorts.

In practice, array pointers tend to be used most effectively in applications of type 1 above, to overcome the limitations of allocatable arrays. In particular, if a derived type is to contain a variable-sized array then it can only be done by using an array pointer. This is the basis of the implementation of the **VARYING_STRING** data type described in Appendix C.

13.6 Exercises 13.B

13.B1 Set up a system for dealing with a derived data type that is to represent sets of intervals on the real line. In other words, each object of this type may represent any number of non-overlapping intervals, each interval being defined by two real numbers (x_1, x_2), where $x_1 < x_2$. (Single-point "intervals" with $x_1 = x_2$ can be excluded for simplicity, i.e. we are dealing with mathematically "open" sets.)

Defined operators should be designed to calculate the sum (union) and product (intersection) of interval sets. There can be a function measuring the total extent of an interval set. Generalized forms of elementary mathematical functions (such as the cube root) can be written which map one interval set onto another.

13.B2 Following on from Exercise 12.B5, set up a derived type to handle sparse matrices using array pointers to achieve maximum flexibility in minimum memory.

CHAPTER 14

Overview

A few remaining features of the Fortran 95 language are described in the early part of this chapter. In particular we explain the use of procedure names as procedure arguments, which is important; and the **GO TO** *statement, which is a powerful statement but generally deprecated. This leads to a consideration of coding conventions and the movement towards defining a "core" Fortran 95 language.*

The later part of the chapter is devoted to a broader discussion of the programming process including the use of structure plans, the general layout of statements within a program unit, and the design of a program as a set of program units of different kinds.

14.1 Procedure names as procedure arguments

So far we have discussed procedures whose dummy arguments are data objects of various kinds. However, it is also possible for a procedure to have, as an actual argument, the name of yet another procedure. This could be useful if, for example, a procedure is to be written to calculate the integral of an arbitrary function. We could have a subroutine with the structure

```
SUBROUTINE Integrate (Func, alimit, blimit, result)
REAL, EXTERNAL :: Func
REAL, INTENT (IN) :: alimit, blimit
REAL, INTENT (OUT) :: result
REAL :: x! local variable
   .
   .
   .
       By references to Func(x), calculate an
       approximation to the integral of that function
       between x=alimit and x=blimit
   .
   .
   .
```

.
.
.

```
END SUBROUTINE Integrate
```

The attribute **EXTERNAL** in the first **REAL** statement tells the subroutine that **Func** is the name of a real-valued function. Note that a dummy argument that is a procedure name may not be given an **INTENT** attribute. In fact it is always the case that the procedure-name information is conveyed in, not out.

The above subroutine could be called with any actual function name as the first argument, as long as that function is also declared **EXTERNAL** in the calling program unit and actually exists as an external or module function. Naturally, the actual argument associated with **Func** must have the same characteristics as **Func**, e.g. in this example it must be a scalar real-valued function with one real scalar argument. A procedure with a procedure-name argument does not necessarily need to be given an explicit interface in the program unit that calls it.

An actual argument could alternatively be the specific name of an intrinsic function, in which case it should be declared with the **INTRINSIC** attribute in the calling program unit: but there are awkward restrictions on the names of the intrinsic functions that may be used in this way, so this is best avoided. In most realistic applications a dummy procedure will correspond to an external or module procedure. Even if actual arguments are intrinsic functions, the corresponding dummy arguments should still be declared as **EXTERNAL** in the procedure itself, because the **EXTERNAL** designation is used there simply to show that a dummy argument is the name of a procedure (be it external, module or intrinsic) rather than a data object.

The next example is inspired by a feature of the functional programming language Miranda:

```
FUNCTION Map (Func, array)
REAL, EXTERNAL :: Func
REAL, INTENT (IN) :: array(:)
REAL :: Map(SIZE(array))
INTEGER :: k
k = SIZE(array)
FORALL (i = 1:k) Map(i) = Func(array(i))
END FUNCTION Map
```

This is a function whose first argument is a function (of a scalar argument) and whose second argument is a rank-one assumed-shape array to all of whose members that function is to be applied. The result is an array of the same length as its second argument. Note that the function **Map** needs an explicit interface, both because it has an assumed-shape argument and also because it has an array-valued result. However, **Map** is not particularly useful in Fortran: although it would allow an array expression such as

```
Map (Cuberoot, dataset)
```

to be used, a better approach to the problem would be to ensure that functions like **Cuberoot** are written as elemental (Section 11.3) so that the expression

```
Cuberoot (dataset)
```

would do the trick by itself. There are other examples of amusing but not-very-useful procedures with dummy-procedure arrays, such as

```
FUNCTION Twice (F,x)
REAL, EXTERNAL :: F
REAL :: Twice
REAL, INTENT (IN) :: x
Twice = F (F (x))
END FUNCTION Twice
```

and

```
FUNCTION Compose (x, A, B, C, D, E, F, G)
REAL :: Compose
REAL, EXTERNAL, OPTIONAL :: A, B, C, D, E, F, G
REAL, INTENT(IN) :: x
REAL :: store
store = x
IF (PRESENT(A)) store = A(store)
IF (PRESENT(B)) store = B(store)
IF (PRESENT(C)) store = C(store)
IF (PRESENT(D)) store = D(store)
IF (PRESENT(E)) store = E(store)
IF (PRESENT(F)) store = F(store)
IF (PRESENT(G)) store = G(store)
Compose = store
END FUNCTION Compose
```

Compose(x) just returns the value of **x**. **Compose(x, EXP)** is equivalent to **EXP(x)**. **Compose(x, EXP, SIN)** is equivalent to **SIN(EXP(x))**, and so on.

In any procedure that calls this function, there must be an explicit interface to **Compose** because there are optional arguments. Each actual argument corresponding to one of the dummy arguments **A–G** must be the name of an external or intrinsic function, or it may be the name of an associated module procedure, or it may even be a dummy procedure name within the context of the calling procedure itself (with an **EXTERNAL** declaration) corresponding in turn to an actual argument in yet another procedure. This rather artificial example illustrates the point:

```
FUNCTION Arbitrary (aleph)
REAL :: Arbitrary, aleph
```

```
REAL, INTRINSIC :: EXP
.
.
.
CALL Caller (EXP)
.
.
.


SUBROUTINE Caller (Z)
REAL, INTRINSIC :: SIN
REAL, EXTERNAL :: Gamma
REAL, EXTERNAL :: Z
INTERFACE
  FUNCTION Compose (x, A, B, C, D, E, F, G)
  REAL :: Compose
  REAL, EXTERNAL, OPTIONAL :: A, B, C, D, E, F, G
  REAL, INTENT(IN) :: x
  END FUNCTION Compose
END INTERFACE
.
.
.
y = Compose (0.4, SIN, Gamma, Z)
.
.
.
```

The effect is to calculate `EXP(Gamma(SIN(0.4)))`, whatever the external function `Gamma` may be.

Incidentally, although a self-reference such as

```
Compose (x, EXP, Compose)
```

may have a clear mathematical meaning (this would be equal to `EXP(x)`), it would not be permissible as a Fortran expression because (a) a Fortran procedure is not allowed to refer to itself, directly or indirectly, unless it is defined with the **RECURSIVE** keyword, and, more to the point, because (b) the characteristics of the real argument `Compose` and those of the dummy argument `B` are different and do not match.

In Fortran, the use of procedure names as the arguments of procedures is in fact a rather awkward and inadequate approach to the larger question of allowing variables to represent procedures. For example, it might be nice to have the possibility of code such as

```
IF (x > 0.0) Trig = SIN
IF (x < 0.0) Trig = TAN
y = Trig (x)
```

but this is not permissible in Fortran. No procedure-name may appear on the right of an assignment statement (like **SIN** and **TAN** above) without arguments that give it a particular value. It is only as a procedure's dummy argument that a variable may "stand in" for the name of a function, and then only to transmit the name into the procedure, not out of it. The code

```
CALL Getfunction(Func)
x = Func(y)
```

to obtain the identity of **Func** from the subroutine and then apply it to **y**, could not arise in Fortran because the subroutine **Getfunction** could not be written: one might start with

```
SUBROUTINE Getfunction (Dummyfunc)
EXTERNAL :: Dummyfunc
   .
   .
   .
```

but then there is no way, in legal Fortran syntax, of associating **Dummyfunc** and thereby **Func** with some actual function. There exist "functional" programming languages that allow function names to be manipulated almost as flexibly as data objects, but Fortran is not one of them, although some proposals for a future version of Fortran (Fortran 2000?) have included "procedure variables".

Nevertheless, in practice the range of real-life problems that Fortran can solve seems undiminished by the fact that it is not a "functional" language in the full sense; and Fortran's existing syntax for procedure-name arguments allows adequately for code to calculate such things as integrals, zero-points, and the maxima and minima of arbitrary functions.

14.2 Varying-length character strings

Fortran allows for just five intrinsic types of data: **REAL**, **INTEGER**, **COMPLEX**, **LOGICAL** and **CHARACTER**, plus the obsolete type **DOUBLE PRECISION**. When data of **CHARACTER** type are declared, the lengths of the character strings must be specified once and for all. For many purposes this is an irksome restriction and it would be more convenient if the programmer could forget about the lengths of strings and leave it to the computer to allocate whatever memory is needed, which could vary during the execution of the program. In fact, Fortran's derived-type facility makes it possible for varying-length strings to be defined and used. Because of the usefulness of varying-length strings, they have been adopted as an auxiliary to the standard Fortran language. Full details are given in Appendix C.

14.3 INCLUDE

An unusual but potentially useful Fortran feature is the "**INCLUDE** line", whose general form is

```
INCLUDE character-string
```

where **character-string** is a character constant (not just the name of a character constant) that is the name of a file containing Fortran source code. The **INCLUDE** line is not, technically, a Fortran statement itself: but before compilation it causes one or more statements to be read from the named file and inserted at the position of the **INCLUDE** line. **INCLUDE** lines may be nested, i.e. the file referred to may itself contain **INCLUDE** lines.

INCLUDE could be used as a form of data input, as in

```
PROGRAM Demonstrate
real :: datastream(100) = (/(0.0, i=1,100)/)
INCLUDE "C:\f95\scratchdata"
  .
  .
  .
```

where the file called **"C:\f95\scratchdata"** might contain Fortran code such as

```
datastream = (/2.4, 3.1, 6.0, ......../)
```

allowing up to 100 real numbers to be input. For general purposes, a utility subroutine could be written like this:

```
SUBROUTINE Fortran95_Data (data)
REAL :: data(:)
INCLUDE "/home/counihan/f95_input_data"
END SUBROUTINE Fortran90_Data
```

while a file is arranged containing

```
data = (/......../)
```

The size of **data** would have to be declared in the program unit that calls the subroutine **Fortran95_Data**.

Because **INCLUDE** works at compilation time, the file to which it refers cannot be written by the program itself while executing. However, if the program runs repeatedly, there is no reason why it should not write a file during one run that will be read via an **INCLUDE** line and form part of the program for the next run.

14.4 GO TO: the pariah of Fortran

All the Fortran statements that we have met so far must start with a letter of the alphabet. However, before that it is possible to have a sequence of digits serving to label the statement, as in the examples

```
1 n=1+INT(x)
341 CALL RANDOM(x)
90 nh6 = Firstroot(g1,g2,g3,g4,g5,g6)
8 i=0; 9 j=0; 10 k=0
```

A label must have at least one non-zero character, it must be separated by at least one blank from the start of the statement itself, it must be unique within its program unit, it may not consist of more than five digits, and it may not have blanks embedded in it. Labels need not be in numerical sequence, although in the examples below they are ordered in the natural way. Labels can be used in Fortran in a number of minor ways that add nothing to the functionality of the language, but they have one important use: to redirect the flow of execution through a GO TO statement, which has the simple form

```
GO TO 341
```

or whatever might be the number labelling the statement you want to go to at that point. The keyword GO TO must be followed by an actual label, not by an expression or variable name. The GO TO statement may be contingent on an IF, as in

```
26 IF (x<0.0) GO TO 27
y = SQRT(x)
```

It can sometimes be handy to have a "do-nothing" statement to hang a label onto; a special statement, CONTINUE, exists for this purpose, so for example

```
27 CONTINUE
```

could complete the previous example.

GO TO statements can be used to write extremely opaque code very concisely, as in

```
READ (*,*) j
j = MAX(1,ABS(j)); k=0
1 If(MOD(j,2).EQ.1) GO TO 2
j=j/2; k=k+1; GO TO 1
2 j=j+k; IF(MOD(j,3).EQ.1) GO TO 3
GO TO 1
3 j=(j-1)/3
WRITE (*,*) j
```

Note that there is scarcely any point in ever labelling non-executable statements such as TDSs. It would be an error to **GO TO** a non-executable statement.

It is arguable that the **GO TO** statement does nothing that cannot be done with more clarity in Fortran in other ways (e.g. by calling a subroutine). However, **GO TO** is seductively simple to use and really comes into its own when you want to stitch a modification into a previously existing program. For example,

```
GO TO 999
  .
  .
  .
999 CONTINUE
```

will simply bypass all the code between those two statements and could be a useful trick when debugging a program. However,

```
Bypass: IF (.FALSE.) THEN
  .
  .
  .
END IF Bypass
```

does much the same thing. Because of the potential for its misuse, the once-ubiquitous **GO TO** statement is deplored by most teachers of Fortran and has become thoroughly disreputable, although it will always occupy a proud place in the history of computing. Nevertheless, **GO TO** (combined with the **IF** statement) can be used to simulate all of Fortran's control structures, the array system, and the procedure call system. In fact, a programming language with full mathematical functionality can be made up from little more that **IF**, **GO TO**, and the simple assignment statement.

Assigned GO TO

A special statement, **ASSIGN**, can be used to associate a particular statement label with an integer variable, as in

```
ASSIGN 10 TO ipoint
```

The integer variable could subsequently be used instead of a statement label in a **GO TO** statement, or instead of a format statement label in an i/o statement.

Computed GO TO

GO TO may be followed by a bracketed list of statement labels, and then by an integer expression, as in

```
GO TO (100, 31, 41, 51) kchoice
```

and the effect is that control passes to the first, second, third, etc. statement in the list according to whether the integer expression (**kchoice** in that example) has value **1**, **2**, **3**, etc. If the integer is larger than the number of labels listed, or is less than **1**, nothing happens.

Arithmetic **IF**

A statement such as

```
IF (handle) 20, 30, 40
```

transfers control to the statement labelled **20**, **30** or **40** according to whether **handle** is negative, zero or positive. The labels **20**, **30** and **40** in this example are arbitrary, but there must be a list of three (not necessarily distinct) labels. The name **handle** is also an arbitrary example: any real or integer expression may appear between the brackets.

14.5 Coding conventions and "Core" Fortran 95

Because of the language's history, Fortran contains a number of obsolescent or unessential features that a new programmer would be well advised to avoid. These are features which are not functionally necessary, i.e. there's nothing you can do with them that you cannot do without them. Many of them, mentioned only for the sake of completeness, are relegated to small type in this book.

It is strongly recommended that the obsolescent features of Fortran be avoided. Additionally, there are many features whose usage is a matter of taste and personal opinion. At the same time as avoiding obsolescent language features, it is a good idea also to adhere to voluntary conventions that will make your code easier and more pleasant to read, and therefore easier for somebody else to read and understand.

Some recommended coding conventions are, like the avoidance of obsolescent features, implicit in the examples given throughout this book (for example, the avoidance of the **DIMENSION** attribute). Some worth highlighting are

1. Stick to the convention described in Section 2.5 and followed in this book for the use of lower-case and upper-case letters – or, alternatively, use a different convention. But do not mix upper case and lower case indiscriminately!
2. Avoid **IMPLICIT** and stick to the default initial-letter convention for naming real and integer variables. (But beware – many Fortran experts disagree strongly with this!) Ideally all variables should be specified in type declaration statements except for the integers that are used as loop indices *within* statements, e.g. within array constructors .
3. If a word already has a meaning in Fortran, e.g. as a keyword in an intrinsic procedure, do not use it as a name for something else.
4. Use only double quotes, not single quotes (apostrophes), to delimit character strings.
5. In expressions and assignment statements with mixed data types, type conversions should be explicit except in the most trivial of cases (e.g. avoid expressions like **x+(1/2)** and **x==0** if **x** is real).

6. Use parentheses freely rather than depending on the rules for the order of operations (e.g. do not use expressions such as **x/2**y/2**).
7. Always label **IF** constructs, **DO** constructs, etc.

This list could be extended considerably. In fact, in many research centres and laboratories where Fortran is used extensively, there are coding conventions that enforce a "house style" of Fortran.

If we go further down this road, it is possible to identify a recommended subset of Fortran 95 – "Core Fortran", if you like – which retains all the elegance and power of the language while rejecting large parts of it that are unessential. "Core Fortran" proposals typically involve rather Draconian restrictions such as:

1. eliminating **GO TO** and statement labels entirely;
2. drastically pruning the i/o facilities;
3. always using generic rather than specific names for intrinsic procedures;
4. making all array dummy arguments of assumed shape, and all character dummy arguments of assumed length;
5. eliminating non-pure functions;

and, again, the list could be continued. No standard "Core Fortran 95" has been agreed by the programming community, but there is a widely-felt need to create a new, compact language out of the best features that Fortran offers.

14.6 Structure plans; a case study in program design

Of necessity, the bulk of this book has been about the syntax of Fortran and the rules the govern how programs *may* be constructed. Little has been said about how they *should* be constructed, or about how to systematically set about finding the Fortran solution to a complex problem. But, very often, the hardest part of a programmer's task is not the actual coding but the process that must precede the coding – finding out how in principle the problem can be solved, or finding the best solution if there is more than one, or perhaps, in some cases, establishing that the problem has no solution. And then, if the program is likely to be a large one, there is the skill of designing it as a set of program units. A simple program might be written straightforwardly as a single program unit, and for a slightly more complex problem a few external procedures might be tacked on to the main program unit when the need for them appears; but a much more systematic design process is needed for large-scale real-life programming.

This section and the next are an attempt to redress this imbalance by drawing attention to some of the skills involved in program design. In this section, we look at the problem-solving process behind the writing of a single-unit program to carry out a certain mathematical task. In particular, we focus on the concept of a "structure plan". In Section 14.7 we will review the structures of the different kinds of program units that might fit together as parts of a large Fortran program.

The problem we consider in this section is the "zero-point" problem. It is sometimes necessary to be able to find the zero-points of functions: in other words, for a given real function $y(x)$, to find where its curve crosses the x axis. Can we write a Fortran procedure to do this? We will analyze this problem in some detail to see how to proceed in defining a problem, deciding on a mathematical method of solving it, setting out a structure plan for a Fortran program, and finally writing the program itself. However, it is important to understand that there is no unique solution to this problem. No two programmers, no matter how experienced, would approach it in exactly the same way or arrive at exactly the same solution. Indeed, there does not even exist an *optimal* solution to the problem as posed. Before trying to optimize the solution, further questions would first have to be asked – is it important that the procedure should work quickly? Is memory space at a premium? With what precision is the zero-point to be found? How should the procedure respond to "pathological" functions, such as those having infinite numbers of zeros? Can the procedure assume that $y(x)$ is continuous? Or that it is differentiable? Questions like this are non-nit-picking: they are the important first step towards solving the problem and writing the program. When the answers to such questions are made explicit, they comprise a detailed "specification" of the procedure or program, i.e. a statement of how the procedure is required to perform under any circumstances. The programmer often discovers surprisingly late that the program specification is ambiguous or neglects certain possibilities, or that the problem itself is badly posed. It is no good asking for a programme to calculate the square root of a number without specifying what you will want if the number is negative – a trivial example, but it is mirrored in far-from-obvious ways in the posing of more complex problems.

But let us proceed. Let us write an external function called **zeropoint**.

What will be the arguments of **zeropoint**? One argument springs to mind, namely the function $y(x)$ whose zeros are to be found. So, we must write a "function of a function", with the function y being represented by a dummy procedure name. In Fortran, let us use **Y** as the dummy procedure name. So, we will have a function whose first line might be

```
FUNCTION Zeropoint (Y)
```

Then, the first declarative statements must specify the characteristics of **Zeropoint** and of **Y**. **Zeropoint** will be of type **REAL**, since we are dealing mathematically with real variables. Should **zeropoint** be a scalar or an array? If the function has more than one zero-point, and we want to find them all, then perhaps **zeropoint** should be an array. For the time being, let us take it that the task is to find just one zero-point. But this question must be borne in mind and perhaps reconsidered at a later stage.

The function **Y**, similarly, is of **REAL** type. Since **Y** is a function it must be declared here as **EXTERNAL**: this is just so that the compiler will know that **Y** is a function rather than an ordinary variable. So we have, so far,

```
FUNCTION Zeropoint (Y)
REAL :: Zeropoint
REAL, EXTERNAL :: Y
```

At this stage it is wise to think a little about how this function will be called from elsewhere. Must there be an explicit interface? What are the constraints on the actual argument corresponding to **Y**?

In fact, as **Zeropoint** stands, the rules of Fortran do not require it to have an explicit interface, although it would need one if **zeropoint** were an array. When **zeropoint** is referenced, the actual argument corresponding to **Y** must be the name of a Fortran function. It may not be a real number or a real constant. To ensure this, the actual argument must, in the calling program, be declared as **EXTERNAL** or **INTRINSIC**, or it must be a module procedure accessed by a **USE** statement or by host association in the calling program. Whichever option is taken, it does not affect the **EXTERNAL** statement in **Zeropoint** itself. In the context of the function itself, **EXTERNAL** is used to indicate the functional character of **Y** even if the corresponding actual argument will be an intrinsic function. In fact, the simplest way to work will be for the functions whose zeros are to be found to be supplied as external functions in Fortran. To avoid any error or inconsistency, they should have the same characteristics as **Y**, i.e. they should be scalar-valued real functions of a single real variable.

The mathematical problem

Well, we have started to write the program, but how are we going to solve the problem? For this, some mathematical knowledge and a little imagination are required. Patience may also be needed: few people would be able to think of a good solution without reflecting on the problem for some time.

One possible way forward is for **zeropoint** to choose random values of a variable **x** in the hope of finding by chance a value of **Y(x)** which is close to zero. This idea immediately raises a number of questions. Can we search the whole range of **x**, from $-\infty$ to $+\infty$? If there is a zero, can we be certain of finding it? With real numbers, the chance of finding an exactly zero value of **Y** is in most cases infinitesimal, so what do we mean by "close to zero"?

In fact, whatever algorithm might be used, a little thought shows that **zeropoint** cannot expect to find a zero-point exactly, but must use some sort of iterative process to approach it. The value of **zeropoint** will therefore be an approximation, albeit a good approximation.

Moreover, without checking the value of **Y(x)** for every possible value of **x**

– an impossibility since **x** is a real number – we cannot be absolutely certain of finding a zero of **Y** even if several zeros exist. It is therefore possible that no value can be assigned to **Zeropoint**. And if no zero exists, then of course no value will be found no matter how good the program.

The problems of searching over an infinite range of x are intractable, mathematically and computationally, and should be avoided. In any case, this problem is avoidable. For example, the zeros of the function $y(x)$ over the whole infinite x range are the zeros of the function $y(\tan(\theta))$ over the finite range $(-\frac{1}{2}\pi, +\frac{1}{2}\pi)$ in θ. By changing variables, an infinite range can be converted to a finite one. It is therefore reasonable to modify the specification of **Zeropoint**, and to ask that it looks for a zero-point only within a certain range. Specifying the range with additional arguments, we could have

```
FUNCTION Zeropoint (Y, xmin, xmax)
REAL :: Zeropoint, xmin, xmax
REAL, EXTERNAL :: Y
```

There is an additional advantage in doing this. The function **Y(x)** may not be defined for all values of **x**, and there may be values for which it is infinite. To avoid errors arising from calls to **Y** in such circumstances, the call to **Zeropoint** can limit attention to a range in which **Y** is known to be defined and finite.

Also, in view of the discussion above, **Zeropoint** should allow for the possibility that no zero-point value is found. One way of doing this is by introducing a fourth argument:

```
FUNCTION Zeropoint (Y, xmin, xmax, f)
REAL :: Zeropoint, xmin, xmax
REAL, EXTERNAL :: Y
LOGICAL :: f
```

and the logical argument **f** will be returned with a true value if and only if a zero-point is found. If it is not, **f** will be false and an arbitrary value (say, zero) will be assigned to **Zeropoint** itself.

This gives us a possible way of dealing with the problem of multiple zeros. If the **Zeropoint** function finds a zero of **Y(x)** at **x=xzero**, then **Zeropoint** could be called again with the interval **(xmin, xmax)** replaced by **(xmin, xzero)**. As long as the specified ranges are interpreted as excluding their boundary points, the latter call will not give a result repeating **xzero** but will return a second zero-point, if there is one, below **xzero**. If there is no such point, then we will know because **f** will be returned false. Having found (or not found) a second zero to the left of **xzero**, we can then turn our attention to the right of it by looking in the interval **(xzero, xmax)**.

It therefore makes sense to confine the specification of **Zeropoint** to the finding of a single zero-point of the function **Y(x)**. Apart from the fact that we could never be certain of finding all the zeros anyway, a program utilizing the

zeropoint function could easily look for additional zeros, if the programmer wished, by invoking **zeropoint** again for the intervals on either side of the first zero to be found. This vindicates the decision above to make **zeropoint** a scalar-valued, not array-valued, function.

A structure plan

But how are we to set about actually finding a zero point? The considerations above are important, but we still have not solved the heart of the problem. There are many different ways in which one might proceed, but one way is first to notice that if **Y(xmin)** and **Y(xmax)** are different in sign, then **Y** must pass through a zero value somewhere in the interval. If the chicken gets to the other side, it must cross the road. Unless **Y** is undefined or has infinite values in the interval, then if **Y** changes sign between two end points it has a zero between them.

This suggests the following program structure for **zeropoint**:

Step 1.   Evaluate **Y(xmin)** and **Y(xmax)**. For the time being, suppose that their signs are opposite so that ...

Step 2.   **Y** has a zero between **xmin** and **xmax**.

Step 3.   Let **xmiddle = (xmax-xmin)/2**, and evaluate **Y(xmiddle)**.

Step 4(a)   If **Y(xmiddle)** has the opposite sign to **Y(xmin)**:
Y has a zero between **xmin** and **xmiddle**.
Replace **xmax** by **xmiddle**.

Alternatively,

Step 4(b)   if **Y(middle)** has the opposite sign to **Y(xmax)**:
Y has a zero between **xmiddle** and **xmax**.
Replace **xmin** by **xmiddle**.

Step 5.   Since **Y(xmin)** and **Y(xmax)** have opposite signs, either 4(a) or 4(b) above must be true. Having replaced either **xmin** or **xmax** by **xmiddle**, we still have an interval within which we know there is a zero of **Y**; but the width of the interval is half what it was at step 2. Now, go back to step 2 (with the halved interval) and repeat steps 2–5 again and again, halving the interval each time, until the width of the interval is so small that, for all practical purposes, the zero-point has been reached.

This is a "structure plan". It is not Fortran, but it is a way of representing the layout of what might evolve into a Fortran procedure. All programmers use structure plans to some extent, often informally, according to their personal notation, without ever having been taught to do so. A structure plan is not a distraction from the business of writing the Fortran or a sign of intellectual weakness, like counting on your fingers: it is usually the quickest way to arrive at a sound program.

The plan above seems to be an acceptable algorithm for finding the value of **Zeropoint**: it is an iterative process which is guaranteed to converge on a suitable point. Since the width of the interval is halved at each iteration, an initial interval given by (say) **xmin=0** and **xmax=1** would give a value of **Zeropoint** precise to within one part in a million after 20 iterations.

The only remaining problem arises at step 1. What if **Y(xmin)** and **Y(xmax)** do not have different signs? If **Y(xmax)** has the same sign as **Y(xmin)**, then a possible course of action would be to search for a value of **x**, between **xmin** and **xmax**, for which **Y(x)** has the opposite sign to **Y(xmin)** and **Y(xmax)**. If such a value of **x** is found (say, **xopp**), then a zero-point exists both in the interval (**xmin, xopp**) and in (**xopp, xmax**). The algorithm of steps 2–5 above could then be applied to either of those two intervals.

So we need a way of searching the **x** interval (**xmin, xmax**) for a value of **Y(x)** of a certain sign. A suitable method would be simply to pick points at random until a value of **Y** is obtained having the desired sign. If, after a certain number of tries, no such point is found, then it can be taken that **Y(x)** possesses no zero in the specified interval and the program must return from **Zeropoint** with the logical "flag" **f** set false. How many tries should there be? Mathematically speaking, one can never be absolutely sure that **Y** does not change sign in the specified interval, as discussed above, but it would be reasonable to give up the search after, say, 10 000 tries.

To implement this procedure, step 1 above could be broken down into the following substeps:

Step 1(a) Evaluate **Y(xmin)** and **Y(xmax)**. If their signs are opposite move directly to step 2.

Step 1(b) Choose a random number (**xopp**) between **xmin** and **xmax**. Evaluate **Y(xopp)**.

Step 1(c) If **Y(xopp)** has the same sign as **Y(xmin)**, go back and repeat step 1(b). Do this up to 10 000 times, after which go to step 6. If **Y(xopp)** has the opposite sign to **Y(min)**, then . . .

Step 1(d) Give either **xmin** or **xmax** the value of **xopp**, and pass on to step 2.
⋮

Step 6.   No zero-point can be found. Set **f** to be false, give **Zeropoint** the value **0.0**, and return.

Note that, in step 1(d), it does not really matter whether **xmin** or **xmax** is replaced by **xopp**, but it would be more efficient to choose so that the resulting interval is smaller. Having arrived at a suitable structure plan, the function as a whole can be constructed as follows:

```
FUNCTION Zeropoint (Y, xmin, xmax, f)
REAL :: Zeropoint, x, x1, x2, xmiddle, gap
```

```
REAL, INTENT(IN) :: xmin, xmax
REAL, EXTERNAL :: Y
LOGICAL, INTENT (OUT) :: f

! 'epsilon' is used to exclude the ends of the interval
(xmin, xmax):
REAL, PARAMETER :: epsilon = 0.000000000001

! 'fraction' determines how precise Zeropoint is to be:
REAL, PARAMETER :: fraction = 0.000001

! number of times we look for Y to have a different sign:
INTEGER, PARAMETER :: number_of_tries = 10000

! logical variables, true if Y is positive:
LOGICAL :: ipos, ipos1, ipos2

! preset f to be true:
f = .TRUE.

! other auxiliary variables:
gap = fraction*(xmax-xmin)
x1 = xmin + epsilon
x2 = xmax - epsilon
x = 0.0

ipos1 = Y(x1)>0.0
ipos2 = Y(x2)>0.0

! Does Y(xmin) have the same sign as Y(xmax)?
Signs: IF (ipos1.EQV.ipos2) THEN
  f = .FALSE.
  ! Look for a Y-value of the opposite sign
  Search: DO itry = 1, number_of_tries
    CALL RANDOM(x)
    x = x1 + x * (x2-x1)
    ipos = Y(x)>0
    IF (ipos.NEQV.ipos1) THEN
      ! We've found one
      f = .TRUE.
      ! Select a new interval
      Select: IF ((x - x1)>(x2 - x)) THEN
        x1 = x
      ELSE Select
        x2 = x
      END IF Select
      EXIT Search
```

```
        END IF
      END DO Search
    END IF Signs
    ! Carry on if a zero-point can be found
    Found: IF (f) THEN
      ! Cut the interval in half
      Slice: DO
        xmiddle = x1 + (x2-x1)/2
        ipos = (Y(xmiddle)>0.0)
        ! Redefine the interval
        IF (ipos.EQV.(Y(x1)>0.0)) THEN
          x1 = xmiddle
        ELSE
          x2 = xmiddle
        END IF
        ! Jump out if we've gone far enough
        IF ((x2-x1)<gap) EXIT
      END DO Slice
      Zeropoint = (x2-x1)/2
    ELSE Found
      Zeropoint = 0.0
    END IF Found
    END FUNCTION Zeropoint
```

This can be regarded as a good first stab at what is required. But this procedure is still very far from perfect. What would be the result of `Zeropoint(TAN, 1.0, 2.0, f)`?

14.7 Program architecture

What about the overall form that a large program unit, or a program consisting of a large set of program units, should have? Unfortunately, in a book of this length it is impossible to give examples of the lengthy programs – running to tens of thousands of statements and more – that have been written to solve real-life problems and that are much closer to the real spirit of Fortran than the very short procedures and code fragments used to illustrate particular points in a textbook such as this.

This section, therefore, gives some indications as to how a large Fortran programme would in practice be designed. We will review the structure that any program unit must have, and particularly the ordering of declarative statements.

A "program unit" may be either a main program, an external subprogram, or a module.

BLOCK DATA

There is another sort of program unit that may occur in Fortran, known as **BLOCK DATA**, intended merely to preset the values of data items. The syntax is

```
BLOCK DATA
   .
   .
   .
END BLOCK DATA
```

where the keyword **DATA** may optionally be followed by a name. The final statement may be abbreviated to **END**. Between the two statements shown, one or more **COMMON** blocks may appear and data items from them may be specified by type declaration statements and/or by **DATA** statements.

A "subprogram" is either a function or a subroutine. Besides external subprograms, it is possible to have "module subprograms" contained within modules.

Statement functions and internal procedures

There also exist statement functions (Section 7.1) and internal procedures (section 7.3).

The general structure of a program unit may be represented by Table 14.1. Within this and the following tables, the number of the table giving the structure of the entity mentioned is included. For example, Table 14.1 includes reference to interface blocks and derived type definitions, whose detailed structures are given in Tables 14.2 and 14.4 respectively. Table 14.1 also includes reference to module subprograms, which are program units whose structures are themselves of the type given in Table 14.1 itself; this is a case where one program unit may contain another program unit.

An **IMPLICIT NONE** statement must appear before any other **IMPLICIT** statement. Apart from **IMPLICIT** statements, Table 14.1 excludes statements whose usage is not recommended. **BLOCK DATA** statements are on the same footing as **PROGRAM** statements. **FORMAT** and **ENTRY** statements may appear anywhere between the **USE** statements and the **CONTAINS** statement. **PARAMETER** statements may appear among **IMPLICIT** statements (but not before an **IMPLICIT NONE**) or among type declaration statements, interface blocks and derived type definition blocks. **DATA** statements are on the same footing as type declaration statements, but may also appear among the executable statements. Internal subprograms are on the same footing as module subprograms.

Within Table 14.1, a module subprogram has the same general structure as an external procedure. An interface block has the general structure shown in Table 14.2, within which an interface body has the general structure shown in Table 14.3 Although it is conceivable that an interface block might contain an interface body needing to contain another interface block (e,g. if a procedure

Table 14.1   The general structure of a program unit.

PROGRAM, SUBROUTINE, FUNCTION or MODULE statement

USE statements

IMPLICIT statements (Section 8.4)

Interface blocks (Table 14.2), derived type definition blocks (Table 14.4), and type declaration statements (TDSs)

Executable statements

CONTAINS statement

Module subprograms   (Table 14.1)

END statement

Table 14.2   The general structure of a interface block.

INTERFACE statement

Interface bodies   (Table 14.3)

MODULE PROCEDURE statements

END INTERFACE

Table 14.3   The general structure of a interface body.

FUNCTION or SUBROUTINE statement

USE statements

IMPLICIT statements

Interface blocks (Table 14.2), derived type definition blocks (Table 14.4), and type declaration statements (TDSs)

END statement

---

has a dummy procedure-name argument that is used as an actual procedure-name argument to another procedure) it is rather unusual.

Derived type definition blocks are of the form given in Table 14.4. Here, a **PRIVATE** statement is allowed only if the block is contained within the declarative part of a module (see cross-reference to Table 14.4 in Table 14.1). Also, the type declaration statements (TDSs) here are restricted in form compared with those of program units.

USE statements, type definition blocks, interface blocks and TDSs are all declarative in character and it is often said that they may appear in any order. However, one may depend on another and therefore they should appear in a logical order. For example, the declaration of a variable of derived type should not precede the definition of that type, and an automatic array should not be declared before other objects on whose properties it depends. The presence of

Table 14.4 The form of derived-type definition blocks.

TYPE statement
PRIVATE statement
Type declaration statements (TDSs)
END TYPE statement

Table 14.5 Simplified (non-module) program unit.

PROGRAM, **SUBROUTINE**, or **FUNCTION** statement
USE statements
IMPLICIT statements
Type declaration statements (TDSs)
Executable statements
END statement

Table 14.6 Derived-type or interface block module.

MODULE statement
USE statements
Derived type definition block (Table 14.4) or interface block (Table 14.2)
END MODULE statement

specification expressions (Section 11.9), evaluated at execution time, blurs the ideal distinction between declarative (compilation-time) and executable (execution-time) statements.

The scheme can be simplified considerably if the programmer chooses that derived type definitions and interface blocks are *always* to be encapsulated in modules, a convention that will also avoid a good deal of unnecessary repetition in a large program, and also that module subprograms are always to be in modules by themselves. Then the general structure of a program unit reduces to that shown in Table 14.5.

It is a good idea to distinguish sharply between the following different types of module:

1. Modules which each contain either an interface block or a derived type definition, as in Table 14.6.
2. Modules containing only data, i.e. TDSs, as in Table 14.7. However, it would be unusual to have **PRIVATE** or **PUBLIC** statements (or the equivalent accessibility attributes in the type declaration statements) in a module of this sort. If would only arise in a case like

268

Table 14.7 Data module.

MODULE statement
USE statements
IMPLICIT statements
PRIVATE or **PUBLIC** statements
Type declaration statements (TDSs)
END MODULE statement

Table 14.8 Subprogram module.

MODULE statement
USE statements
IMPLICIT statements
PUBLIC or **PRIVATE** statements
Type declaration statements (TDSs) for variables to be host-associated among the subprograms following
CONTAINS statement
Module subprograms   (Table 14.5)
END MODULE statement

Table 14.9 Generic external procedure.

MODULE statement
USE statements
Generic **INTERFACE** statement
Interface bodies to external procedures (Table 14.3)
END INTERFACE
END MODULE

```
MODULE Stack
INTEGER, PARAMETER, PRIVATE :: n = 10000
REAL :: array (n)
END MODULE Stack
```

where the programmer wants to declare a large array, and perhaps change its size easily at a later stage, without compromising the use of the name n in any other program unit.

3. Modules containing module subprograms, i.e. with the structure shown in Table 14.8.

4. Modules each containing a generic interface to one or more external procedures (Table 14.9); and finally

269

Table 14.10 Generic module procedure.

MODULE statement

USE statements referring to subprogram modules (Table 14.8)

PRIVATE or **PUBLIC** statements

Generic **INTERFACE** statement

MODULE PROCEDURE statements

END INTERFACE

END MODULE

---

5. Modules each containing a generic interface to one or more module procedures (Table 14.10). The **PRIVATE** and/or **PUBLIC** statements here might be to hide the names of the module procedures themselves, making them accessible only through a defined operator or defined assignment.

It is helpful to use **USE** statements liberally, encapsulating all procedure interfaces and derived types in modules, and it is better to use data modules than to have procedures with confusingly long lists of arguments. Also, it is wiser to use data modules than to rely on host association. However, there is a danger. The undisciplined use of modules leads to a form of "chinese box" programming that can be opaque and difficult for anybody else to understand – a modern counterpart of the vice of "spaghetti programming" that arose from over-use of the **GO TO** statement mentioned in Section 14.5.

The concept of a "scoping unit" may help to clarify the remarks above. A scoping unit can be thought of as a section of a Fortran program within which the variables can have arbitrary names and are not accessible outside the scoping unit. If variables in two different scoping units have the same name, it does not matter and they do not interfere with one another.

A scoping unit is any program unit, but excluding any derived type definition blocks, interface bodies, or (if the program unit is a module) module procedures contained within it. The latter are separate scoping units on their own account.

So, the general program unit in Table 14.1 is a scoping unit, which may contain three sets of other scoping units within it (the module subprograms, the derived type definition blocks, and the bodies in the interface blocks). Consequently, variables that crop up *within* a derived type definition, or that are used *within* an interface block, or which are local variables *within* a module subprogram, are not accessible to (and do not interfere with) the outer program unit in that they are embedded. Of course, the program unit can make use of a derived type – that is why the definition block is there – but it cannot interfere with the variables used to define its internal structure. Nor can the program unit interfere with the variables in an interface block, although of course it can use the keywords that might be defined in such a block.

The simplified program unit in Table 14.5 is a single scoping unit, and the program units in Tables 14.6, 14.7 and 14.9 also each contain essentially a single scoping unit each.

Table 14.8 shows the structure of a module containing subprograms: here, each subprogram is its own scoping unit with its own local variables. As the table indicates, there may be TDSs before the **CONTAINS** statement, and the variables so declared will be available by host association to all the subprograms that follow. It would probably be better programming practice not to have such data and instead to set up a special data module accessible by a **USE** statement in each of the subprograms. In other words, it is recommended that host association be avoided: to associate data from one scoping unit with another, **USE** association and argument association are the simplest and safest methods.

So, it is recommended that in a large program

1. Program units should be organized so that, within reason, each program unit is a single scoping unit. Interface blocks, derived type definitions, and module procedures should be individually modularized. Host association should be avoided.
2. **PRIVATE** and **PUBLIC** statements, and/or the **ONLY** keyword in **USE** statements, should be used to avoid the inadvertent association of data between scoping units.
3. Data modules should be used freely to avoid lengthy or complicated lists of procedure arguments. For example, all the complications associated with optional arguments can be avoided (except when the arguments are procedure names!) by putting the data into a module common to the calling and the called procedures.
4. Keep the main program fairly short, with a simple structure that makes the overall working of the program as clear as possible. Do not try to calculate anything in the main program – just use it as a switchyard for controlling the overall flow of the program. The following style has a lot to commend it:

```
PROGRAM Model
USE Data
CALL Stage1
CALL Stage2
CALL Stage3
END Program Model
```

5. Use functions to carry out self-contained tasks that depend on limited sets of arguments. A valuable rule (but perhaps an unrealistically harsh discipline!) is that *all* functions should be pure if they are not recursive.
6. Use different subprograms to do different sorts of job. For example, try to do all i/o in dedicated subroutines. Also, any processor-dependent code (e.g. something depending on an extended character set) should also be segregated.

7. Module procedures are really valuable only when there is a large group of related procedures (for example, to define and manipulate a derived data type) which can be regarded as general-purpose utilities. Such a module can be developed and maintained as an entity in its own right, and easily plugged into any program. The procedures described in Appendix C are an excellent example of this.

8. When designing a large program it is helpful to take an "object-oriented" approach and to concentrate initially on the data objects that are being dealt with. Derived-type data structures and arrays can be defined and put into modules as the first step. Functions and subroutines can then be written to carry out standard tasks with that data, e.g. reading it or displaying it. The job of programming is then primarily one of data structure design. With the right data structures in place, the actual flow of program execution will then appear much easier to arrange.

14.8 Exercises 14.A

14.A1   The following are variants of the same basic problem:
   (i)   Write a function `Fix(Proc)`, where `Proc` is an external function name, to find a "fixed point" of a complex function of a complex variable. A "fixed point" of a function $f(x)$ is defined as a value of x such that $f(x) = x$.
   (ii) Write a function `Crossover (F, G)` to find the value of `x` for which `F(x) = G(x)`, F and G being real-valued external functions.
   (iii) Write a general function-inverter `Inverse(F, a)` to return the value of `x` for which a specified function has a specified value. In other words, solve `F(x) = a`.

14.A2   Write a function `Infinite_Range_Integral(F)` to calculate the integral of a specified external function between plus and minus infinity. *Hint*: a useful mathematical trick might be to make the range of integration finite by a change of variable. For example, taking the inverse tangent of the variable will reduce the range to $(-\pi/2, +\pi/2)$.

14.A3   Write a real function `Interpol(Intfunc, x)` where `Intfunc` is an integer function of an integer variable and `x` is a real variable. `Interpol` is to generate a value for `Intfunc(x)`, so to speak, by an appropriate interpolation between the values that `Intfunc` has for integers on either side of `x`.

14.A4   The module `ISO_VARYING_STRINGS` is to be implemented in Fortran. You are asked to advise on whether the module should be based on representing a variable-length string by an array pointer or by a linked list of characters. Investigate the question and write a brief report making an appropriate recommendation. See also Exercise 13.A3.

14.A5   Write a program to try to find an even integer that can be decomposed as the sum of two odd primes in only one way, that way being as the sum of two *equal* primes. For example, $6 = 3 + 3$, but this example does not count because we can also have $6 = 5 + 1$.

14.A6   The Gamma function $\Gamma(x)$ is similar to the factorial function $x!$ but can have any real argument. It satisfies the recurrence relation

$$\Gamma(x + 1) = x.\Gamma(x)$$

which implies

$$\Gamma(1 - x) = -x.\Gamma(-x)$$

and these recurrence relations mean that the computation of the Gamma function for any real argument can be reduced to that of computing $\Gamma(x + 1)$ for $0 \leq x \leq 1$. When x is in that range, a fairly good approximation is provided by the power series

$$\Gamma(x + 1) = 1 + a_1 x + a_2 x^2 + \ldots + a_5 x^5$$

with

$a_1 = -0.57486\ 46$
$a_2 = 0.95123\ 63$
$a_3 = -0.69985\ 88$
$a_4 = 0.42455\ 49$
$a_5 = -0.10106\ 78$

Write a Fortran function for $\Gamma(x)$, taking into account that the function is infinite when x is zero or is a negative integer. Use your function to find the location of the minimum of $\Gamma(x)$ where $x > 0$.

14.A7   Stirling's approximation to the Gamma function is

$$\Gamma(x) = e^{-x}.x^{x-(1/2)}.(2\pi)^{1/2}.S(x)$$

where $S(x)$ is the series

$S(x) = 1 + 1/(12x) + 1/(288x^2) - 139/(51840x^3 - 571/(2488320x^4) + \ldots$

higher-order terms being generally negligible. It is valid for large positive values of x. Write it as a Fortran function called **stirling(x)** and investigate the extent to which it differs from the function written in Exercise 14.A6 when **x** is less than large. Modify **stirling(x)** so that it will write an error message and return a zero value if **x** is not large enough for the approximation to be good.

14.A8   Be a real programmer: do the sieve of Eratosthenes as a one-liner! A program to find prime numbers is a common textbook programming exercise, but a more challenging task is to write a single statement that will write out all the prime numbers not exceeding, say, 100.

14.A9   Write a module containing a derived-type definition and miscellaneous procedures for handing data in the form of quaternions.

14.A10   A project on derived types and program design:
        A polyhedron can be defined as the set of finite plane surfaces that are its faces. Simplify this representation by breaking down any faces that are

quadrilaterals (or polygons with more sides) into triangles. A polyhedron is therefore defined by a set of triangles in 3-space. Each triangle is defined by its vertices. To avoid duplicating the coordinates of the vertices, define the polyhedron as (i) the set of points which are its vertices, and (ii) the triangles which are its faces, defined as ordered triplets of (i). Each of the triangles is to have an inside-or-outside orientation defined by the cyclic order of its three vertices. A method must be found to determine this orientation.

We want to have a logical-valued function `Convex(Polyhedron)`, to determine whether or not a polyhedron is convex, and other procedures to calculate things like the volume and surface area of a polyhedron.

CHAPTER 15

High Performance Fortran

Some basic ideas about parallel-processor computing, and the motivation for High Performance Fortran (HPF), are outlined. The HPF extensions to Fortran's syntax, and its additional array-handing procedures, are listed and explained. Then we come to the heart of the chapter, dealing with the HPF directives and related procedures for aligning and distributing arrays of data among processors. We end with an account of "extrinsic" and "local" procedures, including the HPF Local Library.

High Performance Fortran, usually abbreviated to HPF, is a set of extensions to the Fortran language. HPF has been developed – and is still in a state of development – so that programs can be written in such a way that they will run as efficiently as possible on advanced parallel-processing computer systems. HPF is a de facto standard in industry and academia (and what follows is based on version 1.1) but it is not an international ISO standard and the implementation of HPF on particular machines is a matter of gradual development. This chapter is written for those who want to gain an insight into the future of Fortran, and of advanced scientific computing, and for those whose research will require them to write programs for parallel-processing computer systems.

We cannot attempt to describe here all aspects of HPF as comprehensively as Fortran 95 has been described in the rest of this book, but all the procedures and directives associated with HPF are mentioned.

15.1 Parallel processing

High Performance Fortran (HPF) is an emerging standard for the programming of advanced computers capable of carrying out data-parallel computation. "Data-parallel" means that similar instructions are being carried out simultaneously, by parallel processors, on several different sets of data.

Although today's conventional single-processor computers (such as the PC) are very much faster than their predecessors, and they continue to grow faster year by year, speed is still the limiting factor that prevents computers from solving certain problems. Because of the way in which science progresses, the solution to one problem always seems to pose new and more difficult problems demanding still more computing power.

One way to speed up a computation is to divide the task into a number of sub-tasks which can be carried out simultaneously and to build a computer with several processing units instead of just one. If the different processors can be efficiently orchestrated and synchronized, then in principle the speed of a computer system can be increased simply by adding extra processors. As long as hardware is relatively cheap, a system could contain hundreds or thousands of separate processors working in parallel, with a combined computation rate far higher than could be achieved by a single processor in the foreseeable future.

It also happens to be the case that large arrays of parallel processors are especially suited to solving some of the most interesting *kinds* of scientific problems that are of current interest. These are problems involving large arrays of data: examples are the lattices used for calculations in quantum chromodynamics in particle physics, simulations of the global climate system, numerical solutions of Einstein's equations in cosmology, simulations of astrophysical events such as supernova explosions, image processing, and the evolution of diverse ecologies of interacting organisms.

The new technology of parallel computation involves both hardware and software. The software problem is that of efficiently controlling a large number of simultaneous threads of calculation, and doing so through a general-purpose programming system based on a standard language. HPF is part of the attack on that problem.

The style of parallel computing reflected in HPF, and suggested by the types of scientific problem mentioned above, is often referred to as "data-parallel" computing. The idea is that identical or very similar instructions will be executed in parallel on all the elements of a large array of data, as opposed to applying an array of different operations to the same item of data. In the latter case, different processors would be supplied with different sequences of instructions, i.e. with different programs, but in data-parallel computing the processors all execute essentially the same instructions but are supplied with different streams of data.

To carry out data-parallel computing as efficiently as possible, the structure of the arrays of data, which is imposed externally by the nature of the problem, needs to be brought into a correspondence with the physical layout of the array of processors. The former needs somehow to be mapped onto the latter through the software that is the bridge between the abstract problem and the hardware that is being used to solve it. The task of mapping the first set of arrays onto the second – the mathematical onto the physical – is undertaken in HPF with compiler "directives", explained in Section 15.4.

15.2 Pure procedures, **FORALL** and **INDEPENDENT**

Having been developed before Fortran 95 was defined, HPF is an extension of Fortran 90, not of Fortran 95. However, some of HPF's innovations were also incorporated in the extension of Fortran 90 to Fortran 95 and therefore have already been dealt with elsewhere in this book. In particular, these are "pure" procedures (Section 11.2) and the **FORALL** statement and **FORALL** construct (Section 6.5).

Pure procedures, which are constrained to affect only local data, are intended to facilitate parallel computing. If a pure procedure is to be applied to an array of data, then it may be executed simultaneously on separate elements on parallel processors. Elemental procedures, being a sub-category of pure procedures, can also be executed on parallel processors. The keywords **PURE** and **ELEMENTAL** can be regarded as advice to the compiler provided so that the system will "know" that parallel execution can be exploited if the hardware supports it.

The **FORALL** statement and construct are also defined in such a way as to facilitate parallel processing. In a statement such as

```
FORALL (i=1:n) result(i) = Algorithm(data(i))
```

the procedure **Algorithm** must be pure and it must be possible for the assignments to be carried out in any order, or simultaneously, without the result being altered. However, consider a **FORALL** construct such as

```
FORALL (i=1:n)
  data2(i) = Algorithm1(data1(i))
  data3(i) = Algorithm2(data2(i))
  data4(i) = Algorithm3(data3(i))
END FORALL
```

Although this could be executed in parallel for each of the **n** elements of the data arrays, the construct as it stands might still not be optimized for the fastest possible parallel processing. To see why, it must be understood that the code will be executed by:

1. calculating **Algorithm1(data1(i))** for every value of **i**, and then
2. setting every element of **data2** to the corresponding value of **Algorithm1**, and then
3. calculating **Algorithm2(data2(i))** for every value of **i**, and then ...

and so on. This may involve parallelism *within* steps 1, 2, 3 etc., but the calculations and assignments are still sequential from one statement to the next. This is lockstep parallelism, with a synchronization across the processors after each step of the calculation. So, the time taken for the *parallel* calculation of the set **Algorithm1(data1(i))** will be the longest of the times for the individual values of **i**. This is like an army marching at the speed of the slowest.

Synchronization may in some cases be a virtue. With code like

277

```
FORALL (i=1:n)
  data2(i) = Algorithm1(data1(i), data1(n-i+1))
  data3(i) = Algorithm2(data2(i), data2(n-i+1))
  data4(i) = Algorithm3(data3(i), data3(n-i+1))
END FORALL
```

confusion could result if each statement were not fully executed for all values of the index i before proceeding to the next statement. Often, however, it will be possible to relax the synchronization. To achieve this, **FORALL** can be supplemented in HPF with a "directive" taking the form of the line

```
!HPF$    INDEPENDENT
```

and if this is inserted immediately before the **FORALL**, then the compiler is advised that the parallel strands of computation are completely independent of one another, and therefore that strong synchronization is not necessary. If the compiler is capable of making best use of this advice, a considerable saving in execution time may be made.

The line above is not a Fortran statement: it is known as a "directive". Several other HPF directives will be met below in Section 15.4. All HPF directives start with the characters **!HPF$** and it should be noticed that the initial ! means that the whole line will be ignored, as if it were a mere program annotation, by a normal Fortran compiler. So, the presence of HPF directives will not prevent a program from conforming to the Fortran standard, but an HPF compiler will detect the **!HPF$** string and will interpret the remainder of the line as a directive. A directive is not classed as a statement, and should make no difference whatsoever to what is calculated: it is simply advice to the compiler that should lead to an increase in the speed of the calculation. The directive **INDEPENDENT**, before a **FORALL**, does not of itself make the strands of calculation independent of one another: it merely asserts that is the case. If it were not the case (as in the last example above) then **INDEPENDENT** should not be used.

The **INDEPENDENT** directive can also be used with the **DO** construct (Section 6.4). In this context it is even more useful than with **FORALL**, because a **DO** loop normally involves no parallelism at all. But if we have

```
!HPF$ INDEPENDENT
  DO kipper = 1, 1024
        mackerel(kipper) = lemon + kipper**2
  END DO
```

then the compiler is informed that the cycles of the loop could, equivalently, be executed in any order or simultaneously. In this rather trivial example, it could be said that the programmer should have used a **FORALL** instead of a **DO** anyway, or that a good compiler should detect the independence without having to be told: but in more complex instances it can be far from obvious whether or not a **DO** loop can be parallelized.

278

For a DO loop, the INDEPENDENT directive means that no iteration can directly or indirectly affect the result of any other iteration.

With DO loops (but not with FORALL) the INDEPENDENT directive has an extended form including what is known as a "NEW clause". The syntax for this is

```
!HPF$ INDEPENDENT, NEW (list-of-names)
```

where list-of-names is a list of one or more variables occurring in the loop. The NEW clause means that the iterations are INDEPENDENT if the named variables are recreated afresh at each iteration through the loop. This amounts to saying that the named variables are local to the loop and need not be "saved" from one iteration to the next. An example is in the pair of nested DOs

```
!HPF$ INDEPENDENT, NEW (i)
  DO kipper = 1, 1024
    mackerel(kipper) = lemon + kipper**2
!HPF$ INDEPENDENT
    DO i = 1, 1024
      mullet(i, kipper) = mullet(i, kipper) +&
      mackerel(kipper)
    END DO
  END DO
```

where the first directive points out that the variable i does not need to be retained from one cycle to the next of the *outer* loop. That is in fact the case, and the outer loop could therefore be parallelized. This example also illustrates that INDEPENDENT directives may be nested with the DO (or FORALL) blocks that they refer to. The second INDEPENDENT means that the iterations of the inner DO loop above could be executed in any order.

15.3 HPF procedures

The Fortran 95 enhancements of the intrinsic functions MINLOC and MAXLOC, which have already been mentioned in this book, are part of the HPF specification. HPF also specifies a new intrinsic function, ILEN(i), useful for some bit-handing problems:

- ILEN (i) returns an integer equal to one less than the number of bits needed to represent i in "two's complement" notation.

More important are two new intrinsic functions that will tell the program about the arrangement of the individual processors comprising a parallel system:

- NUMBER_OF_PROCESSORS (), with no argument, gives the basic information of how many processors there are. On a conventional PC the result is **1**. Note that the value of **NUMBER_OF_PROCESSORS** is not the total physical number of "chips" in the whole computer system: it is, in effect, the number of parallel processing channels.

- **PROCESSORS_SHAPE ()** never has an argument. Its value is an integer rank-one array specifying the notional geometry of the array of processors, analogous to the "shape" of a data array. If there are 64 processors arranged in the form of a two-dimensional square lattice, then **PROCESSORS_SHAPE** has the value **(/8, 8/)**. The value of **PROCESSORS_SHAPE** corresponds to the logical connectedness among the processors and not necessarily to the geometry of their physical positions. It is quite possible, and for some purposes useful, for the processors to form a multidimensional hypercube even though embedded in three-dimensional space!

  NUMBER_OF_PROCESSORS has an optional argument, *dim*, which if specified points to the *dim*th dimension of the processor array, and the function result is the number of processors along that dimension. In the example just mentioned, **NUMBER_OF_PROCESSORS(1)** and **NUMBER_OF_PROCESSORS(2)** are both equal to **8** and no other argument would be meaningful. The **NUMBER_OF_PROCESSORS** function will not convey any information that is not already implied in the value of the array **PROCESSORS_SHAPE**.

HPF introduces numerous new functions in a library entitled **HPF_LIBRARY**. A number of these are to do with how the data is distributed among the processors (see Section 15.5). Other procedures are simply numerical, and would be relevant on any kind of computer, parallel-processing or not:

- **LEADZ (i)** is an elemental function returning the number of leading zero bits in the representation of the integer **i**.

- **IALL (array, dim, mask)** is a function of an integer array, and carries out a bit-by-bit **AND** combination of the elements along a particular dimension. It therefore has a concertina effect, the result having a rank of one less than that of **array**. The optional argument *dim* indicates along which dimension the elements are to be combined, but if **array** has rank one then *dim* may be absent and **IALL** will reduce the array to a scalar. The logical argument *mask*, if present, means that the **AND** combination is carried out only among those elements of the array corresponding to true values of *mask*; if *mask* is not a scalar, it must have the same shape as the array.

  As an example: if **array = (/5, 6, 7/)**, then in binary it is **(/101, 110, 111/)** and the **IALL** function will produce the number represented in binary by **100**, i.e. the value **4**.

  IALL is rather similar to the bit function **IAND** (Appendix B.2), except that **IAND** combines its two arguments whereas **IALL** combines elements from one (array) argument.

- **IANY** (array, *dim, mask*) does a similar job to **IALL**, reducing a dimension of **array** by carrying out a bitwise combination of its elements; but **IANY** carries out a logical inclusive **OR** combination rather than **IALL**'s **AND**. **IANY** is therefore analogous to **IOR**.

  IANY ((/5, 6, 7/)) produces the binary bit sequence **111**, i.e. its value is **7**.

- **IPARITY** (array, *dim, mask*) has a similar syntax to **IALL** and **IANY**, but yields the parity of each set of bits. **IPARITY** ((/*i, j*/)) is equivalent to **IEOR(i, j)**. **IPARITY** ((/5, 6, 7/)) is equal to **4**.

- **PARITY** (mask,*dim*) works not on bits within an integer but on a logical-type array (**mask**), and its value is a logical scalar or array. If present, *dim* performs the same role as in the functions above, indicating which dimension of **mask** is to be collapsed. The basic operation is the exclusive **OR** combination (i.e. like the **NEQV** operator) across the appropriate elements of **mask**.

- **POPCNT** (i) is an elemental integer function that looks at the sequence of bits within the integer **i** and returns the number of bits that are equal to **1**.

- **POPPAR** (i) is like **POPCNT** but yields the parity of the bit sequence within **i**, i.e. **POPPAR** is equal to **0** for an even number of **1** bits, and to **1** for an odd number.

We now move on to a series of HPF functions that transform or reconstitute arrays of data. These functions are not simple, but they are much less complicated than they will appear at first sight. We will deal with them in three groups, the first being the following:

```
ALL_SCATTER (mask, base, indx1, indx2, ..., indxn)
ANY_SCATTER (mask, base, indx1, indx2, ..., indxn)
COPY_SCATTER (array, base, indx1, indx2, ..., indxn, mask)
COUNT_SCATTER (mask, base, indx1, indx2, ..., indxn)
IALL_SCATTER (array, base, indx1, indx2, ..., indxn, mask)
IANY_SCATTER (array, base, indx1, indx2, ..., indxn, mask)
IPARITY_SCATTER (array, base, indx1, indx2, ..., indxn, mask)
MAXVAL_SCATTER (array, base, indx1, indx2, ..., indxn, mask)
MINVAL_SCATTER (array, base, indx1, indx2, ..., indxn, mask)
PARITY_SCATTER (mask, base, indx1, indx2, ..., indxn)
PRODUCT_SCATTER (array, base, indx1, indx2, ..., indxn, mask)
SUM_SCATTER (array, base, indx1, indx2, ..., indxn, mask)
```

These all have names of the form *xxx*_**SCATTER**, where *xxx* refers in each case to a basic operation similar to one of those carried out by a simpler function that we have already met. For example, **ALL_SCATTER** can be understood as an extension of the Fortran 95 **ALL** function. The **SCATTER** part of the name refers to a process that can be regarded as a generalization of the use of vector subscripts (Section 9.2).

A vector subscript is a way of picking out elements from a rank-one array and arranging them to construct a new array, also of rank one. The vector subscript is itself a rank-one array containing the indices that pick out the desired elements. If

```
kudos = (/91, 92, 93, 94, 95, 96, 97, 98, 99/)
```

and if

```
ipick = (/2, 4, 6, 8, 1/)
```

then, using **ipick** as a vector subscript, **kudos(ipick)** is an array expression equal to

```
(/92, 94, 96, 98, 91/)
```

The *xxx*_SCATTER functions extend the idea of vector subscripts to higher-rank arrays. Where there is an **array** argument, it contains the fundamental data on which the operation is being carried out. The value of *xxx*_SCATTER (**array,...**) will be an array whose shape will in general be different from that of **array**, being the same as that of the array argument **base**. The elements of **base** can be regarded as default values for the elements of the function's result.

Each argument **indx1**, *indx2*, *indx3*, ... is itself an integer array conformable with **array**. So, each element of **array** corresponds to a series of elements of **indx1**, *indx2*, *indx3*, ... However, the number of **indx** integers for each element of **array** must be equal to the rank of **base** and therefore to the rank of the function's result. Thus if **array** has rank two, each element

```
array (m, n)
```

will be associated with the element of **base**:

```
base (indx1(m,n), indx2(m,n), indx3(m,n), ...)
```

Leaving aside the argument *mask*, each of the functions *xxx*_SCATTER (**array,...**) above carries out this association for every element of **array**, i.e. for every value of **m** and **n** spanning the full shape of **array**. In other words, the elements of **array** will be "scattered" into a new array having the shape of **base**. If the optional *mask* argument is present, it must be a logical array conformable to **array**, and only when the corresponding element of *mask* is true will that element of **array** be used.

Notice that the **indx** arrays are generalized vector subscripts, but defined in such as way as to be conformable with the original array rather than with the result – this is opposite to the situation with vector subscripts.

We can now turn to some of the individual functions listed above.

COPY_SCATTER is particularly simple, since it merely copies elements from **array** into the result without carrying out any mathematical or numerical operation. In other words, the association mentioned above is an equality: if

array has rank two and if

```
result = COPY_SCATTER (array, base, indx1, indx2, ..., &
indxn, mask)
```

then its element

```
result (indx1(m,n), indx2(m,n), indx3(m,n), ...)
```

is in general set equal to the element

```
array(m, n)
```

However, if the elements of the **indx** arrays are such that no element of **array** is mapped into a particular element of the result, or if **mask** prevents it, then that element of result will be taken instead from **base**. On the other hand, if the elements of the **indx** arrays are such that several elements of **array** are mapped into the same element of the result, then one of them will be chosen by the processor in an arbitrary way to produce the result of **COPY_SCATTER**.

Now it starts to get easy! The **SCATTER** functions with prefixes **IALL**, **IANY**, **IPARITY**, **MAXVAL**, **MINVAL**, **PARITY**, **PRODUCT**, and **SUM** have results in which each element is obtained by applying the appropriate numerical operation to the element or elements from **array** that are scattered there, together with the corresponding element of **base**. Because **IALL_SCATTER**, **IANY_SCATTER** and **IPARITY_SCATTER** carry out bit-by-bit operations on integers, their arguments must be integers; **MAXVAL_SCATTER** and **MINVAL_SCATTER** may have either real or integer arguments.

Note that the **base** argument in each case serves the purpose not only of determining the shape of the function's result; it also provides default data to ensure that no element of the result will ever be left undefined.

For the special case of a rank-two **array** and a rank-three **base**, the effect of, say, **SUM_SCATTER** could be achieved with the Fortran 95 code

```
result = 0                 !array initialization
check = .FALSE.            !array initialization
DO i=1, SIZE(array, DIM=1)
   DO j=1, SIZE(array, DIM=2)
      IF (.NOT.mask(i,j)) CYCLE
      l=indx1(i, j)
      m=indx2(i, j)
      n=indx3(i, j)
      result(l, m, n) = result(l, m, n) + array(i,j)
      check(l, m, n) = .TRUE.
   END DO
END DO
WHERE (.NOT.check) result = base
```

The **xxx_SCATTER** functions with the prefixes **ALL**, **ANY** and **COUNT** do not have an argument called **array** but the logical argument called **mask** argument takes its place. **ALL** and **ANY** have logical-valued results, carrying out the obvious operations on scattered elements of **mask** with **base, base** being logical. For **COUNT_SCATTER**, **base** is an integer and the function adds the element of base to the number of true elements of **mask** that are scattered to it.

The next group of HPF functions that we must consider are:

```
ALL_PREFIX (mask, dim, segment, exclusive)
ANY_PREFIX (mask, dim, segment, exclusive)
COPY_PREFIX (array, dim, segment)
COUNT_PREFIX (mask, dim, segment, exclusive)
IALL_PREFIX (array, dim, mask, segment, exclusive)
IANY_PREFIX (array, dim, mask, segment, exclusive)
IPARITY_PREFIX (array, dim, mask, segment, exclusive)
MAXVAL_PREFIX (array, dim, mask, segment, exclusive)
MINVAL_PREFIX (array, dim, mask, segment, exclusive)
PARITY_PREFIX (mask, dim, segment, exclusive)
PRODUCT_PREFIX (array, dim, mask, segment, exclusive)
SUM_PREFIX (array, dim, mask, segment, exclusive
```

These functions carry out operations on the data in their first argument in ways very similar to the **xxx_SCATTER** functions described above. One difference is that **PREFIX** functions combine the elements along an indicated dimension (**dim**) rather than taking elements selected by a generalized vector subscript. The other difference is that the prefix functions do not simply combine all the elements of the array along that dimension (which would give a result whose rank would be one less than that of the first argument). Instead, "running totals", so to speak, are kept as the processor works through the elements. The "running total" at each element forms the corresponding element of the result, and the result has the same shape as the original data. As examples, it will be sufficient for us to look at cases where the first argument is a rank-one array and **dim** can therefore be omitted. Disregarding for the moment the later optional arguments,

```
    SUM_PREFIX (/6, 3, 0, 8, 8, 6, 9, 1/)
```

is equal to the array

```
    (/6, 9, 9, 17, 25, 34, 35/)
```

and the phrase "running total" has its literal meaning. **PRODUCT_PREFIX**, applied to the same array, would give

```
    (/6, 18, 0, 0, 0, 0, 0, 0/)
```

These are called "prefix" functions because the results involve the elements of the initial data up to and including that corresponding to the particular element of the result.

An optional *mask* argument allows some of the initial data to be ignored: for example, with

```
k1 = (/6, 3, 0, 8, 8, 6, 9, 1/)
k2 = PRODUCT_PREFIX(array=k1, mask=(k1/=0))
```

k2 would have the value

```
(/6, 18, 18, 144, 1152, 6912, 62208, 62208/)
```

The argument *segment*, if present, allows the prefix calculation to be made separately for different sections of the data. It is of logical type and of the same shape as the data. As we move from one element to the next, the process is restarted (just as at the first element) if and when there is a flip in the value of the corresponding element of *segment*. So, a new segment within the data is started whenever *segment* switches from false to true or *vice versa*. Following the example above,

```
t=.TRUE.
f=.FALSE.
k2 = PRODUCT_PREFIX(array=k1, &
  segment=(/t, t, t, f, f, f, t, t/), exclusive=f)
```

yields

```
(/6, 18, 0, 8, 64, 384, 9, 1/)
```

The argument *exclusive* is a logical scalar that says whether or not the elements at the boundaries are excluded (in effect, masked out) or included in the computations.

Prefix functions having been understood, there is no need to say much here about the "suffix" functions that form the third group:

```
ALL_SUFFIX (mask, dim, segment, exclusive)
ANY_SUFFIX (mask, dim, segment, exclusive)
COPY_SUFFIX (array, dim, segment)
COUNT_SUFFIX (mask, dim, segment, exclusive)
IALL_SUFFIX (array, dim, mask, segment, exclusive)
IANY_SUFFIX (array, dim, mask, segment, exclusive)
IPARITY_SUFFIX (array, dim, mask, segment, exclusive)
MAXVAL_SUFFIX (array, dim, mask, segment, exclusive)
MINVAL_SUFFIX (array, dim, mask, segment, exclusive)
PARITY_SUFFIX (mask, dim, segment, exclusive)
PRODUCT_SUFFIX (array, dim, mask, segment, exclusive)
SUM_SUFFIX (array, dim, mask, segment, exclusive)
```

These perform in exactly the same way as the prefix functions, but the arrays are scanned the other way around. An element of the result depends on the following, not preceding, elements of the initial data.

The bewildered reader may understand what all these functions do, but may wonder who on earth would want to use them and what problems they might solve. Unlike the frequently-encountered mathematical functions of Fortran 95, such as the trigonometrical functions or those for multiplying vectors and matrices, the HPF functions do not seem to correspond to familiar textbook problems. They are, nevertheless, powerful and useful tools for the construction of fast parallel algorithms.

15.4 Data distribution in parallel-processor systems

All the aspects of HPF mentioned so far have been enhancements to Fortran that could lead to valuable increases in program execution speed on a parallel computer system if the compiler is sufficiently sophisticated to take full advantage of them. However, it was assumed that the compiler itself – not the programmer – is aware of the number and configuration of parallel processors and can choose a good way of distributing the computing among the processors. In practice, however, if the optimum computing performance is to be achieved then the programmer must be aware of the configuration of the hardware and will need to give instructions to the compiler so that the arrays of data can be most efficiently "mapped" onto the array of actual processors.

These instructions are given with the help of a set of HPF directives. Apart from **INDEPENDENT** (Section 15.2) the possible directives have the keywords

```
PROCESSORS
DISTRIBUTE and REDISTRIBUTE
ALIGN and REALIGN
TEMPLATE
DYNAMIC
INHERIT
SEQUENCE
```

Like **INDEPENDENT**, any of these would actually appear on a line starting with the string **!HPF$**. With the exceptions of **REDISTRIBUTE, REALIGN** and **INDEPENDENT**, these are classified as "specification directives" and would appear among the declarative statements at the start of a program unit. The other three are "executable directives" and may appear only among executable statements.

The **SEQUENCE** directive is mainly to handle the disposition of data in Fortran-77-style **COMMON** blocks and could be useful if old code is to be converted to run on new parallel computers, but it will not be discussed further here.

Before discussing the above directives in detail, it is necessary to introduce the concept of an abstract array of processors. The abstract processors may be regarded as an intermediate stage between arrays of data (that depend on the particular program) and the actual physical arrangement of processors that comprise the parallel computing system. The distinction between abstract processors and physical processors is crucial. The programmer will wish to "map" the data arrays onto a set of abstract processors whose configuration is defined within the program. However, the abstract processors may have a different shape to the physical processor array and it is left to the compiler to finish the job by mapping the abstract processors onto the physical processors. The intrinsic functions **NUMBER_OF_PROCESSORS** and **PROCESSORS_SHAPE** (Section 15.3) return information about the physical processors: that information could be used by the programmer (or by the program) to decide what arrangement of abstract processors would best suit the problem in hand.

PROCESSORS

The **PROCESSORS** directive is used to declare one or more abstract arrays of processors, specifying an arbitrary name and a shape for each. The specifications of abstract processors are internal to the program unit in which they are declared. Valid **PROCESSORS** directives are

```
!HPF$ PROCESSORS:: hypercube (16, 16, 16, 16)
!HPF$ PROCESSORS:: serial (NUMBER_OF_PROCESSORS())
!HPF$ PROCESSORS:: single
```

The first of these might be used if the mathematical problem were based on data organized in a four-dimensional hypercubic array and if the programmer envisages that, in theory, the calculations could be efficiently organized on an array of processors having that connectivity. The physical processor array might be different (say, a 256×256 square) but the compiler is left to decide how the hypercube might best be projected onto the square.

In the second example above, the programmer envisages simply a one-dimensional sequence of parallel processing channels, and defines its size by taking the actual number of physical processors. The third example invites the compiler to treat the program as though the program were running on a single-processor computer, giving the processor the name **single**.

Having declared the names and shapes of the abstract processor arrays, the programmer need no longer be concerned with the physical processors. All the other directives described below deal with the relationships between the data itself and the abstract processors.

DISTRIBUTE

This is the fundamental directive for indicating the relationship between an array of data and an abstract processor array. Like **PROCESSORS**, it has a syntax not very different from the type declaration statement of Fortran 95: the **DISTRIBUTE** keyword, followed by some additional specifications, and then a double colon (::), followed finally by a list of the data arrays to which the directive refers. (As with the Fortran type declaration statement there is an alternative notation not using the double colon, but that need not concern us here.)

A very simple **DISTRIBUTE** directive is in

```
    PROGRAM Lets_Go
 !HPF$ PROCESSORS :: serial (NUMBER_OF_PROCESSORS())
    REAL :: x (1000)
 !HPF$ DISTRIBUTE (BLOCK) ONTO serial :: x
     .
     .
     .
```

Here, the processors are notionally arranged in a row called **serial**. The data in the array **x** is distributed between those processors. The keyword **BLOCK** dictates the mode of that distribution, and just means that **x** is divided into equal blocks of sequential elements, each block being assigned to one processor. If the number of processors is eight, then **x(1:125)** will go to the first processor, **x(126:250)** to the second, **x(251:375)** to the third, and so on.

In other words, a **BLOCK** distribution divides the array into contiguous chunks, one going to each processor, and each processor's chunk has a number of elements equal to

```
    SIZE(array)/NUMBER_OF_PROCESSORS()
```

The syntax of the **DISTRIBUTE** directive would allow any number of data arrays to be listed after the double colon, all of them being distributed in the same way across the arrangement of abstract processors, which is named immediately before the double colon.

A variation on the above is to specify the number of data-array elements which are to be mapped onto each processor. The number can be specified in brackets after **BLOCK** as in

```
 !HPF$ PROCESSORS :: serial (NUMBER_OF_PROCESSORS())
    REAL :: x (1000)
 !HPF$ DISTRIBUTE (BLOCK(200)) ONTO serial :: x
```

This maps **x(1:200)** onto the first processor, and so on, using five of the processors by the time all of **x**'s elements have been accounted for. If **BLOCK(n)** is specified, **n** must not be so small that there are not enough processors to hold all the elements of **x** with **n** elements per processor.

Leaving aside for now some complications to do with the dummy arguments of procedures, the general form of the **DISTRIBUTE** directive is

```
 !HPF$ DISTRIBUTE (format-list) ONTO processors : array-list
```

where **processors** is the name of the array of processors, and **array-list** is a list of data arrays (all of the same rank) that are being mapped onto the processor array by this directive. The purpose of **format-list** is to show how the distribution should be made: it is a list of indicators each of which must take one of the following forms:

```
BLOCK
BLOCK(number-of-elements)
CYCLIC
CYCLIC(number-of-elements)
*
```

There must be one of these indicators for each dimension of the data arrays. The meanings of **BLOCK** and of **BLOCK(...)** have already been mentioned. In the case of, say, a rank-two array, the code

```
!HPF$ PROCESSORS :: nodes (8, 4)
   INTEGER :: data (1024, 1024)
!HPF$ DISTRIBUTE (BLOCK, BLOCK) ONTO nodes :: data
```

would divide the data among the 32 processors by equal partitions of the first index into eight blocks and the second index into four blocks. So, **data (1:128, 1:256)** would go to one processor, and so on, dividing the square **data** into the rectangular sections

```
data (i*128+1: i*128+128, j*256+1: j*256+256)
```

where **i** runs from **0** to **7** and **j** runs from **0** to **3**. As in our earlier example, the effect of using **BLOCK(...)** would be to require each block to span the given number of elements in each direction.

The keyword **CYCLIC**, in place of **BLOCK**, means that the array elements along that dimension will be distributed around the processors one by one, like dealing cards. So, adjacent array elements will be distributed to different processors. With

```
!HPF$ PROCESSORS :: nodes (8, 4)
   INTEGER :: data (1024, 1024)
!HPF$ DISTRIBUTE (CYCLIC, CYCLIC) ONTO nodes :: data
```

one processor will receive the elements

```
data (1:1017:8, 1:1021:4)
```

and the other 31 will receive similarly separated sets of elements. Specifying **CYCLIC(...)**, with an integer between the brackets distributes the elements not one at a time but two, three or four at a time or whatever the integer is.

The final option mentioned above in a **format-list** is the asterisk (*). This symbol is used to indicate a dimension of the data array that is not to be separated among different processors at all, but should all but kept within one processor. This gives what is called a "degenerate" distribution. For example,

```
!HPF$ PROCESSORS :: triad (3)
  REAL :: t (6,3)
!HPF$ DISTRIBUTE (CYCLIC, *) :: t
```

will put $t(1,1), t(1,2), t(1,3), t(4,1), t(4,2)$, and $t(4,3)$ onto the first processor; $t(2,1), t(2,2), t(2,3), t(5,1), t(5,2)$, and $t(5,3)$ onto the second; and $t(3,1), t(3,2), t(3,3), t(6,1), t(6,2)$, and $t(6,3)$ onto the third.

As a further example, consider

```
!HPF$ PROCESSORS :: fourfold(4)
  REAL :: x(100, 100), y(100, 100), z(100)
!HPF$ DISTRIBUTE (BLOCK, *) ONTO fourfold :: x
!HPF$ DISTRIBUTE (*, CYCLIC) ONTO fourfold :: y
!HPF$ DISTRIBUTE (BLOCK(5)) ONTO fourfold :: z
```

This will distribute the array sections $x(1:25, 1:100)$, $y(1:100, 1:97:4)$, $z(1:5), z(21:25), z(41:45), z(61:65)$, and $z(81:85)$ to the first processor, and so on for the other processors.

Besides the syntax above, it is possible for the **DISTRIBUTE** directive to have its whole *format-list* replaced by, or preceded by, an asterisk. This has a meaning in relation to the distribution of dummy argument arrays in procedures, and is best discussed in the context of the **INHERIT** directive on page 294.

ALIGN

We have seen that the **PROCESSORS** directive defines an array of abstract processors, and the **DISTRIBUTE** directive states how the elements of data arrays should be distributed amongst them. **DISTRIBUTE** allows arrays of data to be split into blocks of adjacent elements, or to be dealt cyclically around the processors, or (using *) not to be separated at all but to go to the same processor. With sophisticated combinations of blocking, cycling or degeneracy along different dimensions, high-rank arrays can be distributed in complex ways so as to suit the mathematical logic of the problem and to speed up program execution by minimizing the amount of intercommunication that has to take place between different processors.

However, it could be a tedious and error-prone task to specify distributions separately for all the data arrays in a program. When groups of arrays represent data with similar structures, it is likely to be easier to align them with one another and then to distribute them all onto the processors with one **DISTRIBUTE** directive. This can be done in HPF with the help of the **ALIGN** directive, which maps one data array onto another. So, the directives

```
!HPF$ DISTRIBUTE (BLOCK, BLOCK) ONTO fourfold :: a
!HPF$ ALIGN WITH a :: b, c, d, e. f
```

will have the effect of aligning all six arrays, **a–f**, with one another and distributing them together across the processor array. In this example the same effect could be achieved just by listing all six arrays at the end of the **DISTRIBUTE** statement, but in more complicated examples the alignments of **b–f** with **a** could differ in detail and would have to be specified by separate **ALIGN** statements, while the final mapping of all the data onto the processors would still be achieved with the one **DISTRIBUTE** directive.

Another example of the **ALIGN** directive is

```
  REAL :: x(1:1000), y(1:1000), z(-499:500)
!HPF$ PROCESSORS :: singlefile(10)
!HPF$ DISTRIBUTE (BLOCK) ONTO singlefile :: x
!HPF$ ALIGN WITH x :: y
!HPF$ ALIGN WITH x(i+500) :: z(i)
```

The last line means that the element **z(-499)** is aligned with **x(1)**, **z(-498)** with **x(2)**, and so on up to **z(500)** and **x(1000)**. Notice that alignments and distributions are always made with reference to particular array indices. In this instance it is not sufficient to write

```
!HPF$ ALIGN WITH x :: z
```

because the directive tries to match the arrays index value by index value, not just lining up their total lengths.

The syntax of the **ALIGN** directive is

```
!HPF$ ALIGN WITH target (subscripts) :: array-names &
  (dummy-subscripts)
```

with *array-names* being the names of the arrays being aligned, and *target* the array to which they are being aligned. It is foreseen that the *array-names* will ultimately be distributed onto the processors through *target*, and therefore they are not allowed to appear separately in **DISTRIBUTE** directives of their own.

The *dummy-subscripts* and *subscripts* in the **ALIGN** directive are primarily to allow for offsets or unusual mappings between the indices of *array-names* and *target*.

Each *dummy-subscript* may be either an asterisk(*), a colon (:), or the name of a dummy integer variable (like the **i** in the example above).

Each *subscript* may be either an asterisk, a *subscript-triplet*, or an *integer-expression*. A *subscript* may refer to a dummy integer variable from the list of *dummy-subscripts*, as in the example of **(i+500)** given above.

As another example using specification expressions, we could have

```
      REAL :: central(n, n), square(n+2*margin, &
         n+2*margin)
!HPF$ ALIGN WITH square(i+margin, j+margin) :: central(i, j)
```

We saw that an asterisk may be used in the **DISTRIBUTE** directive to produce a degenerate distribution, i.e. ensuring that one or more dimensions of an array are not divided between the processors. A similar effect (sometimes called "collapsing" an array) can be achieved by including one or more asterisks among the *dummy-subscripts* of an **ALIGN** directive.

For example,

```
!HPF$ ALIGN WITH targ(i) :: data(i, *)
```

means that each element of **targ** has a complete row of **data** aligned with it. An alternative syntax, using a trivial subscript triplet for **data**, is

```
!HPF$ ALIGN WITH targ(:) :: data(:, *)
```

Unlike **DISTRIBUTE**, the **ALIGN** directive may also be used to replicate an array, or parts of it, by using an asterisk instead of one of the *subscripts* of the *target*. So,

```
!HPF$ ALIGN WITH matrixtarget(:, *) :: vector(:)
```

replicates **vector**, aligning a copy of it with every column of **matrixtarget**.

To see how these directives can be used in practice, the example below is a subroutine to multiply together two square matrices as speedily as possible. The processors are imagined to form a 20×20 array, but it is the compiler's task to map this abstract processor array onto the physical processors.

```
      SUBROUTINE Square_Matrix_Multiplication (a, b, ab)
      REAL, (INTENT, IN) :: a(:,:), b(:,:)
      REAL, (INTENT, OUT) :: ab(:,:)
      INTEGER :: i, j, n = SIZE(a, DIM=1)
!HPF$ PROCESSORS grid (20, 20)
!HPF$ DISTRIBUTE (BLOCK, BLOCK) ONTO grid :: ab
!HPF$ ALIGN WITH ab(:, *) :: a(:, *)
!HPF$ ALIGN WITH ab(*,:) :: b(*,:)
      FORALL (i=1:n, j=1,n) ab(i,j) = DOT_PRODUCT &
         (a(i,:), b(:, j))
      END Subroutine Square_Matrix_Multiplication
```

The first **ALIGN** directive makes **n** copies (*) of every (:) row of **a** and broadcasts the copies along (*) the corresponding (:) rows of **ab**. The second **ALIGN** makes **n** copies (*) of every (:) column of **b**, and puts the copies down (*) the corresponding (:) columns of **ab**. So, when the **FORALL** is executed, the processor that is calculating **ab(i, j)** will have local copies of the elements **a(i, k)** and **b(k, j)** for all values (:) of **k**.

TEMPLATE

Besides aligning data arrays against one another, it can be useful to define a pseudo-array, a "template", against which a variety of data arrays can be sensibly aligned, but without the template occupying any memory space in its own right. The template can then be mapped to the abstract processor array by a **DISTRIBUTE** directive.

A template can be regarded as allowing for another intermediate stage in the process by which mathematical data arrays are ultimately mapped onto the physical processor array. We can visualize the process like that shown in Figure 15.1:

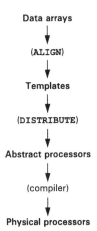

Figure 15.1 A model of the mapping process.

A template is defined by a special directive, **TEMPLATE**, with a syntax very similar to that of **PROCESSORS**. For example,

```
!HPF$ TEMPLATE :: chessboard (8,8)
```

defines a template with the name **chessboard**. It represents data structured in the form of an 8 × 8 matrix, but it occupies no memory itself. A template can be the **target** of an **ALIGN** statement, and it can be distributed to the processors like a data array by a **DISTRIBUTE** directive.

The following code sets up a large square template. It then aligns four smaller data arrays against it, with each data array pushed into one of the four corners of the template.

```
!HPF$ TEMPLATE :: square (64, 64)
   REAL :: bl(10, 10), br(10, 10), tl(10, 10), tr(10, 10)
   ALIGN WITH square (i+54, j):: bl(i, j)
   ALIGN WITH square (i+54, j+54):: br(i, j)
   ALIGN WITH square (i, j):: tl(i, j)
   ALIGN WITH square (i, j+54):: tr(i, j)
```

INHERIT

The **INHERIT** directive is used within procedures to ensure that the data represented by a dummy argument will be appropriately mapped.

When a procedure is called, a dummy argument can in fact be handled in any of three distinct ways: "transcriptive", "prescriptive", or "descriptive". The **INHERIT** directive arises in the first of these, but all three are briefly explained below.

1. Transcriptive mapping means that the distribution of the dummy argument data is "transcribed", i.e. "inherited", from the distribution of the corresponding actual argument data. To achieve this, the procedure must include an **INHERIT** directive naming the dummy argument or arguments for which this is to happen, as in

   ```
   SUBROUTINE Jabber (x)
   REAL, INTENT (IN OUT) :: x (:,:)
   !HPF$ INHERIT :: x
   ```

   which means that the assumed-shape argument **x** takes its distribution, as well as its shape and value, from the actual argument.

2. Prescriptive mapping occurs when the procedure specifies its own distribution for the dummy argument data, regardless of how the actual argument might have been distributed, as in

   ```
   SUBROUTINE Hiho (a)
   REAL, INTENT (IN OUT) :: a(16, 16)
   !HPF$ PROCESSORS :: procs (32, 32)
   !HPF$ DISTRIBUTE (BLOCK, BLOCK) ONTO procs :: a
   ```

   If this happens to match the mapping of the actual argument in the calling program, well and good. If the mapping in the calling program was different, then the argument data will be implicitly remapped on entry to **Hiho** and will be implicitly remapped again on re-entry to the calling program.

3. Descriptive mapping simply consists of specifying within the procedure that the argument data will have a certain distribution, with the requirement that the actual argument must conform to that. This is achieved with a special asterisk notation: in a **DISTRIBUTE** directive, an asterisk must immediately precede the distribution format:

   ```
   SUBROUTINE Silver_Lining (q)
   REAL, INTENT (IN OUT) :: q (16,16)
   !HPF$ PROCESSORS :: procs (32, 32)
   !HPF$ DISTRIBUTE *(BLOCK, BLOCK) ONTO procs :: q
   ```

   The asterisk means that the mapping is assumed from the calling program, although it is specified here anyway. If the actual and dummy arguments have distributions that do not match, it is regarded as an error, unless the procedure has an explicit interface. Interfaces may include HPF directives as well as ordinary Fortran declarative statements. If there is an explicit interface, the compiler will be able to ensure that data array remapping occurs.

REDISTRIBUTE, REALIGN and DYNAMIC

The **REDISTRIBUTE** and **REALIGN** directives have much the same syntax as the **DISTRIBUTE** and **ALIGN** directives, but they allow the redistribution (or realignment) at execution time of data that has already been distributed or aligned. **REDISTRIBUTE** and **REALIGN** can be regarded as executable versions of the corresponding declarative directives.

However, in order for a data array to be realigned or redistributed while the program is executing, i. e. "dynamically", it must have originally been declared to have the HPF attribute **DYNAMIC**. This can be done with a special declarative directive whose syntax is similar to that of **PROCESSORS** or **TEMPLATE**, e.g.

```
!HPF$ DYNAMIC :: arrayname
```

Procedures for data mapping

HPF includes a library of procedures known as **HPF_LIBRARY** that was mentioned in Section 15.3. Most of the functions described in that section are part of **HPF_LIBRARY**. In addition, **HPF_LIBRARY** has procedures that are intended to facilitate the aligning and distributing of data arrays. These procedures are:

- **GRADE_UP (array, dim)**, a function that produces an integer array which is a permutation of the indices of **array**. The permuted indices are such as to re-order the elements of **array** in ascending order of their values.

- **GRADE_DOWN (array, dim)** does the same as **GRADE_UP**, but sorts the elements of **array** in descending order.

- **HPF_ALIGNMENT (alignee, lb, ub, stride, axis_map, identity_map, dynamic, ncopies)** is an inquiry subroutine associated with the **ALIGN directive**. It returns information about the alignment of **alignee**. It can be used to return integer arrays containing the lower bounds (**lb**), upper bounds (**ub**) and strides (**stride**) governing the correspondence between the dimensions of the alignee and its alignment target. The **axis_map** argument is normally an array containing successive integers (**1, 2, 3, ...**) but in a permuted order to indicate if the dimensions of the alignee were permuted when it was aligned to its target. If there is a "collapsed" (i.e. "degenerate") dimension, then that dimension is indicated by a zero value in **axis_map**. The **identity_map** argument is a scalar logical variable used simply to indicate if the alignee was aligned in an identical fashion onto a target of the same shape, and **dynamic** likewise indicates if the alignee has the **DYNAMIC** attribute, i.e. can be realigned dynamically. Finally, the scalar integer **ncopies** is the number of copies that were made of each element of the alignee if replication was involved in the alignment.

- **HPF_TEMPLATE (alignee, template_rank, lb, ub, axis_type, axis_info, number_aligned, dynamic)** is an inquiry subroutine that can largely be understood with reference to **HPF_ALIGNMENT**. **HPF_TEMPLATE** also gives information about the alignment of **alignee**, but it assumes that the alignment was to a template and it gives the information relating to that template. The **axis-type** argument is a character array indicating whether each dimension of the alignee is aligned in a **"NORMAL"**, **"REPLICATED"** or **"SINGLE"** way to the template. If **"NORMAL"**, **axis_info** is an array saying which dimension of the template is aligned to which dimension of the alignee. If **"REPLICATED"**, **axis_info** is like **ncopies** for this particular dimension. The **"SINGLE"** value means that, in this dimension, the alignee is mapped to just one coordinate of the template, in which case **axis_info** says which one.

- **HPF_DISTRIBUTION (distributee, axis_type, axis_info, processors_rank, processors_shape)** is a subroutine whose usage follows the same pattern as **HPF_ALIGNMENT** and **HPF_TEMPLATE**. It is concerned with the ultimate distribution of the **distributee** array onto an abstract processor array. The **axis_type** argument is a character array, as in **HPF_TEMPLATE**, but the values that may be returned are **"BLOCK"**, **"CYCLIC"** and **"COLLAPSED"**. In the first two cases, **axis_info** will contain block sizes (i.e. the integers in brackets after **BLOCK** or **CYCLE** in a **DISTRIBUTE** directive).

15.5 Extrinsic procedures

All the procedures so far described in this chapter, whether written by the programmer or provided as part of HPF, can be imagined to be executed globally for the whole of the computer. Although the computer may consist of a number of parallel processors, and the data may be divided among them, any ordinary procedure is executed centrally and controls all the processors. This is an aspect of the SIMD (single instruction, multiple data) paradigm on which HPF is based.

In reality, however, and depending on the computer's architecture, a compiled procedure may be replicated and executed separately on the different processors. This might already happen behind the scenes, so to speak, under the compiler's control, e.g. for Fortran's simple intrinsic procedures. HPF gives the programmer an explicit method of writing procedures that are to be executed separately on different processors. They are said to be "local" procedures.

Local procedures are one of a new class of procedures called, in HPF terminology, "extrinsic" procedures. If extrinsic procedures are to be called from an HPF program, they must have an explicit interface, and they are defined by specifying **EXTRINSIC** in that interface. The interface to an extrinsic function is of the form:

```
INTERFACE
  EXTRINSIC (HPF_LOCAL) FUNCTION ...
  .
  .
  .
  END FUNCTION ...
END INTERFACE
```

The keyword **HPF_LOCAL**, in brackets, indicates what sort of extrinsic function is being used. As the term suggests, an **HPF_LOCAL** extrinsic function is written in the HPF language and is a local function in the sense explained above, i.e. it will execute locally and independently on individual processors.

There may be other sorts of extrinsic procedures. For example, the syntax is intended to serve as a way of interfacing HPF to programs written in the language C, in which case we might have

```
EXTRINSIC (C) FUNCTION ....
```

The sorts of extrinsic procedures supported by different implementations of HPF will vary. There is no guarantee that **EXTRINSIC (C)** will actually work on a particular installation. However, any HPF-conforming system should allow for local procedures with the **HPF_LOCAL** keyword.

An extrinsic local procedure, in HPF, may look superficially like any other HPF procedure, but when such a procedure is written there are a number of obvious constraints arising from the local nature of its execution. It should work with local data, i.e. data that has been distributed to the particular processor, although one should bear in mind that **ALIGN** directives in the main program may replicate any array data that needs to be broadcast to all the processors. Scalar arguments will be automatically broadcast to all the processors. An extrinsic function interface may specify global arrays as arguments, but each locally-running copy of it will only have access to a section of it that is distributed to one processor, and the dummy arguments must have assumed shape. Local procedures cannot gain access to global data through modules. Local procedures may invoke other local procedures, but not non-extrinsic ("global") HPF procedures. Extrinsic local procedures are not allowed to be recursive and should be pure, although the syntax above does not allow for the **PURE** keyword.

An extrinsic local procedure cannot be invoked from a **FORALL** construct or from within an **INDEPENDENT** loop, because in those circumstances it is already expected that execution will take place in parallel on separate processors – in a way, **FORALL** and **INDEPENDENT** already go part-way (compiler permitting) towards doing the job of local procedures.

The processors are synchronized before a local procedure is invoked, and re-synchronized on return from all the processors. If the local procedure is a scalar-valued function, the values returned from all the processors should be the same, except that the global version of the procedure may be declared to be a vector with one element corresponding to the value returned by each processor.

15.6 HPF local procedures

Although a local procedure is executed separately on a number of processors, it is necessarily written in a single "extrinsic" version, and it might therefore be thought that it must execute in exactly the same fashion on every processor, apart from differences in the values of the data arrays. It might also be thought that a local procedure can obtain no information at all about the global situation. But this is not so: HPF provides a number of special procedures that can be used to give useful and processor-specific information to a local procedure.

- **MY_PROCESSOR()** is an argument-free function returning an integer identifying the local physical processor. All the processors are imagined to be numbered in sequence (**1, 2, 3, ...**).

- **LOCAL_BLKCNT (array, dim, proc)** returns the number of blocks of elements from **array**, along the dimension **dim**, that are distributed to the processor numbered **proc**.

- **LOCAL_LINDEX (array, dim, proc) and LOCAL_UINDEX (array, dim, proc)** return the lower and upper index values of elements from **array**, in the dimension indicated, that are distributed to the processor numbered **proc**.

These procedures obviously enable a local procedure, running on a single processor, to find out which processor it is and to establish which bits of the global data arrays have been distributed to it.

The procedures **HPF_ALIGNMENT**, **HPF_TEMPLATE** and **HPF_DISTRIBUTION**, already described in Section 15.4, will also work when called from local procedures. However, their results will be different – when called locally, they are interpreted in terms of the local data arrays on the particular processor. To give the same global information when called from local procedures, three new procedures have been defined. They, and the others below, are part of a procedure library known as **HPF_LOCAL_LIBRARY**:

- **GLOBAL_ALIGNMENT (array, ...)** is the same as **HPF_ALIGNMENT** but gives the global information when called locally.

- **GLOBAL_DISTRIBUTION (array, ...)** is like **HPF_DISTRIBUTION**.

- **GLOBAL_TEMPLATE (array, ...)** is like **HPF_TEMPLATE**.

- **GLOBAL_LBOUND (array, dim)** is a function that takes as its *array* argument the local (dummy) name of an array, and its value is the lower index bound (in the dimension indicated) of the corresponding whole actual array.

- **GLOBAL_UBOUND (array, dim)** is similar to **GLOBAL_LBOUND**, but returning a lower bound. If *dim* is absent, **GLOBAL_LBOUND** and **GLOBAL_UBOUND** are array-valued, spanning the dimensions of *array*.

- **GLOBAL_SHAPE (source)**, where *source* is a dummy argument, tells the local procedure the shape of the global array of which *source* is a part.

- **GLOBAL_SIZE (array, dim)** is similar to **GLOBAL_SHAPE**, but will return the extent of the global array along the specified dimension.

- **ABSTRACT_TO_PHYSICAL (array, index, proc)** and **PHYSICAL_TO_ABSTRACT (array, proc, index)** are subroutines giving the correspondence between a physical processor (see **MY_PROCESSOR** above), an abstract processor (identified by its indices in the array given in a **PROCESSORS** directive), and data that has been distributed to a particular processor (*array* being its dummy argument name in a local procedure). **ABSTRACT_TO_PHYSICAL** yields the *proc* identifier, the other two arguments having **INTENT (IN)**. **PHYSICAL_TO_ABSTRACT** yields the abstract processor's *index*, the other two arguments having **INTENT (IN)**.

- **LOCAL_TO_GLOBAL (array, l_index, g_index)** and **GLOBAL_TO_LOCAL (array, g_index, l_index, local, ncopies, procs)** are subroutines to convert local indices to global indices, and *vice versa*, for an element of the array argument whose local dummy name is *array*. In **GLOBAL_TO_LOCAL**, the argument *local* is a logical flag saying whether the specified global element is within the local array, and *ncopies* and *procs* will say how many copies there are on other processors if it was replicated.

15.7 Final summary

Work is already being done in preparation for a major revision of Fortran for early next century (Fortran 2000), but the real future of Fortran probably lies in the line of research and development that is represented by HPF. It has no serious competitor as a *de facto* standard language for the advanced parallel-processing computers on which leading-edge scientific research now depends. Since advanced computer systems are now as important to science as new devices for collecting or measuring physical data, HPF is central to the future of many different scientific disciplines. Enjoy using it!

APPENDIX A

Input and output

Fortran's **READ** and **WRITE** statements were introduced in a simple form early in this book so that statements could be written that would pass data from or to the processor's default input or output (i/o)devices. It has been assumed that these default devices are a keyboard and a screen and that the format of the data takes a simple form. Appendix A.1 describes the **READ** and **WRITE** statements more fully, and also a second output statement, **PRINT**. The rules of straightforward "list-directed" i/o and "unformatted" i/o are also explained in detail, as are **NAMELIST** groups.

The full details of Fortran's data edit descriptors and device control descriptors are listed in Appendix A.2, and finally a number of specialized file-handling procedures are covered in Appendix A.3.

The i/o procedures **GET**, **PUT** and **PUT_LINE**, for reading and writing variable-length character strings, are to be found in Appendix C.

The details of i/o are relegated to this appendix because Fortran is not primarily a language for data acquisition, data display, or file handling. Although Fortran's i/o facilities are powerful and extensive, computer users today are more likely to use other tools for these purposes. A programmer who tries to use Fortran for anything more than the most straightforward kinds of i/o is probably using the wrong tool for the job. Fortran's i/o facilities date back to a time when black-and-white fixed-font text printers were essentially the only way of producing output for direct human consumption. This history has left its mark not only on the Fortran language but, more generally, on the ASCII character set itself: the bell character was once the only way of getting a computer to make an intentional sound and the underscore exists because originally one of the very few methods of highlighting text was by underlining it, i.e. by writing the text, then backspacing, and then writing a line of underscores. That is now of interest only to historians of technology.

A.1 Data transfer

A.1.1 READ, WRITE and other statements

The **READ** and **WRITE** statements are essential for any program that is to communicate with the outside world. **READ** and **WRITE** are the Fortran "data transfer statements", by which information is transferred from or to any external medium (keyboard, screen, disk files, printers, or whatever).

The information is usually expected to take the form of a sequence of characters (possibly including special control characters), and in this case the data is said to be in "formatted" i/o records. So far we have always used formatted i/o, and most of this chapter will be devoted to formatted data. However, there is such a thing as "unformatted" i/o, which will be explained in Section A.1.5.

As we shall see, reading and writing data can be a complex and sophisticated task for the programmer. As a general rule it is advisable for those parts of a program that deal with i/o statements to be organized into dedicated subroutines, and they could be kept in a special module. It is usually bad programming practice to scatter data transfer statements across subroutines whose primary functions are something else. Grouping i/o statements together also simplifies matters if the program ever needs to be modified for use on a processor with a different set of i/o devices.

The general forms of the data transfer statement are

> **READ (UNIT=..., FMT=..., ...)** *input-item-list*

and

> **WRITE (UNIT=..., FMT=..., ...)** *output-item-list*

except that **FMT** may be replaced by **NML** in the special case of **namelist** formatting, which will be described in Section A.1.6.

READ or **WRITE** indicates, obviously, the direction of data transfer. **UNIT=** is normally followed by a unit number that is an integer (or a scalar integer-valued expression) indicating which i/o unit is to be used. The idea is that different numbers will point to different devices. The available devices will be system-dependent. More details about i/o units are given in Appendix A.3. Fortunately, to simplify matters the default i/o devices can be selected by inserting an asterisk in place of the unit number.

The **FMT** keyword gives a "format specifier" that will normally be a character expression or character variable as described in Appendix A.2. However, there is a simple kind of default formatting, "list-directed" formatting, which is invoked by putting an asterisk as the format specifier. List-directed formatting, which in fact we have used so far in this book, is described in more detail in Sections A.1.3 and A.1.4.

Between the brackets following **READ** or **WRITE** there may in fact be a fairly lengthy list of control specifications in addition to **UNIT=** and **FMT=**. The additional control specifications are optional, and will arise mostly in connection with reading and writing magnetic disk files and tapes. The control specifications in the brackets can appear in any order, being identified by the keywords **UNIT**, **FMT**, and others. However, the keyword **UNIT** is unnecessary if this specification comes first, and the **FMT** keyword is unnecessary if this specification follows second; hence **READ(*,*)** is equivalent to **READ(UNIT=*, FMT=*)**.

The PRINT statement and abbreviated READ statement

A statement

```
PRINT f, ...
```

where **f** is any format specifier (including, possibly, *) can be used as an alternative to

```
WRITE (UNIT=*, FMT=f) ....
```

Also, it is possible to replace the statement

```
READ (UNIT=*,FMT=f) ....
```

by

```
READ f, ....
```

A.1.2 I/O item lists

The data transfer statement, after the bracketed set of control specifications, has a list of input items or output items. Items for input, in a **READ** statement, must be represented by the names of variables and, if the statement is successful, those variables will thereby be assigned values. In principle, the items may be of any type or dimension, with just one or two technical exceptions mentioned below. Examples of input lists are:

```
namestring
x, y, z
bstring(1:5), bstring(7:7)
address%postcode
address
kounts, (milliamps(j), j = 1, kounts)
```

Here, **namestring** could be one string of characters or could be an array of strings, as long as it has been previously declared as such. When an i/o list contains an array or an array section, it is as though the elements were specified one after another in array element order. However, it is not possible to input data into an assumed-size array.

In the second example above, **x**, **y** and **z** could be three real numbers, but if they have been declared as (say) complex numbers then the equivalent of six real numbers will be input. The third example illustrates that input characters may be assigned to sections of strings. Also, a single derived-type structure-component can be read (**address%postcode**), as can a complete data structure (**address**), but input and output statements are not allowed with derived-type structures containing pointer components. The final example shows how the "implicit-**DO**" notation can be used to control an i/o list: here we have one integer (**kounts**) followed by that number of further integers, namely **milliamps(1)**, **milliamps(2)**, ..., up to **milliamps(kounts)**. The integer variable **j** is an arbitrarily-named dummy index. This example is equivalent to

```
kounts, milliamps(1:kounts)
```

However, something like

```
(milliamps(i), j=1,milliamps(1))
```

would not be allowed as you cannot read a variable and also utilize it within the same item of an i/o list.

Any of the above could equally well appear as output item lists in a **WRITE** statement as long as the variables have previously assigned values. An output item list may also contain constants and expressions, such as:

```
"There is no further data available to you"
"Date: ",nday," ",months(nmonth)," ", nyear+2000-
  &100*INT(nyear/50)
"Sines: ", (SIN(theta(i)), i = 1, 99, 2)
((rmass(i), Prob(rmass(i), errbar(i), rm(i), nalgo), &
  i = 1, 22), nalgo = 1, 3)
```

The second of these consists of a character string constant, an integer variable, another character constant (the blank), an element of a character string array, another blank, and an integer expression that depends on the integer variable **nyear** and invokes the function **INT**. The third example outputs the values of the sines of alternate members of the array **theta**. Implied **DO** loops in i/o may be nested, as illustrated in the final example, and in a **WRITE** statement there is no reason why an external function (e.g. **Prob** above) should not appear.

By using arrays or derived types, very large amounts of data can be handled by short and elegant statements. For example, the statement

```
WRITE (UNIT=laserprinter, FMT=memo) document
```

could do a great deal of work, all the complications being expressed elsewhere in the definitions of **memo** and **document**.

A.1.3 List-directed input

The **FMT** control specification will be explained in more detail in Appendix A.2, but it is often sufficient to use what is called "list-directed" formatting, invoked by inserting an asterisk (**FMT=***). With list-directed formatting, the input or output format is determined by the nature of the i/o item list alone.

Bear in mind that list-directed formatting (like all forms of i/o formatting in Fortran) amounts to a conversion between internal Fortran data and a sequence of characters used by an external device. On input, a sequence of characters is converted into Fortran data objects (real, logical, character or whatever) and on output the conversion goes the other way.

If a single integer number is to be input, then the input format will be simply the number expressed in ordinary decimal form, e.g.

```
365
```

and this is also a valid input format for a real number that happens to have no fractional part. Remember that here we are not talking about Fortran statements but about the form of data input (e.g. through a keyboard) to the processor as it runs the program. For a real number having a fractional part, a decimal point may be used:

```
365.242
```

For convenience with numbers of very large or very small magnitude, a multiplying power of ten may be indicated by putting the exponent after the letter **E** immediately following the number: examples are:

```
2.997925E8
2.997925E+8
6.626176E-34
365242E-3
```

of which the first two are equivalent to one another and the last is exactly equivalent to the example in the previous paragraph. If a complex number is to be input, then its real and imaginary parts are enclosed together in brackets; valid forms of complex numbers are:

```
(0,1)
(-0.5, 1.73205)
(41975.9, 3.7E6)
```

If a series of numbers is input, their types must match the names listed in the **READ** statement and the numbers can be separated by commas. For example, the Fortran code

```
INTEGER :: k; REAL :: days, root3
COMPLEX :: omega, zero
```

> .
> .
> .

```
READ (UNIT=*, FMT=*) k, days, root3, omega, zero
```

will be satisfied by the input data

```
365, 365242E-3, 1.73205, (-0.5, 1.73205), (0,0)
```

Blanks alongside a comma are not significant and may be omitted, as in the data

```
365,365242E-3,1.73205,(-0.5,1.73205),(0,0)
```

but one or more blanks may be used (outside a complex number) as separators by themselves instead of commas:

```
365 365242E-3 1.73205 (-0.5,1.73205) (0,0)
```

An "end of record" (i.e. the **enter** or **return** key on a keyboard) normally has the effect of a blank and so this may be used as a separator or a terminator: so all the above examples should be understood as having the **return** key pressed after the final character of the line. It is possible for every item to appear on a separate line:

```
365
365242E-3
1.73205
(-0.5, 1.73205)
(0,0)
```

Arrays of numbers, or derived data types formed out of numbers, may be input in the same way. If we have

```
INTEGER :: nwars(6)
.
.
.
READ (UNIT=*, FMT=*) nwars
```

then the data may be put in as

```
1914, 1918, 1939, 1945, 1998, 2007
```

If the input data is of type logical, it is sufficient if it consists of letters **T** (for **TRUE**) and/or **F** (for **FALSE**) separated like numbers by blanks or commas, e.g. for seven logical items we may have

```
T,F,F,F,T,T,F
```

or

```
T F F F T T F
```

but the **T** or **F** may be immediately preceded by a decimal point, and other arbitrary characters may follow it before the next separator, so

```
TRUE FALSE FALSE FALSE TRUE TRUE FALSE
```
and
```
.T .F .F .F .T .T .F
```
and also
```
.TRUE. .FALSE. .FALSE. .FALSE. .TRUE. .TRUE. .FALSE.
```
are all equivalent valid input formats.

Things can be a little more complicated if character constants are to be input. A pair of statements like

```
CHARACTER(20) :: title, forename, surname
    .
    .
    .
READ (UNIT=*, FMT=*) title, forename, surname
```

will be satisfied by the input

```
Bishop Thomas Finnegan
```

because the blanks (which could equally well be commas) will act as separators between the three character strings. However, ambiguities could arise if the strings themselves are supposed to contain blanks or commas (or slashes). To get over this, it is possible to use double or single quotes when a character string is input, just as we do when specifying a character constant in Fortran itself. In other words,

```
"Bishop" "Thomas" "Finnegan"
```

will have exactly the same effect as the previous example, and

```
"Air Vice-Marshal" "Howard" "Tudor Jones"
```

will correctly include the spaces in the first and third items. The usual rules for character string constants apply: a double quote may appear as part of a string delimited by single quotes (apostrophes); a single quote may occur as part of a string delimited by double quotes; a doubled double quote can be used to represent a (single) double quote within a string delimited by double quotes; and a doubled single quote can be used to represent a (single) single quote within a string delimited by single quotes. A string delimited by either single or double quotes may run from one record (i.e. one line) to the next, as long as the end-of-record does not appear between doubled (single or double) quotes within the string.

If this seems complicated, remember that when character input is contained within one line, does not involve any blanks, slashes, or commas, and does not start with a quote or apostrophe, then there is no need for it to be enclosed in quotes (single or double) at all.

It remains to be said that, with list-directed character string input, an input string longer than that declared for the list item will be truncated from the right; if it is shorter, the list item will be padded out with blanks to the right. This is just the same as happens in character assignment statements when strings of different length are equated.

Whatever the type of the input data, null values can be input by having no characters between successive commas, e.g. for six integers of which only the first four are actually input

```
1914, 1918, 1939, 1945,,,
```

or, if the line is ended by pressing enter/return, we can have

```
1914, 1918, 1939, 1945,,
```

Remember that a blank is purely cosmetic when it is next to a comma. In the above example, the first four integers are specified but the last two are not altered within the program: a null value does not change anything and an undefined value will remain undefined. A null value is not equivalent to a zero or (for character data) a blank. If items in an input list have been preset to certain values by assignment statements before the **READ** statement, null inputs will leave the preset values unchanged.

It is sometimes convenient to input a series of identical values. This can be done by a "multiplier", or "repeat specification", as in

```
3*0 3*1 3 5 5*T 3*F 7*Yes
```

which is equivalent to the collection of integer, logical and character string inputs

```
0 0 0 1 1 1 3 5 T T T T T F F F Yes Yes Yes Yes Yes Yes Yes
```

In general, if the form **r*** (where **r** is an unsigned positive integer) immediately precedes any input value, the value is regarded as having been input **r** times. (For this reason, a character string being input naked, i.e. not enclosed in quotes or parentheses, may not begin with numeric digits followed by an asterisk.) If the **r*** is immediately followed by a blank, then a series of **r** null values is understood, e.g.

```
1914 1918 1939 1945 2*
```
or
```
1914,1918,1939,1945,2*
```

are equivalent to the example given earlier. At the end of a list, another way of inputting null values is with a slash as in

```
1914 1918 1939 1945/
```

The slash always terminates the execution of a list-directed input statement, with null values for any remaining items, unless of course the slash is part of a character string delimited by quotes or apostrophes.

A.1.4 List-directed output

A statement such as

WRITE (UNIT=*, FMT=*) *o/p item list*

will output the values of the listed items according to a simple convention similar to that which we have seen for list-directed input. Integer numbers appear in the obvious format, and logical items appear as **T** or as **F**. Real numbers appear in decimal form, if necessary with an exponent (i.e. an **E** suffix and power of ten) if they are very large or very small: the number of decimal places given, and the exact criterion for using the exponent notation, are processor-dependent. Complex numbers will be in parentheses, with a comma between the real and imaginary parts. Integer, real and complex data items will be separated by commas and/or blanks, but character strings will normally appear without separators or surrounding quotes or apostrophes.

A.1.5 Unformatted i/o

Formatted i/o, in Fortran, involves some sort of transformation between data as it is stored internally in the processor and data as it is stored or displayed externally. Whatever the internal form, the external form can always be regarded as a sequence of characters divided into records. The "records" may simply be lines, as on a printed page, and the characters will almost always be separate bytes coded according to a convention such as ASCII.

Unformatted i/o, by contrast, involves no conversion of the structure of the data: it is transferred to or from the external medium in the same form that it has within the processor. The internal form is a technical matter and Fortran does not care about the details of it. In general, unformatted records can only be read by the same processor, or the same type of processor, that wrote them: general portability between processors cannot be assumed.

The advantage of unformatted i/o is that it is likely to be faster and more efficient than formatted i/o, and it is easier for the programmer because no format specification or namelist specification is needed.

In practice, unformatted i/o does not arise in Fortran with data coming from a keyboard or going to a display device such as a screen or printer. It can arise if, say, data is being dumped onto a tape for periodic backup purposes, or if data needs to be transferred between disk files.

Unformatted i/o is achieved simply by omitting the **FMT** specifier in an i/o statement.

To be on the safe side, especially where derived-type data structures are concerned, unformatted data should be written and read with similar data item lists. If **Decay_Modes** is a data structure (not involving pointers), and if **disk99** is the number of a disk unit, then we could have

```
WRITE (UNIT=disk99,REC=1) Decay_Modes
   .
   .
   .
READ (UNIT=disk99,REC=1) Decay_Modes
```

These statements could be used to store the data temporarily outside the processor's memory. The meaning of **REC** will be mentioned in Appendix A.3.

A.1.6 Namelists

A data transfer statement such as

```
READ (UNIT=..., NML=..., ...)
```

provides a concise method of reading (or writing, in the case of a **WRITE** statement) a set of data the structure of which is defined elsewhere in a special kind of statement, a **NAMELIST** statement. Because the **NAMELIST** statement gathers data together under a collective group name, there is no need to specify an i/o list in this data transfer statement. Neither is it necessary to have a format specifier. When namelists are used for input or output, the data is given in the input or output records in a standard annotated form described below. Namelist output is especially convenient as a way of dumping out data when a program is being debugged.

The **NAMELIST** statement is a specification statement with the syntax

```
NAMELIST / group-name / group-object-list
```

where *group-name* is a name constructed according to the usual Fortran rules. The *group-object-list* is simply a list of the names of variables. These variables can be of a mixture of types, including arrays and derived types, but they must have been declared (or be implicitly defined) previous to the **NAMELIST** statement. Examples are

```
NAMELIST /Years/ nwars, nfloods, nfamines
NAMELIST /Person/ title, forename, surname
NAMELIST /Coordinates/ x, y, z
```

A single **NAMELIST** statement can include more than one group, as in

```
NAMELIST /Months/ birthmonths, deathmonths &
   /Years/ nbirthyears, ndeathyears
```

and one group can be continued later on a second or successive **NAMELIST** statement, e.g.

```
NAMELIST /Person/ bmonth, dmonth, nbyears, ndyears
```

would append four more items to the group */Person/* defined in the earlier example. There is no reason why the same item of data should not crop up in two or more different namelist groups.

The sets of data in the above examples could be input or output by statements like

```
READ (UNIT=*, NML=Years)
WRITE (UNIT=*, NML=Person)
```

or

```
READ (UNIT=*, NML=Coordinates)
```

but note that group names cannot be manipulated or switched about by assignment statements: group names can only occur in **NAMELIST**, **READ** or **WRITE** statements and they cannot be passed as arguments of procedures. In some respects a namelist group is similar to a derived-type data structure, but derived types can be manipulated and assigned with much more flexibility.

If we return to the example above, the statement

```
READ (UNIT=*, NML=Coordinates)
```

will invoke the input of three real numbers, thereby assigning values to the variables x, y and z. The input must take a form like

```
&Coordinates x=3.8, y=-6.6, z=0 /
```

i.e. on a keyboard the user must type an ampersand followed by the group name, then a blank (or a number of blanks), then a series of values. Each value must be specified by the name of a group member followed by an equals sign followed by the value itself. The group members need not all be specified, nor need they be in the original order; so we could input

```
&Coordinates y = 0.332, x = 4.9 /
```

in which case the value of z would not be changed. The value specifications are separated from one another by commas and/or one or more blanks, and the set must be terminated with a slash. The values themselves must be specified according to the same rules as for list-directed input, described earlier in this chapter, except that character input must always be enclosed in quotes or apostrophes, as in

```
&Security Keyword="Carthaginian" /
```

Array elements may be specified. We could have, for example,

```
LOGICAL :: leaps(2000)
NAMELIST /Calendrical/ leaps
leaps = false
READ (UNIT=*, NML=Calendrical)
```

with the actual input

```
&Calendrical leaps(4:2000:4) = 500*T /
```

311

so the program presets as false all members of a logical array called **leaps** and at execution time the user sets every fourth member to be true. The great advantage of namelist input is that the program user can decide at execution time to change any selection of variables as long as their names have been included in the namelist group.

It is much more straightforward to use namelists for output rather than input, since with output the program user does not need to remember any names or syntax. A statement like

```
WRITE (UNIT=*, NML=Coordinates)
```

could output the following data:

```
&COORDINATES X=4.9, Y=0.332, Z=0.0 /
```

Fortran 95 Feature not in Fortran 90

On input, namelist data can have, following one or more name/value pairs, an exclamation mark followed by comment as in

```
&Calendrical leaps(4:2000:4) = 500*T /! i/p record 21
```

A.2 Data editing and formatting

A.2.1 Introducing formats

So far we have only considered data transfer statements in which the format of the data is determined by default conventions according to the nature of the data, i.e. "list-directed" formatting with **FMT=***. However, for complete flexibility the programmer can control the format through the **FMT** specifier. The **FMT** specifier should take the form of a character expression. Below, most of our examples will refer to **WRITE** statements, but the same rules generally apply to **READ**.

Suppose there is just one object in the i/o item list, and we are writing its value onto the standard output device:

```
WRITE (UNIT=*, FMT=format1) datum
```

Before the execution of this statement, **format1** (which is an arbitrary name) must have been assigned a character value, e.g. by

```
format1 = "(I10)"
```

Here, quotes are present because the variable **format1** is being set to the character constant

```
(I10)
```

and this character constant is known as the "format specification". The parentheses are a feature of the syntax needed for any format specification. Inside the parentheses we have in this example the single "edit descriptor"

```
I10
```

and this means that the output item is an integer and can occupy up to ten spaces, i.e. the specification allows for an integer of up to ten digits to be printed or displayed, or nine digits with a minus sign. In other words, **datum** should be an integer not greater than **9999999999** and not less than **-999999999**. If **datum** were going to be a real number, we would need something like

```
format1 = "(F10.4)"
```

The edit descriptor **F10.4** means that **datum** is real (the **F** stands for "floating point"), that a total of ten spaces are allowed, and that the value will be shown rounded to four decimal places. For example, if **datum** is equal to **22.0/7** then the above will display four blanks followed by

```
3.1429
```

In general a format specification takes the form of a bracketed list of edit descriptors, where the total number of edit descriptors should normally match the number of data items in the i/o item list. For example, for a series of three real numbers and one integer we could have the format specification

```
(F10.4, F10.4, F10.4, I10)
```

and the blanks between the edit descriptors are not significant. To abbreviate things, there is a simple notation for repeating identical edit descriptors: the number of them is put immediately before the letter **F** or **I**, so the above example is equivalent to

```
(3F10.4, I10)
```

Repetitions may be nested using brackets, i.e. we could have something like

```
(3(2I10,F10.4))
```

which is an abbreviation for

```
(I10, I10, F10.4, I10, I10, F10.4, I10, I10, F10.4)
```

and this would present the nine numbers side by side over 90 spaces.

Here is a more complete example:

```
REAL :: volume(3), weight(3)
INTEGER :: number(3)
   .
   .
   .
```

```
format99 = "(3I6,6F8.3)"
   .
   .
   .
WRITE (*, FMT=format99) number, weight, volume
```

So far only the simplest edit descriptors have been mentioned for integer and real-number data (**I** and **F** editing). There are in addition many other types of edit descriptor in Fortran. In practice, format specifications often consist of long lists of edit descriptors of different sorts. They fall into three classes, namely:

(a) data edit descriptors;
(b) character string edit descriptors; and
(c) control edit descriptors.

These will be explained in turn in the sections following.

In addition we could say that there is a fourth class (d) consisting only of the null edit descriptor where there is nothing between the brackets, as in

```
WRITE(*, FMT="()")
```

which has the effect of writing an empty record (or, on input, skipping over a record). So the statement

```
READ (*, FMT="()")
```

should just pause the execution of the program until the **return** key is pressed.

A.2.2 Data edit descriptors and character edit descriptors

The letters **I** and **F** discussed above are special cases of "data edit descriptors" Data edit descriptors guide the input or output of the data items listed at the end of the **READ** or **WRITE** statement. Each edit descriptor starts with a letter depending on the nature of the data and how it is to be edited. The possible initial letters are listed below.

I   Integer data (decimal form)
B   Integer data (binary form)
O   Integer data (octal form)
Z   Integer data (hexadecimal form)
F   Real or complex data (simple decimal form)
E   Real or complex data (exponential notation)
L   Logical data
A   Character data
G   Generalized editing (for data of any type).

For **I** editing, as we have seen, the letter **I** is followed immediately by an integer specifying the total number of character positions used to display the data item. For example, on input, **I6** will read a decimal integer from a field of six characters, i.e. with up to six digits or five digits and a sign. On output, **I6** will display an integer in a field six characters wide, if necessary with leading blanks. **B**, **O** and **Z** editing is very similar to **I** editing except that the integer is displayed or stored in binary, octal or hexadecimal form. For example, **B10** will edit an integer in binary form up to a maximum value of **1111111111**, i.e. (in decimal) up to **1023**.

Note that binary, octal and hexadecimal editing have nothing to do with how the integers are stored within the processor's memory. The descriptors **I**, **B**, **O** and **Z** would all apply to data of the same Fortran integer type. The editing simply determines the external display or storage format.

For output with **I**, **B**, **O** and **Z** editing it is possible to display leading zeros so that each data item has a certain specified minimum number (**m**) of digits. This is done by adding the integer **m** after a decimal point, e.g. the descriptor **4I10.8** might display

    00079451 00175600 10905502 00000000

given the data **79451**, **175600**, **10905502**, and **0**. So, the general forms of integer edit descriptors are **Iw, Iw.m, Bw, Bw.m, Ow, Ow.m, Zw**, and **Zw.m**, where **w** is the total field width and **m** is used to arrange leading zeros. Obviously **m**, if present, cannot exceed **w**.

The integers **w** and **m**, and similar elements of the other edit descriptors mentioned below, must appear in Fortran as actual integers and not as variables or expressions.

An **F** edit descriptor is used for real-number data (or two of them could be used for a complex number). The general form is **Fw.d**, where **w** is an integer giving the total field width. On output, there will be a decimal point in the appropriate position followed by **d** places of decimals. On input, if there is a decimal point, **d** could mean that the final **d** digits are interpreted as the fractional part of the number, but if a decimal point appears explicitly in the input stream then the value of **d** is irrelevant. Also on input (but not output) the actual data item may include an exponent as described under **E** editing below.

E editing has exactly the same effect as **F** editing for input. **E7.0** and **F7.0** will both take a real number from a field seven characters wide. On output, however, **E** editing writes the data in exponential notation, i.e. with a power of ten so that very large or very small numbers can be represented compactly. This is best illustrated by examples: the edit descriptor **E10.4** could display numbers in the form

    -.5000+009   (meaning -500 million)
    -.3408-015   (-0.34×10^{-15})
    .1000+129   (10^{128})

    .1000+000   (0.1)
    .0000+000   (0)

So, the number appears as an optional sign followed by a decimal fraction less than **1** but not less than **0.1**, followed after a + or - sign by a power of ten (exponent) which determines the magnitude of the number. In these examples up to three digits are allowed for the exponent, but if necessary more can be allowed by an extension to the edit descriptor: the general form is **Ew.dEe**, and **e** gives the maximum number of digits in the exponent (default three). The above examples are therefore equivalent to **E10.4E3**.

There is a further elaboration of **E** editing, relevant for output, known as **EN** ("engineering")editing. The general form **ENw.d** will display a real number across a field of **w** characters in exponent notation but with the exponent being always a multiple of three. To do this the number appears first in the range from **1** to **999** with a fractional part specified to **d** places of decimals. With **EN12.4** the number of seconds in a year would appear as **31.5360+006**, and half a millionth would appear as **500.0000-009**. The extended form **ENw.dEe** extends the possible magnitude of the exponent as mentioned in the previous paragraph.

Finally, there is a another variation known as **ES** editing (general forms **ESw.d** and **ESw.dEe**) which is like **E** editing but displays one significant figure before the decimal point. With **ES12.4**, therefore, the last example would appear as **5.0000-007**.

L editing is for transmitting data of logical type. The letter **L** is followed by an integer giving the number of character positions taken up by the data item. The item is represented, on output, by a right-justified letter **T** or **F** representing the values **.TRUE.** or **.FALSE.** respectively. The edit descriptor **8L4** could produce the output

    T   T   F   T   F   F   F   F

On input, the **T** (or **F**) may be preceded by a decimal point and may be followed by other characters, as in the case of list-directed input. Thus, forms like **.T**, **.T.**, **TRUE** and **.TRUE.** would all be acceptable inputs as long as the field width is adequate.

For data of character type the **A** edit descriptor is used. (This is not quite the same thing as a "character edit descriptor" that will be explained at the end of this section.) The letter **A** can be followed by an (integer) field width, and that number of characters are directly transferred in or out.

Character editing is particularly simple because we are, in effect, doing the trivial job of converting a character string into a character string, whereas all the other data edit descriptors have to carry out a conversion between a character string and some other data type. The letter **A** need not be followed by a field width: if it is not, the length of the string is taken to be the length of the corresponding data item as listed in the **READ** or **WRITE** statement. If a field width is specified and is not equal to the length of the corresponding list item, then characters may be lost or padding blanks may be inserted, so it is generally best just to use the descriptor **A** by itself to transfer a character string of any length.

As an alternative to all the data edit descriptors mentioned so far in this section, **G** ("generalized") editing can be used for data of any type. A descriptor of the form **Gw.d** or **Gw.dEe** will output a real number in exactly the same way as **Ew.d** or **Ew.dEe**. If the data is of integer, logical or character type, the **d** and **e** parameters are ignored, and **Gw.d** (or **Gw.dEe**) is equivalent to an **Iw**, **Lw** or **Aw** descriptor.

Fortran 95 Feature not in Fortran 90

The possibility of specifying zero field width has been introduced for **IBOZ-** and **F** descriptors, with the meaning of the *minimum* field needed to accommodate whatever data there is. It is possible to have a double zero, e.g. with **F0.0** meaning that as many digits are displayed as are necessary to show the actual data item.

Hollerith data: a Fortran 90 Feature excluded from Fortran 95

For formatted output there is another type of edit descriptor, **nH**, for writing a specific string of characters. Such a string is sometimes called "Hollerith" data. The descriptor **nH...** causes the output of a string of **n** characters immediately following the letter **H**. So, **8HOVERFLOW** is equivalent to **'OVERFLOW'** and **8HMartin's** is equivalent to **'Martin''s'**.

Hollerith editing is outmoded and unnecessary and should be avoided in new programs. It has been eliminated from the Fortran 95 standard.

A "character string edit descriptor" is a kind of descriptor that, technically, is not a data edit descriptor because it does not correspond to an item in an i/o item list and therefore does not transfer a data object. A character string edit descriptor is simply a character constant, specified explicitly between quotes or apostrophes, and is used only with a **WRITE** statement to output a fixed set of characters. For example,

```
"The result is "
```

is a character string edit descriptor, and could be included within a format specification like

```
presentation = "('The result is ', F10.4, ' ', A)"
```

to guide the output statement

```
WRITE(*, FMT=presentation) result, units
```

In fact this format specification actually has two character string edit descriptors, the second containing only a blank character to write a space between the number **result** and the word **units**.

It is always possible to use character data instead of a character string edit descriptor. Instead of

```
f = "('Execution terminating.')"
WRITE(*, FMT=f)
```

we could have

```
f = "(A)"
signoff = "Execution terminating."
WRITE(*, FMT=f) signoff
```

Bear in mind that character variables must be declared and must have defined lengths, so in the above examples **f** and **signoff** must have previously appeared in **CHARACTER** type declaration statements. This could of course be avoided by having simply

```
WRITE(*, FMT="('Execution terminating')")
```

and remember that the need to count characters can be avoided by statements like

```
CHARACTER(*) :: f = "('Execution terminating.')"
    .
    .
    .
WRITE(*, FMT=f)
```

The FORMAT statement:

The format specifier in an i/o statement need not only be a character expression or an asterisk. It may alternatively be a statement label (Chapter 14). In that case the labelled statement must be of a special kind, a **FORMAT** statement, which gives the format specifier. For example,

```
101 FORMAT (3(8X,F12.4))
    WRITE (UNIT=3, FMT=101) a, b, c
```

is equivalent to

```
CHARACTER(*) :: f101 = "(3(8X,F12.4))"
    WRITE (UNIT=3, FMT=f101) a, b, c
```

It is also possible to have the name of an integer variable as a format specifier, but the variable must be assigned (by an **ASSIGN** statement) to the label of a **FORMAT** statement.

A.2.3 Control edit descriptors

Control edit descriptors, as their name suggests, are useful to control i/o devices but they do not themselves refer to individual i/o data items. Fortran's control edit descriptors are listed below:

Tn	Tabulate to character position n in the i/o record
TLn	Tabulate n characters to the left
TRn	Tabulate n characters to the right
nX	Skip forward n characters
/	Skip to start of next record
:	Stop i/o immediately if the i/o list is finished
S	Plus signs optional (numeric output only)
SP	Plus signs written (numeric output only)
SS	Plus signs omitted (numeric output only)
BN	Ignore blanks (numeric input only)
BZ	Treat blanks as zeros (numeric input only)
kP	Scale numbers by 10^k

With the first four of these, **n** is a positive integer that must be specified explicitly. For example, **T1** will move to the first character of the current record. With printed output,

```
WRITE (UNIT=iprint, FMT="(3(T1, A))") word, word, word
```

will write the word **word** in bold (three times superimposed) at the beginning of the line. Note that **TL** (leftward tabulation) cannot move further left than the beginning of the record. **TRn** and **nX** are equivalent to one another. On output, **TR1** and **1X** are both equivalent to the character string edit descriptor containing one blank (" ").

The slash (/) skips to the start of the next record, and may be preceded by an integer greater than one if it is to be repeated. So,

```
WRITE (UNIT=iprint, FMT="(6/)")
```

leaves six blank lines. Slash editing (or format reversion, mentioned below) is used whenever one i/o statement is to transfer more than one record. For example,

```
WRITE (UNIT=mtape, FMT="(50(A,/))") strings
```

writes 50 records (followed by a final empty record) if there are 50 elements in the array **strings**.

The colon (:) is useful if it is not known in advance how long the i/o item list will be. So if **keynumbers** is an array of any size, but not greater than 100,

```
WRITE (*, FMT="(:,'keynumbers ',/,T10,100(I6,:,/,T10))") &
   keynumbers
```

will output all the elements of **keynumbers** but will not execute the / and **T10** after the final element. The first colon means that nothing at all is written if **keynumbers** is a size-zero array. The same effect could be achieved with

```
WRITE (*, FMT="(:,'keynumbers ',100(/,T10,I6))" &
   keynumbers
```

Usually, if a format specification allows for more data items than are actually present in the i/o list, the statement terminates only when an unfulfillable data edit descriptor is encountered, and this may mean that some unnecessary control or character string edit descriptors are executed.

Incidentally, if a format specification allows for fewer data items than are present in the i/o list, then a process known as "reversion" occurs and the processor runs through the format specification (or the last bracketed section of it) again as often as necessary. So in fact,

```
WRITE (*, FMT="(:,'keynumbers ',/,(T10,I6))") keynumbers
```

would work just like the example above, irrespective of the size of the array **keynumbers**. When a format specification involves nested brackets, format reversion only goes back over the edit descriptors within the current level brackets, so in the above example it is **(T10,I6)** that is repeated, not the whole format specification. Reversion always involves moving forward to the next i/o record, so we have **(T10,I6)** and not **(/,T10,I6)** in the above example. Simpler examples of format reversion are

```
WRITE (UNIT=mtape, FMT="(A)") strings
READ (UNIT= mtape, FMT="(A)") strings
```

both of which will transfer as many records (each interpreted as a single character string) as there are elements in the character array **strings**.

When numbers are output, positive numbers may or may not be preceded by plus signs. The **S**, **SP** and **SS** descriptors control this. **SP** means that subsequent positive numbers written by the **WRITE** statement will have plus signs, **SS** means that the plus signs will be omitted, and **S** lets the processor decide. **BN** and **BZ** refer to the interpretation of non-leading blanks in numeric input. **BN** means that they will be ignored, i.e. it does not matter if the digits of a number are interspersed with blanks or followed by blanks. **BZ** means that blanks in or after a number are treated as zeros.

The **kP** descriptor is for use in conjunction with **F** editing. The number **k** must be an integer, interpreted as a power of ten, and with subsequent **F** editing (without exponent) real and complex data items are scaled up (for output) or down (for input) by that factor.

A.2.4 Exercises A.2

A.2.1 Which of the following are valid format specifications? And which are valid edit descriptors?

(i) `"(F10.4)"`	(ii) `(F10.4)`	(iii) `F10.4`
(iv) `8(F10.4)`	(v) `8F10.4`	(vi) `(8F10.4)`
(vii) `((F10.4))`	(viii) `(F10.6,I8)`	(ix) `()`
(x) `"3()"`		

A.2.2 Write a format specification to output a four-digit integer, followed by three real numbers, all neatly spaced out over an 80-column line. Assume that the real numbers do not exceed a value of **1000.0** and must be specified to two decimal places.

A.2.3 Write a **WRITE** statement, incorporating the format specification, to output an integer variable called **n** in decimal, binary and octal form on one line, the three forms suitably separated with blanks. Assume that **n** does not exceed (in decimal) **99**.

A2.4 What is the output from:

  (i) `WRITE (*, "(2L2,2X)") (/.TRUE.,(.FALSE.,k=1,3)/)`
 (ii) `WRITE (*, "(A4,:,TR1)") "Cause", "of", "death"`
(iii) `WRITE (*, "(2F7.4)") SQRT(2.0), SQRT(3.0)`
 (iv) `WRITE (*, "(B6,1X,I6.6)") 40, 40*40`
  (v) `WRITE (*, "(2E12.4)") SQRT(2.0), 40.0*40.0`
 (vi) `WRITE (*, "('FA',L1,'E')") 2+2<5`

A.2.5 Write a **WRITE** statement to produce the output
        T E R M I N A T I O N
   (i.e. underlined and with spaces between the letters) given a character string called **caption** such that
       `caption = "TERMINATION"`

A.3 File handling

A3.1 Units, files and records

Little has been said so far about the nature of input and output devices. The following sections cover a number of ways in which it is possible to control i/o devices and files. The statements concerned are **OPEN, CLOSE, BACKSPACE, ENDFILE, REWIND** and **INQUIRE**. Also, we will mention here a number of special control specifications that can be used with the **READ** and **WRITE** statements.

Terms such as "unit", "file" and "record", although often used loosely, have precise technical meanings. A "record" is to be understood simply as a sequence of data items, usually in the form of characters. A record may have any length, and if it is a sequence of characters then the "length" is defined simply as the number of characters in it.

For example, a single line of printed characters is usually regarded as a "record". A sequence of characters from a keyboard would usually constitute a single input record. In general a record does not have to end with any particular kind of character, even though the end of a record may be indicated to Fortran by pressing the **enter** or **return** key (keyboard input) or by the slash (**/**) edit descriptor.

There are two types of "file", external and internal. "Internal" files are explained in Section 9.5. An "external" file is a set of data having a physical existence external to the program. It is rarely necessary to work with internal files, and so the word "file" is usually used by itself to refer to an external file. For example, you might say that a magnetic tape contains a "file" of data.

A file may consist of any number of records (including zero!) and may have, as its final record, a special "endfile record". The word "file" is usually used to refer to a durable set of machine-readable data, as opposed to something ephemeral like a screen display or the tapping of a keyboard. As we shall see, a file can have a name in Fortran. Most commonly, files are stored on magnetic media, i.e. disks or tapes. Some processors may store files on other media such as optical discs or in special areas of memory ("RAM disks").

An important distinction must be made between "sequential access" and "direct access" files. A sequential-access file has a beginning and an end, and the data items must be read or written in sequence. When such a file is first opened it will be positioned at the beginning. As a general rule, sequential-access files consist of "formatted" records, i.e. each record consists of a sequence of characters. "Unformatted" records (Section A.1.5), on the other hand, are most often of direct-access type.

Historically, the concept of sequential access arose from the use of magnetic tapes: obviously a magnetic tape has to be wound from one end to the other, although backspacing and rewinding are possible. By contrast, a direct-access file corresponds to something like a magnetic disk where any part of the file can be reached very quickly.

It is assumed that a direct-access file is divided into records, and that any record can be read or written independently of the others. However, it is not possible to dive into the middle of a record: each record must be read or written from the first character. For reference purposes, the records of a direct-access file are numbered, but the numbering need not correspond to physical positions on the surface of the disk. The physical layout of data on a disk is a matter for the operating system, not for Fortran, and a sophisticated system may switch records about in complicated ways to optimize the utilization of space on the disk. In a direct-access file the records must all have the same length and they must be numbered: otherwise the operating system would have to be inordinately complicated. The record numbers must be positive integers. In the case of a direct-access file there is no such thing as an "endfile record".

A sequential-access file, such as a file on a magnetic tape, can have records of varying lengths. Unless otherwise specified (and we shall see soon how these things are specified) all files are assumed by Fortran to be sequential-access files. The keyboard, for example, is treated like a sequential-access file, since the records must be input in a particular order – the real-time order – and the records may vary in length. It is possible for a sequential-access file to have zero length.

A possible feature of a sequential-access file is "non-advancing" i/o, as opposed to the usual "advancing" i/o. Usually, a **WRITE** or **READ** statement will transfer data to or from an exact number of records. Even if a **READ** statement only looks at the data in the first part of a record, nevertheless the unit will have physically passed over the whole of the record. So, between two i/o statements a file will always be positioned between two records. If you want to examine two parts of a record separately, you must either read the record twice (using **BACKSPACE**, Section A.3.3) or you must read the whole thing once and store in memory the information that you are not ready to analyze. "Non-advancing" i/o offers an alternative: you can read or write a record on a character-by-character basis, executing i/o statements several times as you move through one record. This is called "non-advancing" because the file does not advance automatically to the end of the record after a **READ** or **WRITE**, which is the usual procedure.

In Fortran, external files are associated with "units". A "unit" is an i/o device, such as a printer, a tape drive, a barcode reader, or whatever. The definition of a unit is quite independent of the particular data that happen to be flowing through it. A processor will have access to a range of different units, usually numbered by different non-negative integers, except that a standard input device and a standard output device may be referred to by asterisks.

It must be remembered that a "unit" is not the same thing as a "file". A unit is a channel by which the processor may access a file.

A.3.2 Opening and closing files

In the earlier part of this book, **READ** and **WRITE** were the only types of i/o statement mentioned. It could be imagined that the input device was the keyboard and the output device was a VDU or perhaps a printer. There was no need to do any more than **READ** or **WRITE** to transfer the data, and distinctions between, say, direct-access and sequential-access files did not arise. In general, however, it is not possible to **READ** or **WRITE** a file without first executing a special setting-up statement, **OPEN**. The **OPEN** statement is used to connect a file to a numbered unit and to decide certain options. It is most commonly used with magnetic tape or disk files. The syntax is simply

```
OPEN (connection-specification-list)
```

where **connection-specification-list** is a selection of specifications, separated by commas, of the sort

UNIT = ...	the unit number (compulsory!)
IOSTAT = ...	for error-checking
FILE = ...	to specify the file's name
STATUS = ...	new file or old?
ACCESS = ...	**SEQUENTIAL** or **DIRECT**

FORM = ...	FORMATTED or UNFORMATTED
RECL = ...	record length
BLANK = ...	NULL or ZERO
POSITION = ...	ASIS, REWIND or APPEND
ACTION = ...	READ, WRITE or READWRITE
DELIM = ...	APOSTROPHE, QUOTE or NONE
PAD = ...	YES or NO

None of these may appear more than once in the same **OPEN** statement. They need not all be present, but there must be a **UNIT** specifier. In many cases an **OPEN** statement will only involve a small number of the possible options. A typical **OPEN** statement might be

```
OPEN (UNIT=6, IOSTAT=ncheck, FILE="april.dat", &
  STATUS="NEW", ACCESS="DIRECT", &
  FORM="FORMATTED", RECL=512)
```

What do the specifiers mean? Taking them in the order listed above, each is discussed at more length below.

- **UNIT** This specifier must be set to an integer expression. It would be quite possible to have, say,
  ```
  OPEN (UNIT= ndisk1, ....)
  ```
  with **ndisk1** being an integer to be specified as a parameter at the start of the program. The particular meanings of the unit numbers will be processor-dependent. It is not possible to have **UNIT=*** in an **OPEN** statement, i.e. opening the processor's default i/o unit.

- **IOSTAT** This supplies the name of a scalar integer variable that, on execution of the statement, will be given either:
  1. a positive value if an error condition is encountered;
  2. negative values if an end-of-file or an end-of-record condition is encountered; or
  3. the value zero otherwise.

  In fact only case 1 or case 3 may occur as a result of the **OPEN** statement, but it will be seen that the **IOSTAT** specifier can also be used with other statements such as **READ** and **WRITE** and then case 2 may arise. In case 2, the end-of-file condition can only be relevant to a sequential-access file, and the end-of-record condition can only be relevant to a sequential-access file with non-advancing i/o. With a direct-access file, case 2 is never relevant.

- **FILE** This specifier lets the programmer state a name for the file as a scalar character expression. It is not always needed: for example, magnetic tape files or printers do not usually have names. However, processors usually require disk files to be named. To read an existing file from a disk, it will be necessary to know its name and, to write a new file, a name must be supplied. The convention for constructing names will depend on the processor. It is possible to specify the filename either as a constant expression (like **"april.dat"**) or through the name of a variable.

- **STATUS** This is a character string (or a character expression) that must be either **"OLD"**, **"NEW"**, **"SCRATCH"**, **"REPLACE"**, or **"UNKNOWN"**. **OLD** means that a named file already exists, **NEW** means that it does not yet exist, and **REPLACE** creates a fresh file and deletes any old file of the same name. **SCRATCH** is used for a file that has not been given a name, creating a "scratch" file for temporary use as the program executes: a scratch file is deleted when the program terminates or when a **CLOSE** statement (below) is executed for the unit. The **UNKNOWN** option, which is the default if **STATUS** is omitted, simply means that the status is processor-dependent.

  For **STATUS**, and for the other specifiers below which call for character expressions, there is no distinction between upper and lower case and any trailing blanks will be ignored.

- **ACCESS** This is a character expression which is equivalent to either **"SEQUENTIAL"** or **"DIRECT"**, specifying whether this is a sequential-access or direct-access file. The default is **SEQUENTIAL**.

- **FORM** This specifier determines whether the file is formatted or unformatted, and it must be a character expression equal to **"FORMAT-TED"** or to **"UNFORMATTED"**. The default is **FORMATTED** for a sequential-access file, or **UNFORMATTED** in the case of direct access.

- **RECL** This specifier, which is set to an integer expression, gives the record length. For formatted records this means the number of characters in a record. In the direct-access case, **RECL** is the length of every record, and must be specified. In the sequential-access case records may be of variable length and **RECL** is taken to be the maximum record length: it may be omitted, in which case a processor-dependent default value takes effect.

- **BLANK** A specifier applicable to formatted input files, which is set to a character expression equal to either **"NULL"** or **"ZERO"**, the former being the default. **NULL** means that blanks are ignored in numeric data (except that a whole field of blanks is treated as a zero) and **ZERO** means that blanks are treated as zeros.

- **POSITION** This is a character expression equal to **"REWIND"**, **"APPEND"** or **"ASIS"**, and it can be specified in the case of an existing sequential-access file. It determines whether the file will be positioned at its start or at its end. **REWIND** positions it at the start, and **APPEND** at the end. The **ASIS** option, which is the default, leaves the file positioned wherever it was.

- **ACTION** This permits the file to be restricted to read-only or write-only use. **ACTION** may have the character values **"READ"**, **"WRITE"** or **"READWRITE"**. The first two are self-explanatory. **READWRITE**, the default, permits both reading and writing to take place on this file.

- **DELIM** This may have one of the character values **"APOSTROPHE"**, **"QUOTE"** or **"NONE"**, and it has a significance in relation to list-directed or namelist character-string data output. It specifies whether character strings will be displayed between apostrophes (single quotes), between quotes (double quotes), or without any delimiters.

- **PAD** This is a character expression equal to **"YES"** or **"NO"**. It determines whether or not a formatted input record should be padded out with blanks if it is shorter than expected. If **NO**, the record's length must match what the **READ** statement demands. The default is **YES**.

The list of specifiers above may seem long and confusing at first sight, but in practice the **OPEN** statement is not difficult to use. A simple procedure is:

1. Specify the **UNIT** number. This will depend on the particular configuration of the processor being used.
2. Does the unit refer to a sequential-access file, such as a printer or a tape drive? Or is it a direct-access file such as a disk file? If the latter, skip to step 5. For sequential access, continue with step 3. If you do not know, there is an intrinsic function **INQUIRE** that can tell you (Section A.3.5).
3. If direct access is not specified, files are taken by default to be sequential access. And, unless otherwise specified, sequential-access files are taken by default to be formatted. Formatted sequential-access records may vary in length, but there will be a processor-dependent maximum record length. The **INQUIRE** function can tell you the processor's maximum record length.
4. The specifiers **BLANK**, **DELIM** and **PAD**, which are for formatted records, are not of great interest. They can almost always be omitted. The optional **POSITION** specifier, for a sequential file, is an opportunity to position the file at its starting point (**"REWIND"**, equivalent to the **REWIND** statement) or at its end (**"APPEND"**).
   Skip to step 6.
5. For direct access, specify **ACCESS="DIRECT"**. A direct-access file is taken by default to be unformatted. For direct access, it is necessary to specify the record length using the **RECL** specifier.
6. A file-name may be given using the **FILE** specifier, but a file name is usually only needed in the case of direct-access disk files. The specifiers **STATUS** and **ACCESS** may be useful for protecting files from being inadvertently overwritten. Remember that when **STATUS="SCRATCH"**, the file should not have a name.

7. The **IOSTAT** specifier is not compulsory but should be included if the code is to be watertight.

Here are a few examples of **OPEN** statements:

```
OPEN (UNIT=7, ACCESS="DIRECT", RECL=128, &
  FILE='studentgrades.dat', ACTION=READ)
OPEN (UNIT=14, POSITION="APPEND", &
  IOSTAT=k_error_unit_14)
OPEN (UNIT=ndiskb, ACCESS="DIRECT", &
  RECL=nrecs, FILE=fstring)
OPEN (UNIT=4, ACCESS="DIRECT", &
  RECL=idata_unit(4), STATUS="SCRATCH")
```

After a file has been opened, records may be written or read and other operations may be performed as described below. Finally, the **CLOSE** statement may be used to disconnect the file from a unit. The syntax is similar to that for **OPEN**:

```
CLOSE (specification list)
```

but the specification list for **CLOSE** is taken from

UNIT = ...	the unit number (compulsory!)
IOSTAT = ...	for error-checking, as for **OPEN**
STATUS = ...	**KEEP** or **DELETE**?

The optional **STATUS** specifier may be set either to **"KEEP"** or **"DELETE"**. In the latter case, the file will be deleted when **CLOSE** is executed. Note that a file opened with **STATUS="SCRATCH"** is always deleted on closure anyway. The default **STATUS** is **"KEEP"**.

Some examples of **CLOSE** statements are:

```
CLOSE(UNIT=6, IOSTAT=ncheck)
DO k=1,6; CLOSE(k); END DO
CLOSE(UNIT=14, IOSTAT=k_error_unit_14)
CLOSE(UNIT=ndiskb, STATUS="DELETE")
```

A.3.3 **BACKSPACE, ENDFILE** and **REWIND**

These are the "file positioning statements" and their functions should be clear from their names. They are applicable only to sequential-access files, and in particular magnetic tapes. The syntax can be illustrated by the **BACKSPACE** statement, which takes the form

```
BACKSPACE (UNIT=..., IOSTAT=...)
```

where the **UNIT** specifier is compulsory and **IOSTAT** is as usual optional. **UNIT** and **IOSTAT** have the same meanings as for the **OPEN** statement. **BACKSPACE** moves the file back to the start of the previous record if there is one. The **REWIND** statement moves the file back to the start of the first record. **ENDFILE** writes an endfile record. However, an endfile record will be written automatically after a **CLOSE** statement or simply if a program terminates normally after writing on the file has taken place.

A.3.4 I/O control specifications

So far **READ** and **WRITE** statements have been considered of the form

        READ (*UNIT=..., FMT=..., ...*) *input-item-list*
and
        WRITE (*UNIT=..., FMT=..., ...*) *output-item-list*

and for namelist groups **NML** has been explained as an alternative to **FMT**. If the data is unformatted, neither **FMT** nor **NML** will be present. The following additional specifiers may be included:

IOSTAT = ...	as for **OPEN**
REC = ...	record number
ADVANCE = ...	advancing or nonadvancing i/o
SIZE = ...	number of characters to be read

If **IOSTAT** is present it allows the program to detect an i/o error or the end of a record or of a file as was described for the **OPEN** statement earlier.

- **REC** If **REC** is present the file must be of direct-access type and **REC** specifies the number of the record that is to be written or read. Records in a direct-access file do not have to be written or read in any particular order (that is what direct access means, of course) and so the i/o statement has to include the record number. If **REC** is not present the file is of sequential-access type.

- **ADVANCE** This is an option available when formatted sequential files are being written or read. The default option, **ADVANCE="YES"**, the most common situation, simply means that the i/o statement will read or write one record, moving the file from the start of one record to the start of the next: it is not possible to read or write a fraction of a record and stop part way through. The option **ADVANCE="NO"** means that "non advancing" i/o will take place, i.e. the file does not automatically advance to the start of the subsequent record. The effect of this is to make it possible to read or write a record piece by piece. Individual characters can be transferred, the exact number of them depending on the format specification and the i/o item list.

- **SIZE** In the case of a **READ** statement, with formatted sequential non-advancing input, the **SIZE** specifier may be used to give the name of an integer variable that will yield, after the statement has been executed, the number of characters transferred.

Some examples of i/o statements are:

```
WRITE (UNIT=*, FMT=format, IOSTAT=icheck) (title(k), &
  data(:,k), k=1,6)
READ (UNIT=4, REC=1) dump
READ (UNIT=11, FMT=f4, ADVANCE="NO", SIZE=nchars) string
READ (*, FMT="(A1)", ADVANCE="NO") char
```

The last of these reads a single character from the keyboard. Because **ADVANCE="NO"** the statement is not expecting to input a complete record and therefore the data is transferred without any need for the **return** or **enter** key to be pressed.

A.3.5 INQUIRE

Some of the statements mentioned above, especially **OPEN**, may require a knowledge of the detailed properties of the i/o unit being referred to. However, the Fortran programmer does not have to look up all these details in the processor's user guide: there is a statement called **INQUIRE** which permits the program, at execution time, to find out most of the necessary information automatically. In fact **INQUIRE** can yield a bewilderingly large array of information. The statement's syntax is simple enough:

```
INQUIRE (specification-list)
```

In many respects the **specification-list** is similar to what we have already seen for **OPEN** and other statements above. The specification list for **INQUIRE** must include either **UNIT=...** or **FILE=...**, but not both, specifying either a unit number or a filename. If a unit is specified, we have what is said to be the "inquire by unit" form of the statement. If a filename is given, it is "inquire by file". (There is a third possibility, "inquire by output list", mentioned at the end of this section.)

With "inquire by unit", the keyword **UNIT=** may be omitted if the unit specifier is the first in the list, i.e.

```
INQUIRE (3, EXIST=being_3)
```

is a permissible statement to check the existence of unit 3. In any **INQUIRE** statement the unit number must be specified by an integer expression, not by an asterisk, and consequently the default i/o devices cannot be referred to.

After **UNIT** or **FILE**, other items in the specification list are of the usual form

```
SPECIFIER = variable-name
```

and depending on the specifier the variable may be of integer, character or logical type. The possible specifiers are listed below, and they are all optional, but none of them may appear more than once in the statement. The variables named must all be scalars. They will be given values when the statement is executed.

IOSTAT = ...	as for OPEN
EXIST = ...	does the unit/file exist?
OPENED = ...	file and unit connected?
NUMBER = ...	what is the unit number?
NAMED = ...	does the file have a name?
ACCESS = ...	as for OPEN
SEQUENTIAL = ...	can this be sequentially accessed?
DIRECT = ...	can this be directly accessed?
FORM = ...	as for OPEN
FORMATTED = ...	is formatted i/o possible?
UNFORMATTED = ...	is unformatted i/o possible?
RECL = ...	maximum record length
NEXTREC = ...	number of next record
BLANK = ...	as for OPEN
POSITION = ...	as for OPEN
ACTION = ...	as for OPEN
READ = ...	can the file be read?
WRITE = ...	can the file be written?
READWRITE = ...	are reading and writing both allowed?
DELIM =- ...	as for OPEN
PAD = ...	as for OPEN

It should be stressed that all the specifiers in the above list are for the program to obtain information from the processor, not to supply information to it. For example, the ACCESS specifier here is working in the opposite direction to that in the OPEN statement.

Except for those already explained earlier, more details of the above specifiers are given below:

- EXIST This specifies a logical variable that will be true if the file, or unit, exists, and false otherwise.
- OPENED This is also a logical variable. In an "inquire by file" statement it is true if the named file is connected to a unit. In "inquire by unit" it is true if the unit has a file attached.
- NUMBER In an "inquire by file" statement, this is an integer equal to the file's unit number. If the file cannot be found it is set to -1.
- NAMED In "inquire by unit", this logical variable says whether or not there is a named file at this unit.

- **SEQUENTIAL** This will be a character string equal to **"YES"** if the file/unit can be used in sequential-access mode, and **"NO"** if it can only be used in direct access. The processor may answer **"UNKNOWN"**!
- **DIRECT** This is similar to **SEQUENTIAL**. A character string is set to **"YES"** if the file/unit may be used in direct-access mode, and to **"NO"** if it may not.
- **FORMATTED** This is a character string equal to **"YES"** if formatted records are possible, and **"NO"** if it is restricted to unformatted use.
- **UNFORMATTED** The opposite of **FORMATTED**: **"YES"** means that unformatted i/o is possible, **"NO"** means that i/o must be formatted.
- **RECL** This specifies an integer, the processor's maximum record length for this file/unit. This cannot be exceeded by the **RECL** specified for the same unit in an **OPEN** statement.
- **NEXTREC** When a direct-access file is being written or read, it can be useful to know the number of the next record. The integer specified by **NEXTREC** is one greater than the number of the last record, or is equal to **1** if none have yet been written or read.
- **READ** This is a character string set to **"YES"** if the file/unit may be read from, and **"NO"** otherwise.
- **WRITE** This is equal to **"YES"** if writing is possible, and **"NO"** if it is not. For example, this specifier will give **"NO"** if the unit is a keyboard, because a keyboard is an input device. You cannot write onto a keyboard!
- **READWRITE** **"YES"** is given if, and only if, the file/unit can be used both for reading and writing.

INQUIRE is an extremely useful statement because it can be used to interrogate a processor and yield information on the basis of which other i/o statements can be constructed to make the best use of the facilities available to the processor. **INQUIRE** is the key to writing good, portable and crashproof i/o code. A few examples of **INQUIRE** statements are

```
INQUIRE (UNIT=laser_printer, RECL=linelength)
INQUIRE (UNIT=3, IOSTAT=j, FORM=sform)
INQUIRE (FILE=scratch_disk_output, NEXTREC=k)
```

The following subroutine could be used to set up and read a named disk file:

```
SUBROUTINE Peruse (filename, nrec)
USE Data, ONLY: input => stringbank
CHARACTER(*), INTENT (IN) :: filename
INTEGER, INTENT (IN) :: nrec
INTEGER :: n_unit, icheck
LOGICAL :: q

INQUIRE (FILE=filename, IOSTAT=icheck, EXIST=q, &
```

```
          NUMBER=n_unit)
      File: IF (icheck/=0) THEN
        filename="FAULTY"
      ELSE
        Existence: IF (.NOT.q) THEN
          filename="NOTFOUND"
        ELSE
          OPEN (UNIT=n_unit, IOSTAT=icheck, &
          FILE=filename, ACCESS="DIRECT")
          Opening: IF (icheck/=0) THEN
            filename="ERROR1"
          ELSE
            READ (UNIT=n_unit, REC=nrec, IOSTAT=icheck) input
            IF (icheck/=0) filename="ERROR2"
          ENDIF Opening
        ENDIF Existence
      ENDIF File
      END SUBROUTINE Peruse
```

So far two forms of the **INQUIRE** statement have been described: "inquire by unit" and "inquire by file". A third form uses the syntax

```
    INQUIRE (IOLENGTH=integer) output-list
```

where **integer** is the name of a scalar integer variable and **output-list** is a list of data such as could appear in a **WRITE** statement. The purpose of this statement is to ascertain the record length that the processor would require to output the data with an unformatted **WRITE** statement. The integer variable specified by **IOLENGTH** will be set to the necessary record length, and could then be used to open an output file with records of sufficient length, as in

```
    INQUIRE (IOLENGTH=n) stringbank
    OPEN (UNIT=k, ACCESS="DIRECT", RECL=n, STATUS="SCRATCH")
    WRITE (UNIT=k, REC=1, IOSTAT=nasty) stringbank
```

The ERR, END and EOR specifiers

In the **OPEN, CLOSE, READ, WRITE, BACKSPACE, ENDFILE, REWIND** and **INQUIRE** i/o statements the list of specifications may include **ERR=...** with the number of a statement label being given. The effect is to transfer control to a statement with that label if there is an error as the i/o statement executes.

Similarly, in a **READ** statement there can be an **END=...** specification giving the label of a statement to which control passes if the end of the file is encountered.

There can also be an **EOR=...** specification in a **READ** or **WRITE** statement being used for non-advancing i/o. Control then passes to the labelled statement if the end of the record is reached.

A.3.6 Exercises A.3

A.3.1 Write **OPEN** statements:
  (i) To open a magnetic tape scratch file on unit 7.
  (ii) To open a magnetic tape file on unit 3, positioning it at the end of the file so that more data can be appended.
  (iii) To open a direct-access disk file called **s_sheet_45** on unit 2, the record length being 256. Then write a **CLOSE** statement to close the file and discard it.

A.3.2 Write statements to:
  (i) Write the 20 elements of an array called **datasave** as 20 records in an unformatted file on unit 5. (Use a **DO** loop.)
  (ii) Read the first 10 characters of a record on unit 1, without advancing further through the record. The 10 characters are to be interpreted as two five-digit integers.
  (iii) Inquire which of the units 1 to 10 exist on the processor, and which may be used for unformatted i/o. (Use a **DO** loop.)
  (iv) Inquire whether a file called **tempora** is attached to a unit, and what the number of the unit is.

APPENDIX B

Bits

Besides Fortran's intrinsic data types (**INTEGER, REAL, COMPLEX, CHARACTER** and **LOGICAL**) it is possible to manipulate data in the form of individual binary bits. Bits are similar in some ways to **LOGICAL** data, in that both are restricted to two possible values, called **.FALSE.** or **.TRUE.** for **LOGICAL** and 0 or 1 for a bit. However, lengthy sequences of binary data can be handled much more naturally and flexibly as bits than in **LOGICAL** form. Bits are packed within data of integer type, and stored in memory much more economically than **LOGICAL** data.

To handle bits, Fortran provides the intrinsic functions **BIT_SIZE, IBSET, IBCLR, IBITS, ISHFT, NOT, IAND, IOR**, and **IEOR**, and the subroutine **MVBITS**. These procedures manipulate sets of bits that have to be declared as data of integer type.

B.1 Inside integers

A non-negative integer i may be regarded as a sequence of "bits" or binary digits w_k as in

$$i = \sum_k w_k 2^k = w_0 + 2w_1 + 4w_2 + 8w_3 + \ldots$$

with the sum running from $k = 0$ to a value $s - 1$, where s is the number of bits. This formula can be taken to relate an integer i to the sequence of bits $w_0, w_1, \ldots, w_{s-1}$.

It is important to know how many bits can be contained in each integer, i.e. what is the processor's value of s, and this is given by a special inquiry function **BIT_SIZE(I)**. The argument **I** is any integer. The statement

```
numbits=BIT_ SIZE(1)
```

will therefore tell the program the number of bits per integer on the processor being used. Typically this might be 32 or 64.

The function **BTEST(I,POS)** looks into the integer **I** and tests whether the bit in position **POS** is **0** or **1**. The argument **POS** corresponds to the index k in the equation above, and so it must be an integer in the range from 0 to $s - 1$. **BTEST** itself has logical value, i.e. **BTEST(I=64, POS=k)** has the value **.TRUE.** if and only if **k=6**.

BTEST is an elemental intrinsic function, as are the other bit functions mentioned below, and may therefore have an array as argument and result. Taking **POS** as an array, on a 32-bit processor, we could have

```
INTEGER :: ibitstring; LOGICAL :: bdigits(32)
 .
 .
 .
bdigits = BTEST (I=ibitstring, POS=(/ (i, i=0,31) /))
```

converting **ibitstring** (an integer corresponding to a sequence of 32 bits) into the logical array **bdigits**.

The functions **IBSET(I,POS)** and **IBCLR(I,POS)** are used to reset individual bits within the integer **I**, the result being the modified version of **I**. **IBSET** sets the bit in position **POS** equal to **1** (if that is not already its value) and **IBCLR** clears the bit to **0**. If **POS** were an array spanning the whole of the integer **I**, as in the previous example, then **IBCLR** would clear all the bits in **I** to zero.

There is a function **IBITS(I,IPOS,LEN)** which forms a new integer by picking out a subset of the bits within **I**, i.e. a number **LEN** of bits starting at position **POS**. The result **IBITS** is obtained by right-justifying the chosen bits and setting the others to **0**. So, for example, **IBITS(I=munch,POS=0,LEN=8)** picks out the first byte from munch, and **IBITS(I=munch,POS=8,LEN=8)** picks out the second byte. When using **IBITS**, the sum of **POS** and **LEN** cannot exceed the total number of bits in **I** that would be given by the function **BIT_SIZE**.

B.2 Bit logic

To carry out logical operations on bits there are the intrinsic functions **NOT(I)**, **IAND(I,J)**, **IOR(I,J)**, and **IEOR(I,J)**. The first of these simply yields the complement of **I**, i.e. **NOT(17)=238** on an eight-bit machine. The other functions have two arguments and form the logical "and", "or", and "exclusive or" combinations on a bit-by-bit basis. So, if

$$i = \sum_k w_k 2^k \qquad \text{and} \qquad j = \sum_k y_k 2^k$$

the ws and ys being binary digits, then

$$\text{NOT}(i) \quad = \quad \sum_k (1 - w_k) 2^k$$

$$\text{IAND}(i, j) \quad = \quad \sum_k w_k y_k 2^k$$

$$\text{IOR}(i, j) \quad = \quad \sum_k (w_k + y_k - w_k y_k) 2^k$$

and $\quad \text{IEOR}(i, j) \quad = \quad \sum_k (w_k + y_k - 2 w_k y_k) 2^k$

There are two intrinsic functions to shift the bits around within an integer. **ISHFT(I,SHIFT)** shifts the bits within **I** by a number of places given by **SHIFT**. They go left if **SHIFT** is positive, and right if **SHIFT** is negative, and bits that fall off the end are lost, while places vacated at the other end are filled with zeros. Another function, **ISHFTC(I,SHIFT)** does a circular shift so that bits pushed off one end of **I** appear at the other end. In fact, **ISHFTC** may have a third argument, **SIZE**, in which case the circular shift occurs only among the **SIZE** bits at the right. So, **SHFTC(I=90,SHIFT=-2,SIZE=8)** just operates on the first byte of **I** and has the value **150**.

Finally, there is an intrinsic elemental subroutine called **MVBITS (FROM, FROMPOS, LEN, TO, TOPOS)** which will do the job of taking a sequence of bits (of length **LEN**) from the integer **FROM** (starting with bit position **FROMPOS**) and copying it into the integer **TO** (starting at position **TOPOS**). The statement

```
CALL MVBITS(FROM=source, FROMPOS=0, LEN=16, TO=dest, &
    TOPOS=16)
```

uses the first two bytes of **source** to replace the third and fourth bytes of **dest**.

B.3 A warning

In Fortran, when we use the intrinsic procedures described above, bits are assumed to be packed into non-negative integers according to the equation at the beginning of Appendix B.1. That equation is fundamental to the working of the procedures. However, variables of integer type in Fortran are not normally represented according to that equation but according to another, processor-dependent, scheme that must of course allow for negative as well as positive numbers.

In other words, the basic equation is valid only in the context of the bit manipulation procedures. If a bit-pattern is set up according to that equation, the value of the integer i will not necessarily be the same as the value we would get if the same bit-pattern were interpreted for the purposes of ordinary Fortran integer arithmetic. In fact if **ibitstring** defines a string of bits by that equation, then its value when regarded as a 32-digit binary number is given by

```
intval = SUM (MERGE (&
  TSOURCE=(/(2**k, k=0,31)/), &
  FSOURCE =(/(0, k=0,31)/), &
  MASK=BTEST(I=ibitstring, POS=(/(i,i=0,31)/))))
```

and this is not necessarily equal to **ibitstring**'s value when regarded as being of Fortran's integer type!

The following subroutine is an example of how a "non-advancing" input statement could be used to read a stream of bits. Since there is no requirement for format conversion, character-type editing is used, and one character at a time is input. It is assumed that one character represents one byte (eight bits) and that four characters (32 bits) can be stored in the "integer" **ibitstring**. The subroutine reads 32 bits, but with null bytes if there is an end-of-file, an end-of-record or an input error.

```
SUBROUTINE Instream (ibitstring, n_unit, icheck)
INTEGER :: ibitstring, n_unit, icheck=0
CHARACTER :: char(4), cnull=ACHAR(0)
DO k = 1, 4
  READ (UNIT=n_unit, FMT="(A)", &
  ADVANCE="NO", IOSTAT=icheck) char(k)
  IF (icheck==0) CYCLE
  char(k) = cnull
  EXIT
END DO
ibitstring = TRANSFER(SOURCE= char(1)//char(2)//char(3)&
  //char(4), MOLD=1)
END SUBROUTINE Instream
```

The **TRANSFER** function here is taking a concatenation of four characters (32 bits) and designating it as the "integer" **ibitstring** so that it could subsequently be used in the context of the intrinsic bit manipulation functions. The arithmetical value of **ibitstring** is irrelevant.

APPENDIX C

ISO_VARYING_STRINGS

Full details are given in this appendix of the data type **VARYING_STRING**, a standard modular extension to the Fortran language. The rationale and structure of the type are explained, and the operators and intrinsic procedures that can operate on it. After some examples of its use, there is a brief critique of the **ISO_VARYING_STRINGS** module.

C.1 Rationale

Since the publication of the Fortran 90 language by the International Standards Organization (ISO), an auxiliary standard has been accepted and published that adds a new data type to the language. The new data type is called **VARYING_STRING**. It allows for character strings of variable length to be manipulated, instead of just the fixed-length strings allowed with data of type **CHARACTER**.

Of course **CHARACTER**-type strings can be of any length, but the length of any particular variable of **CHARACTER** type must be declared in a type declaration statement and cannot subsequently be altered. The use of a specification expression, or an asterisk in the case of a procedure's dummy argument, provides only very limited leeway with the length of a character string. It has long been felt that this is an irksome restriction and that Fortran should allow character strings to have lengths that can vary dynamically as a program runs. The **VARYING_STRING** data type now provides this. When a **VARYING_STRING** variable is declared, the number of characters in the string is not, and indeed cannot be, specified. The programmer may write programs manipulating character strings without ever having to worry about their lengths.

Since **VARYING_STRING** data is an extension to Fortran, and not yet a required part of the language, the necessary facilities are in a module that is optional to the programmer. The module is called **ISO_VARYING_STRINGS**, and any program unit that is to have access to it must include the statement

```
USE ISO_VARYING_STRINGS
```

This module contains the definition of the **VARYING_STRING** data type together with a number of functions and subroutines that can be used to manipulate **VARYING_STRING** data. The names of these functions and subroutines are standardized and are given below.

ISO does not specify exactly how the module **ISO_VARYING_STRINGS** should be written. In principle, it could be written in a language other than Fortran and it need not be the same on all processors. The ISO standard only specifies what the module must do, not how it should do it. The situation is similar to that for Fortran compilers. However, **ISO_VARYING_STRINGS** can in fact be written in Fortran 90. In a version written by J. L. Schonfelder, the **VARYING_STRING** type is defined by code equivalent to

```
TYPE VARYING_STRING
  PRIVATE
  CHARACTER(1), POINTER :: chars(:)
END TYPE VARYING_STRING
```

which is to say that it is implemented as a pointer to a rank-one deferred-shape array, each element of that array being a single character. However, the user need not know these details and should not make any presumptions about the internal structure of the type.

C.2 The **VARYING_STRING** data type

Like any user-defined derived type, a variable of **VARYING_STRING** type must be declared by a type definition statement such as

```
TYPE (VARYING_STRING) :: forenames(2), surname, &
  qualifications(:)
```

This example also serves to illustrate that, like other data types, **VARYING_STRING** variables may be scalars or arrays, including assumed-shape arrays. The array **qualifications** represents an arbitrary number of character strings, each having arbitrary (and differing) numbers of characters.

The internal structure of **VARYING_STRING** data is **PRIVATE** to the **ISO_VARYING_STRINGS** module. Structure components (using the **%** notation) cannot therefore be used, and neither should structure constructors such as

```
surname = VARYING_STRING ((/"S","m","i","t","h"/))
```

because no assumptions should be made about the layout of the components of the data.

In principle the programmer could ascertain the structure of **VARYING_STRING** data by reading the code of the local implentation of the **ISO_VARYING_STRINGS** module or by using the **TRANSFER** function, but it would not be wise to assume that a **VARYING_STRING** argument can be used with **TRANSFER** and it is best avoided for the sake of program portability. However, this is no handicap: a range of procedures is provided to facilitate the use of **VARYING_STRING** data much more elegantly than with structure components and structure constructors. Some of these procedures extend the meanings of the intrinsic Fortran operators for assignment, concatenation and comparison so that they can be applied to **VARYING_STRING** data. Others are extensions of existing intrinsic procedures (such as **LEN**) normally only applicable to **CHARACTER** data. Additionally, there are some completely new procedures specifically for working with **VARYING_STRING** data.

C.3 Operators

The assignment operator (=) can be used between data of **VARYING_STRING** and **CHARACTER** types. Given, for example, the declarations

```
TYPE (VARYING_STRING) :: v, w
CHARACTER(6) :: c
```

then the assignment operator (=) can be used between **VARYING_STRING** and **CHARACTER** data in statements such as

```
v = w
v = c
c = v
```

If the variable on the left is of **VARYING_STRING** type (the first two cases above) then it takes on the length of the expression on the right whether that is itself **VARYING_STRING** (v=w) or **CHARACTER** (v=c). In the third case above (c=v), the string **v** will be either truncated or padded with blanks to yield the correct length for the **CHARACTER** string on the left. Note that the successive statements

```
c = v
v = c
```

will have the effect of truncating or padding **v** to the length of **c** (i.e. to six characters in this example).

VARYING_STRING data can therefore be constructed with assignments such as

```
v = "Smith"
```

The concatenation operator (`//`) can also be applied to **VARYING_STRING** data. With the above examples, the concatenations **v//w**, **v//c** and **c//v** are all legal and are expressions of **VARYING_STRING** type.

The comparison operators **==**, **/=**, **<**, **<=**, **>** and **>=** (and their equivalent forms **.EQ.**, etc.) can also be applied to **VARYING_STRING** data or to combinations of **VARYING_STRING** and **CHARACTER** data. The results are logical expressions having the same meanings as if the operators were applied to **CHARACTER** data.

However, with **VARYING_STRING** data all these operators are defined only for scalars. They cannot be used on arrays of variable-length strings. To concatenate arrays of such strings, for example, it would be necessary to construct a more complicated expression such as

```
(/ (v(i)//w(i), i=1,SIZE(v)) /)
```

Here, with **v** and **w** being arrays of **VARYING_STRING** type, **v(i)** and **w(i)** are elements of the arrays and are therefore scalars. The concatenation **v(i)//w(i)** is therefore valid and it is a scalar expression of **VARYING_STRING** type. The array constructor (`/.../`) yields an array of **VARYING_STRING** type equal in size to **v**, here assumed equal in size also to **w**.

C.4 Extensions of intrinsic procedures

The module **ISO_VARYING_STRINGS** contains procedures that allow the following functions to be called with scalar arguments of **VARYING_STRING** type. In the descriptions below, **v** and **w** represent **VARYING_STRING** variables or expressions and **c** represents a **CHARACTER** variable or expression. In this list, italicized arguments are optional.

- **LEN(v)**   Returns the length of the string (integer valued)
- **CHAR(v, *length*)**   Carries out type conversion, **VARYING_STRING** to **CHARACTER**. If the optional integer argument ***length*** is absent, **CHAR** is returned as a **CHARACTER** string containing the same characters, and having the same length, as **v**. If ***length*** is present, **v** is truncated or padded to make **CHAR** the specified length.
- **ICHAR(v)**   As for the intrinsic function **ICHAR(c)**, the argument must have length **1** and the result (an integer) is the position of that character in a processor-dependent sequence.
- **IACHAR(v)**   As **ICHAR(v)** above, but with the result being based on the ASCII character numbering sequence.
- **TRIM(v)**   Removes trailing blanks from **v**.
- **LEN_TRIM(v)**   Ascertains the number of characters in **v** not counting trailing blanks.
- **ADJUSTL(v)**   Replaces leading blanks by trailing blanks.

- **ADJUSTR(v)**   Replaces trailing blanks by leading blanks.
- **REPEAT(v, ncopies)**   **ncopies** must be a non-negative integer, and the function value is **v//v//v ... v//v**, being that number of copies of **v** concatenated together.
- **LLT(v, w)**   A logical function corresponding to that for **CHARACTER** data. The result is **.TRUE.** if **v** is "logically less than" **w**. This function also works with arguments of mixed **VARYING_STRING** and **CHARACTER** types, i.e. for **LLT(v, c)** and for **LLT(c, v)**.
- **LLE(v, w)**   Analogous to **LLT**.
- **LGE(v, w)**   Analogous to **LLT**.
- **LGT(v, w)**   Analogous to **LLT**.
- **INDEX(v, w, *back*)**   Returns an integer which is zero if **w** is not a substring of **v** but otherwise is the starting position (or the first starting position, if there is more than one) of the substring **w** in **v**. If the optional logical argument *back* is present and is true, then the function picks out the last such starting position if there is more than one occurrence of the substring **w** in **v**. Like **LLT**, this function also works if one of its string arguments is of **CHARACTER** type.
- **SCAN(v, w, *back*)**   Like **INDEX** above, but finding the position in **v** of any single character from **w** if **v** contains such a character.
- **VERIFY(v, w, *back*)**   Like **INDEX** above, but finding the position in **v** of a character that is *not* among those comprising **w**. **VERIFY** is zero if all the characters in **v** are also to be found in **w**.

C.5 New procedures for **VARYING_STRING** data

The procedures below do not correspond to existing intrinsic functions. Again, **v** and **w** are **VARYING_STRING** scalars and italicized arguments are optional.

VAR_STR(c)
An inverse to **CHAR**, this function takes a string of **CHARACTER** type as argument and returns the corresponding string of **VARYING_STRING** type.

GET(unit, v, set, separator, maxlen, iostat)
The subroutines **GET**, **PUT**, and **PUT_LINE** are very important innovations in Fortran because they provide for the first time a simple and modern alternative to the old-established set of i/o procedures **READ**, **WRITE** and **PRINT**. I/o procedures have to be provided as part of the **ISO_VARYING_STRINGS** package because otherwise it would be impossible to read or write **VARYING_STRING** data without first converting it to another type. A **VARYING_STRING** variable may not appear in a **READ**, **WRITE** or **PRINT** statement because the

internal structure of such a variable (i.e. how the characters are laid out) is not specified by the ISO standard and will be found to be **PRIVATE** to the **ISO_VARYING_STRINGS** module.

GET has one argument which must be present (**v** of **VARYING_STRING** type) and five arguments which are optional.

GET causes a sequence of characters to be read from the input unit number specified by the integer **unit**, or from the standard input device (normally a keyboard) if the argument **unit** is not present. The characters read are placed in the string **v**.

The input stream can be terminated by the occurrence of any one of the termination characters specified by comprising the string **set**, which may be of either **CHARACTER** or **VARYING_STRING** type. If **set** is present, there may also be an argument **separator** which would be of **VARYING_STRING** type and would be returned to indicate which character from **set** was actually encountered if indeed input had been halted in that way (and would be a zero-length string if it had not). Alternatively, input may be halted not by encountering a special character but when a certain specified maximum number of characters, **maxlen**, have been read from the input record.

If the argument **maxlen** is not present, the input stream will be terminated at the end of the current input record or file. The integer argument **iostat** can be used to check what happened: it will be returned with a negative value if an end-of-file is reached, with a different negative value if an end-of-record is reached, as zero if the record has not been read to its end, or with a positive value if some sort of reading error has occurred. The argument **separator**, if present, would be returned as a zero-length string.

A subsequent call to the **GET** subroutine will continue with the reading of the current record (if it had not reached its end) or will start on the next record.

Although most of **GET**'s arguments are optional, there should be no confusion between them: **unit** is present if the first argument is an integer, then comes the string **v**, if there is a second string it is **set**, and if there is a third string it is **separator**. Then, a second integer argument will be **maxlen**, and a third will be **iostat**. You cannot have **separator** without **set**, and you cannot have **iostat** without **maxlen**.

Although **GET** is designed for **VARYING_STRING** data, it can also be used for data of other types by performing a type conversion to **CHARACTER** data (using **CHAR**) and then, if necessary, to another data type by using the **TRANSFER** function or by writing and reading an auxiliary internal file. Similar comments apply to the **PUT** and **PUT_LINE** subroutines described below.

GET, **PUT**, and **PUT_LINE** read and write formatted sequential files, but unfortunately (since the unit number must be an argument of integer type) not internal files.

PUT(*unit, v, iostat*)

This is a subroutine that is an inverse of **GET** in the sense that it writes a string of characters **v** to an external file which, if not the default output unit, is specified by the unit number **unit**. If there is a current record, the string is appended to it, but otherwise a new record is started. The argument *iostat*, if present, is returned zero or positive according to whether the writing operation was successful or led to an error condition.

PUT_LINE(*unit, v, iostat*)

This subroutine is very similar to **PUT** except that, when the string **v** has been written, the output record is terminated and the file is moved to the start of a subsequent record. With screen output, **PUT_LINE** would move to the start of the next line after writing **v**, while **PUT** would stay on the same line unless it had reached the end of it.

INSERT(v, *istart*, w)

The argument **istart** being an integer, this function inserts the string **w** into the string **v** immediately before the character at position **istart** within **v**. If **istart** is less than **1**, **w** is inserted at the beginning as if **istart=1**. If **istart** is greater than **LEN(v)**, **w** is appended to **v**. **INSERT** is a function whose value is of **VARYING_STRING** type. It makes no difference if one or both of **v** and **u** are of **CHARACTER** type instead of **VARYING_STRING**.

REPLACE(v, *istart, ifinish, target*, w, *every, back*)

This function may replace one or more substrings within **v** by copies of the string **w**. If the second argument is an integer, it is *istart* and this represents the position in **v** before which **w** will be inserted. If the third argument is an integer it is *ifinish*, and **w** replaces the characters from position *istart* going rightward to position *ifinish* in **v**. However, if *ifinish* is less than *istart* or greater than the length of **v**, then the string **w** is simply added at the beginning or end of **v** without any deletion of characters.

If *ifinish* is absent, **w** replaces its own length's-worth of **v**'s characters (or whatever number remain, if fewer) going rightward from position *istart*. If *istart* is less than **1** it is treated as if it were equal to **1**, and if it is greater than the length of **v** then **w** is simply appended to **v**.

Alternatively, if **REPLACE**'s second argument is a string, the string is *target* and the function looks for occurrences of *target* within **v**, searching from right to left. The first occurrence of *target* within **v**, if there is one, will be replaced by a copy of **w**. If the argument **w** is followed by a true logical argument, *every*, then all distinct occurrences of *target* are replaced by copies of **w**. A second logical argument, *back*, may follow *every*, and if *back* is true then the search for *target* is carried out from right to left through **v**.

The **REPLACE** function can therefore work in either of two modes according to whether the replaced string is identified by its position (if *istart* is

345

present) or by its content (if *target* is present). The logical arguments *every* and *back* may only be present if *target* is present, and *ifinish* may only be present if *istart* is.

As in the case of the **INSERT** function, the string arguments in **REPLACE** may be of either character type but the result is always of **VARYING_STRING** type. Examples are:

REPLACE("aaaa","aa","b") is equal to **VAR_STR("baa")**

REPLACE("aaaa","aa","b",.TRUE.) is equal to **VAR_STR("bb")**

REPLACE("aaaa","aa","b",.FALSE.,.TRUE.) is equal to
  VAR_STR("aab")

REPLACE("aa","a","bb",.TRUE.) is equal to **VAR_STR("bbbb")**

REMOVE(v, istart, ifinish)

REMOVE(v) removes all the characters from **v**, leaving a zero-length string.

REMOVE(v, istart) removes all the characters from **v** starting from position *istart*, *istart* being an integer. The function's result is what is left.

If the integer *ifinish* is not less than *istart*, then **REMOVE(v, istart, ifinish)** will remove from **v** the characters from position *istart* to position *ifinish*. If *ifinish* is less than *istart*, no characters are removed.

The argument v may be of either character type. An example is:

  REMOVE(text, LEN(text))

which cuts off the last character of **text**.

EXTRACT(v, istart, ifinish)

This function yields the substring of **v** that would be removed if the **REMOVE** function were called with the same arguments. Examples are:

  EXTRACT(text, LEN(text))

which gives the final character of **text**, and

  EXTRACT(text,2)

which cuts off the first character of **text**, i.e. extracts the rest of **text**, from the second character on.

SPLIT(v, w, set, separator, back)

This is a subroutine which runs through **v** looking for the occurrence of a character from among those specified by being members of the string **set**. When such a character is found (or at the end of **v** if none is), the characters that were to the left of it form the string **w** and only those to the right of it are retained in **v**. If *separator* is present, and a character from **set** was encountered, *separator* is returned with that character.

The logical argument *back*, if present and true, causes the search for a character from **set** to be carried out from right to left through **v**. In this case **v** will remain with the leftmost part, and **w** the rightmost part, of the original **v**.

The arguments **v, w** and *separator* must be of **VARYING_STRING** type; **set** may alternatively be of **CHARACTER** type.

An example is as follows: after

```
Type (VARYING_STRING) :: title, name
```

the code fragment

```
title = "Alexander the Great"
CALL SPLIT(title, name, " ")
```

has the same effect as

```
title = "the Great"
name = "Alexander"
```

but

```
title = "Alexander the Great"
CALL SPLIT(title, name, "")
```

has the same effect as

```
title = ""
name = "Alexander the Great"
```

because in the latter case **set** contains no characters, and therefore no character from **set** is encountered in **v** (i.e. in **title**), and therefore all the characters from **v** are decanted into **w** (i.e. into **name**).

C.6 Programs using `ISO_VARYING_STRINGS`

As a very simple example of the use of the **VARYING_STRING** data type, the following program reads text from the keyboard word by word, assuming that words are separated either by blanks or by the end of a line. The words are then displayed on the screen, one to a line. The program stops when the word **terminate** is typed.

```
PROGRAM Wordfinder
USE ISO_VARYING_STRINGS
TYPE (VARYING_STRING) :: word

! Set up a string containing the non-alphabetic characters:
CHARACTER(*), PARAMETER :: &
   set = "`!""£$%&*()_-+={}[]:@~;'#<>?,./|\¬^1234567890 "

! Read the words
Words: DO
```

```
! Read in one word
CALL GET (word, " ")

! Remove any non-alphabetic characters
Characters: DO
  ipos = SCAN(word, set); IF (ipos==0) EXIT Characters
  word = REMOVE(word, ipos)
END DO Characters

! If appropriate, display the word on screen
IF (word=="terminate") EXIT Words
IF (word/="") CALL PUT_LINE (word)

END DO Words

END PROGRAM Wordfinder
```

The program below does much the same job, but it reads characters one at a time from the keyboard and forms words by concatenating sequences of adjacent alphabetic characters.

```
PROGRAM Wordfinder_II
USE ISO_VARYING_STRINGS
TYPE (VARYING_STRING) :: word, onekey

! Set up strings containing the alphabetic characters:
CHARACTER(26), PARAMETER :: &
  uppercase = "ABCDEFGHIJKLMNOPRSTUVWXYZ", &
  lowercase = "abcdefghijklmnopqrstuvwxyz"

! Read the words
Words: DO

! Read in one word
word = ""
Word: DO

! Read in one keystroke
CALL GET (onekey, 1)

! A blank ends a word
IF (onekey==" ".OR.onekey=="") EXIT Words
! Note that a null input may arise at the end of a
! record
! It is assumed that no word is split between two
! records

! Replace any upper-case letter by its lower-case
equivalent
ipos = VERIFY (uppercase, onekey)
```

```
IF (ipos/=0) onekey = EXTRACT (lowercase, ipos, ipos)

! Ignore non-alphabetic characters
ipos = VERIFY (lowercase, onekey)
IF (ipos==0) CYCLE Words

word = word//onekey

END DO Words

! If appropriate, display the word on screen
IF (word=="terminate") EXIT Words
IF (word/="") CALL PUT_LINE (word)

END DO Words

END PROGRAM Wordfinder_II
```

Arguably, **Wordfinder_II** is a better-designed program than **Wordfinder** because (a) it reads the data in character by character in the first place, while **Wordfinder** reads complete words and then has to scan through them; and (b) **Wordfinder_II** checks positively that characters are alphabetic, instead of depending on a possibly incomplete list of non-alphabetic characters. Both programs are somewhat inelegant in using both character data types: with **ISO_VARYING_STRINGS** being used, there is a case for not using **CHARACTER**-type data at all (except to specify constants such as **""**). Also, both programs fail to check against i/o errors by utilizing the *iostat* argument of **GET** and **PUT_LINE**.

The following example shows a way of implementing a derived data type in Fortran to represent sets of discrete objects. The sets can be of any size, and the problem of modelling them can be simplified and solved economically using **ISO_VARYING_STRINGS** as a tool.

```
MODULE Sets
! This module defines a new data type, "Set", together
! with a number of associated operators and procedures.
! An entity of type Set is a finite set of unordered
! distinct elements. Since a set may have any number of
! elements, this module is coded with the help of the
! VARYING_STRING type defined in ISO_VARYING_STRINGS.
! Internally, a set will be represented by an ordered
! sequence of positive integers separated by commas, e.g.
!
! 2,5,17,18,19,572,1024
!
! but coded as a VARYING_STRING data object
!
! VAR_STR("2,5,17,18,19,572,1024")
```

```
!
! together with an integer that is the number of
! elements in the set.
!
! It is assumed that integers will be used as set-member
! identifiers, i.e. each potential member of a set can
! be uniquely identified by an integer label. Each
! member may also involve further data. For example, if
! the sets are the members of different golf clubs then
! their names and addresses, handicaps,etc. will have to
! be stored somewhere. The association between a
! member's identification number and that data is not
! the concern of this module. This module merely
! manipulates sets of identification numbers.
!

USE ISO_VARYING_STRINGS
! Enables VARYING_STRING type to be utilized.

PRIVATE
! Entities within this module will normally be
! inaccessible outside it.

TYPE Set
  PRIVATE
  ! The components are private even if Set itself is
  ! made public.
  TYPE (VARYING_STRING) :: stringset
  INTEGER :: multiplicity
END TYPE Set

PUBLIC :: Set, Construct, Union
! These entities are to be accessible outside the
! module.

CONTAINS
! Module procedures are as follows:

FUNCTION Construct (integers)
! Constructs a set out of the array of integers provided
! as argument.

TYPE (Set) :: Construct, temporary
INTEGER, INTENT (IN) :: integers(:)
TYPE (VARYING_STRING) :: build

CHARACTER(100) :: internal_file
! Identification numbers may have up to 100 digits.
```

```fortran
CHARACTER(100) :: item
! Sets may have up to 100 members

INTEGER :: itemp1 (SIZE(integers)), &
itemp2(SIZE(integers)), number, n

! First, order the integers and eliminate duplicates.
! Duplicated entries are replaced by negatives.

itemp1 = integers
n = 0

number = SIZE(integers)

Order: DO i = 1, number
  max = MAXLOC(itemp1)
  itemp2(number+1-i) = itemp1 (max)
  itemp1 (max) = -1
END DO Order

Duplicates: DO i = 2, number
  IF (itemp2(i)==itemp2(i-1)) itemp2(i) = -1
END DO Duplicates

build= VAR_STR("")
IF (number/=0) THEN
  DO i = 1, number
    IF (itemp2(i)<0) CYCLE
    n = n+1
    WRITE (internal_file, "(I100)") itemp2(i)
    READ (internal_file, "(A100)") item
    build = build // TRIM(ADJUSTL(item))
    build = build // ","
  END DO
END IF

temporary%stringset = Remove (build, LEN(build))
temporary%multiplicity = number
Construct = temporary
END FUNCTION Construct


FUNCTION Union (s1, s2)
! Returns the union of the two sets s1 and s2

TYPE (Set) :: Union
TYPE (Set), INTENT (IN) :: s1, s2
VARYING_STRING :: contents1, contents2
CHARACTER(100) :: internal_file
CHARACTER(100) :: item
```

351

```
INTEGER :: integers1(s1%multiplicity), &
integers2(s2%multiplicity)
INTEGER :: number1, number2, icount1, icount2, icount3, &
 numbers_full_3, more
INTEGER :: integers3(s1%multiplicity + s2%multiplicity)

Trivial: IF (s1%multiplicity==0) THEN
  Union = s2
ELSE IF (s2%multiplicity==0) THEN
  Union = s1
ELSE

  ! Unpack s1 and s2

  contents1 = s1%stringset
  number1 = s1%multiplicity
  DO i = 1, number1
    CALL SPLIT(contents1, item, ",")
    WRITE (internal_file, "(A100)") item
    READ (internal_file, "(I100)") integers1(i)
  END DO

  contents2 = s2%stringset
  number2 = s2%multiplicity
  DO i = 1, number2
    CALL SPLIT(contents2, item, ",")
    WRITE (internal_file, "(A100)") item
    READ (internal_file, "(I100)") integers2(i)
  END DO

  ! Now combine integers1 with integers2 and construct
! Union
  Pairs: DO
    icount1 = 1
    icount2 = 1
    icount3 = 1
    IF (integers1(icount1)<integers2(icount2)) THEN
      integers3(icount3) = integers1(icount1)
      icount1 = icount1 + 1
      icount3 = icount3 + 1
    ELSE IF (integers1(icount1)>integers2(icount2)) THEN
      integers3(icount3) = integers2(icount2)
      icount2 = icount2 + 1
      icount3 = icount3 + 1
    ELSE IF (integers1(icount1)==integers2(icount2)) &
      THEN
```

```
      integers3(icount3) = integers2(icount2)
      icount1 = icount1 + 1
      icount2 = icount2 + 1
      icount3 = icount3 + 1
    END IF
    IF(icount1>number1.OR.icount2>number2) EXIT Pairs
  END DO Pairs

  IF (icount1==(number1+1).AND.icount2==(number2+1)) &
      THEN
    ! Enough of integers3 has been filled and
    numbers_full_3 = icount3-1
  ELSE IF (icount1>number1) THEN
    ! fill out integers3 with the remainder of integers2
    more=number2-icount2+1
    integers3(icount3:icount3+more-1 ) = &
      integers2(icount2:number2)
    numbers_full_3 = icount3+more-1
  ELSE IF(icount2>number2) THEN
    ! Fill out integers3 with the remainder of integers1
    more=number1-icount1+1
    integers3(icount3:icount3+more-1) = &
      integers1(icount1:number1)
    numbers_full_3 = icount3+more-1
  END IF
  Union = Construct (integers3(1:numbers_full_3))
 END IF Trivial
 END FUNCTION Union

 END MODULE Sets
```

C.7 Deficiencies of ISO_VARYING_STRINGS

Although the **VARYING_STRING** data type is a great improvement on the **CHARACTER** type, it is interesting to notice that the specification of **ISO_VARYING_STRINGS** is a compromise designed to allow the module to be written in Fortran. So, **VARYING_STRING** is a derived type like any other, albeit with its internal structure hidden (to avoid inadvertent name clashes) by **PRIVATE** statements within the module.

Consequently, **ISO_VARYING_STRINGS** has one or two disadvantages. It is not possible to write constants of **VARYING_STRING** type. So, a statement like

```
word = ""
```

(from the example program `Wordfinder_II` above) involves the implicit use of **CHARACTER** data because `""` is a **CHARACTER** constant. To avoid implicit or unexpected type conversions, **VARYING_STRING** constants should ideally be written using **VAR_STR**, e.g. in the form

```
VAR_STR("abcdefghijklmnopqrst")
```

The procedures listed in this appendix are strictly speaking module procedures, not intrinsic procedures or external procedures. Functions like **LEN** and **CHAR** are therefore classed as module procedures when their arguments are of one type but are intrinsic procedures with another type. This could conceivably make a difference to code which uses the **INTRINSIC** statement. Functions such as **CHAR** and **IACHAR** are elemental as intrinsic functions, but not as they are extended by **ISO_VARYING_STRINGS**. Also, the assignment operator cannot be used elementally with **VARYING_STRING** arrays. So, **VARYING_STRING** arrays cannot always be manipulated as easily as **CHARACTER** arrays.

Another disadvantage of **ISO_VARYING_STRINGS** arises because the natural way for the module to work is by using **ALLOCATE** statements with array pointers to allocate sufficient memory space to hold the strings. However, there is then no easy way of deallocating the space when the corresponding variable is no longer needed. For example, on return from a subroutine that uses large arrays of non-saved local data of **VARYING_STRING** and **CHARACTER** types, the space taken up by the **CHARACTER** arrays will in principle be released, but the space taken up by the **VARYING_STRING** arrays would not be deallocated and therefore could not be used to store any other data while the program is running. So, **ISO_VARYING_STRINGS** is likely to be wasteful of computer memory, at least if it is written using array pointers in Fortran 90 (see the comment at the end of Section 12.1 concerning automatic deallocation in Fortran 95).

These remarks are not intended to discourage the use of **ISO_VARYING_STRINGS**, merely to make it clear that **VARYING_STRING** is a derived type and has the same limitations of any other derived type defined in Fortran. If, in a future version of the language, **VARYING_STRING** is adopted as an additional intrinsic type, then a good feature will have evolved into an excellent one – which is what the evolutionary philosophy of Fortran is all about.

Fortran 95's new features: summary

The new features of Fortran 95, which were not present in Fortran 90, are summarized below:

D.1 FORALL (Section 6.5)

FORALL statements and FORALL constructs can be regarded as like DO loops but without the time sequence implied in DO. FORALL is intended to allow for parallel execution. Examples of the FORALL statement are

```
FORALL (i=1:n, i/=13) square(i,i) = backdiag(n-i)
FORALL (j=1:n-1, Test(r(j))==.TRUE.), r(j) = Fun(r(j)) &
  + Fun(r(j+1))
```

In FORALL assignments, the right-hand sides are all calculated before any of the left-hand sides are changed. Any procedures that arise, like Test and Fun above, must be pure (see Appendix D.5).

D.2 Enhancements to WHERE (Sections 4.9 and 6.6)

WHERE statements and constructs may now be nested within one another and within FORALL constructs. In a WHERE construct, masks may be applied not only to the WHERE statement itself but also to ELSE WHERE statements.

D.3 Initialization of pointers (Sections 8.7 and 13.1)

Variables which are pointers may be initialized with the NULL function (see Appendix D.8).

D.4 Default initialization of derived types (Section 12.5)

Data of derived type may be initialized within the derived type definition. This default initialization applies to all variables of the type and can be overridden for individual variables by initialization of the usual sort in type declaration statements. For example,

```
TYPE Default_zero_real
  REAL :: r = 0.0
END TYPE
```

defines a new type of real variable which, unlike **REAL**, is always automatically initialized to zero.

D.5 Pure procedures (Section 11.2)

A pure function calculates its value but does not alter the values of its arguments or of any other variables accessible from outside it. A pure subroutine may affect the values of **INTENT (IN OUT)** or **INTENT (OUT)** arguments.

Pure functions may be used in specification expressions (Section 11.9).

D.6 Elemental procedures (Section 11.3)

Elemental procedures are pure procedures which are defined in terms of scalar arguments but which may be referenced elementally in array assignments. So, in Fortran 95, the programmer may write procedures, like the intrinsic elemental procedures, that can be called with scalar or array arguments.

D.7 Automatic deallocation of allocatable arrays (Section 12.1)

To avoid memory loss, allocatable arrays (unless declared with the **SAVE** attribute) will be automatically deallocated on return from the procedure in which they occur.

D.8 New and enhanced intrinsic procedures (Appendix F)

- **MINLOC** and **MAXLOC**   These functions have been extended so that their arguments correspond to those of **MINVAL** and **MAXVAL**.
- **CEILING** and **FLOOR**   These may now be called with a **KIND** keyword.
- **NULL**   This is a new function that evaluates to a disassociated pointer.
- **SIGN**   This function may distinguish between positive and negative zero

if the processor supports the distinction.

- **CPU_TIME** This new intrinsic subroutine may, in the case of parallel processing, return an array giving the timings of the individual processors.

D.9 Newly obsolescent features

Computed **GO TO**, statement functions, **DATA** interspersed with executable statements, assumed character length functions (which can be recoded as subroutines), fixed-form source code, and assumed-size arrays have been added to the official list of Fortran's obsolescent features.

They join the rarely-used features that were declared to be obsolescent in Fortran 90, i.e. the arithmetic **IF**, a syntax for returning from a procedure to a particular labelled statement, and some irregular ways of terminating **DO** loops.

D.10 Deletions from Fortran 90

Fortran 95 deletes some of the features that were labelled as obsolescent in the Fortran 90 standard, i.e. **PAUSE, ASSIGN**, assigned **GO TO**, real indices for **DO** loops, branching to an **END IF** from an outer block, assigned integers as **FORMAT** specifications, and **H** editing.

With the advent of user-written elemental subroutines (Appendix D.6) defined assignment statements (in **WHERE**) are now restricted to being elemental.

Fortran 95 statements

This appendix is in two parts. Appendix E.1 lists a "core" of Fortran 95 statements whose usage is recommended. Appendix E.2 lists statements that, although neither illegal nor officially obsolescent, are not recommended. The distinction between "recommended" and "non-recommended" statements is a matter of opinion, and sometimes merely style, on which Fortran specialists have differing views.

E.1 Recommended statements

- Scoping unit boundaries

`PROGRAM`	`END PROGRAM`
`SUBROUTINE` `PURE SUBROUTINE` `ELEMENTAL SUBROUTINE` `RECURSIVE SUBROUTINE`	`END SUBROUTINE`
`FUNCTION` `PURE FUNCTION` `ELEMENTAL FUNCTION` `RECURSIVE FUNCTION`	`END FUNCTION`
`MODULE`	`END MODULE`
`TYPE`	`END TYPE`

- Program unit control statements

```
              USE
           INTERFACE
       MODULE PROCEDURE
         END INTERFACE
            CONTAINS
              CALL
   EXTERNAL                        PRIVATE
   INTRINSIC                       PUBLIC
```

- Type declaration statements

```
   REAL              INTEGER           COMPLEX
   LOGICAL           CHARACTER         TYPE (...)
```

- Memory management statements

```
   ALLOCATE                          DEALLOCATE
   Pointer assignment (=>)           NULLIFY
```

- Assignment statement (=)

- Execution control statements

```
   SELECT CASE       IF                DO
   CASE              ELSE IF           DO WHILE
   END SELECT        ELSE              CYCLE
                     END IF            EXIT
                                       END DO
   WHERE
   ELSE WHERE        FORALL
   END WHERE         END FORALL        STOP
```

- Input/output statements

```
   OPEN      READ      BACKSPACE      INQUIRE
   CLOSE     WRITE     REWIND         ENDFILE
```

- Pseudo-statements

```
   INCLUDE                    Comment line (! ...)
```

- Alphabetical list

ALLOCATE	Dynamically allocates memory to arrays or to pointers.
Assignment statement (=)	Gives a value to a variable.
BACKSPACE	Moves an i/o file back by one record.
CALL	Invokes a subroutine.
CASE	Specifies a range of values for a **CASE** expression.
CHARACTER	Declares data of character type.
CLOSE	Closes an i/o unit.
Comment (!)	For program annotation.
COMPLEX	Declares data of complex type.
CONTAINS	Heads a set of module procedures.
CYCLE	Jump to the bottom of a **DO** loop.
DEALLOCATE	Deallocates a pointer or an allocatable array.
DO	Starts a **DO** loop.
ELEMENTAL FUNCTION	Starts an elemental function
ELEMENTAL SUBROUTINE	Starts an elemental subroutine
ELSE	Heads the final catch-all block within an **IF** construct.
ELSE IF	Heads an alternative block within an **IF** construct.
ELSE WHERE	Heads an alternative block within a **WHERE** construct.
END DO	End of a **DO** loop.
END FORALL	End of a **FORALL** construct.
END IF	End of an **IF** construct.
END INTERFACE	End of an interface block.
END FUNCTION	End of a function subprogram.
END MODULE	End of a module.
END PROGRAM	End of the main program.
END SELECT	End of a **CASE** selection construct.
END SUBROUTINE	End of a subroutine.
END TYPE	End of a derived type definition block.
END WHERE	End of a **WHERE** construct.
ENDFILE	Writes an end-of-file record.
EXIT	Jump out of a **DO** loop.
EXTERNAL	Declares that a name refers to a procedure.
FORALL	Heads a **FORALL** construct or **FORALL** statement.
FUNCTION	Starts a function subprogram.
IF	Conditional statement.
IF ... THEN	Heads a block of conditional statements

361

INCLUDE	Inserts a file of additional Fortran statements.
INQUIRE	I/o unit general status inquiry.
INTEGER	Declares data of integer type.
INTERFACE	Start of an interface block.
INTRINSIC	Declares that a name is that of an intrinsic function.
LOGICAL	Declares data of logical type.
MODULE	Starts a module.
MODULE PROCEDURE	Declares names of module procedures.
NULLIFY	Disassociates a pointer.
OPEN	Opens an i/o unit or file.
Pointer Assignment (**=>**)	Points a pointer to a target.
PRIVATE	Bars access of data from outside the module.
PROGRAM	Starts the main program.
PUBLIC	Permits access of data from outside the module.
PURE FUNCTION	Starts a pure function.
PURE SUBROUTINE	Starts a pure subroutine.
READ	Causes data to be input.
REAL	Declares data of real type.
RECURSIVE FUNCTION	Starts a function which may refer to itself.
RECURSIVE SUBROUTINE	Starts a subroutine which may call itself.
REWIND	Go back to the first record of an i/o file.
SELECT CASE	Starts a **CASE** construct.
STOP	Halts execution immediately.
SUBROUTINE	Starts a subroutine.
Type declaration (...: :...)	The general data-declaration statement.
TYPE (Typename)	Declares data of a specified derived type.
TYPE Typename	Starts a derived type definition block.
USE	Summons the contents of a module.
WHERE	Heads a **WHERE** statement or a **WHERE** construct.
WRITE	Causes data to be output.

E.2 Non-recommended statements

E.2.1 Miscellaneous statements

The following are discouraged either because they are regarded as linguistically obsolescent (e.g. the arithmetic **IF**), or because they have been superseded by newer Fortran syntax (e.g. data modules have superseded **COMMON**), or because of inelegance.

Arithmetic **IF**	A switchable **GO TO** choosing between three labelled statements.

ASSIGN	Assigns a statement label to an integer variable.
Assigned **GO TO**	A **GO TO** with a variable statement label.
BLOCK DATA	Introduces a block data subprogram.
COMMON	Declares data to be accessible from more than one program unit.
Computed **GO TO**	A switchable **GO TO**, specifying several labelled statements.
CONTINUE	A dummy statement, to carry a label.
DATA	Gives values to variables
DOUBLE PRECISION	Type declaration statement for the obsolete **DOUBLE PRECISION** type.
END	Terminates a program unit (use suffixed **END**s instead).
END BLOCK DATA	End of a **BLOCK DATA** unit.
ENTRY	Alternative entry point to a procedure.
EQUIVALENCE	Declares more than one name for the same area of memory.
FORMAT	A labelled statement containing an i/o format specification.
GO TO	Jump to another statement.
IMPLICIT	Changes the initial-letter data type convention.
IMPLICIT NONE	Withdraws the initial-letter data type convention.
NAMELIST	Specifies data to be included in a **NAMELIST** group.
PAUSE	Causes program execution to pause.
PRINT	Writes data to a default output unit.
RETURN	Alternative point of exit from a procedure.
SEQUENCE	Declare sets of data to be stored sequentially in memory.
Statement function	A form of one-line internal function.

E.2.2 Attribute specification statements

In spite of the initial-letter convention which allows **REAL** and **INTEGER** variables to be used without the need for a type declaration statement (TDS), it is recommended that virtually all data (and function names) should be declared in TDSs. Consequently, the following statements are unnecessary because these attributes can be specified within the TDS for the data involved.

ALLOCATABLE	Declares an array to be allocatable.
DIMENSION	Declares data to be arrays of a specified shape.
INTENT	Declares dummy argument data to be incoming/outgoing.
OPTIONAL	Declares a dummy argument to be optional.
PARAMETER	Declares a named constant.
POINTER	Declares a data item to be a pointer.

SAVE   Declares subprogram data to be retained on return.

TARGET   Declare that a data item may be the target of a pointer.

E.2.3 Type-specific function statements

It is best to avoid altogether the variants of the **FUNCTION** statement which have a prefix indicating the type of the function's result. The type should instead be specified by a type declaration statement after a **FUNCTION** statement. So, the only prefixes used before the **FUNCTION** keyword should be **ELEMENTAL, PURE,** or **RECURSIVE.**

Fortran 95 intrinsic procedures

This appendix lists all the Fortran 95 intrinsic procedures. It does not include the functions defined in **ISO_VARYING_STRINGS** (Appendix C) or in High Performance Fortran (Chapter 15). In Appendix F.1 "specific" (as opposed to generic) function names are not listed: the different specific names, whose use is not recommended, are listed in Appendix F.2.

F.1 Recommended intrinsic procedures

"Intrinsic" procedures are one of the six or seven classes of procedures in Fortran:

- Intrinsic procedures
- External procedures
- Module procedures
- Dummy procedures (no independent existence)
- Extrinsic procedures (HPF only)
- Internal procedures
- Statement functions

and are themselves divided into four sub-classes:

- Elemental functions
- Inquiry functions
- Transformational functions
- Subroutines

Of these, the elemental functions are most numerous and are used mainly for manipulating data and making standard calculations. They have the feature that they may be used with either scalar or array arguments, correspondingly returning either scalar or array values.

Elemental functions

- Numeric functions:

ABS	ANINT	CONJG	MAX	MODULO
AIMAG	CEILING	FLOOR	MIN	NINT
AINT	CMPLX	INT	MOD	REAL

- Mathematical functions:

ACOS	ATAN2	EXP	SIN	TAN
ASIN	COS	LOG	SINH	TANH
ATAN	COSH	LOG10	SQRT	

- Character functions:

ACHAR	IACHAR	LEN_TRIM	LLE	SCAN
ADJUSTL	INDEX	LGE	LLT	TRIM
ADJUSTR	LEN	LGT	REPEAT	VERIFY

- Logical function:

LOGICAL

- Bit manipulation functions:

IAND	IBITS	IEOR	ISHFT	BTEST
IBCLR	IBSET	IOR	ISHFTC	NOT

- Floating-point manipulation functions:

EXPONENT	RRSPACING	FRACTION	NEAREST	SCALE
SPACING	SETEXPONENT			

- Vector and matrix multiplication functions:

MATMUL	DOTPRODUCT

Inquiry functions

- Argument presence inquiry function:

PRESENT

- Character inquiry function:

LEN

- Kind inquiry functions:

KIND

- Numeric inquiry functions:

DIGITS	EPSILON	HUGE	MINEXPONENT
RADIX	RANGE	TINY	MAXEXPONENT PRECISION

- Bit inquiry function:

BIT_SIZE

- Array inquiry functions:
  LBOUND   **UBOUND**   **SHAPE**   **SIZE**   **ALLOCATED**
- Pointer inquiry function:
  ASSOCIATED

Transformational functions

- Character functions:
  REPEAT   **TRIM**
- Kind functions:
  SELECTED_INTEGER_KIND   **SELECTED_REAL KIND**
- Transfer function:
  TRANSFER
- Array reduction functions:
  ALL   **ANY**   **COUNT**   **MAXVAL**
  MINVAL   **PRODUCT**   **SUM**
- Array construction functions:
  MERGE   **PACK**   **SPREAD**   **UNPACK**
- Array reshape function:
  RESHAPE
- Array manipulation functions:
  EOSHIFT   **CSHIFT**   **TRANSPOSE**
- Array location functions:
  MINLOC   **MAXLOC**
- Pointer function:
  NULL (*Fortran 95*)

Intrinsic subroutines

- Bit-copying:
  MVBITS
- Timekeeping:
  DATE_AND_TIME   **SYSTEM_CLOCK**
  CPU_TIME (*Fortran 95*)
- Random numbers:
  RANDOM   **RANDOMSEED**

Alphabetical list

All the intrinsic procedures are listed below (but see also Appendix F.2). After each procedure name there is a bracketed list of arguments. All the arguments of all the intrinsic procedures have keywords, and it is by the keywords that they are indicated here (but in lower case, contrary to our usual convention for quoting keywords). Optional arguments are italicized. In some complex cases, the descriptions are followed by references to sections in this book where more details are given.

It should noticed that all trigonometric functions, and their inverses, refer to angles in radians.

To indicate data types, the following abbreviations are made:

I = Integer	R = Real	Z = Complex
C = Character	S = Character string	L = Logical

Where no data type is indicated, the type is irrelevant. A number of procedures (ALLOCATED, ASSOCIATED, CSHIFT, EOSHIFT, MERGE, NULL, PACK, PRESENT, RESHAPE, SOURCE, SIZE, SPREAD, TRANSFER, TRANSPOSE and UBOUND) may have arguments of any type, not excluding derived types. The PRESENT function, moreover, may have a dummy procedure name as argument.

F.2 Non-recommended procedures

Strictly speaking this section deals not with non-recommended procedures but non-recommended procedure *names*. The list below (p. 375) gives several type-specific names for functions that exist (and are listed in Appendix F.1) under different generic names. The names below are not essential since the functions can always be invoked through the generic names in Appendix F.1 (see Section 5.8).

In addition, the "double precision" functions DBLE and DPROD have been included in this list: they are unnecessary since the old double precision data type is not recommended.

Argument and result types follow the abbreviations listed at the start of Appendix F.1, with the addition of D for double precision data.

Fortran 96 intrinsic procedures

Name	Argument type	Result type (for functions)	
ABS(a)	R, I or Z	R or I	Absolute value
ACHAR(i)	I	C	ASCII character
ACOS(x)	R	R	Inverse cosine, $\cos^{-1}(x)$
ADJUSTL(string)	C	C	Replace leading blanks by trailing blanks
ADJUSTR(string)	C	C	Replace trailing blanks by leading blanks.
AIMAG(z)	Z	R	Imaginary part
AINT(a, kind)	R	R	Truncate to a whole number by removing fractional part $AINT(-a) = -AINT(a)$
ALL(mask, dim)	L, I	L	True if all elements of **mask** (or all elements along dimension **dim** are true (Section 5.7)
ALLOCATED(array)		L	True if array is allocated
ANINT(a, kind)	R	R	Nearest whole number
ANY(mask, dim)	L, I	L	True if any element of **mask** (or any element along dimension **dim** is true. (Section 5.7)
ASIN(x)	R	R	Inverse sine, $\sin^{-1}(x)$
ASSOCIATED(pointer, target)		L	Is **pointer** associated with **target**?
ATAN(x)	R	R	Inverse tangent, $\tan^{-1}(x)$
ATAN2(y, x)	R, R	R	Inverse tangent, $\tan^{-1}(y/x)$, but in the range $(-\pi, +\pi)$ reflecting the signs of both **x** and **y**. Other inverse trigonometrical functions have results in the range $(-\frac{1}{2}\pi, +\frac{1}{2}\pi)$
BIT_SIZE(i)	I	I	Number of bits in an integer. (Appendix B.1)
BTEST(i, pos)	I	L	Tests the bit in position **pos** within the integer **I**. (Appendix B.2)
CEILING(a, kind)	R	I	The integer equal to **a** or immediately above it in the positive direction. The **kind** parameter is a *Fortran 95 feature not in Fortran 90*.
CHAR(i, kind)	I	C	The character in the **i**th position in the processor's sequence.
CMPLX(x, y, kind)	I/R/Z, I/R, I	Z	Constructs (or changes the **kind** of) the complex number **x** + **i**y.
CONJG(z)	Z	Z	Complex conjugate, z^*.
COS(x)	R or Z	R or Z	Real or complex cosine, $\cos(x)$.
COSH(x)	R	R	Hyperbolic cosine, $\cosh(x)$.
COUNT(mask, dim)	L, I	I	Number of true elements of **mask**, or the number along dimension **dim**. (Section 5.7)

Name	Argument type	Result type (for functions)	
CPU_TIME(time)	R	Subroutine	A measure of the processor time in seconds. The result is a scalar in standard Fortran 95, but a parallel processor might return an array of times. This is a *Fortran 95 intrinsic procedure absent in Fortran 90.*
CSHIFT(array, dim, shift)		As array	Performs circular shift of elements of **array**. (Section 5.7)
DATE_AND_TIME(all, count, msecond, second, minute, hour, day, month, year, zone)	Is	Subroutine	Timekeeping subroutine. (Section 5.1)
DIGITS(x)	I or R	I	Number of significant digits in a number of **x**'s type and kind.
DIM(x, y)	Is or RS	I or R	MAX(x − y, y − x)
DOTPRODUCT(vector_a, vector_b)	I, R, Z or L	I, R, Z or L	Vector product.
EOSHIFT(array, dim, shift, boundary)		As array	Shifts off elements of an array. (Section 5.7)
EPSILON(x)	R	R	A very small positive number.
EXP(x)	R or Z	R or Z	Exponential function e^x.
EXPONENT(x)	R	I	"Exponent" part of the internal representation of **x**. (Section 5.8)
FLOOR(a, kind)	R	I	Integer equal to or immediately below **a** (in the negative direction, even when **a** is negative). The **kind** argument is a *Fortran 95 feature not present in Fortran 90.*
FRACTION(x)	R	R	"Fractional" part of the internal representation of **x**. (Section 5.8)
HUGE(x)	I or R	I or R	Largest representable positive number of **x**'s type and kind.
IACHAR(c)	C	I	ASCII code number of the character **c**.
IAND(i, j)	Is	I	Bit-by-bit logical intersection of **i** with **j**. (Appendix B.2)
IBCLR(i, pos)	Is	I	Sets to zero the bit in position **pos** within **i**, returning the modified value of **i**. (Appendix B.1)
IBITS(i, pos, len)	Is	I	Forms an integer from a sequence of **len** bits, starting from position **pos**, within **i**. (Appendix B.1)
IBSET(i, pos)	Is	I	Like **IBCLR**, but sets the bit to 1. (Appendix B.1)
ICHAR(c)	C	I	Processor's sequence number for the character **c**.
IEOR(i, j)	Is	I	Exclusive **OR** between the bits within **i** and **j**. (Appendix B.2)
INDEX(string, substring, back)	C, C, L	I	Starting position of substring within string. (Section 8.2)
INT(a, kind)	I, R or Z	I	Converts to (or changes the kind of) an integer, reducing a real number (or the real part of a complex number) to the nearest integer of lower magnitude.

Name	Argument type	Result type (for functions)	
IOR(i. j)	Is	I	Inclusive OR between the bits within i and j. (Section B.2)
ISHFT(i, shift)	Is	I	Shift the bits within i by shift places. (Appendix B.2)
ISHFTC(i, shift, size)	Is	I	Perform a circular shift, by shift places, on i (or on the size rightmost bits of i). (Appendix B.2)
KIND(x)	Intrinsic	I	Kind parameter of x.
LBOUND(array, dim)	dim=I	I	Lower bound(s) of an array. (Section 12.2)
LEN(string)	C	I	Number of character in a string (or in any element of string, if it is an array).
LEN_TRIM(string)	C	I	Number of characters in string, disregarding trailing blanks. Note that although LEN is an inquiry function, LEN_TRIM is an elemental function. Although both may have array arguments, only LEN_TRIM may have an array value.
LGE(string_a, string_b)	CS	L	True if string_a is "lexically greater than or equal to" string_b in terms of ASCII code sequences. (Section 8.2)
LGT(string_a, string_b)	CS	L	"Lexically greater than". See LGE and Section 8.2.
LLE(string_a, string_b)	CS	L	"Lexically less than or equal to". See LGE and Section 8.2.
LLT(string_a, string_b)	CS	L	"Lexically less than". See LGE and Section 8.2.
LOG(x)	R or Z	R or Z	Natural logarithm of x. If real, x> 0, and if complex, x ≠0.
LOGICAL(1, kind)	L, I	L	Converts between kinds of logical values.
LOG10(x)	R	R	Logarithm to base 10, i.e. $\log_{10}(x)$, for x > 0.
MATMUL (matrix_a, matrix_b)	I, R, Z or L	I, R, Z or L	Matrix multiplication of two same-type matrices. (Section 5.7)
MAX(a1, a2, a3,....)	I or R	I or R	The maximum value from among the arguments. There is no maximum number of arguments, but all must be of the same type and kind.
MAXEXPONENT(x)	R	I	Maximum "exponent" in the internal representation of x. (Section 5.8)
MAXLOC(array, dim, mask)	I or R, I, L	I	Location of the maximum-valued element within array. (Section 5.7). *The argument dim is a Fortran 95 feature absent in Fortran 90.*
MAXVAL(array, dim, mask)	I or R, I, L	I or R	The maximum value from among elements of array. (Section 5.7)
MERGE(tsource, fsource, mask)	mask=L	As tsource and fsource	Pick elements from tsource or from fsource according to the value of mask. (Section 5.7)

Name	Argument type	Result type (for functions)	
MIN(a1, a2, a3, ...)	I or R	I or R	Like **MAX**, but minimum.
MINEXPONENT(x)	R	I	Minimum exponent in the internal representation of **x**. (Section 5.8)
MINLOC(array, *dim*, *mask*)	I or R, I, L	I	Like **MAXLOC**, but minimum. *The argument dim is a Fortran 95 feature not present in Fortran 90.*
MINVAL(array, *dim*, *mask*)	I or R, I, L	I or R	Like **MAXVAL**, but minimum.
MOD(a, p)	Both I or R	I or R	Remainder when a is divided by **p**. (Section 5.3)
MODULO(a, p)	Both I or R	I or R	a modulo **p**. (Section 5.3)
MVBITS(from, frompos, len, to, topos)	Is	Subroutine	Takes a sequence of bits from within the integer **from** and copies it into part of the integer **to**. (Appendix B.2). Exceptionally for Fortran, the dummy arguments **to** and **from** may be associated with the same actual arguments.
NEAREST(x, s)	R, R	R	Finds the closest other representable number to **x** in the direction indicated by the sign of **s**.
NINT(a, kind)	R, I	I	Nearest integer to **a**. (Section 5.3)
NOT(i)	I	I	Bit-by-bit logical complement of **i**. (Appendix B.2)
NULL(mold)			A disassociated pointer of the same type and kind as **mold**. If **mold** is absent, the type must be determined from the context in which **NULL** is called. **NULL** *is a Fortran 95 intrinsic function absent in Fortran 90.*

An example of NULL:

```
REAL, POINTER :: pointer_a, pointer_b, &
     pointer_z => NULL()
INTEGER, POINTER :: i_point_c
pointer_a => NULL()
CALL Genroute (w, x, NULL(pointer_b))
CALL Genroute (y, z, NULL(i_point_c))
```

The first call to **NULL** needs no argument because it is to initialise a pointer (**pointer_z**) of declared type. The second call also needs no argument because **pointer_a** is of pre-declared type. In the third and fourth cases, **Genroute** is imagined to be a generic subroutine name whose third argument could be a pointer of any type. So, **NULL** is given arguments of which the types (but not the associated values) will determine the specific procedures that will be entered.

Name	Argument type	Result type (for functions)	
PACK(array, mask, vector)	**mask=L**	As **array**	Takes elements from **array**, for which **mask** is true, in array element order, to form a rank-one array. (Section 5.7)
PRECISION(x)	R or Z	I	Decimal precision (i.e. number of significant decimal places) provided for numbers of **x**'s type and kind. (Section 5.4)
PRESENT(a)		L	Whether the dummy argument called **a** is present as an actual argument.
PRODUCT(array, dim, mask)	I/R/Z, I, L	I/R/Z	Multiplies the elements of **array** for which **mask** is true along the dimension **dim**. A zero-sized array has **PRODUCT = 1**. (Section 5.7)
RADIX(x)	I or R	I	The numerical base for representing numbers of **x**'s type and kind. (Section 5.8)
RANDOM(harvest)	R	Subroutine	Returns a random number in the range $0 \leq$ **harvest** < 1.
RANDOMSEED(size, put, get)	Is	Subroutine	Initializes random number generator. (Section 5.6)
RANGE(x)	I, R or Z	I	Order of magnitude of the largest representable number of **x**'s type and kind. (Section 5.4.
REAL(a, kind)	I/R/Z, I	R	Converts to real type, or between kinds of real type. (Section 5.3)
REPEAT(string, ncopies)	C, I	C	Concatenates **ncopies** copies of **string**.
RESHAPE(source, shape, pad, order)	**shape** and **order** = I	As **shape**	Changes the shape of **array**. (Section 9.1)
RRSPACING(x)	R	R	Inverse of the spacing between representable real numbers. (Section 5.8)
SCALE(x, i)	R, I	R	Scales up **x** by the **i**th power of the internal representation base. (Section 5.8)
SCAN(string, set, back)	C, C, L	I	Scans through **string** looking for characters from **set**. (Section 8.2)
SELECTED_INTEGER_KIND(r)	I	I	The smallest kind parameter needed for an integer to have **R** decimal digits.
SELECTED_REAL_KIND(p, r)	Is	I	The smallest kind parameter needed for a real number to have a precision of **P** digits and a magnitude of **R** powers of ten. (Section 5.4)

Name	Argument type	Result type (for functions)	
SETEXPONENT(x, i)	R, I	R	In terms of its internal representation, set x's exponent to i. (Section 5.8)
SHAPE(source)		I	The shape (as a vector of integers) of the array source. Source may not be an assumed-size array.
SIGN(a, b)	Both I or R	I or R	Changes the sign of a to that of b. *Fortran 95 feature not in Fortran 90*: if the processor distinguishes between "positive" and "negative" representations of zero, then the SIGN function may distinguish between them in the argument b.
SIN(x)	R or Z	Same as x	Sin(x)
SINH(X)	R	R	Sinh(x)
SIZE(array, dim)	dim = I	I	Number of elements in array, or its extent along the dimth dimension.
SPACING(x)	R	R	Spacing between adjacent representable numbers in the vicinity of x.
SPREAD(source, dim, ncopies)	dim and ncopies = I	As source	Replicates (ncopies times) the dimth dimension of source, thereby increasing the rank by 1. (Section 5.7)
SQRT(x)	R or Z	As x	Square root of x (x ≥0).
SUM(array, dim, mask)	I/R/Z, I	As array	Adds the elements of array for which mask is true along the dimension dim. (Section 5.7)
SYSTEM_CLOCK(count, count_rate, count_max)	IS	Subroutine	Counts clock ticks. (Section 5.6)
TAN(x)	R	R	tan(x)
TANH(x)	R	R	tanh(x)
TINY(x)	R	R	Tiniest possible positive (non-zero) representable number.
TRANSFER(source, mold, size)	size = I	As mold	Changes the type interpretation of what is physically stored in source. (Section 9.5)
TRANSPOSE(matrix)		As matrix	The transpose of matrix.
TRIM(string)	C	C	Removes trailing blanks from string.
UBOUND(array, dim)	dim = I	I	Upper bound of array's index in the dimth dimension (or in all dimensions). (Section 12.2)
UNPACK(vector, mask, field)	mask = L	As vector	Distributes the elements of a rank-one array. (Section 5.7)
VERIFY(string, set, back)	C, C, I	I	Checks in string for the characters contained in set. (Section 8.2)

Name	Generic name	Argument type	Result type
ALOG(x)	LOG	R	R
ALOG10(x)	LOG10	R	R
AMAX0(a1, a2, a3,..)	REAL(MAX)	Is	R
AMAX1(a1, a2, a3,..)	MAX	Rs	R
AMIN0(a1, a2, a3,..)	REAL(MIN)	Is	R
AMIN1(a1, a2, a3,..)	MIN	Rs	R
AMOD(a, p)	MOD	R, R	R
CABS(a)	ABS	Z	R
CCOS(x)	COS	Z	Z
CEXP(x)	EXP	Z	Z
CLOG(x)	LOG	Z	Z
CSIN(x)	SIN	Z	Z
CSQRT(x)	SQRT	Z	Z
DABS(x)	ABS	D	D
DACOS(x)	ACOS	D	D
DASIN(x)	ASIN	D	D
DATAN(x)	ATAN	D	D
DATAN2(y. x)	ATAN2	D, D	D
DBLE(a)	DBLE	I, R or Z	D
DCOS(x)	COS	D	D
DCOSH(x)	COSH	D	D
DDIM(x, y)	DIM	D, D	D
DEXP(x)	EXP	D	D
DINT(a)	AINT	D	D
DLOG(x)	LOG	D	D
DLOG10(x)	LOG10	D	D
DMAX1(a1, a2, a3,..)	MAX	Ds	D
DMIN1(a1, a2, a3,..)	MIN	Ds	D
DMOD(a, p)	MOD	D, P	D
DNINT(a)	ANINT	D	I
DPROD(x, y)	DPROD	R, R	D
DSIGN(a, b)	SIGN	D, D	D
DSIN(x)	SIN	D	D
DSINH(x)	SINH	D	D
DSQRT(x)	SQRT	D	D
DTAN(x)	TAN	D	D
DTANH(x)	TANH	D	D
FLOAT(a)	REAL	I	R
IABS(a)	ABS	I	I
IDIM(x, y)	DIM	I, I	I
IDINT(a)	INT	D	I
IDNINT(a)	NINT	D	I
IFIX(a)	INT	R	I
ISIGN(a, b)	SIGN	I, I	I
MAX0(a1, a2, a3,..)	MAX	Is	I
MAX1(a1, a2, a3,..)	INT(MAX)	Rs	I
MIN0(a1, a2, a3,..)	MIN	Is	I
MIN1(a1, a2, a3,..)	INT(MIN)	Rs	I
SNGL(a)	REAL	D	R

Answers to selected exercises

Chapter 2

2.A1 **A, $, %, :, ;**, and **>** are in the Fortran character set.

2.A2

(i)   6561

(ii) **6/12** is evaluated first, and because it is an integer expression it is truncated to zero. Answer: **4**

(iii) **2****(**-1**) is evaluated first, and being an integer it is truncated to zero. Since you cannot divide by zero the expression is illegal.

(iv) Exponentiations go right-to-left. Answer: **512**

(v)   Because divisions of integers give results that are truncated to integers, the answer is **1**

(vi) **32**   (vii) **3**   (viii) **2048.0**

(ix) **1.0**   (x)   **1.0**

2.A3

(i)   **(a+b+c+d+e)/5.0**   (ii)   **((a**2 + b**2 + c**2)/3.0)**0.5**

(iii) **100.0*b/(a+b+c+d+e)**   (iv)   **(a*b)**0.5**

2.A5
```
PROGRAM Larger
REAL :: a, b, x
WRITE (*,*) "Input two numbers: "
READ (*,*) a, b
x=a
IF (a<b) THEN
  x=b
END IF
WRITE (*,*) "The larger number is ", x
END PROGRAM Larger
```

Using a function introduced later, five lines of the above could be abbreviated to

```
WRITE (*,*) "The larger number is ", MAX(a,b)
```

2.B1   The valid names are **aramaic, zhq5, p998530, top_mark**, and (having no more than 31 characters) **state_population_estimate_1997**. Others are invalid because the currency symbol, the apostrophe and the blank space are not allowed as parts of names, and although a name may include digits it may not start with a digit.

2.B3
```
PROGRAM Quad
WRITE (*,*) "Input the coefficients of the quadratic: "
READ (*,*) a, b, c
d = b**2 - 4.0*a*c
IF (d<0) THEN; WRITE (*,*) "Solutions are unreal"
  ELSE; d=SQRT(d)
  e=(-b+d)/(2.0*a); f=(-b-d)/(2.0*a)
  WRITE (*,*) "The solutions are: ", e, f
END IF
END PROGRAM Quad
```

Chapter 3

3.A1

(i)	62	(ii)	−2	(iii)	0
(iv)	−2	(v)	520	(vi)	0

3.A2

(i)	0.666	(ii)	24000.0	(iii)	10.0
(iv)	27E8	(v)	101E−7	(vi)	1E−16

3.A3

(i)	−2.6	(ii)	95.8	(iii)	5.8
(iv)	−9.0	(v)	5.8	(vi)	−7.111
(vii)	0.25				

3.A4
```
PROGRAM Lsd
REAL :: x, bob,
INTEGER :: ipounds, ishillings, ioldpence
WRITE (*,*) "Input a sum in pounds and pence, expressed &
  &as a decimal number"
READ (*,*) x              ;          ipounds = INT(x)
bob = 20.0*(x-ipounds)    ;          ishillings = INT(bob)
ioldpence = NINT(12.0*(bob-ishillings))
WRITE (*,*) "The equivalent in pounds, shillings and &
  & old pence is £", ipounds," ",ishillings,"s &
  & ",ioldpence,"d"
END PROGRAM Lsd
```

3.B1

(i)	Illegal (a number must include a digit)					
(ii)	Real	(iii)	Real	(iv)	Integer	
(v)	Real	(vi)	Integer			

(vii)   Illegal (a real number must have a digit in the "significand" preceding the exponent letter)

(viii) Character (with no relationship to the **ACHAR** function!)

(ix)   Illegal (embedded blank not allowed)

(x)   Illegal (commas not allowed within numbers)

(xi)   Character

(xii)   This is a legal expression but not a legal constant

(xiii) Real   (xiv)   Real   (xv)   Character

(xvi)   Real, of kind **big**

(xvii) Complex   (xviii) Integer

(xix)   Illegal (There must be an "exponent" after the **E**)

(xx)   Integer (Fortran specifies no maximum number of digits)

3.B2

(i)   `REAL :: power1, power2, creeper`

(ii)   `INTEGER :: kappa, kappa_prime`

(iii)   `REAL(KIND=3) :: finetune`

(iv)   `CHARACTER(4) :: v, w`

3.B3
```
COMPLEX:: c1, c2, c3, z = (-2, 0), power = (1/3, 0)
c1 = z**power
c2 = (-ABS(c1), 0.0)
c3 = CONJG(c1)
```

When a complex number is raised to a complex power, say **x**y**, the result is equivalent to **EXP(y*LOG(x))**. The **LOG** of a complex number is the principal value with imaginary part in the range $\pm\pi$. In the above example **LOG(z)**, i.e. **LOG (-2, 0)**, has the value **(LOG(2)**, π**)** and so **c1** is set approximately equal to **(1.09, 0.63)**, i.e. with magnitude 1.26 and argument $\pi/3$ radians. Then, **c2** is set to **(-1.26, 0)** and finally **c3** is set to **(1.09, -0.63)**.

3.B5

(i)   The order of operator precedence is such that **.NOT.** is evaluated first, and then **.NEQV.** and **.EQV.** are evaluated left-to-right. The answer is **.TRUE.**.

(ii)   This expression is equivalent to that in (i) above, whatever the values of the variables. Answer: **.TRUE.**.

(iii)   **.FALSE.**

(iv)   **.TRUE.**

3.B6   `(ABS(n1-n2)-ABS(m1-m2))>=ABS(k)`

3.B7
```
PROGRAM Stringy
CHARACTER(12) :: first, second, check = "satisfactory"
WRITE (*,*) "Type in two strings each of 12 characters"
READ (*,*) first, second
IF (second==check) THEN
  WRITE (*,*) first
ELSE
  WRITE (*,*) second, " is unsatisfactory"
```

```
          END IF
          END PROGRAM Stringy

3.B8    PROGRAM Trapezium
        REAL :: a, b, c, d
        REAL :: area1=0.0, area2=0.0, areasq1=0.0, areasq2=0.0
        WRITE (*,*) "Input the lengths of the sides of a trapezium &
        & in cyclic order"
        READ (*,*) a, b, c, d
        IF (a==c.AND.b==d) THEN
           WRITE (*,*) "That is a parallelogram"
        ELSE
           ! We don't know which pair of sides are parallel
           IF (d/=b) areasq1 = ((a**2-c**2)**2/(d-b)**2 &
              + a**2 + c**2 -(d-b)**2) * (b+d)**2/16.0
           IF (a/=c) areasq2 = ((b**2-d**2)**2/(a-c)**2 &
              + b**2 + d**2 -(a-c)**2) * (a+c)**2/16.0
           IF (areasq1>0.0) area1 = SQRT(areasq1)
           IF (areasq2>0.0) area2 = SQRT(areasq2)
           IF (area1==0.0.AND.area2==0.0) WRITE (*,*) &
              "That is not a real trapezium"
           IF (area1==0.0.NEQV.area2==0.0) WRITE (*,*) &
              "The area is ", area1+area2
           IF (area1/=0.0.AND.area2/=0.0) WRITE (*,*) &
              "Possible values for the area are ", area1, " and ", area2
        END IF
        END PROGRAM Trapezium
```

Chapter 4

4.A1
(ii)   `INTEGER :: n(60) = (/(-1, i=1,30),(1, j=1,30)/)`
(iii) `REAL :: powers(10) = (/(3.14159265358**m, m=1,10)/)`

4.B1
(i)   `"at"`   (ii)   `"mull"`   (iii)   `"g"`   (iv)   `"wat"`

4.B2
(i)   `CHARACTER(0) :: null`
(ii)   `CHARACTER(24) :: s1, s2, s3`
(iii) `CHARACTER(*) :: me = "Eisenstein"`
(iv)   `CHARACTER, PARAMETER :: bs = ACHAR(92)`

4.B3
(ii)   `CHARACTER :: c(11) = (/("abracadabra"(1:k), k=1,11)/)`

4.B4   `REAL :: p1(10), p2(10), greatness(10)`
       `COMPLEX :: z(10)`
       `READ (*,*) p1`

```
      READ (*,*) p2
      z = CMPLX(p1,p2)
      greatness = abs(z)
      WRITE (*,*) z(MAXLOC(greatness))
```

4.B5
  (i)   (/"light", "trick"/)   (ii)   (/"beach", "shore"/)
  (iii) (/"hazel", "witch"/)   (iv)   (/"gh", "ic"/)
  (v)   (/"t"/)

4.B7   .
       .
       .

```
      REAL :: x(n), y(n), z(n), r(n), theta(n), phi(n)
```
       .
       .
       .

```
      r = SQRT(x**2 + y**2 + z**2)
      theta = ACOS(z/r)
      phi = ATAN2(y, x)
      max = MAXLOC(r)
      WRITE(*,*) "The point nearest to the origin is at:"
      WRITE(*,*) " r = ", r(max)
      WRITE(*,*) " theta = ", theta(max)
      WRITE(*,*) " phi = ", phi(max)
```
       .
       .
       .

4.B8   ```WHERE (MOD(n,2)==0) n = n/2```

4.B9
```
      PROGRAM Stringpull
      CHARACTER(20) :: string
      CHARACTER :: blank = " ", asterisk = "*"
      LOGICAL :: trailers= .TRUE.
      READ (*,*) string
      DO k=20,1,-1
        IF (string(k:k) /= blank) trailers = .FALSE.
        IF (string(k:k) == blank . AND .. NOT . trailers) &
           string(k:k) = asterisk
      END DO
      WRITE (*,*) TRIM(string)
      END PROGRAM Stringpull
```


Chapter 5

5.A1
  (i)
```
      PROGRAM Secant
      REAL :: angle, radians, cosine, sec, c = 57.29577951
```

```fortran
      WRITE (*,*) "Input the value of an angle in degrees: "
      READ (*,*) angle
      radians = angle / c
      cosine = COS(radians)
      IF (cosine==0.0) THEN; sec = HUGE(0.0)
      ELSE; sec = 1.0/cosine
      END IF
      WRITE (*,*) "The secant of the angle is ", sec
      END PROGRAM Secant
```

(ii)   .
        .

```fortran
      arcsinh = LOG(x + SQRT(x**2 + 1))
```
        .
        .

(iii)   .
        .

```fortran
      REAL :: log16, ..., ratio = LOG(16.0)
```
        .
        .

```fortran
      log16 = LOG(x) / ratio
```
        .
        .

5.A2
```fortran
      PROGRAM Interest
      REAL :: p, r, t, permonth, factor, total
      INTEGER :: months
      WRITE (*,*) "Principal: "; READ (*,*) p
      WRITE (*,*) "Rate: "; READ (*,*) r
      WRITE (*,*)   "Time: "; READ (*,*) t
      ! If r is the annual interest rate then
      ! the annual growth factor is 1+r
      ! So, the monthly growth factor is
      permonth = EXP(LOG(1.0+r)/12.0)
      ! The number of months is
      months = INT(12*t)
      ! So the principal grows by a factor
      factor = permonth ** months
      ! giving a total sum to the nearest pound
      total = NINT(p * factor)
      WRITE (*,*) "Final sum: ", total
      END PROGRAM Interest
```

5A4
```fortran
      CHARACTER(9) :: mname
```
        .
        .
        .
```fortran
      CALL DATE_AND_TIME (MONTH=m)
      IF (m==1) mname == "January"
      IF (m==2) mname == "February"
      IF (m==3) mname == "March"
```

```
IF (m==4) mname == "April"
IF (m==5) mname == "May"
IF (m==6) mname == "June"
IF (m==7) mname == "July"
IF (m==8) mname == "August"
IF (m==9) mname == "September"
IF (m==10) mname == "October"
IF (m==11) mname == "November"
IF (m==12) mname == "December"
WRITE (*,*) "The month is ",TRIM(mname)
```

This can be done much more elegantly using an array of character strings (Chapter 7).

5.A5   `result = LOG((COSH(x),SINH(x)))`

5.A8
```
PROGRAM Smalls
REAL :: eps, thoutimes, ntens, epssq
eps = EPSILON(0.0)
thoutimes = 1000.0 * eps
ntens = 3 - NINT(LOG10(thoutimes))
! thoutimes is used only to make sure that the
! argument of LOG10 is not too small
WRITE (*,*) "EPSILON has the order of magnitude"
WRITE (*,*)   "10**(-",ntens,")"
epssq = eps ** 2
IF (epssq>TINY(0.0)) THEN
  WRITE (*,*) "Its square is distinct from zero"
ELSE
  WRITE (*,*) "Its square is, in effect, zero"
END IF
END PROGRAM Smalls
```

5.A9   `IF (a*b<0.0) a=-a`

5.B1   `MERGE(TSOURCE=.TRUE., FSOURCE=.FALSE., MASK=(n==1))`

Chapter 6

6.A2
```
SELECT CASE (IACHAR(string(1:1)))
CASE(97:121)
  string(1:1) = ACHAR(IACHAR(string(1:1)) - 32)
CASE(65:90)
  CONTINUE
CASE(32)
  string = string(2:)
CASE DEFAULT
  string(1:1) = "X"
END SELECT
```

6.A3
```
initialcode = IACHAR(string(1:1))
IF (initialcode >= 97.AND.initialcode <= 121) THEN
   string(1:1) = ACHAR(initialcode - 32)
ELSE IF (initialcode >= 65.AND.initialcode <= 90) THEN
   CONTINUE
ELSE IF (initialcode == 32) THEN
   string = string(2:)
ELSE
   string(1:1) = "X"
END IF
```

6.A4
```
INTEGER :: n, nsr, ncr
REAL :: en, ensr, encr, eps = EPSILON(1.0)
LOGICAL :: square = .FALSE., cube = .FALSE.
   .
   .
   .
en = REAL(n); ensr = SQRT(en); encr = en**(1.0/3.0)
IF (ensr-INT(ensr) < eps) square = .TRUE.
IF (encr-INT(encr) < eps) cube = .TRUE.
IF (square.AND..NOT.cube) THEN
   WRITE (*,*) "The number is a perfect square but not a &
   & perfect cube"
ELSE IF (cube.AND..NOT.square) THEN
   WRITE (*,*) "The number is a perfect cube but not a &
   & perfect square"
END IF
```

6.B1
```
nfac = 1
DO j = 1, n
nfac = nfac * j
END DO
```

6.B3
```
n = LEN(string); number = 0
DO j = n, 1, -1
number = number + (IACHAR(string(j:j)) - 48) * 10**(n-j)
END DO
```

6.B6
```
PROGRAM Vowels
CHARACTER(30) :: word
CHARACTER :: v(5) = (/"a", "e", "i", "o", "u"/)
READ (*,*) word
DO k = 1, LEN_TRIM(word)
   DO m = 1, 5
      IF (word(k:k) == v(m)) THEN
         WRITE (*,*) v(m)
         EXIT
      END IF
   END DO
END DO
END PROGRAM Vowels
```

```
6.B9   PROGRAM Average
       REAL :: addin, totin=0.0, endmark=9999999
       INTEGER :: numin=0
       WRITE (*,*) "Input a series of numbers, and &
         &show when you have finished by giving 9999999"
       Number: DO
       READ (*,*) addin
       IF (addin/=endmark) THEN
       totin = totin + addin; numin = numin + 1
       ELSE; EXIT Number
       END IF
       END DO Number
       WRITE (*,*) "The average is ", totin/numin
       END PROGRAM Average
```

Chapter 7

```
7.A1   REAL FUNCTION Sphere (radius)
       REAL :: radius, fourthirdspi = 3.14159265358 * 4.0 / 3.0
       Sphere = fourthirdspi * radius * radius * radius
       END FUNCTION Sphere
```

```
7A2    COMPLEX FUNCTION Arcsine (z)
       COMPLEX :: z, eye = (0.0, 1.0)
       Arcsine = -eye * LOG(eye*z + SQRT(1.0 - z*z))
       END FUNCTION Arcsine
```

```
7.A10  INTEGER FUNCTION Luck (i)
       REAL :: x
       INTEGER :: n1, n2
       Luck = 0
       DO
       CALL RANDOM(x); n1 = 1 + INT(6.0 * x)
       CALL RANDOM(x); n2 = 1 + INT(6.0 * x)
       Luck = Luck + n1 + n2; IF (n1 /= n2) EXIT
       END DO
       END FUNCTION Luck
```

```
7.B1   SUBROUTINE Order (r1, r2, r3)
       REAL :: r1, r2, r3, r(3), ar(3)
       r = (/r1, r2, r3/)
       ar = ABS(r)
       r1 = r(MAXLOC(ar))
       r3 = r(MINLOC(ar))
       r2 = SUM(r) - r1 - r3
       END SUBROUTINE Order
```

385

Chapter 8

8.A1

(i)	11	(ii)	" "	(iii)	o	
(iv)	32	(v)	.FALSE.			

(vi)   This has a processor-dependent value since the character α is not in the ASCII character set.

(vii)   .FALSE.   (viii)   .TRUE.

8.A2

```
initialcode = IACHAR(x(1:1))
IF (initialcode>47.AND.initialcode<58) THEN
   x = x(2:LEN(x))
END IF
```
Alternatively, the SCAN function does the job in one line:
```
IF (SCAN(x(1:1),"0123456789")==1) x=x(2:LEN(x))
```

8.A3   `WRITE (*,*) ADJUSTL(x)`

8.B1

(i)   `COMPLEX :: xbanks(30)`

(ii)   `LOGICAL, OPTIONAL :: check1, check2, check3`

(iii) `REAL, SAVE :: matrix_name(20, 20), vector_name(45)`

(iv) `INTEGER, PARAMETER :: squares(0:99) = (/(k**2, k=0,99)/)`

(v)   `CHARACTER(12) :: julius(:,:)`

(vi) `REAL :: inverse_squares(100) = (/(1.0/REAL(m**2),-&`
       `m=1,100)/)`

(vii) `CHARACTER(*), PARAMETER :: moniker = "Abigail Sara Lemoine"`

Chapter 9

9.A2
```
INTEGER FUNCTION Logpack(data)
LOGICAL :: data(32)
INTEGER :: i
DO k = 0, 32
IF(.NOT.data(k)) THEN
   i = IBCLR(i,k)
ELSE
   i = IBSET(i,k)
END IF
END DO
Logpack = i
END FUNCTION Logpack
```

9.A4
```
chessboard = RESHAPE(SHAPE=(/8,8/), &
SOURCE=(/six_rows,((/.TRUE.,.FALSE!/), k=1,8)/)))
```

9.A5

   (i)   (/"a","o","u"/) (ii)   (/"e","i"/)   (iii)   (/4,5/)

  (iv)   (/"o","e"/)   (v)   (/"ae","oe","ue"/)

Chapter 10

10.A1

```
MODULE Year
CHARACTER(9):: daynames(7) = &
(/"Monday","Tuesday","Wednesday","Thursday","Friday", &
  &"Saturday","Sunday"/)
CHARACTER(9):: monthnames(12) = &
(/"January","February","March","April","May","June", &
  &"July","August","September","October","November", &
  &"December"/)
INTEGER:: daynumbers (12) = (/31,28,31,30,31,30,31,31, &
  30,31,30,31/)
END MODULE Year
```

10.A2

```
MODULE Constants
REAL, PARAMETER :: pi = 2.0 * ASIN(1.0)
REAL, PARAMETER :: e = EXP(1.0)
INTEGER, PARAMETER :: ipow2(20) = (/(2**k, k=1, 20)/)
END MODULE Constants
```

10.A3

```
MODULE Sheet
CHARACTER(12) :: strings(30, 10)
CHARACTER :: contents(30,10)
  !  'contents' is blank if the corresponding cell is empty,
  !     = "c" if it contains a word
  !     = "i" if it contains an integer
  !     = "r" if it contains a real number
CONTAINS
  INTEGER FUNCTION Number (irow, icolumn)
  INTEGER :: irow, icolumn, n
  INTEGER :: ivalue, idefault = 0
  IF (contents(irow, icolumn) == "i") THEN
    READ (strings(irow, icolumn), "I12") n
    Number = n
  ELSE
    Number = idefault
  END IF
  END FUNCTION Number
END MODULE Sheet
```

Chapter 11

11.A4
```
RECURSIVE REAL FUNCTION Sinpow(n, x1, x2) RESULT (v)
INTEGER :: n
REAL :: x1, x2, value
SELECT CASE (n)
   CASE (3:)
      value = Sinpow(n-2, x1, x2) * REAL(n-1) / REAL(n)
      value = value - SIN(x1)**(n-1) * COS(x1) / REAL(n) &
         + SIN(x2)**(n-1) * COS(x2) / REAL(n)
   CASE (2)
      value = 0.5*(x1-x2) - 0.25*SIN(2.0*x1) + &
         0.25*SIN(2.0*x2)
   CASE (1)
      value = COS(x2) - COS(x1)
END SELECT
v = value
END FUNCTION Sinpow
```

11.B2
```
FUNCTION Mean (n1, n2, n3, n4, n5, n6, n7, n8, &
   n9, n10, n11, n12)
INTEGER, OPTIONAL :: n1, n2, n3, n4, n5, n6, n7, n8, n9, &
   n10, n11, n12
INTEGER :: Mean, nargs, nsum; nargs = 0; nsum = 0
IF (PRESENT(n1)) THEN; nsum = nsum + n1; nargs = nargs &
   + 1; END IF
IF (PRESENT(n2)) THEN; nsum = nsum + n2; nargs = nargs &
   + 1; END IF
IF (PRESENT(n3)) THEN; nsum = nsum + n3; nargs = nargs &
   + 1; END IF
IF (PRESENT(n4)) THEN; nsum = nsum + n4; nargs = nargs &
   + 1; END IF
IF (PRESENT(n5)) THEN; nsum = nsum + n5; nargs = nargs &
   + 1; END IF
IF (PRESENT(n6)) THEN; nsum = nsum + n6; nargs = nargs &
   + 1; END IF
IF (PRESENT(n7)) THEN; nsum = nsum + n7; nargs = nargs &
   + 1; END IF
IF (PRESENT(n8)) THEN; nsum = nsum + n8; nargs = nargs &
   + 1; END IF
IF (PRESENT(n9)) THEN; nsum = nsum + n9; nargs = nargs &
   + 1; END IF
IF (PRESENT(n10)) THEN; nsum = nsum + n10; nargs = &
   nargs + 1; END IF
IF (PRESENT(n10)) THEN; nsum = nsum + n11; nargs = &
   nargs + 1; END IF
IF (PRESENT(n12)) THEN; nsum = nsum + n12; nargs = &
   nargs + 1; END IF
Mean = NINT(REAL(nsum)/REAL(nargs))
END FUNCTION Mean
```

The above is not particularly elegant and it requires an interface to be provided. A much more elegant version, not needing an interface, could be written if the argument were an assumed-shape array instead of a set of scalars. This makes a good supplementary exercise! However, the function would then have to be called with an array name or an array constructor as the actual argument, i.e. the function would have to be referenced by a statement like

```
klose = Mean((/5,4,8,6,9/))
```

rather than having `Mean(5,4,8,6,9)`.

11.B3
```
FUNCTION Cross (v1, v2)
REAL :: Cross(3), v1(3), v2(3)
REAL, PARAMETER :: x(3) = (/1.0,0.0,0.0/), &
  y(3) = (/0.0,1.0,0.0/), z(3) = (/0.0,0.0,1.0/)
Cross = x * (v1(2)*v2(3) - v1(3)*v2(2)) &
  + y * (v1(3)*v2(1) - v1(1)*v2(3)) &
  + z * (v1(1)*v2(2) - v1(2)*v2(1))
  END FUNCTION Cross
```

11.B5
```
FUNCTION Geomean (a, b)
REAL :: a, b, geo, Geomean
geo = SQRT(ABS(a*b))
IF (a*b < 0.0) geo = -geo
Geomean = geo
END FUNCTION Geomean

INTERFACE OPERATOR (.X.)
  REAL FUNCTION Geomean (a, b)
  REAL :: a, b
  END FUNCTION Geomean
END INTERFACE
```
If **a** and **b** are of opposite sign, this function copes by defining a "geometric mean" with a negative value.

11.B8
```
SUBROUTINE Rescale (array, average)
REAL, OPTIONAL, INTENT(IN) :: average
REAL, INTENT (IN OUT) :: array(:)
REAL :: factor
IF (PRESENT(average)) factor = average / SUM(array)
IF (.NOT.PRESENT(average)) factor = 1.0/SUM(array)
array = array * factor
END SUBROUTINE Rescale
```

11.B9
```
CHARACTER FUNCTION Pick (string)
CHARACTER(*) :: string
INTEGER :: n, k; REAL :: x
n = LEN(string); CALL RANDOM (x); k = 1 + INT(x*REAL(n))
Pick = string(k:k)
END FUNCTION Pick
```

Chapter 12

12.A1

(i)
```
COMPLEX, ALLOCATABLE :: cmatrix (:,:)
CHARACTER(12), ALLOCATABLE :: rivernames (:)
```

(ii)
```
ALLOCATE (cmatrix(4,4))
ALLOCATE (rivernames(200))
```

(iii)
```
IF (ALLOCATED(rivernames)) DEALLOCATE(rivernames)
ALLOCATE (rivernames(150))
```

12.A2
```
ALLOCATE (characters(LEN(string))
characters = (/(string(k:k), k=1, LEN(string))/)
```

12.A3

(i) `(/1,1901,1,0/)`   (ii) `(/12,150,20,200/)`

(iii) `(/1,50,20,200/)`   (iv) `(/1,2050,20,199/)`

(v) `(/50,20,200/)`   (vi) `(/2050,20,199/)`

(vii) `1`   (viii) `40000`

(ix) `3`   (x) `2`

12.B1

(i)
```
TYPE Species
  CHARACTER(12) :: name
  REAL :: weight, extent, height
  INTEGER :: legs
  LOGICAL :: marine
  END TYPE Species
```

(ii) `TYPE (Species) :: panda, shark, whale, butterfly`

(iii) `TYPE (Species) :: big_cats(15)`

(iv)
```
whale = Species("cetus_____", 4578.0, 12.71, 2.86, &
  0, .TRUE.)
```

(v)
```
big_cats(5) = Species("snow_leopard", 46.0, 1.35, 0.69, &
  4, .TRUE.)
```

(vi) `whale%weight = 4287.0`

(v) `big_cats(5)%marine = .FALSE.`

12.B2

(i)
```
TYPE Person
  CHARACTER(40) :: name
  INTEGER :: nbirthday(3)
END TYPE Person
```

(ii)
```
TYPE Couple
  TYPE (Person) :: husband, wife
  INTEGER :: nmarriage(3)
END TYPE Couple
```

(iii)
```
TYPE Family
  TYPE (Couple) :: parents
  TYPE (Person) :: children(8)
END TYPE Family
```

(iv)   `robinson%parents%nmarriage(3)`
        `robinson%parents%wife%name`

12.B4   ```
        FUNCTION Addition (x, y)
        TYPE Fuzzy
          REAL :: evalue   !   expectation value
          REAL :: error   !   statistical error
        END TYPE Fuzzy
        TYPE (Fuzzy) :: Addition
        TYPE (Fuzzy), INTENT(IN) :: x, y
        TYPE (Fuzzy) :: a
        a = Fuzzy(x%evalue + y%evalue, SQRT(x%error**2 &
          + y%error**2))
        Addition = a
        END FUNCTION Addition

        INTERFACE OPERATOR (+)
          FUNCTION Addition (x, y)
          TYPE Fuzzy
            REAL :: evalue   !   expectation value
            REAL :: error   !   statistical error
          END TYPE Fuzzy
          TYPE (Fuzzy) :: Addition
          TYPE (Fuzzy), INTENT(IN):: x, y
          END FUNCTION Addition
        END INTERFACE
        ```

12.B6   ```
        SUBROUTINE Intchar(n, string)
        INTEGER, INTENT (OUT) :: n
        CHARACTER, INTENT (IN) :: string
          n=IACHAR(string(1:1))
        IF (n<0.OR.n>127) n = 0
        END SUBROUTINE Intchar

        INTERFACE ASSIGNMENT (=)
          SUBROUTINE Intchar(n, string)
          INTEGER, INTENT (OUT) :: n
          CHARACTER, INTENT (IN) :: string
          END SUBROUTINE Intchar
        END INTERFACE
        ```

Chapter 13

13.A2   ```
        FUNCTION Snakehead(vector) RESULT (head)
        TYPE (Link), POINTER :: Snakehead, beta, gamma
        TYPE (Link), TARGET :: alpha
        REAL :: vector(:)
        alpha%x = vector(1)
        beta => alpha
        ```
        ```

```
DO i = 2, SIZE(vector)
  ALLOCATE (gamma)
  beta%nextlink => gamma
  gamma%x = vector(i)
  NULLIFY (gamma%nextlink)
  beta => gamma
END DO
head => alpha
END FUNCTION Snakehead
```

Chapter 14

14.A8
```
WRITE (*,*) &
PACK((/ (i, i=1,100) /), &
ALL (&
RESHAPE(SHAPE=(/100,100/), &
SOURCE=(/(&
(MOD((MOD(j,100)+1),INT(j/100+1)))/=0) &
.OR.(INT(j/100)==0).OR.((MOD(j,100)+1)==(INT(j/100)+1)) &
, j = 0, 9999)/) &
), 2 &
) &
)
```

Appendix A

A.2.1
   (i)   Technically this is not a format specification, it is a character string that is
          a format "specifier". But...
   (ii)   (F10.4) is a valid format specification. A format specification always
          includes parentheses around it.
   (iii) F10.4 is a valid edit descriptor, but not a format specification. The point
          is that a format specification should control all the data that passes when
          an i/o statement is executed, and in general will contain a list of edit
          descriptors within parentheses.
   (iv, v) 8(F10.4) and 8F10.4 are equivalent, representing a set of eight identi-
          cal edit descriptors.
   (vi)   (8F10.4) is a valid format specification.
   (vii) ((F10.4)) is illegal.
   (viii) (F10.6,I8) is a valid format specification.
   (ix)   () is a valid format specification, representing an empty i/o list. It could
          be used to skip over an input record or to write out an empty record.
          However, the slash edit descriptor (/) is usually used for this purpose.
   (x)   "3()" is invalid. For three empty records, the format specifier "(3/)"
          could be used.

A.2.2   `(8X, I4, 3(13X, F7.2), 8X)`

A.2.3   `WRITE (*, FMT="(I2,10X,B7,10X,O3)") n, n, n`

A.2.4
  (i)   `T F T F T F`
       (This has one blank at the start and two blanks at the end.)
  (ii)   `Caus of deat`
       (no trailing blanks).
  (iii) `1.4142 1.7321`
       (one leading blank but no trailing blanks)
  (iv) `101000 001600`
  (v)   `0.1414E+01   0.1600E+04`
       (two leading blanks)
  (vi) `FATE`

A.2.5   `WRITE (*, FMT="(A,TL1,'_',:,' ')") (/(caption(k:k), k=1,`
          `LEN(caption))/)`

A.3.1
  (i)   `OPEN (UNIT=7, STATUS="SCRATCH")`

  (ii) `OPEN (UNIT=3, STATUS="OLD", POSITION ="APPEND", &`
       `ACTION="WRITE")`

  (iii) `OPEN (UNIT=2, FILE="s_sheet_45", RECL=256, &`
       `ACCESS="DIRECT", FORM="FORMATTED")`
       `CLOSE (UNIT=2, STATUS="DELETE")`

A.3.2
  (i)   `INQUIRE (UNIT=5, RECL=max)`
       `OPEN (UNIT=5, FILE="savedata", STATUS="NEW", &`
       `ACCESS="DIRECT", RECL=max)`
       `DO k=1, 20`
       `WRITE (UNIT=5, REC=k) datasave(k)`
       `END DO`

  (ii) `CHARACTER(5) :: i1,i2`
       `INTEGER :: k1, k2`
          .
          .
          .
       `READ (UNIT=1, ADVANCE="NO", FMT="(2A5)") i1, i2`
       `READ (i1, FMT="(I5)") k1`
       `READ (i2, FMT="(I5)") k2`
       This reads ten characters from unit 1, and then reads the strings i1 and
       i2 as internal files to interpret them as integers.

Index